AF333502

Economic Policy and the Financial Crisis

The consequences of the global economic crisis which started in the United States in 2007–08 are still being felt in most of the advanced economies, and the mainstream tools of recovery are not having the required results. It seems that many of the after-effects of the crisis, including the instability of the financial markets, increasing public debts and limited economic growth, require new solutions from both economic policy and theory. Lower aggregate demand during the crisis increased the pressure on firms to be more competitive and at the same time, the crisis in the banking system has had a negative impact on the willingness of financial institutions to give credit to companies for investment. Therefore, the key issue for current economic policy is to find a balance between the stabilisation of public finance and maintaining the momentum of long-term growth.

This book offers an evolutionary-developmental analysis, combining elements of neo-Schumpeterian economics, institutional economics and post-Keynesian economics, to show that selection processes within an economy, and the institutional rules shaping those processes, are substantially more important than usually recognised by evolutionary economic theory. Two major challenges for economic theory and policy, in particular, have emerged during the crisis. The first is the rise of unemployment coupled with growing public deficits. The second is the financial instability which threatens the permanence of economic development. This book examines the performance of the advanced economies since the crisis and explores why some of them have been more successful in tackling these challenges than others. It is argued that the reasons for the varied performances of these economies lie in the economic policies which were introduced before and in the aftermath of the crisis and the differences in the regulation of their labour markets.

This volume will be of interest to students and academics in the areas of macroeconomics, public economics and public management.

Łukasz Mamica is Senior Lecturer in Public Economy and Innovation Policy at the Krakow University of Economics, Poland.

Pasquale Tridico is Professor of Labour Economics and Jean Monnet Professor of European Integration Studies at the University Roma Tre, Italy. He is currently General Secretary of the European Association for Evolutionary Political Economy.

Routledge frontiers of political economy

Economic Policy and the Financial Crisis

Edited by Łukasz Mamica and Pasquale Tridico

LONDON AND NEW YORK

First published 2014
by Routledge
2 Park Square, Milton Park, Abingdon, Oxon OX14 4RN

and by Routledge
711 Third Avenue, New York, NY 10017

Routledge is an imprint of the Taylor & Francis Group, an informa business

British Library Cataloguing in Publication Data
A catalogue record for this book is available from the British Library

Library of Congress Cataloging in Publication Data
Economic policy and the financial crisis/edited by Lukasz Mamica and Pasquale Tridico.
  pages cm
  Includes bibliographical references and index.
  1. Financial crises–Government policy. 2. Economic policy.
  3. Economic development. 4. Global Financial Crisis, 2008–2009.
  I. Mamica, Lukasz. II. Tridico, Pasquale
  HB3722.E286 2014
  330.9'0512–dc23   2013036595

ISBN: 978-0-415-70731-2 (hbk)
ISBN: 978-1-315-88693-0 (ebk)

Typeset in Times New Roman
by Wearset Ltd, Boldon, Tyne and Wear

Printed and bound in the United States of America by Publishers Graphics, LLC on sustainably sourced paper.

Contents

Figures

Tables

Contributors

Editors

Łukasz Mamica is Senior Lecturer at the Krakow University of Economics, Poland. He teaches Public Economy and Innovation Policy at the Faculty of Public Economy and Administration. In 2011 he was Lecturer at Vienna University of Economics and Business. He is the author of many publications on such topics as innovation policy, economic change, competitiveness policy including two monographs on the institutional role of research and development units in innovation policy and the role of industrial design as a factor of a firm's competitiveness. For ten years he has been supervising regional innovation strategies in the Malopolska Region. He has also been involved, due to his expertise, in several research projects funded by the European Commission.

Pasquale Tridico is Jean Monnet Professor at the University Roma Tre, Italy. He is Lecturer in Labour Economics, European Labour Market and Welfare Systems and Development Economics at the Department of Economics of the University Roma Tre (Rome, Italy), and General Secretary of the EAEPE. In the academic year 2010–11 he was a Fulbright Research Scholar at New York University. He is author of several articles on institutional economics, labour markets, varieties of capitalism and financial crisis, including two edited books with S. Fadda, (*Financial Crisis, Labour Markets and Institutions*, Routledge, January 2013; *Institutions and Economic Development after the Financial Crisis*, Routledge, October 2013). He is also author of the book *Institutions, Human Development and Economic Growth in Transition Economies* (Palgrave, August 2011).

Contributors

Andrea Bernardi, Manchester Metropolitan University, UK.

Sébastien Charles, University of Paris 8, France.

Silvano Cincotti, Professor, DIME, University of Genova, Italy.

Leszek Cybulski, Wroclaw University of Economics, Poland.

Amitava Krishna Dutt, Notre Dame University, United States.

Tomasz Geodecki, Krakow University of Economics, Poland.

Anna Greenwood, University of Nottingham, Ningbo, China.

Hardy Hanappi, Vienna University of Technology, Austria.

Dany Lang, University of Paris 8, France.

Martina Lavagnini, University Roma Tre, Italy.

Łukasz Mamica, Krakow University of Economics, Poland.

Antonella Mennella, University Roma Tre, Italy.

Anastasia Nesvetailova, City University London, UK.

Niall O'Higgins, University of Salerno, Italy and IZA, Bonn, Germany.

Ewa Pancer-Cybulska, Wroclaw University of Economics, Poland.

Pavel Pelikan, Prague University of Economics, Czech Republic.

Marco Raberto, DIME, University of Genova, Italy.

Malcolm Sawyer, University of Leeds, UK.

Andrea Teglio, Universitat Jaume I, Campus del Riu Sec, Castellon, Spain.

Pasquale Tridico, University Roma Tre, Department of Economics, Italy.

Faruk Ülgen, University of Grenoble, France.

Acknowledgements

This book is a collection of selected papers presented at the 24th Annual Conference of the EAEPE (European Association for Evolutionary Political Economy), held at the Krakow University of Economics, in Poland, 18–21 October 2012. The conference main title was 'Economic Policy in Times of Crisis'. We wish to thank all the participants to that conference, the local organisers (Jerzy Hausner and Łukasz Mamica) and the EAEPE for the wonderful inspiration and opportunity.

About the book

The main objective of this book is to illustrate possible policies, institutions and regulation tools backed by an heterodox approach, able to stimulate economic development and stable growth after the financial crisis. Two major challenges emerged during the crisis: the rise of unemployment with growing public deficits and the financial instability threatening economic development. These two challenges are the primary focus of the book. The book is divided into three parts. Part I has a theoretical approach in the definition of relevant theories explaining the crisis from a macroeconomic point of view. The recovery from the current economic crisis requires first of all theoretical progress in evolutionary and institutional economic theories in order to elaborate an appropriate policy paradigm and a new global governance by means of an evolutionary-developmental analysis, which combines elements of neo-Schumpeterian economics, institutional economics and post-Keynesian economics. In this part we focus also on labour markets and on economic institutions as main variables able to explain better and worse performance among advanced economies. Part II on financial policies, institutions, regulations and tools at the micro level, which are considered appropriate for exiting the crisis. Part III explores both economic competitiveness and possible sustainable development paths of countries, illustrating case studies, experiences and alternative micro-experiences, suggesting that economic sustainability is a key variable in the process of econonomic development, including during crises.

Introduction

Łukasz Mamica and Pasquale Tridico

Book objective and general overview

The global economic crisis which started in the United States in 2007–08 is still having negative effects and consequences in most of the advanced economies. Among those consequences, unstable situations in financial markets, increasing public debts and limited economic growth require new solutions in economic policy. Many traditional tools of growth recovery do not bring positive results and show that both the background of current the crisis and expected policy recommendations are different than in the past. During the crisis, among advanced economies some countries perform better than others, and the reasons for these differences lie in the policies that were introduced and in the labour market institutions. We will explore those policies and will also classify countries on the basis of their socio-economic models, which affect the policies implemented.

The main objective of this book is to illustrate possible policies, institutions and regulation tools backed by a heterodox approach, able to stimulate economic development and stable growth after the financial crisis. In particular, two major challenges for economic theory and policy emerged during the crisis. The first is the rise of unemployment notwithstanding growing public deficits. The second is the financial instability threatening the permanence of economic development. These two challenges are the primary foci of the book.

First, this book shows, generally speaking, that fundamental theoretical progress is needed to understand the current state of deep crisis. Evolutionary economic theory is often misinterpreted as the narrow task of providing some fine-tuning on the assumptions of microeconomics concerning a firm's innovation behaviour. The book contributes to this debate by means of an evolutionary-developmental analysis, which combines elements of neo-Schumpeterian economics, institutional economics and post-Keynesian economics. This analysis shows that selection processes within an economy, and the institutional rules shaping them, are substantially more important than usually recognised, along with the major role played by aggregate demand.

Second, the book shows that the capitalist financial sector remains prone to failures that can seriously damage entire economies and economic development. This has initiated a new debate about the old question: by what regulations, if any, could such failures be prevented, or at least mitigated? While the United States is still far from the introduction of a radical innovation in the regulatory system, in the EU this debate causes a division, as some of its members, in particular France, favor stronger and more extensive regulations than others, most prominently the United Kingdom.

At the micro level, lower aggregate demand during the crisis imposes pressure on firms to be more competitive. At the same time, the crisis in the banking system has a negative impact on the willingness of financial institutions to give credit to companies for investment. The key issue of the current economic policy is to find a balance between stabilisation of public finances and maintaining the momentum of long-term growth which, because of the global market, should be based mainly on innovation. Within limited financial sources for innovation, special attention should be given to relatively low-cost activities connected with design (mainly, but not exclusively, in its industrial dimension).

At the macro level, the book will consider some impacts of financialisation on investment, profit share, the level of demand and the labour market. From consideration of those impacts, it will be argued that (1) fiscal support from the level of demand through reversal of austerity policies is a necessary component of a recovery strategy, (2) attention should be paid to the revival of investment and whether a sufficient revival of investment is possible in light of recent trends and environmental issues related to rapid growth, (3) re-building the productive potential is a further necessary component for recovery, and (4) focused public job creation programmes are also required. Within the macro context, one of the topics that the book touches on is the problem of comparing the effectiveness of policy based on fiscal consolidation versus policy of loosening the fiscal pressure during recessions, resorting to an accommodative monetary policy. Moreover, as regards the labour market impact, our findings conclude that countries which performed better during the economic crisis are countries which do not have a flexible labour market and have managed to keep stable employment levels and aggregate demand. These conclusions may have a strong impact in terms of policy making.

Strategies for economic recovery

The longevity of the current economic and financial crisis confirms that it is different from the one observed after the Great Depression of the 1930s. In Europe, because of the common currency shared by a number of EU member countries and differences in their economic competitiveness, devaluation is not a simple tool for recovery. Massive public interventions in the market at the beginning of the financial crisis were connected with huge increases to public deficits. If we add to this high levels of public debts, which in some European countries like Ireland, Portugal, Italy and Greece are higher than 100 per cent of GDP, it is obvious that stimulating economic recovery by increasing public spending is not a simple solution. A strategy is needed which involves public investments along with public policies such as reform of labour markets (i.e. integration of labour and development policies), financial regulation, sustainable development, innovation stimuli, a sound mix of coordinated monetary and fiscal policies and institutional strategies towards better governance for both public issues and private business. Chapter by chapter, throughout the book, these strategies, policies and institutions will be analysed.

Governments obtaining finance from markets, and the big fluctuations in costs accompanied by the huge impact of private rating agencies, are the next factors which harm the possibility of pursuing effective long-term economic policy. The experiences of implementing austerity measures which can reduce public deficit in the short term are negative and are accompanied by increases in unemployment and the decline of GDP, which can also lead to political destabilisation. The consequences of cuts in public spending can therefore cause more negative impacts on economic growth and, in effect, increase budgetary problems.

At the same time we have observed the consequences of ageing populations on social security systems, and in many countries the real decline of welfare state instruments. The falling fertility rate in most EU countries during the economic crisis may significantly weaken the competitive potential of Europe. There are increased numbers of voices claiming that economic recovery cannot be based solely on free market mechanisms. Effects of public spending and related fiscal, budget and monetary policies should be calculated from the perspective of social aims such as poverty reduction or employment. Employment, specifically, requires decisive action as, in some EU countries like Spain and Greece, the unemployment rate among people below 25 is higher than 50 per cent. There is a fundamental question as to what type of mechanisms are most effective at improving the economic situation and stimulating youth labour markets in Europe.

The length of the current crisis has a strong impact on citizens' state of mind and may lead to different kinds of frustrations and protests. Sometimes these frustrations are slowly formalised, like in the case of the so-called Occupy Wall Street Movement. In this book we try not only to put forward a structural approach to analyse the crisis; we put forward also a general framework of alternative policies and institutions different from the mainstream approach and we suggest also single and specific policies solutions at the micro level, such as credit unions, financial regulation, worker and consumer co-operatives in contributing to the sustainability and growth of economies in time of crisis, decent work, and firm competitiveness and innovation. As regards this last issue, within global market conditions, an economy's competitiveness is the most effective way to maintain standard of living. This is especially important for developing economies. During the crisis, limitations of available sources for R&D have had a negative impact on innovativeness. From 2006 onwards we can observe, for example, the permanent decline of patent applications to the European Patent Office in the European economy's 27 countries. Firms are looking for cheaper methods of achieving higher competitive positions, for example through advanced design or reducing labour costs and wages.

All these challenges provide the framework for discussion about necessary changes in economic, social and fiscal policy, enabling the return to stable economic growth.

The structure of the book

The book is divided into three parts. Part I has a theoretical approach in the definition of relevant theories explaining the crisis from a macroeconomic point of view. The recovery from the current economic crisis requires, first, theoretical progress in evolutionary and institutional economic theories in order to elaborate an appropriate policy paradigm and a new global governance. In this part we focus also on labour markets and on economic institutions as main variables able to explain better and worse performance among advanced economies. Part II focuses on financial policies, institutions, regulations and tools at the micro level, which are considered appropriate for exiting the crisis. Part III explores both economic competitiveness and possible sustainabile development paths of countries, illustrating case studies, experiences and alternative micro-experiences, suggesting that economic sustainability is also a key variable in the process of econonomic development, including during crises.

In particular, Chapter 1, which is the main theoretical chapter of the book, Hardy Hanappi shows that fundamental theoretical progress is needed to understand the current state of deep crisis. Evolutionary economic theory is often misinterpreted as the narrow task of providing some fine-tuning of the assumptions of micro-economics concerning a firm's innovation behaviour. The more methodologically inclined scientific community at least would add that evolutionary economics is part of complexity research, that the interaction of non-equilibrated micro-units eventually will lead to surprisingly simple structured macroeconomic patterns. To experiment with economic complexity it always needs simulation of mostly heterogeneous sets of agents, which in turn produces a Babylon of outcomes of simulation runs. Traditional macroeconomists typically find it difficult even to communicate with researchers in evolutionary macroeconomic simulation models; two different languages, parallel worlds, seem to exist. The aim of the chapter is to improve mutual understanding, and to show how far evolutionary economic simulation can advance political economy by explaining traditional macroeconomics as a (mostly rather implausible) special case of its own more general approach.

In Chapter 2 Pasquale Tridico aims to explore why some countries perform better than others in managing the current economic crisis. He elaborates on this question using the Crisis Management Index, taking into consideration GDP and labour market performance among EU member states. He concludes that countries that performed better during the economic crisis of 2007–11 are countries that do not have a flexible labour market and have managed to keep stable employment levels. These countries combine a very good mix of economic policies and social institutions oriented to stabilise the level of consumption and the aggregate demand. Coordination mechanisms, higher levels of financial regulation and monitoring are also important features of these economies. Clearly, this group of countries, the author argues, identifies better, in the EU, a coordinated market economy model.

In Chapter 3, written by Malcolm Sawyer, the focus is on the creation of conditions for full employment after the financial crisis. Sustainable growth rates at pre-crisis levels may not be possible. Full employment requires an appropriate level of aggregate demand which is sustainable and is not reliant on unsustainable consumer debt, nor dependent on high rates of investment unsustainable through rising capital-output ratio and/or involving an environmentally unsustainable growth rate. In the next few years higher rates of investment will be required to repair the damage of the financial crisis and to enable shifts in the composition of output. In the longer term investment rates could be anticipated to be lower. The attainment of a high level of demand would be much assisted by a egalitarian shift in the distribution of income and would require a sustained budget deficit.

Chapter 4 by Amitava Krishna Dutt, Sébastien Charles and Dany Lang questions the assumption made by many policymakers and economists, who have argued that firms should be allowed to hire and fire workers more easily and quickly. While orthodox economists have argued that such reforms have a positive effect on growth and distribution by increasing employment growth, heterodox economists point to the dangers of having greater employment flexibility. Existing Kaleckian models are unable to address these issues because they assume away long-term labour and allow employment to be short-term and adjust freely with output. This chapter introduces long-term labour into Kaleckian models to address the issues of employment flexibility and dual labour markets with long- and short-term labour. It suggests that increasing employment flexibility is likely to have adverse growth and distributional impacts.

In Chapter 5 Niall O'Higgins argues that young people have undoubtedly been hit hard by the ongoing recession in Europe, albeit with much cross-country variation. Using the Okun Law-inspired framework, he tries to gain some insight on the role of institutions in shaping young people's experiences in the region during what has now been dubbed the 'Great Recession', but which might better be known as the Second Great Depression. The chapter opens with an overview of the main changes in young people's labour market outcomes which have occurred since 2007. After a brief summary of findings on the role of labour market institutions in youth labour markets, an empirical analysis of the latest regression is undertaken. The analysis is based around the estimation of 'Okun Law' type relations between variations in GDP and a series of labour market indicators. The main purpose of the analysis is to look at differences in the relationship between GDP and labour market outcomes across countries with differing institutional set-ups. The analysis also considers the change in these relationships over time and how this is related to labour market institutions.

Chapter 6 by Pavel Pelikan has two objectives: to produce new arguments for an actual policy issue and thus demonstrate the fruitfulness of a new theory. The theory is a recently proposed generalisation of Darwinism termed 'evolutionary-developmental economics', which recognises individuals to be rational only boundedly and unequally. The issue is old, but actualised by the recent financial crises: by what government regulations, if any, could such crises be prevented, or at least mitigated, and what regulations would, or actually did, make the crises even worse? The theory relates financial regulations to the institutional rules produced by economic evolution that shape and guide economic development. The recognition of rationality inequalities brings to the fore the institutional rules that shape selection processes. Regulations needed for successful development are found to be certain general institutional rules, including a sharp antitrust law and a small financial transaction tax, whereas specific government controls, including government ownership of investment banks, are found most likely harmful. The regulations are found to clash with many vested interests, but also to be essential for avoiding new institutionally disruptive crises, and thus allowing capitalist institutional frameworks – the only adaptively efficient ones – to be evolutionarily sustainable.

Chapter 7 by Anastasia Nesvetailova argues that the scale and scope of the phenomenon of shadow banking, and its constitutive relationship with the 'official' banking system, is leading scholars and regulators to rethink some of the major concepts of finance, such as money, collateral, risk and arbitrage. This chapter suggests that a similar analytical effort is needed when drawing lessons about the role of 'liquidity' in light of the crisis and the developments in the shadow banking industry. Today, major paradigms of financial economics and financial regulation tend to place the ultimate source of 'liquidity' in the realm of the financial market. Such a vision, for instance, has been the foundation of the Basel Accord approach to banking regulation, which had assumed perfect and available market liquidity. The crisis of 2007–09, sparked off by an international liquidity crunch and having been transformed into a crisis of the 'shadow banking' industry, has revealed the limitations of such approaches. The aim of this chapter is to offer a conceptualisation of liquidity not as an exclusive function of price, but as a complex legal mechanism underpinning the economic cycle. Following the insights of the early theorisations of liquidity developed in the 1930s–1940s, the author suggests that any investigation of liquidity in the context of an economic system is 'a study of the mechanisms which make particular forms of wealth acceptable'. Revising the insights of the early socio-legal studies of liquidity to the phenomenon of shadow banking, the chapter shows that the financial crisis is best understood as an outcome of the conflict between market liquidity mechanisms on the one hand, and financial innovation mechanisms through shadow banking, on the other.

In Chapter 8 Faruk Ülgen analyses negative consequences of massive public interventions in markets at the beginning of financial crises connected with huge increases of public deficits and unemployment. Stressing negative consequences of financing the public debt by speculation-oriented financial markets, he bases his proposal for economic recovery on functional finance of Abba Lerner and the financial instability hypothesis of Hyman Minsky. Ülgen, in a critical way, refers to austerities, which can reduce public deficit in the short term but can cause more negative impacts on economic growth, employment and, in effect, increase budgetary problems. He does not see the economic recovery based only on the free-market mechanism. Effects of public spending and related fiscal, budget and monetary policies should be estimated from the perspective of social aims like employment or poverty reduction. Ülgen stress also that financing of the public debt and public spending should not be exposed only to speculative funding operations. The state should play an active role in economic growth using integrated fiscal–budgetary–monetary tools – what can be summarised in Minsky's idea that 'The recovery rests on big government'.

In Chapter 9 Marco Raberto, Andrea Teglio and Silvano Cincotti show that fiscal policy has been the subject of fresh interest in recent times as an important stabilising tool available to policy makers in a scenario where conventional monetary policy has been shown to lose its traditional efficacy in dealing with recessions. In particular, as a consequence of the deterioration of public finances following the economic crisis and the bailout of part of the banking system, most European economies are now subject to fiscal consolidation policy measures, despite still poor economic conditions after the Great Recession of 2008–09. In this chapter the authors compare two different fiscal policy approaches by performing a computational experiment with the Eurace agent-based model. On one hand we have the fiscal consolidation, or austerity programme, where a deficit–GDP ratio of 3 per cent is targeted by raising taxes and cutting public expenditures if needed, even during recessions; on the other hand we consider the policy of loosening the fiscal pressure during recessions, resorting to an accommodative monetary policy. Results generally show a better performance of the loose fiscal policy with some warning concerning the combination of monetary expansion with too-relaxed banking regulations leading to an over-indebtedness of the private sector.

Chapter 10 by Tomasz Geodecki addresses the importance of invention and technology transfer for economic growth. The discussion starts with the clear-cut distinction between innovation and invention introduced by Schumpeter. He also discusses the concept of measuring the effects of innovation using parameters of efficiency of factors of production, employed by Solow. He offers an overview of how the perception of these determinants of technical change has evolved, and presents different views on the role of research and development activity in the innovation process and their implications for measuring innovation. The empirical part of the chapter presents a regression analysis of labour productivity, with research and development, technology transfer and other characteristics correlated with technical change adopted as explanatory variables. The analysis was carried out both for technologically advanced economies and less developed ones. It has been observed that in the former group the most important are research and development (R&D) activities, while in the latter the main focus is on technology transfer and features complementary to material investment. In the time of crisis, the leading determining factors can change. Moreover, the roles of the countries can be switched from the catching-up countries to the technology frontier group.

Chapter 11 by Łukasz Mamica argues that the relatively high costs of production in developed countries imposes pressure on many firms' management to maximise the use of non-price competitive factors. Design among technological and organisational innovations is one such element. The chapter shows that the popularity of using design as a factor of firms' competitiveness during times of financial crisis is growing, while other more expensive actions are limited. The international research done in ten countries also confirmed that consumers are ready to pay for good-quality design. The average amount of money said to be paid for a product characterised by a higher quality of design was about 27 per cent of its price.

In Chapter 12 Martina Lavagnini and Antonella Mennella argue that the international economic crisis of this century seriously compromises the labour market variables of a great many European countries: an increase of unemployment and inactivity (in particular youth unemployment) and a decrease of employment have been observed, especially in some Mediterranean countries like Italy, Greece and Spain, where labour market conditions were already poor before the crisis. A worsening of labour market variables can produce a decline of working conditions due to the increased pressure of unemployment. This can induce workers to accept bad conditions, for example in terms of legality of the job or physical safety, in order to protect their working positions. In this sense, the economic crisis can impact on 'decent work' characteristics and worsen variables that define it. Interpreting the concept of decent work harmoniously with Sen's capability approach, work 'can be a liberator' unless some working defects prevent that. The aim of this chapter is to introduce an approach to the ILO decent work concept, defining the variables that characterise 'decent work' in a developed country like Italy. Elements identified in the basic-relations fairness proposal are grouped into three profiles, which are prioritised into two levels. On the basis of this concept, an analysis is made about which policies concerning decent work variables should be implemented to foster it into a wider scenario of actions to recover from the crisis.

In Chapter 13 Andrea Bernardi and Anna Greenwood argue that the current financial crisis triggered not only economic recession, but also an ideological and political crisis, which has quickly become characterised as one of the most profound of Western capitalism. Since 2008, in protest against what was perceived to have been a man-made economic catastrophe, several grassroots movements and political organisations attacked capitalism and its motifs, targeting prominent symbols such as Wall Street, or the other sites of big banks and corporations in both Europe and North America. The apex of the crisis, with monetary instability and uncertainty on sovereign debts, was reached in 2012. Unbeknown to most observers this was also the United Nations' international year of cooperatives. After describing the so-called Occupy Wall Street Movement and their requests, this chapter argues that alternative actors, such as credit unions, workers' and consumers' cooperatives could contribute more to the sustainability, fairness and growth of economies in times of crisis. The successes of co-operative firms in both Western and developing market economies has been all too frequently neglected. Even though cooperatives were not spared the detrimental effects of the recession, they revealed themselves more resilient than capitalist actors in the current and past crises. It is the central contention that cooperative movements and protest movements have several points in common, a fact which makes their lack of dialogue all the more regrettable. The authors suggest that the Occupy Wall Street Movement should productively devote more interest and support to the cooperative model of ownership, rather than focusing its efforts on naive methods and ideological proposals.

Finally, in Chapter 14 Leszek Cybulski and Ewa Pancer-Cybulska argue that unemployment in the European Union reaches a record high at the beginning of the second decade of the twenty-first century. Most forecasts warn that even with the improving economic situation unemployment will remain permanent. The economic situation is the most important key to solving the problems of the labour market. Therefore, the starting point for the considerations of this chapter is examining the impact of the recession and protracted economic stagnation on changes in employment. Although macroeconomic trends are most influential in nature, the measures undertaken under the European Employment Strategy (EES) are definitely insufficiently intensive and flexible, which causes their low effectiveness. The causes of this poor performance, in our opinion, have their roots in the genesis of the EES, i.e. partly in the decision-making inertia and, most significantly, in the excess of legitimate goals that are difficult to reconcile. In view of the over-regulation of the EU economy and narrowing of the field of decisions by means of long-term action programmes, which are insufficiently socially consulted, there remains little room for the EU and the member states to run flexible and discretionary employment policies.

Part I

Theory, policies and institutions to exit from the crisis

A macroeconomic approach

1 Bridges to Babylon

Critical economic policy – from Keynesian macroeconomics to evolutionary macroeconomic simulation models

Hardy Hanappi

Comments and explanations of the worldwide social crisis, reaching from economic and political turmoil to a multi-faceted cultural decline, are flooding the information environment. It is not just the sheer quantity that has arrived at an all-time high; it is also the vehemence of the style of contributions, which is impressive. It shows that scientists and the popularizing media across many disciplines are learning that the last five years are turning out to be the prelude to a major reshaping of human society. But unfortunately enough, the core sciences needed to structure the discourse, namely the three social sciences (political science, economics, sociology), proved unable to provide even the basics of a common language able to debate the newly emerging phenomena. The division of labor in scientific work, which dominated the after-war development, has left a completely disjoint field of specialists expressing themselves in a multitude of professional jargons. Moreover, the institutionalized rules for successful academic careers further amplified the tendencies to ever more singular formal and informal styles, producing academic islands and insider schools. Travels between these islands became cumbersome and ruined chances to get tenure at a respectable academic institution. As soon as a unifying event, e.g., the current global crisis, occurs and scientists are asked for explanations it suddenly becomes visible: The tower of Babel erected by scientists is inhabited by tribes whose languages have been confounded – not by an anxious God afraid of losing its omnipotence (as in the ancient legend), but as a joint product of the misunderstood primacy of the methodological principle of steadily increasing specialization and a loss of public support for synthetic theory building. We are confronted with a scientific Babylon, an arcane church built of highly sophisticated pieces of knowledge, which nevertheless remains mute – amidst the white noise of singular comments – with regard to a sensible understanding of contemporary global political economy.

This chapter will only to a limited extent point at the shortcomings of mainstream economics; there already exists an enormous amount of valuable critique, in theoretical investigations as well as with respect to empirical research. In the current political situation what is needed even more is to collect and to synthesize the existing valid pieces of the knowledge puzzle "political economy." In other words, to build and to rebuild bridges: bridges built of a language enabling mutual understanding between the tribes living on the island of science – Babylon; but also bridges that enable intellectual travel from the ivory tower of knowledge development to the mundane mainland of ordinary inhabitants of the planet – and back. This idea was the motive for stealing the strange title of the chapter from an album of a famous rock and roll band.

As a preparatory device, bridge-building needs the fundament of a set of entities, or pillars, which can be connected to the diverse theoretical continents. What are the elements to which political economy refers to? Figure 1.1 provides the proposal on which all of what follows will be based.

At the lowest level the human species consists of individual members of the species (i), which interact physically in a material environment. To enable their reproduction as species, i.e., beyond the short lives of the individuals, human societies are a cooperating unit with the capability of internal communication. For thousands of years this unit has used a language element, a sign, for the social value of a procedure or the product of a procedure. The material carrier of this sign of social value is called "money" (cf. Hanappi 2013a). The level above the individuals shows the social institutions which are necessary to regulate the primary metabolism of the species: state institutions (eventually divided into Montesquieu's three functions:[1] PLM, LEG and EXE), production units (eventually divided into state-governed and private firms, the latter again distinguished as[2] TNCs and SMEs) and households (eventually divided along the dominant form of income[3]: HHO, HHS, HHB and HHW). To the right of this national setting the fact that nations collide – increasingly are forced to find forms of survival between dominance and cooperation – is summarized by a box labeled "Global environment." In macroeconomics of open economies this box typically

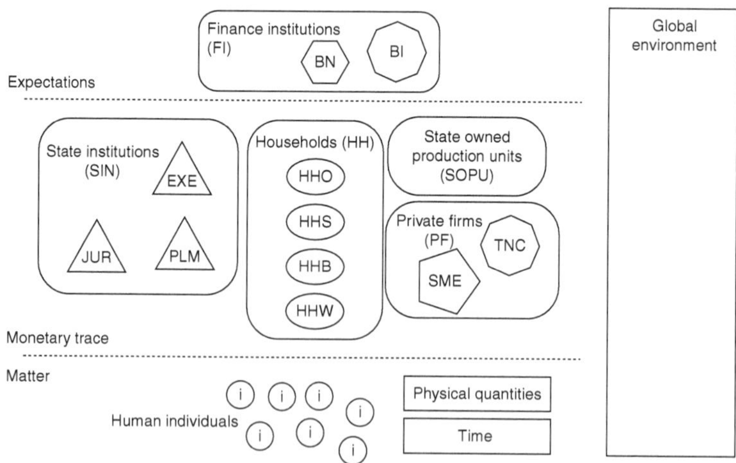

Figure 1.1 The entities of political economy.

would be filled with just another copy of all the entities on the left to depict the two-country case. Note that for each of the two countries a different content of production units, households and state elements can be specified. More on this topic follows in Section 4. Finally, on top of the figure the entities driving the meta-rules of finance are shown (eventually divided into local national players and large, globally acting entities); again Section 4 will elaborate on this issue. The level of granularity of Figure 1.1 has been chosen in a way that should show some major network structures typically used in theory building on this set of entities, while avoiding too much detail.

Equipped with this set of entities, the bridge-building exercise[4] can be started.

1 Macroeconomics (from Walras to Keynes and back)

The last grand attempt for a unified economic approach, linking Keynes' ideas on macroeconomic aggregates with the standard microeconomic optimization framework, was the so-called "neo-classical synthesis" developed[5] from 1947 till the 1970s. Starting with the Walrasian component, a sensible point of departure is to highlight how the marginalist revolution of 1874 (led by Leon Walras, Stanley Jevons and Carl Menger) had been a response to classical political economy, in particular a refusal to its final zenith in the work of Karl Marx. Put in a nutshell, the latter had claimed that aggregation along the lines of class distinctions provides a *theory of exploitation*. In short, the *driving force of capitalism* is the total of *firm owners' activities to maximize profits*, and total profits are the difference between total *revenues* and total *cost*. The limits to *increase revenues* – the product of quantity sold times the (average) price of a unit – are given by production technology, market conditions (competition) and constraints on the demand side (taste and income, and wealth of potential consumers). On the other hand, *total cost* can be *minimized* if the major component of cost, i.e., wage cost, is as small as possible. This can be guaranteed by *permanent unemployment* with which a competitive labor market[6] forces the wages of employees down to a subsistence level, while simultaneously firm owners try to introduce new technologies which allow them to reduce the number of workers needed for a given amount of output. Fewer workers at lower wages results in a lower wage sum, which then subtracted from higher revenues will provide higher profits. The price–wage system sketched in this synopsis is the core of the exploitation theory of classical political economy, not just in Marx's work but across the whole generation of authors.[7]

The authors of the marginalist revolution proposed a completely different theory of prices. This was possible by first narrowing the scope of theory: Consider just the aggregate of all households (HH), and its demand for a given finite set of physical products owned by different firm owners (PF) and focus only on the physical correlates of these two stereotypes.

While the larger picture of Figure 1.1 is dramatically reduced compared to Figure 1.2, there is at the same time a false generalization that takes place. Each household is set equal to a single human individual (i) which can choose to

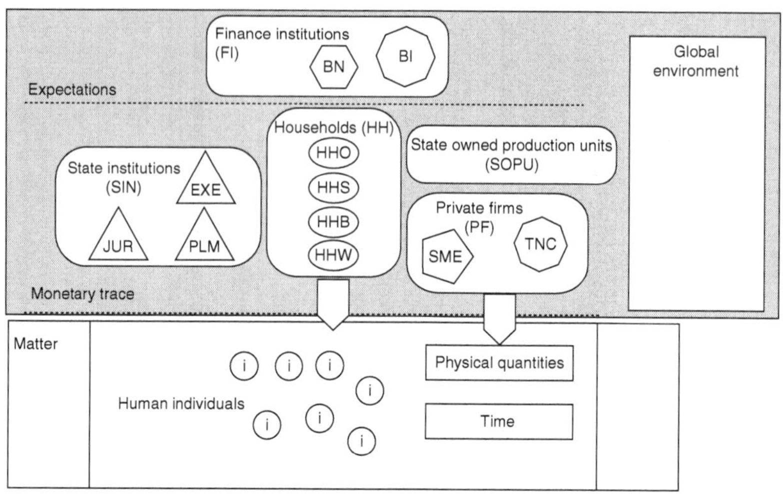

Figure 1.2 Marginalist reduction.

allocate its income to buy from the set of predetermined physical goods also owned by physical individuals (i). This theory of prices thus starts with the assumption that there exists an atomistic material structure of smallest entities (individuals) which possess quantities of goods. To get dynamics into this picture, which then can be interpreted as the emergence of a price structure, an additional innate property has to be ascribed to each atom:[8] a preference order concerning the different goods. If what they possess differs from what atoms would prefer to possess, then algorithms for exchange processes can be specified – see Figure 1.3.

For certain specifications of preference orders, which look plausible as long as no new commodities are introduced, it was possible to show that there exist exchange relations, which can eliminate all possibilities of improving the utility of any one atom without reducing the utility of at least one other atom – such a state of affairs was dubbed the Pareto optimum. Despite the fact that proofs and generalizations (of specifications of functional forms, etc.) of this type of issue took almost 100 years till finally Gerard Debreu and Frank Hahn presented the full model in the late 1960s, which was mainly an enormous mathematical effort, it soon was also used as an ideological weapon to argue for the superiority of "markets" over "planning." To arrive at the concept of a "market," first the emergence of "prices" in the system displayed in Figure 1.3 has to be explained. In this framework the ratio of the quantities of two different goods exchanged by two atoms is called the price of one good in terms of the other good. What had been understood by classical political economy as money, which is provided by a political authority to a society which uses it as a material sign of social value, is no longer part of the metaphor. Instead of being the social value reflected in

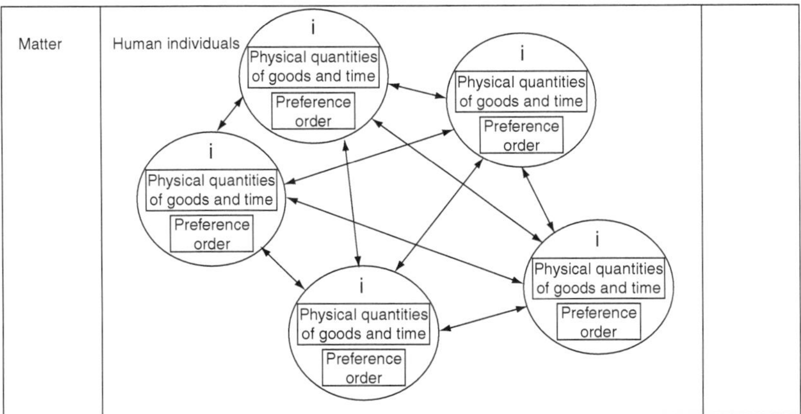

Figure 1.3 Marginalist (false) generalization.

the monetary value of an amount of coins needed to buy a unit of a good, i.e., a price in the sense of classical political economy, now a price is an exchange relation between two commodity owners that is determined by a certain abstract exchange algorithm. The two metaphysical constructs – the innate preference order and the hypothesized exchange mechanism which leads the group of atoms to its Pareto optimum – generate a third metaphysical element: the market. For laymen in economics the interpretation used to hide the involved mysticism usually refers to the idea of an auctioneer helping to figure out all Pareto-improving possible exchanges before any actual exchange takes place. But even more troublesome than the evidently helpless attempt to eliminate ideas of exploitation by reinterpreting prices as the dubious outcome of even more dubious invisible auctioneers was that including labor time as a commodity following the same logic as any other commodity made the theory unable to discuss unemployment and crisis at all.[9]

When in 1929 the Great Depression struck, the Walrasian component of the neoclassical synthesis had to be amended by new elements immediately. Ideological hegemony of the capitalist class was challenged not just by a Stalinist misinterpretation of Marx's classical political economy (reducing it to some emphasis on socialist planning and "socialism in one country" measures), but also was confronted with a Fascist paradigm which laid emphasis on a strong and aggressive influence of state power and command economy features. It was John Maynard Keynes and his Cambridge circle who re-introduced a well-defined dose of state influence and necessary aggregation into the Walrasian framework, which he had learned from his teacher Alfred Marshall. The macroeconomic turn initiated by Keynes actually clarified, or at least laid bare, several of the weak points of the false generalizations of the marginalist approach. The best example is the central system of difference equations, which determines the "price–wage" vector, p_t, i.e., the vector of relative exchange ratios.

$$p_t = p_{t-1} + mkt((q_t^s(.) - q_t^d(.)), x_t). \tag{1}$$

The suggested market mechanism, here collapsed into algorithm $mkt(.)$, has to guarantee that prices converge to a vector that makes the wishes for exchange, here $(q_t^s(.) - q_t^d(.))$, vanish. In such a state of affairs prices would not change any more and the market mechanism would have produced what in the natural sciences had been called equilibrium.[10] Once the "auctioneer" has found this vector, all exchanges between the atoms, i.e., the owners of goods and time, can simultaneously take place. But why does an atom possess a certain amount of goods and time? In the original version captured in Figure 1.2 it is clear that only a short episode in economic life is considered: All households have received their income (without specified source) and now only want to know which goods and services to buy (without specifying how these were made available) from the set of private firms (without specifying why these exist at all). With the false generalization displayed in Figure 1.3, which assumes that this narrow spotlight is the central problem of political economy, it becomes impossible to discuss why then in a general crisis like the Great Depression some atoms, the unemployed, desperately want to exchange their time for goods and cannot do so, while other preconditions like the set of production units start to shrink dramatically. To be able to get such phenomena in the picture again some elements of Figure 1.1 have to be re-introduced. This was Keynes' innovative theoretical idea.

On the demand side of the wishes, $q_t^d(.)$, Keynes extended the atomistic view by adding additional elements which occur at the aggregate level only: demand by state institutions (government expenditure) and intermediate demand by firms (including, in particular, investment demand). The latter enabled a link back to the supply side of exchange wishes, $q_t^s(.)$, since a change in the particular category of goods called "means of production" implied also a change in what the owner could offer as supplied goods. To transport these changes into the world of exchanges between owners of goods and time a new collapsed representation of the production process was needed: the *production function*. It served as an explanatory short-cut for the exchange of time (in that case called labor-time) and goods (in that case called physical output of the production process).

In a subtle way these theoretical innovations had re-introduced an old distinction between the atoms used in the false generalization of the marginalist system: Some smallest entities (atoms) maintain a production function which can augment their utility function, while others do not.[11] And there exists one additional large social entity called the state, which is able to express the wishes of the ruling class by directly interfering in the exchange processes of the system. As a consequence of the observed crisis dynamics this additional entity was needed to achieve a newly visible goal of the system (apart from an automatic convergence to Pareto optimality which obviously was endangered), namely "stability." On an aggregate level the three different types of atoms could then again be treated like three micro-units: firms, households, state. They could be characterized by some innate properties, like a "socio-psychological" propensity to consume, and their aggregate behavior was thought to be measurable by econometric techniques. Since aggregate flows collected by national statistical offices are just the monetary traces of past decisions on quantities, Keynes' macroeconomics had to become a monetary theory again (see Figure 1.4).

With the aggregates of $q_t^d(.)$ and $q_t^s(.)$ now transformed in a way that in principle allowed for persistent overshooting of exchange wishes, that is explaining deflation and unemployment without having to return to a theory of exploitation, the immediate cure to this fragility of capitalism was an action of the political sovereign, the state, which implicitly assumed its unbound monetary authority. The state could use the money which it gave authority to – and could produce itself. This was a very irritating consequence of early Keynesian macroeconomics. It opened up the debate on sources and repercussions of finance, indeed a Pandora's Box of new problems. Luckily enough, the assumption that the aggregate household entity only spends a certain, constant share of its income for consumption allowed defining the remaining part as the flow of household savings. Call this, plus the newly injected state money, the total additional money supply, M_t^s; it can be added to the already existing stock of money. On the other hand, the entity "firm," the entity "household" and the entity "state" might also need additional money – though this implies some schizophrenia (or better: disaggregation) of state and household taking credit and saving at the same time. To handle this exchange of money – the material representative of social value – a new kind of entity enters the scene of political economy: *financial intermediaries*, vulgo *"banks."* This new set of entities handles the transfer[12]

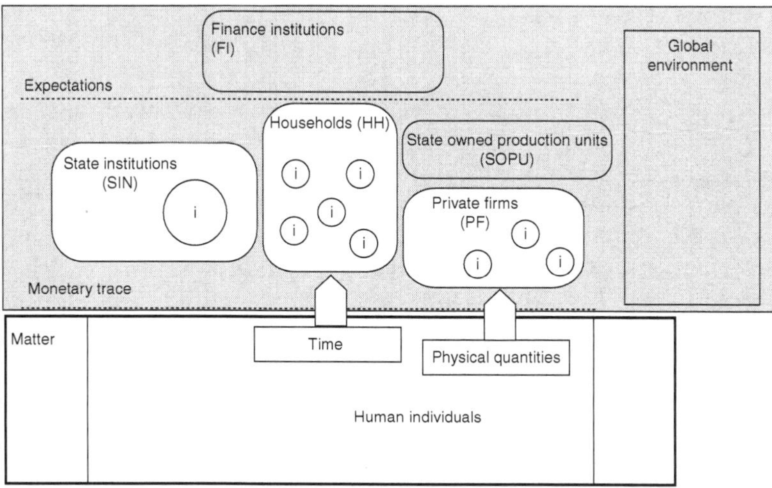

Figure 1.4 Keynes' return to aggregates.

of aggregated total money needed ($\bar{M}_t^d = \bar{M}_{t-1}^d + M_t^d$) and the aggregated total money offered ($\bar{M}_t^s = \bar{M}_{t-1}^s + M_t^s$).

In its simplest version Keynes' model had four behavioral suggestions. The entity HH determines its monetary demand for consumption (equation (2.1)). The entity PF determines its monetary demand for investment goods (equation (2.2). The entity SIN determines its monetary demand for goods and services bought by the state (equation (2.3)). Finally, the new aggregate entity, which it had become necessary to introduce, namely the financial intermediary (FI), also has to be characterized by a behavioral rule. Like the stylized firm owner, this entity has a utility function, which is transformed into a profit-maximizing rule: Pay as little an interest rate as possible for money disposed and ask an interest rate as high as possible for money given as credit. This new entity is of particular theoretical interest because it breaks open Keynes' more static, short-run consideration. Giving credit necessarily involves expectations on future time periods and a well-defined repayment plan agreed upon in the present.[13] But for the simplest model, John Hicks' famous formalization of Keynes' ideas, it was sufficient just to highlight one immediate thought: The more money demand exceeds money supply, the higher all interest rates will be. Taking one interest rate, r_t, as a representative of the whole profile, equation (2.4) shows this behavioral rule of the entity FI. By focusing on this element of the behavior of financial intermediaries, another aspect is completely lost, the difference between interest paid for savings and interest taken for credit, a difference which banks typically try to maximize. Classical political economy had conceptualized this difference as the part of the profit (made by the owner of a firm exploiting workers and other resources) which had to be given to money owners to get the exploitation process pre-financed. Comparing the interest rate for credit with the profit rate (the ratio between profits and the stock of capital employed) would measure the relative strength of the two fractions of the ruling class, financial intermediaries and firm owners (see Hanappi 2012a, appendix 1 for details). This reminder on exploitation theory evidently is lost when applying only equation (2.4). But it remains to be argued how total money demand is determined. In this respect Keynes proposes two influences: (1) the usually assumed proportionality of money needed to the amount of total output (transaction demand), and (2) a so-called "speculative demand for money" which is based on a trade-off that owners of firms face: If they use their money to buy bonds representing the ownership of another firm, then they hold less money, and vice versa. Keynes' tricky shortcut then is to assume that these bonds provide an interest rate, which is again equal to r_t. The aggregate entity FI therefore consists of hybrid members who are partly not only bankers but owners of private firms (shareholders) too. The interest rate r_t – this mysterious construct needed to consolidate the equilibrium framework inherited from Walras – is thus the crux of Keynesian theory, the variable behind which exploitation theory is hidden.

Returning to system (1) it remains to explain variable x_t and algorithm *mkt*. Variable x_t simply can be used to catch all processes not endogenously determined. This sounds trivial but is rather revealing if one considers that the most significant developments of the last 300 years fall under this category of "exogenous trajectories not explained by the model" e.g., technical progress, introduction of new commodities, demographic changes and population growth, institutional developments, development of communication and information, etc. Variable x_t therefore should be seen as the ignored territory that a new theory of political economy should start to explore.

The key to the connection between the two components of the neoclassical synthesis is the algorithm *mkt* in system (1). This algorithm has to be constructed in a way that guarantees convergence of the price–wage vector for every admissible starting value of this vector. A typical specification thus would reduce the absolute value of the difference between the actual value of a certain price p_t^j and its equilibrium value $p^{j,*}$ with every step of the iteration. Whatever specification is chosen – be it a tâtonnement process steered by an auctioneer, or be it some bargaining in the communication sphere – as long as it leads to the equilibrium price–wage vector it qualifies as a central ingredient of the neoclassical synthesis. In this case this algorithm is given the name "the market" and is treated like an independent entity, which has just one goal, namely to produce the equilibrium vector. Since actual exchange is assumed to take place only after the equilibrium vector has been found, it is evident that grand harmony is modeled as long as only the actual trajectory of exchanges is considered. Exchange always only occurs at terms formerly agreed upon; no room for involuntary enforcements is left.[14] In fact, the choice of the precise mechanism *mkt* can even be omitted (assuming that economic interpretation will always find a plausible market mechanism) and system (1) will only deal with situations where prices and wages are at their equilibrium levels. In that sense the price–wage system does not play a crucial role any more and all variables can be considered to be measured in "real" terms.

Recall now that (2.1)–(2.3) determine aggregate demand as follows:

$$\text{(Consumption)} \quad C = C(c,Y), \frac{\partial C}{\partial Y} > 0 , \tag{2.1}$$

with c being a socio-psychological constant, and Y being total income.

$$\text{(Investment demand)} \quad I = I(Y^*,r), \frac{\partial I}{\partial Y^*} > 0, \frac{\partial I}{\partial r} < 0 , \tag{2.2}$$

with Y^* being total demand expected by the entity firm, and r the interest rate on bonds (see the discussion above). Investment demand of the aggregate entity firm will move in the same direction as their expectation of future total demand, though it remains open how it does the actual forecasting. On the other hand, investments financed by credit will be reduced if the interest rate for credit rises.[15]

$$\text{(Government expenditure)} \quad G = G(T), \frac{\partial G}{\partial T} > 0 , \tag{2.3}$$

which is assumed to be the exogenously chosen variable of fiscal policy. What is chosen to be expended can always be financed as tax income, T, of the state.

External finance by increasing government debt is not considered, but higher taxes will only be possible with higher total income (*Y*).

$$\text{(Interest rate setting)} \quad \frac{m^S}{P} = M^S = M^D(Y^*, r) \quad \text{with} \quad \frac{\partial M^D}{\partial Y^*} > 0, \frac{\partial M^D}{\partial r} < 0$$

(2.4)

What in macroeconomic textbooks is usually considered to be an equilibrium condition for the money market has to be re-interpreted as a description of the behavior of entity FI: For any given expected output Y^* the financial intermediaries will react to a difference between money supply M^S and money demand M^D by raising or lowering interest rates appropriately.

The sum of the demand components represents aggregate demand (measured in money): $q^d = C + I + G$. Contrary to aggregate demand, which comes from three sources (all kinds of households, firms and state institutions), aggregate supply is offered only by firms (goods) and physical human individuals (time). Moreover, both formats (physical quantity and labor time) are transformed into items with monetary values only after having been processed by a special algorithm organized by the special atomic agents constituting the macro-entity "firm." This algorithm is the defining characteristic possessed by these agents and is called *production function*, call it *pfct*. In a first stage this algorithm (the production function) is thought to work on a physical level, organizing the time-spending activities of employees and material inputs in a way that leads to new physical output quantities. In the second stage the output (goods and services) is priced and offered as q^s. The process of pricing takes place in an environment which firms perceive and use to determine their profit-maximizing price strategies. Let the algorithm *cmcd* (a mnemonic abbreviation for "consider market conditions") describe this second stage of pricing. Then these assumptions can be expressed as follows:

$$\text{(Production function)} \quad q^s = q^s(cmcd(pfct(material, time))). \tag{3}$$

It is revealing to reconsider at this point of the argument how the Walrasian component of the neoclassical synthesis working with the help of the assumed algorithm *mkt*(.) treats the labor market. As (1) shows, for any given x_t only those situations are further considered in which $q^d(.) = q^s(.)$. And it is most remarkable that this singling out of relevant equilibrium positions occurs on the level of the monetary traces of physical processes (see Figure 1.1). But to be able to fulfill this task of equalization, the macro-atoms on this level have to set actions which profoundly change the situation on the physical level. In particular, the firm entity might not be able to influence *cmcd* strongly enough to adjust to the demand side and therefore will try to modify *pfct*. This can either result in technical progress or – in particular for falling demand – falling capacity utilization and firing of employees. On the other hand changes in *pfct* also can be expected with any new investment, a process described in (2.2). By recognizing these consequences of Keynes' theoretical innovations, and incorporating them into an enlarged general equilibrium model of Walrasian type, the neoclassical synthesis started its way back to marginalist theory. The famous result that the marginal productivity of a *pfct*, rewritten in terms of money, has to be equal to the ("real") wage paid for one unit of labor time input ignores all consequences for physical human individuals. And these consequences do not reappear on the demand side either, as long as the macro-entity "household" is just a conglomerate of different social characters crudely lumped together. The technical assumption of general equilibrium in the world of voluntary monetary exchanges does *not* provide a *wrong* picture of possibly emerging disequilibria in the world of physical quantities – it simply provides no picture at all!

In Figure 1.5 the possible connections mentioned in passing in Keynes' texts are included only as broken lines. The mainstream interpretation first formalized by John Hicks centers on the determination of a static equilibrium brought about by endogenous changes of income Y and interest rate r. An explanation of economic crisis in this framework therefore comes only in sight if some variables are driven (by exogenous forces) to levels which make the assumed behavioral rules implausible. From a formal point of view this is plausible: If only linear dynamics are used, then the model-builder only has the choice of modeling convergence or some special types of divergence. If convergence is chosen, then a crisis can only be understood as exogenous shock. Indeed this property bedevils equilibrium models till today.

Despite these mostly ignored shortcomings, which the incorporation of Keynesian ideas into the Walrasian equilibrium framework brought about, it nevertheless opened up a rather important debate on refinements of monetary economic theory.[16] Moreover, the emerging difficulties concerning the aggregation of single-firm and single-household behavior into the physiognomy of a

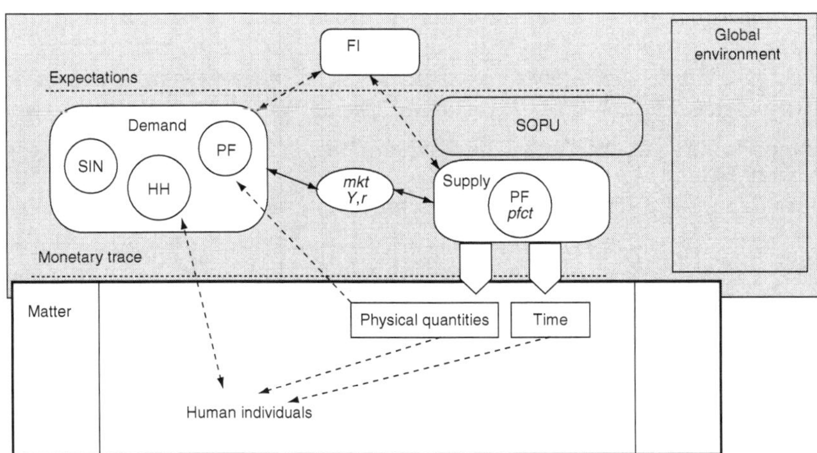

Figure 1.5 Keynes' macroeconomic dynamics.

macro-entity produced a large amount of interesting theory, though in the end the task of a microfoundation of macroeconomics has never been achieved. It thus seems to be fair to assess this last grand effort of a neo-classical synthesis[17] as an interesting but *failed* approach to get rid of the original tenets of classical political economy.

2 Change of techniques (from Marx to Schumpeter and back)

One of the reasons why the renaissance of macroeconomic reasoning vindicated by Keynes and the proponents of the neoclassical synthesis got stuck was the self-imposed restriction to reduce its significance to short-run issues. On the one hand the assumed short time horizon facilitated the formulation of a macro-economic framework that could consider many slower-changing variables as constants. But on the other hand the focus on a momentous spotlight completely misses the long-run characteristics of the capitalist mode of production. This deficiency was quickly discovered by the macroeconomists of the first generation after Keynes, who soon proposed macroeconomic growth models.

Based on Robert Solow's archetypical model the longer run was conceptualized as equilibrium growth (Solow 1956). By letting investment flows change the way material inputs and labor time can be transformed into output (the intermediating concept was called "capital stock") finally a "Golden Rule of Accumulation" was derived which claimed that the propensity to consume could be thought of as being adapted to maximize the equilibrium growth path of the consumption of the macro-entity household (Phelps 1966). How this change of a (short-run) socio-psychological constant can be brought about opened up the economists' views to consider political science questions concerning taxes and psychological questions concerning consumption incentives. Moreover, the effect of technical progress was timidly introduced as a permanent and automatic shift of the production function, which – according to the respective properties of this shift – would modify the equilibrium growth path. In an analogous way, constant growth of labor time supply could be included. Though there is a lot of valuable mathematical detail in this standard growth theory literature, the qualitative status remained within the spell of the neoclassical synthesis as summarized in Figure 1.5.

A more serious attempt to break this spell came from Richard Goodwin, who generalized Roy Harrod's model of growth instability (see Harrod 1939) to produce a model of an oscillating share of investment (in output) and a simultaneously oscillating share of employment (in an exogenously growing total supply of labor time). Included in this combined growth regime is an exogenously assumed constant growth rate of labor productivity, a special type of technical progress (Goodwin 1967). In a later extension of his model, Goodwin was able to substitute oscillations of labor productivity increase for the assumption of its constant growth, thus mimicking long-run Kondratieff cycles (Goodwin 1990). It is remarkable that Goodwin and his followers had to start to build *non-linear dynamic models* – with a toolset borrowed from the natural sciences – to achieve their goals.

As shown in Figure 1.6, the non-linear dynamics (a Lotka–Volterra system) produces oscillations in the two variables u (the share of output of firm owners) and v (the share of labor supply actually employed). Firm owners use all their profits for investment and there is a steady exogenous increase of labor productivity. The unemployment rate fluctuates as the exogenously assumed growth of labor time supply encounters oscillating employment rates determined by firm owners.

This widens the scope of traditional Keynesianism considerably and indeed throws an interesting spotlight on the nature of persistent business cycles. What is even more important is the relationship which Goodwin introduced to make a feedback of unemployment rates on the real wage level plausible. A *political process* (namely wage bargaining based on *bargaining power*) influencing current unemployment rates is brought into play: The higher the unemployment rate, the less bargaining power a union has and the lower the real wage will be. What is implicitly emerging in this dynamic is also a fluctuation of consumption possibilities of physical individuals. Despite its monetary roots – Goodwin was a collaborator of Schumpeter *and* Keynes – this model therefore has implications for the material side of workers' lives, both with respect to time and with respect to available physical goods. One drawback of the highly stylized formulation – it consists of only seven equations – is that the class of exploiting firm owners is only included as one simple behavioral rule: immediately invest all profit.[18] The cycle that is produced is a metaphor for the omnipresence of oscillations in an environment of continuously growing labor productivity.

With respect to an explanation of a deep global crisis, the model nevertheless is not very illuminating. In that respect Harrod's early knife-edge growth model

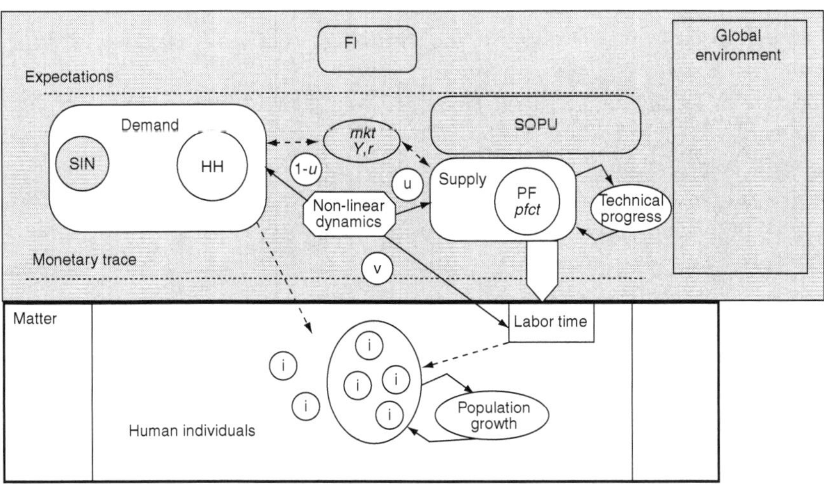

Figure 1.6 Goodwin's surrogate class struggle.

might even be a more telling contribution: In that model any small deviation from the equilibrium path (the knife edge) is amplified and necessarily leads to disaster.

A similar idea can be found 100 years earlier in Karl Marx's work. In his communist manifesto, written in 1848, Marx praises the productivity increases that capitalism, in particular "big industry," is bringing about. He assures that capitalism is a necessary stage – a mode of production – of the development of human society exactly because these productivity increases are its historical mission. But at the same time the very success of this mission generates new contradictions: crises along different dimensions, class dynamics and class struggles. In the end these increasing difficulties and incompatibilities will start to dominate – the capitalist mode of production will be fundamentally revolutionized. This story reads somewhat similar to Harrod's knife-edge model, which due to its unstable growth path sooner or later is doomed to diverge to a system breakdown. Marx's central idea – actually derived from Marx's Hegelian philosophical background – that contradictory developments (welfare-enhancing productivity increase and welfare-destroying class struggles and alienation dynamics) are parallel and interwoven social processes had been completely lost since classical political economy was erased by the marginalist doctrine in the late nineteenth century. Even so-called "Marxist-Leninist circles" and neo-Ricardian interpreters of Marx did not pay too much attention to Marx's (Hegelian) methodological background. Keynes used to ignore Marx's contribution completely, calling him just a "minor neo-Ricardian."

It was Keynes' greatest contemporary rival, Joseph Schumpeter, who was one of the few economists that understood the deep methodological truths hidden for such a long time in Marx's approach. Schumpeter's theory of innovation, including social innovation, is a radical turn to the disequilibrium approach: There is a process running parallel to equilibrating forces of market dynamics[19] which accumulates new ideas and solutions to the many unforeseen contradictory consequences of prevailing developments that in the end leads to a sudden "swarming of innovations" – a revolution in the moment when interdependent problems culminate in a global crisis. With respect to the time that is needed till the great crisis ends, the accelerating divergent (as historical mission even "necessary") growth process, Schumpeter was as oblique as Karl Marx. Both only insisted on the general pattern of social evolution-revolution. Modern evolutionary economists, with the help of recently developed mathematical tools and a new simulation paradigm, are already on their way to further improving this Marx–Schumpeter line of thought.

Using again Figure 1.1 (changed to Figure 1.7), the focus in this line of argument is on the interplay of two divergent growth tendencies linked by the two processes of exploitation and innovation. The first process, *exploitation*, takes place on the level of monetary traces by the repeated excess of revenues over wages, which is called profits of the owners of the means of production. But this process is rooted and secured by a political process governed by state institutions, which guarantee (by a monopoly on the use of coercive force) that the

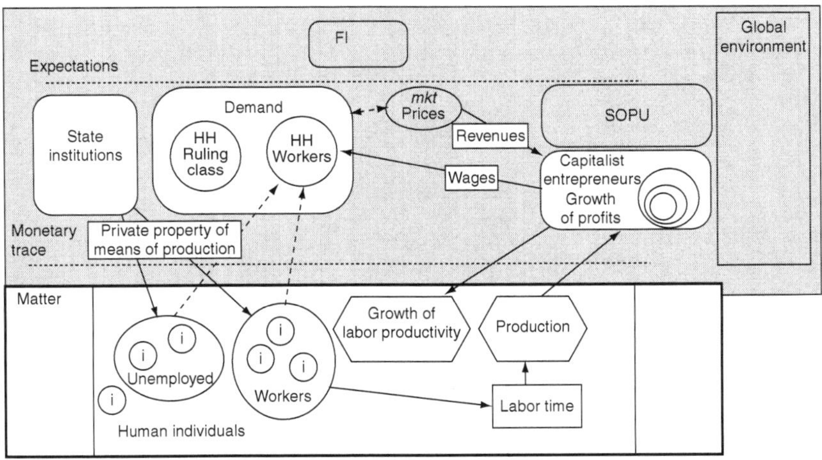

Figure 1.7 Marx–Schumpeter dynamics in political economy.

private property of the means of production remains intact. Politics is back in the picture.[20] Since the "reserve army of unemployed workers" (Marx) helps to keep wages low, a continuous surplus of profits will be the rule. A class of exploiters can be distinguished from a class of exploited. But as can be seen in Figure 1.7, this also has implications for the material level: Human individuals, which are unemployed, nevertheless need material inputs for their daily reproduction. The monetary mechanism thus influences the class structure of the human species on a material level: it divides the species into antagonistic classes, which reduces welfare. Parallel to this process some owners of means of production will be forced by competition to introduce new methods of production, eventually providing new commodities and services. This is the process of *innovation*, which is by and large welfare increasing.[21] Note that technical progress takes place on the material level, and therefore allows for being kept alive even if alternative arrangements on the monetary level are institutionalized.

The essence of this dynamic can also be sketched by a simple dynamic model linking profit rate evolution and labor productivity levels (see Figure 1.8). Here, the two are linked by a simple logistic function (factor in the area of period doubling, see note 22). If one adds an index for the stability of this system, which approximates the level of class struggle mainly by using the variance of experienced distributional changes, then it becomes visible how increased labor productivity (right-hand scale) will lead to the instability of this mode of production; e.g., by assuming that an index of instability higher than 3 (right-hand scale) will imply general revolt.

Neither Marx nor Schumpeter had much to say about what might happen as soon as the system becomes unstable. In principle both referred to the same period of time in history, namely the second half of the nineteenth century until

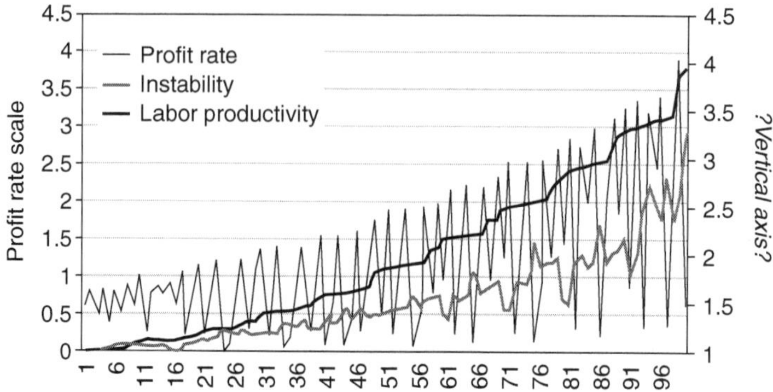

Figure 1.8 Marx–Schumpeter dynamics as a logistic system.

World War I. Their major contribution certainly can be found in the general methodological intuition: Historical eras proceed by combining countervailing forces to enhance net welfare for a limited number of decades. Then they break down under the weight of their own success.[22]

3 Expectations using models (from von Neumann to Sargent and back)

That there are crucial differences between the physical phenomena studied by the natural sciences and phenomena involving living entities has been recognized since ancient times. But in the interwar period the breathtaking successes of theoretical physics lead several of the most advanced pioneers in the natural sciences to reformulate the fundamental question "What is Life?" Erwin Schrödinger wrote an extremely influential book with this title and John von Neumann set out to construct a new formal language to be able to study the strategic interaction between social entities.[23] The crucial point in John von Neumann's approach was his insight that social atoms – either physical human individuals or larger social entities – are able to base their decisions on internal model building, which includes anticipation of the model-building activities of other social atoms.

For a social scientist this complicates his own scientific model building enormously: For an adequate picture of the object of investigation (the model-building social entity) many more assumptions are needed, e.g., to limit the infinite regress of using models including models, in turn including models.... Specifying the limits of information processing capacities of social entities and at the same time explaining how these models are generated and maintained is a task which is still far from being accomplished today. The social sciences, in particular economic theory and political economy, do not have the necessary theory of communication and information they should be based on.

John von Neumann and Oskar Morgenstern were aware of this deficiency and as a first step proposed a framework for the much simpler world of parlor games.

In this world the players, the rules of the game, the available information, the possible actions of players and finally success and failure are all well-defined and understood by all participants. It is surprising and exciting that despite this extreme narrowing down of what actually occurs in social settings, and despite the fact that von Neumann tried his best to limit the formal toolset he used to the well-known mathematical apparatus, they nevertheless arrived at a theory which produced fundamentally new results. Unfortunately, their work occurred at a time when the rising tide of the neoclassical synthesis swept away all competing approaches. Moreover, soon a new generation of very apt – though barely innovative – young mathematicians eagerly started to integrate parts of game theory into the neoclassical framework. In the early 1970s game theory as an important topic for economic theory had disappeared behind a veil of ignorance.

Expectation-building processes using models only reappeared in economic theory in the early 1980s, when the so-called New Classical Macroeconomics of Robert Lucas and Thomas Sargent set out to fight the Keynesian insistence on the importance of state intervention.[24] Interestingly, this counterstrike did not work with a return to the times of model-less, blind reaction, but instead with the introduction of extremely correct model-building processes of all participants. What later was dubbed "hyper-rationality" is the assumption that all atomic agents in a Walrasian economy are equipped with the same true model of all the features of the economy. This includes the assumption that there exists such a true model and immediately implies that any learning process is excluded since it is not necessary. Furthermore, this approach restricts its own use to experiments with exogenous shocks coming from unexplained outside sources. The notorious technical difficulties that can arise with such experiments are solely based on the properties of the different stochastic terms added to the equations in the hyper-rational model.[25]

With respect to old-style Keynesian models this approach doubtless was successful. For example, Keynes' argument that workers would accept lower real wages brought about by an inflationary process initiated by monetary policy rests on the assumption that workers cannot distinguish between nominal and real wages, whereas firm owners can. Assuming that all agents use the same true model makes such an argument impossible. For most other active policies of the state an analogous encounter could be formulated. In short, the assumption of hyper-rationality was equivalent to the proposal that an institution-free Walrasian economy was stable and optimal! All that policy makers should do is to guarantee the free and unconstrained interplay of market forces.[26] Figure 1.9 provides a summary.

The central role is played by the one and only true model. It contains all the information displayed in the Walrasian framework in the lower part of Figure 1.9, and all entities use it to determine simultaneously and in advance their equilibrium choices. This model resides in the upper (expectations displaying) part of the figure and is distributed (black arrows) over all entities. It therefore constitutes *equilibrium in expectations*; all forecasts produced with this model necessarily will be correct.

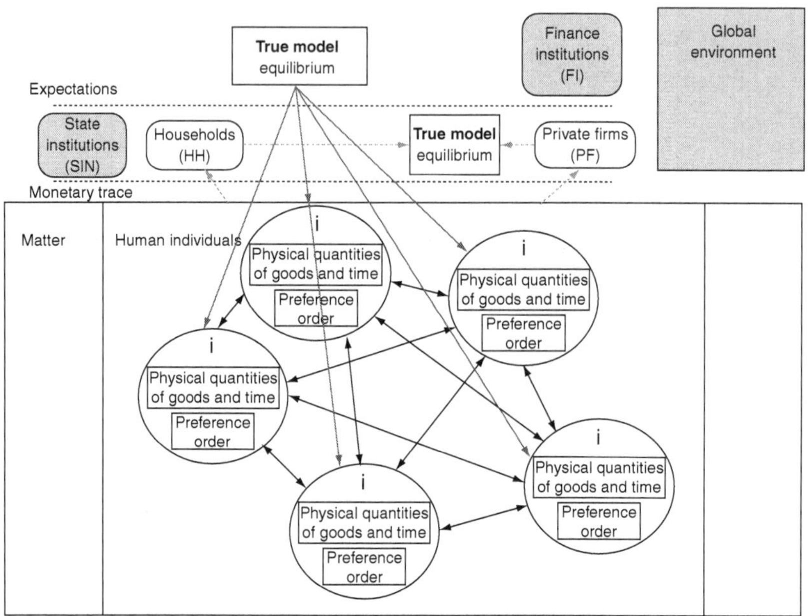

Figure 1.9 Introducing rational expectations.

Moreover – with some strong assumptions on the functional forms of production functions and other behavioral functions[27] – it is also possible to construct (dotted arrows) an aggregate agent "private firm," an aggregate agent "household" and money and bond market mechanisms which allow this true model actually to stay in *equilibrium in the real world* of monetary traces. The upshot of these complicated arguments is that, like in the original Walrasian approach, the innate preference orders of the set of all human individuals together with the exogenously given constraints on production techniques will lead to satisfaction of all participants (equilibrium in expectations as well as equilibrium in exchange wishes in the real world) as long as only free and voluntary market exchange is guaranteed. In other words, no class structure dynamics and their consequence of institutional evolution exist since all differences between the smallest atoms of society, the individuals, are assumed to be innate and have never-changing preference orders.

The school of new classical macroeconomics in essence thus just restates the main argument of the authors of the marginalist school:[28] Walras, Jevons and Menger. But it nevertheless adds an important new ingredient, namely the suggestion that agents use internal models of the economy to determine their actions. It is only the very specific way they specify these internal model-building processes which lets them fall back into a secular micro-theology of an eternal general equilibrium inhabited by omniscient individuals. This treacherous fatalism not only reveals the hidden policy agenda of new classical macroeconomics; it also leads to the general impotence of this approach to deal with accumulation or crisis.

As a consequence, a re-orientation of macroeconomic theory towards older traditions became unavoidable as soon as the deep crisis of 2008 struck.[29] The progressive element in the "rational expectations" approach – namely to introduce the use of internal models – was taken over by a new generation of economists and was enriched by adding ideas from the almost forgotten theory of strategic games of Neumann and Morgenstern. The models built by heterogeneous agents, agents at several levels of social institutions, could be specified differently and studied in detail by the use of sophisticated computer simulation.[30] Game theory, which started as a new mathematical treatment used for parlor games, is now a helpful complement to simulation wherever some modeled strategic conflicts allow for the shortcut of an analytical treatment. And in reverse this new field of evolutionary economics, which makes extensive use of simulations, often inspires new research in game theory. The whole new branch of evolutionary game theory seems to be a good candidate for a methodological pillar of the new theory of political economy, which is needed to guide us through this deep global crisis – and beyond.

How internally generated, maintained and updated models govern the behavior of different types of heterogeneous social agents is at the center of the renaissance of a theory of political economy which is currently in the making. The new classical macroeconomics had the omnipresence of truth as the beginning and end of their theory. This resembles the first step of the philosopher Hegel's famous dialectics where it is stated that the truth must appear.[31] But Hegel then, as step two, added an antithesis to further develop the overall process, to describe its dynamics by introducing countervailing forces (i.e., "negation"). Here, not a single social agent possesses a true model and it is not even clear how such a thing can exist. Nevertheless, agents try to improve their internal models, to modify them into more adequate tools (Hegel's third step of a "synthesis," necessary to return to a better understanding of the original thesis in step one). This procedure, of course, just describes the ordinary process of scientific accumulation of knowledge for given limitations of perception and information-processing capacity. It is exactly that part of the evolution of living systems which characterizes the human species. By returning to the game theoretic research program of Neumann and Morgenstern's game theory – now enhanced by newer techniques and tailored to investigate political economy – the step from (religious) belief systems toward (scientific) knowledge-improvement systems is reiterated.

An evolutionary political economy characterized in this way is promising not only to reunite micro-, meso- and macroeconomics, but also will have to synthesize the many different areas of the social sciences, which in the name of necessary division of scientific labor have become isolated islands of little-known professional jargon. Figure 1.10 sketches these high aspirations of evolutionary political economy.

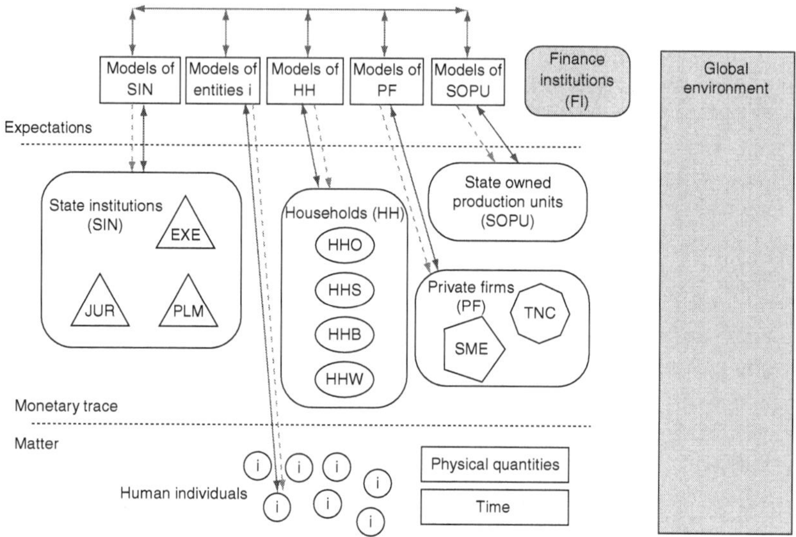

Figure 1.10 Aspirations of evolutionary political economy.

The solid arrows pointing in both directions shall indicate that all conscious entities maintain internal models to explain the past and forecast the future. They use them to determine their actions at a specific point in time (dashed arrows). Moreover, all social agents *communicate*: All models are generated and modified (indicated by the grey arrows on top) by the interaction of the social agents in the communication sphere. The latter thus is a constitutive element of political economy.[32]

Needless to say, the just-sketched research program of evolutionary political economy – including the necessary model of the communication sphere – has only just started to be worked on.

4 Structural breaks and the emergence of larger entities

What remains to be explored to cover all elements introduced in Figure 1.1 are just two closely related items: international finance and the global environment. At first sight it might be surprising that they are related, but they are so because they both point at the same missing concept in the argumentation given so far: *the emergence of novelty*.

To begin with, the end of Section 2 of this text is a possible trigger. There, some emphasis was laid on the importance of studying systems with diverging essential variables, which after a finite time will break down. This type of dynamic, it was argued, is the archetype of living social systems. But as the history of life on earth vividly shows, this usually is not the end of the story. The breakdown of a certain regime is not necessarily a full stop (as in the case of the dinosaur); it might be followed by a rather quick but nevertheless fundamental change in the direction of evolution – and these fast "revolutionary dynamics"[33] might give birth to a novel, again longer-enduring, regime. As shown in Figure 1.11, revolutionary dynamics are fast and intermittent episodes between the major long-term stages of evolution.[34] They are characterized by the creation of new entities, the destruction of some old entities, the establishment of new relations between them, the fixing of new (institutional) compromises (institutions) and a set of new goals and visions guiding the new system. If the revolution succeeds, i.e., the species survives its transformation into a novel form, then this new form often is *larger* – with respect to space as well as with respect to the number of constituting elements (members and their tools).

In political economy the size of the relevant social entity developed from small wandering tribes to village communities, to city states and to nations. Just recently nation states started to form continental units and slowly a global political economy comes into sight.

The parallel process in the communication sphere often is described as the stepwise emergence of consciousness. Even in the biography of a single human individual the traces of this stepwise enlargement can be found: member of a family, member of a city community, member of a national community, member of a continental community and, finally, member of mankind. Each of these steps is contingent on certain and rather sudden additional links appearing in the communication sphere.[35] Some authors of the French Enlightenment had anticipated these jumps in social consciousness as general humanism. Karl Marx, thinking in Hegelian categories of creation by antagonistic forces, saw the emergence of class consciousness of the progressive class as the intermediating carrier of global consciousness of the human species. If indeed countervailing forces are the sources of an implementation of a new, more humanitarian global solution for the species, then they will have to materialize in a global compromise with dominantly progressive – i.e., global welfare enhancing – policy. Currently one of the best candidates[36] with the worst reputation for this splendid task is an institution with only a vague material correlate:[37] international finance. There appears the novelty needed – and not just needed to complete Figure 1.1.

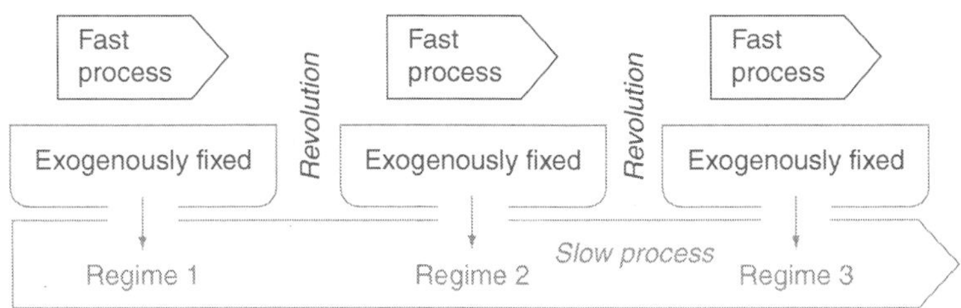

Figure 1.11 Typical profile of life dynamics (source: Hanappi, 2013d).

The second fundamental novelty involved has been labeled "global environment." In the simple world of national macroeconomic models the sub-species of open-economy macro-models was introduced by adding a copy of the first model and linking both with the help of a trade function.[38] Later, more complicated models allowed for more channels of interaction; if these models concentrated more on the real side of the economy (Figure 1.3 and the lower part in Figure 1.1) they contributed to the branch of a "pure theory of economic trade," if they were based more on the monetary traces (Figure 1.5) they belonged to "balance of payment theory." In the first case again, given preferences and technologies were thought to determine a general equilibrium toward which a flexible exchange rate would lead the convergence process.[39] In the second case more variety produced by the instruments of monetary policy – now including, e.g., interference in foreign exchange markets – can be mimicked. But as the events since 2008 showed, even in this second case major questions of global coordination and the emergence of international institutions and their possible instruments were clearly out of reach of the standard formulations of these models. The global economic and monetary environment still needs to be conceptualized.[40]

It is clear that for this global concept several pressing environmental problems will also have to be taken on board. In this area a lot of model building has developed more recently, though little influence on the standard models of mainstream economics can yet be seen.[41] The new approach of evolutionary political economy proposed above should contrast this ignorance by carefully looking for cooperation. As with the case of monetary open-economy macroeconomics, a shift in focus toward the modeling of antagonistic forces, conflicts and possible (sometimes institutionalized) temporary compromises is needed.

In other words, there is a lot of future theoretical work hiding behind the two semi-blind spots of "finance institutions" and "global environment." The hope is that the current crisis speeds up development and makes breakthroughs easier – though it is certainly more risky to determine in which direction they lead.

5 Conclusion

The selection of building blocks of political economy presented above surely is missing many refinements that proponents of any of these streams of thought would have liked to include. But the general line of argument, namely that many different schools have built on many different – often disconnected – parts of the tower of Babel, this line of argument can hardly be denied. Opening this Pandora's Box there also seems to be hope: As the new languages of computer simulation, game theory, network analysis and fractal analysis (to name only a few) are advancing and recombining, there seems to be a chance to arrive at a set of models that match the vision displayed in Figure 1.1 – a dynamic mirror image of the set of globally relevant entities, which can help to guide political action.

Once this research program has its first successes, many of the models briefly hinted at in this text will look as minor accomplishments; sometimes even producing more confusion than clarification. But like it or not, progress moves on by pulsation – in theory-building too. In times of revolutionary dynamics an outbreak of diversity, a diversity of hypothesis and proposals occurs, which ranges from proposals to return to antediluvian regimes to completely utopian plans. Out of this wide-ranging field (in quantity and quality), solutions will have to be picked, and picked soon. The better we know the rooms and vistas in the tower of Babel, the map of Babylon, the better we will be equipped to make wise decisions. This text on the bridges to Babylon is meant to help a bit.

Notes

1 That is: (1) the legislative force of "parliament," PLM; (2) the jurisdiction, LEG, and (3) the executive force, EXE. Using algorithmic terms rather than political science jargon, these refer to rule-set makers, rule-set surveyors and rule executors.
2 For the distinction between transnational corporations, TNCs, and small- and medium-sized enterprises, SMEs, in Europe, see Hanappi (2012, appendix 4).
3 Households with dominant income coming from firm owners, HHO, have to be distinguished from households of workers, HHW, as already pointed out by Kaldor's proposal for consumption functions with different propensities to consume (Kaldor 1966). Today two other large groups of dominant income have to be distinguished: households of state employees, HHS, and households of those employed in banking and finance, HHB.
4 As will be noted, the arguments will mainly follow the discourse led in economic theory, and will touch upon parallel debates in sociology and political science only sporadically.
5 As a starting point for the work on a "neoclassical synthesis" Paul Samuelson's PhD thesis can be considered (Samuelson 1947).
6 Note that the assumption of the feasibility of permanent unemployment implicitly includes the assumption of a state fraction of the ruling capitalist class, which guarantees the existence of the rules of private property of means of production as a necessary ingredient of a "competitive" labor market. It is this fraction of the ruling class which is allowed to use coercive force to secure the rules of the market. This feature of classical political economy is responsible for the adjective "political" and distinguishes it from the later-emerging discipline of "economics."
7 Different earlier authors focused on different aspects of exploitation: Adam Smith investigated why some nations, like England, were able to exploit other nations – and found a reason in outstanding technological progress by advanced division of labor in factories. David Ricardo put emphasis on division of labor by international trade and added the importance of getting rid of "unproductive," non-capitalist classes of rentiers.
8 In Walras' time this preference order was still insufficiently specified. It followed some intuitive ideas best formulated by Stanley Jevons, who suggested the existence of some psychologically rooted laws of human behavior. Only with the work of John von Neumann and Oskar Morgenstern was a consistent formal theory of utility constructed (Neumann and Morgenstern 1944).
9 In Fadda and Tridico (2013) an interesting collection of contributions tackling the special role of labor markets from a non-neoclassical perspective can be found.
10 More on the methodological side of this procedure can be found in Hanappi (2013c).
11 How this difference between entities came about in the first place – what was called "primary distribution" in classical political economy – can remain out of focus for Keynes because he explicitly restricts his analysis to the short-run difficulties of a given primary distribution. It is this limiting of the time scale which in the sequel

ensures that all questions of ownership and exploitation, which were so important in classical political economy, can safely be ignored again.

12 Note that both aggregates are *stock* variables of utmost significance for the political economy of a society; they reflect not only the current relation between new credit and new savings, but indeed incorporate the entire history of surplus and debt.

13 More on this issue can be found in Sections 3 and 4.

14 With respect to wages, Keynes personally felt uneasy with the consequence that unemployment is explained as a voluntary choice of workers. Nevertheless, this conclusion is straightforward for the authors combining the two components of the neoclassical synthesis.

15 Here, Keynes seems to acknowledge the conflict between the two fractions of the ruling class. If the average interest rate received by just possessing a bond of (any) firm is rising, then firm owners might use their profits to jump on this bandwagon rather than investing in their own firm – with a risky expected internal rate of return. In other words, the firm owners' fraction of the ruling class loses members and power.

16 The standard formal representation of Keynes' macroeconomic dynamics, Hicks' IS-LM model, is kept in equilibrium by endogenous adjustment of two variables: total income Y and the interest rate r. The latter variable is a catch-all notion indicating the importance of purely financial dynamics. During the Great Depression Keynes had experienced that deteriorating financial dynamics were the trigger event signaling the overall disaster. Despite this farsighted intuition, Keynes own treatment of financial dynamics remained rather eclectic.

17 In popular journalism the adjective "neoliberal" has recently often been used to summarize some economic policies implicitly recommended by the neoclassical synthesis. *This should be avoided* since the word combines two positively connoted words – "neo" and "liberal" – bearing no relationship to the actual background of the concerned policies. "Neo" is just proclaiming to be fashionable and "liberal" refers to anti-feudal attitudes, which since the end of World War I have been an outdated moralist relict. The actual importance, advantages and disadvantages of the neoclassical synthesis, is lost by renaming its political content as "neoliberal."

18 Apart from this, the model is completely void with respect to financial processes. Since (following his teacher Keynes) Goodwin assumes all variables to be real values, there seems to be a hidden Walrasian equilibrium image in the background (see Figure 1.6).

19 Schumpeter's early book influenced by his teacher von Wieser is devoted to the praise of the Walrasian approach (Schumpeter 1908). Only after 1910 did he discover the force of disequilibrium arguments. When he first used them he personified them in the allegoric personality of the "entrepreneur." Later in life he became more and more influenced by reading Marx – despite the evident fact that he politically usually proposed conservative policies (see Catephores 1994).

20 As has often been noted, Schumpeter was very well aware that capitalism is mainly endangered on a political level. Contrary to Keynes, he thought that economic stability is *not* the main problem of this mode of production. Keynes considered capitalism's political instability only as a consequence of some economic adjustments that could be overcome.

21 An unhappy side-effect of innovation usually is the additional technological unemployment it might entail.

22 If the threshold of instability greater than 3 is used for system breakdown, then this system grows from period 1 to period 99. It is characterized by a logistic equation for profit rates, $\pi_t = 3.51 \cdot \pi_{t-1} \cdot (L_t - \pi_{t-1})$, where there exists a feedback on the limiting productivity level, $L_t - L_{t-1} + \tau_t \cdot (\pi_t - \pi_{t-1})$. The labor productivity level is not allowed to fall and innovative force τ_t – measuring how efficient firm owners are able to translate profit growth into technical progress – follows an exogenously given pulsation

circling every seven periods between 1 per cent and 16 per cent. The latter assumption reflects Schumpeter's idea of swarming of innovations. No empirical foundation is used; the example just shows the possible qualitative features of this simple set of assumptions.

23 Compare Schrödinger (1944), Neumann and Morgenstern (1944) and Hanappi (2013b).

24 The coincidence of fashions in economic theory and the prevailing policy in major capitalist countries is no surprise. The conservative roll-back that started with Margret Thatcher, Helmut Kohl and Ronald Reagan was in need of theories justifying their privatization policies – and found and funded them.

25 The mandatory use of rational expectations (RE) for several decades worked as an entry barrier to major US journals in economic theory. The difficulty of mastering stochastic modeling of this kind usually hid the rather trivial content of the proposed models.

26 From this perspective it is extraordinarily cynical that Thomas Sargent received the Nobel Prize in economics in 2011, after three years of deepest crisis had shown how disastrous his approach to macroeconomics had been.

27 See Sargent (1980) for details.

28 Therefore the name "new classical macroeconomics" is a misnomer. This school indeed is contradicting almost all major issues of classical political economy, a school, which easily could be – but should not be – confused with what was somehow obscurely labeled "classical macroeconomics" in this context.

29 Post-Keynesianism added new elements to the standard interpretation of Keynes to tackle the new crisis. Indeed, Keynes' original texts prove to be a steady source of original – though often eclectic – ideas.

30 See Hanappi (2013c) for more details on these developments.

31 "Das Wahre muß erscheinen," wrote Hegel. Of course, the truth now is assumed to be the structure of the set of preference orders and Hegel's belief in God now is the belief in an infinitely fast (automatic) market mechanism.

32 In Hanappi (2003) two spheres were distinguished: the communication sphere (here "expectations") and the material sphere (here "matter" and "monetary traces"). The second describes the primary metabolism of the human species, while the former describes its secondary metabolism.

33 See Hanappi (2013d) for some details on this idea.

34 The many fast processes occurring during a certain regime are usually kept in line by the authoritative institutions of this regime; the coercive forms of a regime are thus "exogenously fixed" by the need to keep it on track. Nevertheless, there is a slowly ascending countervailing force of diverging essential variables, which in the end leads to the breakdown. The sequence of regimes follows a much slower historical dynamic.

35 At this point of the argument a second thought on the importance of the internet and the widespread availability of mobile phones might be appropriate – and can lead to original new policy proposals.

36 Of course, the search for a new and global revolutionary class – the material counterpart to global consciousness – is high on the agenda of social researchers working in the Hegel–Marx–Schumpeter–Gramsci tradition (see Hanappi and Hanappi-Egger 2012, 2013).

37 This is the reason why in Figure 1.1 "finance institutions" are put in the upper layer of entities based on expectations. They indeed operate completely on the basis of beliefs in certain internal models and the forecasts they produce. Global consciousness will need global finance to realize innovative reproduction of the species.

38 Early prototypes can be found in many macroeconomic textbooks (e.g., Denburg and McDougall 1968). This type of trivial extension usually spreads policy effects over both countries, weakening the original impact observed in a closed economy.

39 With "Rational Expectations" this convergence process then again can be assumed to take place in advance in the brains of all agents only, so all actually observed economies are always in equilibrium.
40 Referring again to Hanappi (2003), this concerns the "global primary metabolism," whereas "international finance" refers to the "global secondary metabolism."
41 Some pivotal contributions were already provided by Herman Daly (1996) and Georgescu-Roegen (1999) more than ten years ago – without much influence on standard economic theory. As an example of an interesting, more recent contribution, see Heinberg (2011).

References

Catephores G., 1994, "The Imperious Austrian: Schumpeter as Bourgeois Marxist," *New Left Review*, 205, pp. 3–30.

Daly H., 1996, *Beyond Growth: The Economics of Sustainable Development*, Beacon Press, Boston, MA.

Denburg T. and McDougall D., 1968, *Macroeconomics*, Kogakusha Company, New York.

Fadda S. and Tridico P. (eds.), 2013, *Financial Crisis, Labour Markets and Institutions*, Routledge, London.

Georgescu-Roegen N., 1999, *The Entropy Law and the Economic Process*, Universal Publishers, New York.

Goodwin R., 1967, "A Growth Cycle." In: C.H. Feinstein (ed.), *Socialism, Capitalism and Economic Growth: Essays Presented to Maurice Dobb*. Cambridge University Press, Cambridge, pp. 54–58.

Goodwin R., 1990, "Schumpeter, Keynes and the Theory of Economic Evolution," *Economia e Banca, Annali Scientifici*, 3, pp. 69–94.

Hanappi H., 2003, "Evolutionary Economic Programs," invited paper at the "Ausschuß für Evolutionäre Ökonomie" of the "Verein für Socialpolitik," July. Available at: http://ftp.econ.tuwien.ac.at/hanappi/Papers/eep.zip (accessed 4 December 2013).

Hanappi H., 2012a, *Can Europe Survive? Ten Commandments for Europe's Next Ten Years*, Papers for Evolutionary Political Economics (PEPE), No. 9-2012.

Hanappi H., 2013a, *Money, Credit, Capital and the State: On the Evolution of Money and Institutions*, updated version, MPRA Paper No. 47166.

Hanappi H., 2013b, "The Neumann–Morgenstern Project." In: H. Hanappi (ed.), *Game Theory Relaunched*, InTech Publishers, n.p., pp. 4–25.

Hanappi H., 2013c, *Future Methods of Political Economy: From Hicks' Equation Systems to Evolutionary Macroeconomic Simulation*, MPRA Paper No. 47181.

Hanappi H., 2013d, "Evolutionary Dynamics in Revolutionary Times," in S. Fadda and P. Tridico (eds.), *Institutions and Economic Development after the Financial Crisis* (forthcoming). Available at: http://ftp.econ.tuwien.ac.at/hanappi/Papers/Hanappi_2012e.pdf (accessed 4 December 2013).

Hanappi H. and Hanappi-Egger E., 2012, "Social Identity and Class Consciousness," working paper at Economics (TU Vienna). Available at: http://ftp.econ.tuwien.ac.at/hanappi/Papers/Hanappi_Hanappi-Egger_2012a.pdf (accessed 4 December 2013).

Hanappi H. and Hanappi-Egger E., 2013, "Gramsci Meets Veblen: On the Search for a New Revolutionary Class," paper presented at the ASSA (American Social Science Association) Annual Meeting, San Diego, 4–6 January.

Harrod R., 1939, "An Essay in Dynamic Theory," *Economic Journal*, 49, pp. 14–33.

Heinberg R., 2011, *The End of Growth: Adapting to Our New Economic Reality*, New Society Publishers, Gabriola Island.

Kaldor N., 1966, "Marginal Productivity and the Macroeconomic Theories of Distribution," *Review of Economic Studies*, 33, 4, pp. 309–319.

Neumann J. and Morgenstern O., 1944, *Theory of Games and Economic Behavior*, Princeton University Press, Princeton.

Phelps E., 1966, *Golden Rules of Economic Growth*, Norton, New York.

Samuelson P.A., 1947, *Foundations of Economic Analysis*, Harvard University Press, Cambridge, MA.

Sargent T., 1980, *Macroeconomic Theory*, Academic Press Inc., New York.

Schrödinger E., 1944, *What is Life?*, Cambridge University Press, Cambridge.

Schumpeter J., 1908, *Das Wesen und der Hauptinhalt der theoretischen Nationalökonomie*, Duncker & Humboldt, Berlin.

Solow R., 1956, "A Contribution to the Theory of Economic Growth," *Quarterly Journal of Economics* 70 (1): 65–94.

2 Why did some countries perform better than others during the current crisis?[1]

Pasquale Tridico

1 The economic crisis in the European Union

The economic crisis which started in the US financial sector in 2007 is today a global crisis which involves almost all sectors and labour markets (Tridico 2012; Posner 2009; Stiglitz 2010; OECD 2010). Mass unemployment emerged in the United States and Europe (Krugman 2008; Wolff 2010). After a recession of GDP in the EU, with an average of –4.2 per cent in 2009, many EU Member States have yet to recover. GDP is stagnating, yet the unemployment level is not declining (Fitoussi and Stiglitz 2009; Barba and Pivetti 2009). Besides that, there are other problems such as low levels of consumption, bank liquidity problems, low levels of private investment, lack of trust and negative expectations in the financial market and between banks and investors, as well as high public deficits and debts. Despite the variety of problems, synthesized by Figure 2.1, national governments in advanced economies, and in particular in the EU, seem to focus, as I will argue below, mostly on a single problem, sovereign debt (Fitoussi and Saraceno 2010).

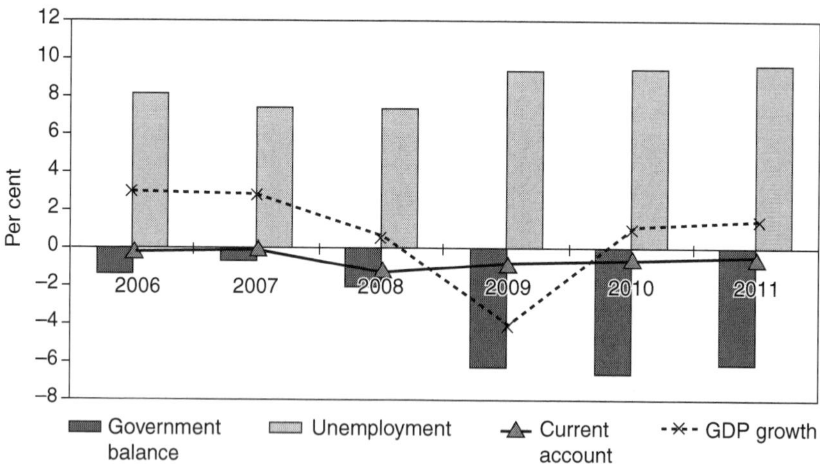

Figure 2.1 EU economy, an overview 2006–11 (source: Eurostat).

The Greek crisis, which emerged in May 2010, showed how EU Member States are much more concerned with national issues than EU integration, in particular during times of crisis (Frangakis 2010).[2] The lack of coordination and financial solidarity emerged dramatically, and the issue of European imbalances is wrongly regarded as a problem of laziness against effort, virtuous balance against bad discipline, Mediterranean corruption against North European integrity (Cesaratto 2011). This does not help to see the real problem behind the deficit–surplus issue within the EU, which is a single market. A single market (with many imperfections) and a common currency within a non-Optimal Currency Area (OCA) at the very least needs labour coordination, budget centralization and fiscal policy harmonization (Wray 2010). In addition, the strong 'internal devaluation' (i.e. wage moderation) that Germany carried out in the past ten years, along with other mercantilist policies, and the cooperation of the European Central Bank (ECB) monetary policies, allowed German exports to increase dramatically (Cesaratto 2011). Such policies were not really in the spirit of EU integration and solidarity. Consequentially, the EU situation today looks fragmented. On one side, Greece and the other Mediterranean countries suffer from the efficiency of North European firms. Free competition and the single market affected the domestic markets in those countries, which were lagging behind in terms of competitiveness and technology at the creation of the Eurozone and the single market. Moreover, the Maastricht criteria and the stability pact appreciated the euro and contributed to the declining foreign competitiveness of South European economies. On another side, the poorer economies in the EU cannot use monetary policies and exchange rate manipulation to gain competitiveness. They are unable to use state aid and firm subsides, nor fiscal policies which are constrained by the Maastricht criteria. Hence, markets have to regulate imbalances despite the fact that labour mobility, single markets and budget centralization are strongly limited in the EU. It follows that surplus and deficit are the two results of the same problem: an imperfect single market and an imperfect currency union. In the EU, Germany's surplus could not exist without Greece's deficit (and similar). Greece should accept, within the EU rules, the German market super-competition, which is historically rooted and state supported, despite the fact that she cannot use policies to enhance competitiveness of Greek firms. Unless these imbalances are covered by a central EU plan, it would not be convenient for Greece to accept European monetary union constraints.

Besides the problem of imbalance in the current account and of the sovereign debt sustainability, the EU is strongly affected by economic problems such as mass unemployment and slow GDP growth, which make imbalances and debt more severe issues.

Among the EU Member States, the situation is very varied. For GDP performance we can divide the 27 Member States into four groups (see Figure 2.2):

1   Group 1 – the worst one – is made up of countries which have experienced a deep recession with a cumulative negative GDP performance during the period from 2007 to 2011 (Greece, Latvia, Ireland, Italy, Denmark, Portugal and Estonia).

2   Group 2 is countries whose GDP is just above 1 per cent between 2007 and 2011 (the United Kingdom, Spain, France and Finland). This is the average situation in the EU27.
3   Group 3 is countries which had a cumulative GDP growth for the period between 2007 and 2011 between 1 and 2 per cent (meaning very modest growth per year, on average between 0.2 and 0.5 per cent).
4   Group 4 is countries which, relatively, had a stronger performance in terms of GDP growth, with a cumulative growth rate between 2.2 per cent (Malta) and 4.3 per cent (Poland, the best performer, which contrary to all other Member States did not experience a single year of recession during the period 2007–11).

Interestingly enough, initial conditions in terms of GDP per capita of the countries did not matter in the performance during the crisis, meaning that we did not observe, as predicted by the neoclassical approach, that poorer countries grew faster or richer countries grew slower. Instead, as Figure 2.3 shows, among the best performers one can find both richer countries, like Germany, Austria and Luxembourg, and poorer countries, like Poland, Slovakia and Malta.

However, in this chapter I will also take into consideration labour market performance in order to rank overall EU country performances. This will allow for a deeper analysis of the crisis.

2 The crisis in the EU labour markets

Following the various performances of the EU economies, one can state that EU labour markets were differently affected by the crisis. However, the performance

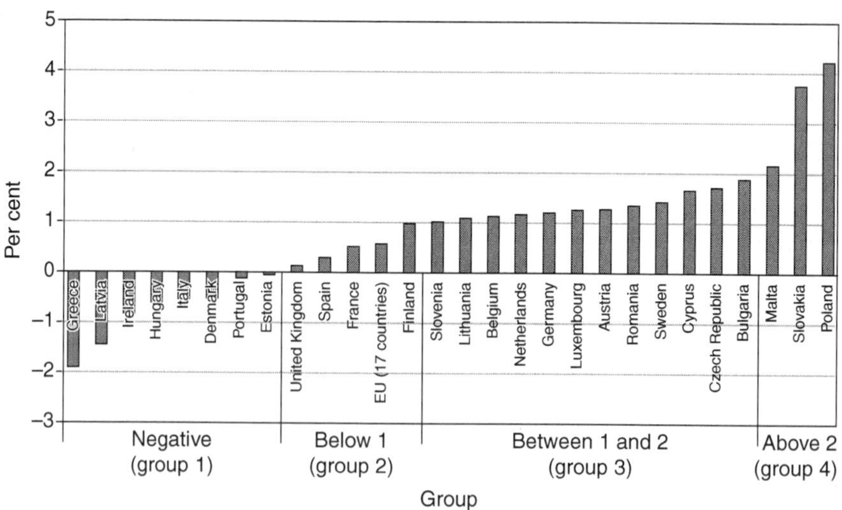

Figure 2.2 Economic crisis in the EU27: cumulative GDP growth 2007–11 (source: Eurostat (own elaboration)).

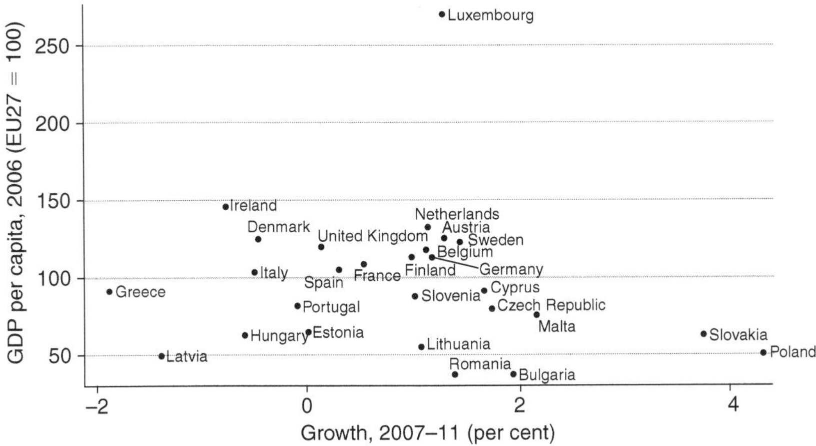

Figure 2.3 GDP per capita 2006 (EU27=100) and cumulative growth 2007–11 (source: Eurostat (own elaboration)).

in the labour market does not reflect strictly the performance of GDP. In some countries where social institutions and trade unions are stronger, unemployment increase was not dramatic and social costs of the crisis were less significant. In particular, beside Poland and Malta (which experienced higher growth of GDP over 2007–11), this is the case of Germany, Austria and Luxembourg, despite only a modest increase of GDP in the period. Not surprisingly, in countries where labour flexibility is very high, unemployment increased dramatically. Even in the Scandinavian countries, which in the last decade adopted a so-called flexicurity model – like Denmark, Sweden and Finland – employment decreased and unemployment reached very high levels (around 7 per cent). However, the most dramatic figures in terms of unemployment and employment fall are in the countries where a flexibility model, *tout court*, was adopted or is more persistent, such as Ireland, Estonia, Lithuania, Latvia, Spain and the United Kingdom (Figure 2.4).

At the same time, unemployment rates followed the same trend: in most of the EU countries it increased enormously. It reached dramatic levels in Spain (around 20 per cent) and in Greece, Latvia, Lithuania, Estonia and Ireland (around 15 per cent). Such a dynamic is real and is not at all affected by demographic trends such as reductions of labour forces, chances in the population or reduction of people looking for jobs. Instead, absolute numbers such as employed and unemployed, in the Survey of Labour Forces, worsened. Figure 2.5 shows the dramatic increase of unemployment rates in most of the EU, with the exception of countries like Austria and Germany and another few where unemployment declined.

Such a variegated situation underlines a different rate of elasticity of employment reduction to the recession of the GDP. Such elasticity is negative and

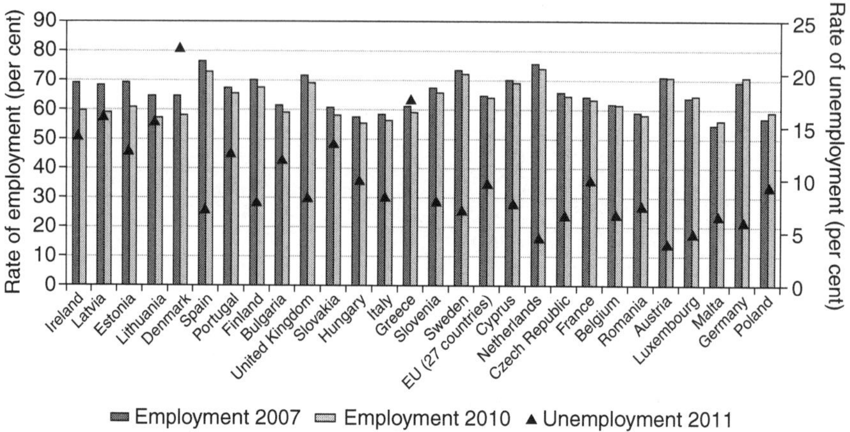

Figure 2.4 Rates of employment (left) 2007–10 and unemployment 2011 (right) (source: Eurostat (own elaboration)).

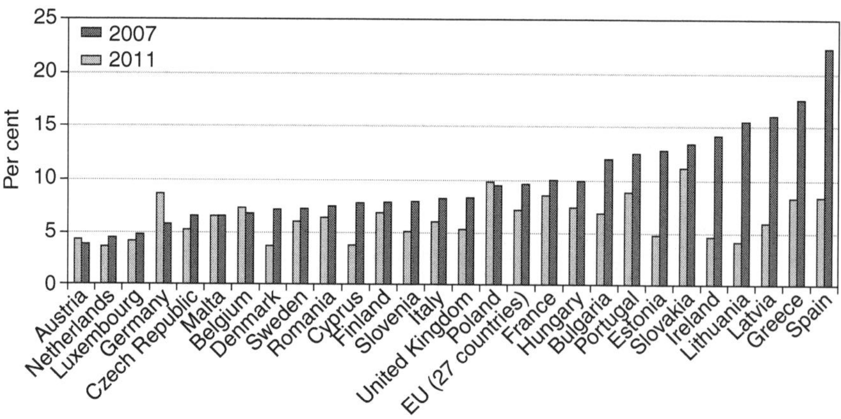

Figure 2.5 Unemployment rates 2007 and 2011 (source: Eurostat (own elaboration)).

higher in Spain, Estonia, the United Kingdom, Portugal, Ireland and Lithuania (see Figure 2.6). These countries are followed by: Finland, Slovenia, the Netherlands, Sweden, Bulgaria, France, Cyprus, the Czech Republic and Slovakia. In those countries employment declined relatively more than the decline of GDP. Austria, Poland, Luxembourg and Malta (which are in general, together with Germany, the best-performing countries) had a GDP growth relatively higher than employment growth. Finally, the case of Germany is extraordinary: this country experienced an employment growth relatively higher than the growth of

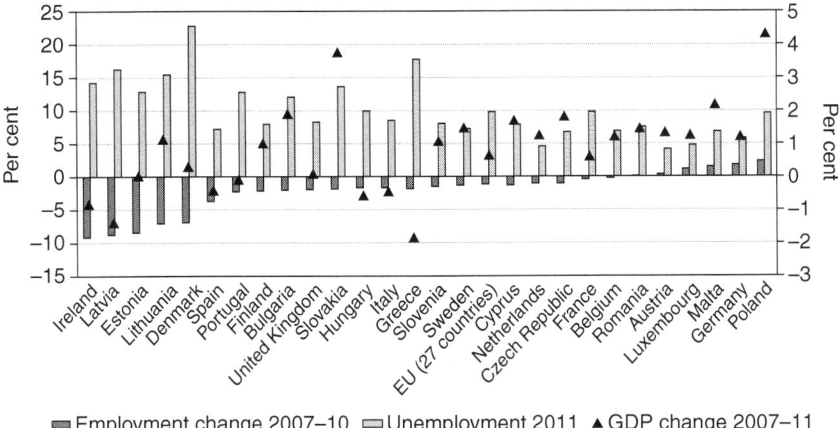

Figure 2.6 Percentage of employment change (left), unemployment rate (left) and GDP growth (right) during the crisis (source: Eurostat (own elaboration)).

GDP, and this highlights the importance of the labour nexus in Germany and the strategic role of trade unions in industrial relations.

A general overview, country by country, is offered in Table 2.1, with a detailed description of the impact of the crisis on the economy and on the labour market. Out of 27 Member States, only Poland did not experience a single year of recession during the critical period of 2007–11. Eight countries – Estonia, Spain, France, Italy, Portugal, Romania, Sweden and the United Kingdom – experienced a so-called double-dip, with two years of recession in the same period. Ireland, Greece and Latvia experience multiple dips, and the rest of the EU had at least one year of GDP recession (in 2009). From Table 2.1 the worst situation in terms of numbers of years of recession and magnitude of the fall can be found in the following groups of countries:

1   Estonia, Latvia, Lithuania (Baltic countries – small and open economies strongly dependant on the outside and high deficit in the current account).
2   UK and Ireland (Anglo-Saxon competitive capitalist countries – financially exposed, with very flexible labour market, inequality and lower public expenditure in social dimensions).
3   Spain, Greece, Portugal and Italy (Mediterranean countries – which combine features of the two groups above).

To some extent Denmark, Sweden and Finland were badly affected by the crisis. The reason is very likely attributed to the strong flexibility in the labour market, which allowed firms to fire workers during recessions, so deepening the crisis from an employment point of view. However, the stronger initial conditions of those countries in terms of GDP levels, active and passive labour policies, as

Table 2.1 EU countries during the crisis 2007–11

Countries with relatively higher GDP cumulative growth 2007–11	Countries with employment stable or increasing	Countries with employment reduction (2007–11)	Countries with high recession (cumulative 2007–11 below 0)	Countries with high unemployment (above 8 per cent)	Countries with stagnating cumulative GDP 2007–11 (between 0 and 1)	Countries with lower unemployment
Slovenia	Belgium	Ireland	Greece	UK	UK	Austria
Lithuania	Romania	Latvia	Latvia	Italy	Spain	Netherlands
Belgium	Austria	Estonia	Ireland	Poland	France	Luxembourg
Netherlands	Luxembourg	Lithuania	Hungary	Hungary	Finland	Germany
Germany	Malta	Spain	Italy	France		Czech Republic
Luxembourg	Germany	Denmark	Denmark	Bulgaria		Malta
Austria	Poland	Portugal	Portugal	Portugal		Belgium
Romania		Finland	Estonia	Estonia		Denmark
Sweden		Bulgaria		Slovakia		Sweden
Cyprus		United Kingdom		Ireland		Romania
Czech Republic		Slovakia		Lithuania		Finland
Bulgaria		Hungary		Latvia		Cyprus
Malta		Italy		Greece		Slovenia
Slovakia		Greece		Spain		
Poland		Slovenia				
		Sweden				
		Cyprus				
		Netherlands				
		Czech Republic				
		France				

Source: own elaboration.

well as welfare, made the crisis less costly in terms of social and human costs. This positioned the countries for a faster recovery, thanks to strong labour market programmes, automatic stabilizers, better education, training and job search programmes.

In regards to the Mediterranean countries, the economic crisis is commonly deepened by structural problems such as low productivity, scarce innovation, exposure to the housing sector – badly affected by the crisis – and higher levels of public debt. Moreover, poor labour market policies, higher inequality and labour flexibility, introduced massively in those four countries in the last decade, reduced consumption capacity and made aggregate demand more unstable than in other EU countries, deepening the crisis from a deflationary point of view.

When we consider the flows of employment changes with absolute values, the situation does not change much, meaning that the variation of the values goes in the same direction and magnitude as the variation of the rates. For instance, employment in Spain decreased by more than two million, while in Germany it increased by more than 1.5 million; these figures correspond, respectively, to −11.8 per cent of employment in Spain and +4 per cent of employment in Germany.

However, some more details and explanations are needed. The top seven countries in maintaining employment flows as positive are again the same: Luxembourg, Malta, Poland, Germany, Austria, Denmark and Belgium in that order. The bottom seven countries in losing jobs are Ireland, Latvia, Lithuania, Spain, Bulgaria, Greece and Portugal. The only exception here to the usual rank on the bottom is Bulgaria, which lost relatively more jobs than other countries, despite the fact that GDP growth in Bulgaria during the same period was relatively higher.

3 Measuring the crisis: the Crisis Management Index

In order to evaluate the crisis on a cross-country basis, I have designed an index which would allow for an assessment of the impact of the crisis simultaneously on the GDP performance (recession and recovery) and on the labour market (employment, unemployment and labour productivity).

The Crisis Management Index (CMI) takes into consideration both employment and GDP aspects. Using such an index would allow for a better consideration of the performance of countries during the crisis. This avoids biases and distortions, such as the fact that countries could have experienced low recession but very bad unemployment or employment reduction. A situation like that, for instance, can be observed clearly in the United States, where despite relatively lower recession than the EU in terms of GDP, during 2007–11 it experienced much worse performance in the labour market (Tridico 2011).

The CMI goes from a maximum of 0.4 (the best) for Austria to a minimum of −22 (the worst) for Spain. Values are assigned according to performances during 2007–11 in terms of magnitude and dynamics of: GDP fall, employment changes, unemployment and employment elasticity effects. Since the first three variables capture all the same aggregate effects, I use only one of them, unemployment, and I combine it with the elasticity variable (CMI=$U+g/n$). This allows also avoidance of collinearity in the building of the index.

Theoretically speaking, the building and the use of such an index is rather new. However, its building is based on a strong empirical intuition. Moreover, the comparison is made with the same index for all the EU27 countries, so that it can be considered a consistent method, at least among the countries analysed. In other words, such an assessment allows for a consistent comparison solely between the 27 Member States and consequently for a rank where the situation of each country can be coherently analysed in comparison to other Member States, and does not aim to be a general theoretical framework of analysis for all countries in the world.

The CMI in the last column of Table 2.2 is the sum U plus the ratio g/n. The best values are for Austria, Luxembourg, Germany, Malta, Poland, the Netherlands and Belgium (the top seven). At the opposite end of the spectrum (between −22 and −12.5) one can find Spain, Greece, Latvia, Lithuania, Ireland, Portugal and Estonia, the bottom seven. Figure 2.7 shows the rank and the index for all countries.

The question that I will elaborate on in regards to the CMI ranking is what leads these countries to perform so differently? Why are the worst-performing countries performing so poorly? What contributed to the better performance of the top seven countries (which by the way are not the usual suspects, meaning the Scandinavia countries)? In order to answer these questions I have analysed data and correlations between selected variables and have elaborated on a model which estimates the CMI. The main hypotheses of my model are:

1 Labour flexibility worsened unemployment and employment levels during the crisis, since elasticity of employment reduction to recession, in countries with higher flexibility, is higher.

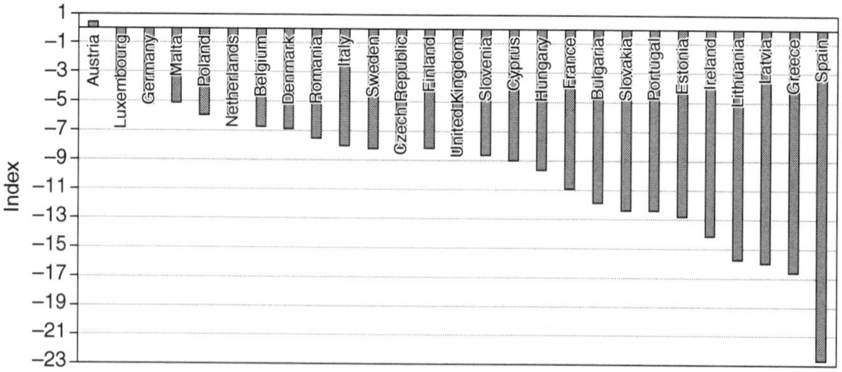

Figure 2.7 The Crisis Management Index, 2007–11 (source: own elaboration on Eurostat data).

Table 2.2 Relevant dimensions for the Crisis Management Index

Countries	GDP (g) change 2007–11	Employment (n) changes 2007–10	Unemployment 2011 (U)	Labour elasticity/Labour productivity × g/n	CMI = U + g/n
Top seven countries					
Austria	1.3	0.3	−3.9	4.33	0.43
Luxembourg	1.28	1	−4.8	1.28	−3.52
Germany	1.18	1.7	−5.8	0.69	−5.11
Malta	2.16	1.5	−6.6	1.44	−5.16
Poland	4.9	2.3	−8	2.13	−5.87
Netherlands	1.14	−1.3	−5	−0.88	−5.88
Belgium	1.12	0	−6.7	0.00	−6.70
Denmark	−0.5	−3.7	−7.1	0.14	−6.96
Romania	1.36	0	−7.5	0.00	−7.50
Italy	−0.52	−1.8	−8.3	0.29	−8.01
Sweden	1.42	−1.5	−7.2	−0.95	−8.15
Czech Republic	1.72	−1.1	−6.6	−1.56	−8.16
Finland	0.96	−2.2	−7.8	−0.44	−8.24
United Kingdom	0.1	−2	−8.3	−0.05	−8.35
Slovenia	1	−1.6	−8	−0.63	−8.63
Cyprus	1.64	−1.3	−7.8	−1.26	−9.06
Hungary	−0.62	−1.9	−9.9	0.33	−9.57
France	0.52	−0.5	−9.9	−1.04	−10.94
Bulgaria	1.9	−2	−10.9	−0.95	−11.85
Slovakia	3.72	−1.9	−10.4	−1.96	−12.36
Bottom seven countries					
Portugal	−0.12	−2.2	−12.5	0.05	−12.45
Estonia	−0.04	−8.4	−12.8	0.00	−12.80
Ireland	−0.82	−9.2	−14.2	0.09	−14.11
Lithuania	1.08	−7.1	−15.5	−0.15	−15.65
Latvia	−1.44	−9	−16.1	0.16	−15.94
Greece	−1.9	−1.8	−17.6	1.06	−16.54
Spain	0.26	−7	−22.6	−0.04	−22.64

Source: own elaboration on Eurostat data.

Note

A value >1 indicates that GDP increases more than employment; a value between 1 and 0 indicates that the increase of employment (or its reductions) was bigger than the increase (or the decrease) of GDP; a negative value indicates that despite the increase of GDP, employment decreased. This indicator can be considered a dynamic measure of labour productivity. However, its reverse is also an indicator of labour elasticity to GDP change.

2   Inequality, in particular during the crisis, emerges as a detrimental variable, lowering income opportunities for middle classes, weakening consumption and therefore leading to unstable aggregate demand, with further negative consequences on GDP performance.

3   Exposure to foreign banks increases financial instability because with the crisis foreign capital was the first to exit, leaving the country in danger of a lack of liquidity, lack of additional investments and further negative consequences on GDP.

4   The higher the weight of the housing sector in the economy, the deeper the impact of the crisis in the GDP fall, since the first victim of the financial crisis was the housing sector and the building construction industry. Such a sector is usually very labour intensive, so consequences in terms of employment can also be dramatic, as was witnessed in Spain.

5   Active policies are very important for a fast recovery of GDP since job training and education can help workers to easily transition to other sectors of the economy, with benefits for employment levels.

6   Trade unions are essential social institutions to cope with the panic and lack of trust that can emerge during a crisis. The objective of trade unions is usually to maintain higher levels of employment and to fight against mass-firing tendencies of firms. Such behaviour can be rational for firms during a crisis in order to minimize losses, but can be detrimental for the negative spiral of the economy, with further deflationary pressures and further recession of the GDP. A strong trade union which manages to maintain higher levels of employment, at the expense of profit erosion for firms, would contribute, at the macro level, to reducing the negative impact of crisis on consumption, aggregate demand and GDP.

7   Passive policies are essential to introduce automatic stabilizers, which would avoid a collapse in consumption, a reduction in the aggregate demand and a further GDP decline.

8   A high level of credit in the system is a bad symptom, in particular if the level of savings is very low. Typically, the situation of the United States and other Anglo-Saxon economies shows that the magnitude of the bubble was high where credit was vast. Consequently, when the bubble bursts the negative consequences on the financial sector and on the banking system are at their worst.

9   A low level of saving, in the long run, is detrimental for the sustainability of the appropriate level of investments which boost economic growth.

10   The financialization of the economy shapes the regime of the economic system and may negatively affect the economic growth in the long run: a finance-led regime of growth, driven by consumption and credit only, is not sustainable in the long run, because investments and savings are needed. A finance-led regime of growth may be able to guarantee growth thanks to credit for consumption and financial investments (as happened in the United States in the past 20 years), but in the long run may cause excess production, instability of aggregate demand and deflationary pressures.

The hypotheses listed above are useful to build our model, where the dependent variable is the CMI and the independent variables are elements of those ten hypotheses.

We have deeply analysed two groups of countries: the countries which performed better during the crisis (the top seven countries in the order: Austria, Poland, Luxembourg, Malta, Germany, Netherlands and Belgium) and the countries which performed the worst (the bottom seven countries in the order: Spain, Latvia, Ireland, Lithuania, Estonia, Greece and Portugal).[3] We have tried to show why the countries that performed better did so, and the division in two groups, best and worst, helps to this purpose, because it reveals clearly the main features of the best-performing countries and the main features of the worst-performing countries. In the following comparative correlations we take into consideration the following variables: inequality, employment protection legislation, financialization, active and passive labour market policies, saving, and trade union density. All of these variables were correlated with the CMI for the worst- and best-performing countries.

It appears very clear, from the correlation shown in Figure 2.8, that the top seven countries with the highest CMI have the lowest inequality level, while in the opposite corner, with the highest inequality level (measured by the Gini coefficient in 2007) one can find the bottom seven countries.

A similar story can be found with the relation between the CMI and the Employment Protection Legislation (EPL 2008), the indicator of the OECD which measures the level of worker protection in the labour market and consequently the level of labour flexibility. This indicator shows the level of protection offered by national legislation with respect to regular employment, temporary employment and collective dismissal. In other words, regulation which allows employers the freedom to fire and hire workers at will (OECD

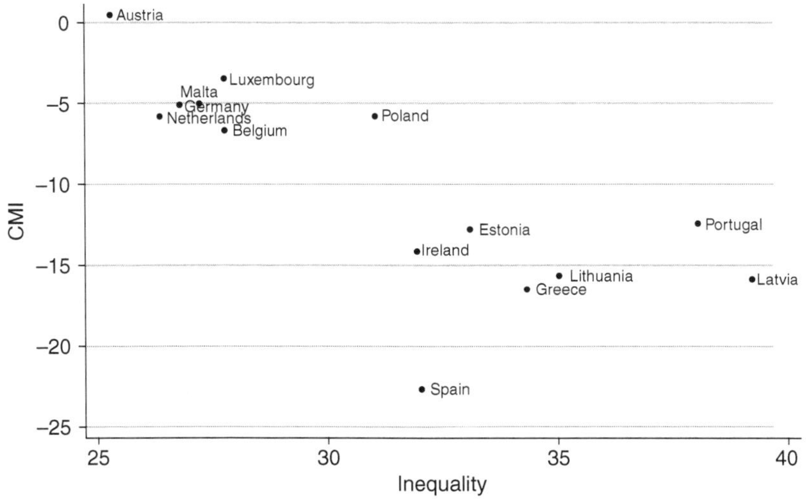

Figure 2.8 Correlation scatter CMI and inequality (source: own elaboration).

2004).[4] The average indicator decreased consistently in the last two decades – which indicates more labour flexibility (Tridico 2009; Leon and Realfonzo 2008; Nickell 1997). The top seven with the highest CMI have the highest EPL level (lower labour flexibility), while in the opposite corner, with the lowest EPL (highest labour flexibility) one can find the bottom seven (Figure 2.9).

Interestingly enough, the correlation scatter between CMI and the level of financialization of the economy just before the crisis in 2006–07 shows similar results, with the bottom seven having the highest level of financialization (Figure 2.10). The variable financialization is the value of market capitalization in the stock exchange as a percentage of GDP. The market capitalization (also known as market value) is the share price multiplied by the number of shares outstanding. Listed domestic companies are the domestically incorporated companies listed on the country's stock exchanges at the end of the year. Listed companies do not include investment companies, mutual funds, or other collective investment vehicles. Not surprisingly, the only exception among the top seven countries with the lowest levels of financialization is Luxembourg.[5]

Active and passive labour market policies (percentage of GDP for expenditure on labour market policies 2008) are consistent with the hypothesis as they travel in the expected direction. Poland is an exception as this country spends relatively little in terms of labour market policies. The case of Poland is not unexpected because our hypothesis states that labour market policies help countries recover from crisis, whereas Poland did not experience a recession during the period analysed so labour market policies were not required as strongly as in the rest of the EU. In Spain, on the contrary, with the extraordinary highest unemployment level in the EU (around 20 per cent), the active and passive labour market policies, as they are automatic stabilizers, were very consistent during the crisis (Figure 2.11).

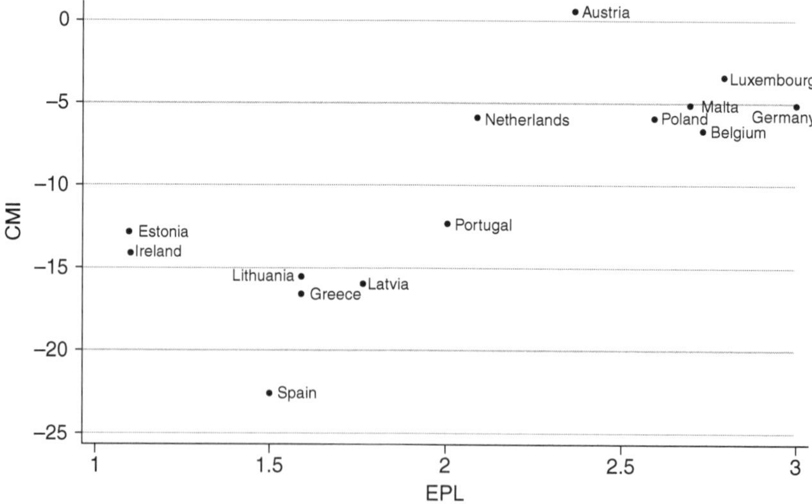

Figure 2.9 Correlation scatter CMI and EPL (source: own elaboration).

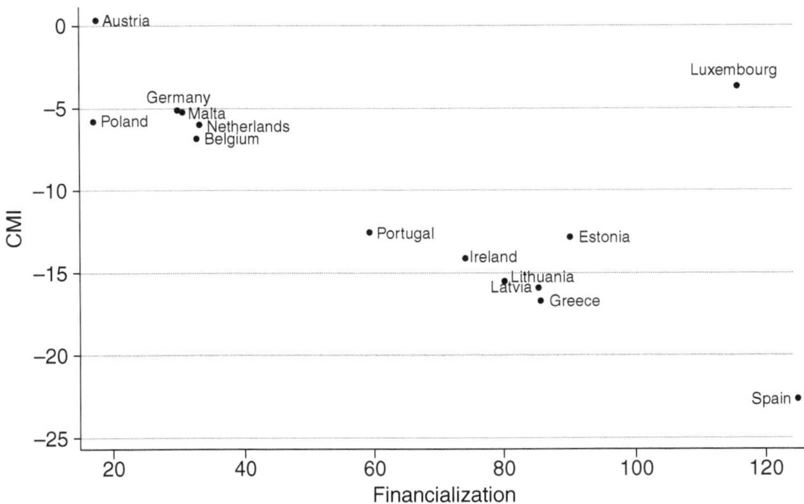

Figure 2.10 Correlation scatter CMI and financialization (source: own elaboration).

Another relevant variable which appears in our hypothesis is the level of savings (in 2008). A low level of savings, in the long run, would inhibit investment and growth. In this case the only exception is Spain, which has a relatively high level of savings, equal to Poland, which has the lowest level among the top seven (Figure 2.12).

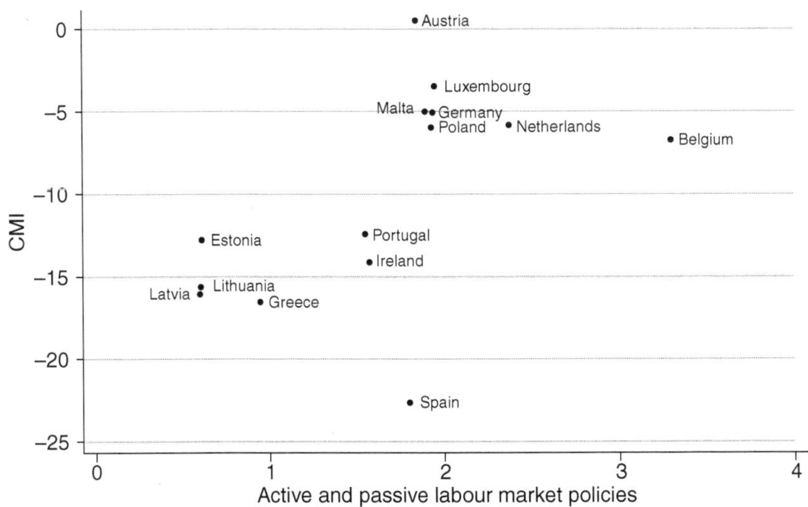

Figure 2.11 Correlation scatter CMI and active and passive labour market policies (source: own elaboration).

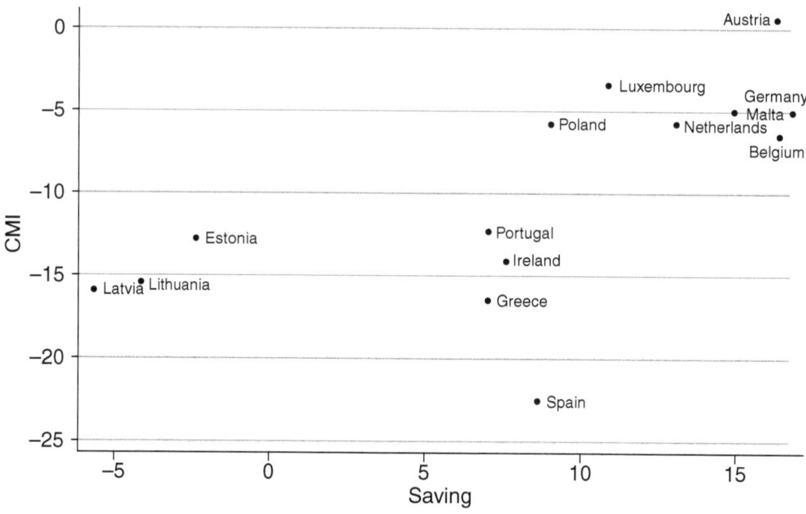

Figure 2.12 Correlation scatter CMI and saving (source: own elaboration).

As I have argued above, among the ten hypotheses trade union density is a relevant variable as well. In this case, without exception, the top seven have the highest trade union density level (membership average percentage 2006–10 of employees) and this has helped to keep higher levels of employment and aggregate demand during the crisis (Figure 2.13).

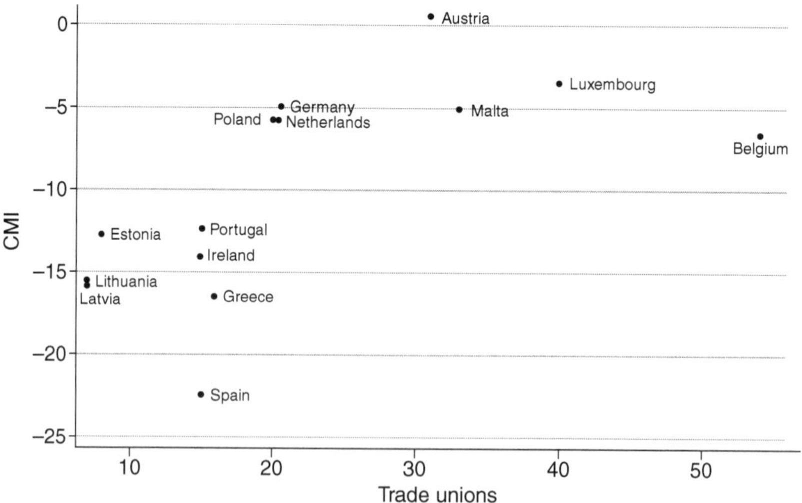

Figure 2.13 Correlation scatter CMI and trade unions (source: own elaboration).

4 The model: explaining the CMI

Following the hypotheses and correlation figures above, I am now able to put forward a model, with a simple regression analysis, an OLS cross-country model, investigating the variables which determine the highest CMI, considered as dependent variables.

The model is the following:

$$CMI = c + B_1 \times EPL - B_2 \times TW - B_3\,Ineq + +e,$$

where c is the constant, B_1, B_2 and B_3 are the coefficients of the correspondent variables; *EPL* is the Employment Protection Legislation Index in 2008 (which measures the level of labour flexibility); *TW* is the percentage of temporary in the total of employment (in 2008), *Ineq* is the Gini coefficient in 2008 which indicates the income distribution and the inequality in the society.

I have tested this model in two ways: first with a simple OLS cross-section regression, using average values of those variables for the period 2007–11 (the crisis time) and 27 observations (as many as there are EU Member States); and second, and more fundamentally, with a more sophisticate GLS model of panel data of six years: 2006, 2007, 2008, 2009, 2010 and 2011, and 162 observations (27×6). Results are very consistent, robust and statistically significant, as Table 2.3 shows.

Table 2.3 Regression table, panel data

Variable	Coefficient (standard errors)	P-values
EPL	1.615307 (0.7324882)	0.027
Temporary work	−0.1578564 (0.0694321)	0.023
Inequality	−0.2716993 (0.107862)	0.012
Constant	4.225772 (3.638554)	0.245
Year 2006	−0.5277289 (0.9971861)	0.597
Year 2008	−3.037997 (0.9973313)	0.002
Year 2009	−10.86284 (0.9978834)	0.000
Year 2010	−4.382909 (0.9970402)	0.000
Year 2011	−6.065116 (0.9974051)	0.000

Year 2007 dropped because of collinearity
R^2:
within = 0.5610
between = 0.2293
overall = 0.4880
Wald chi^2(8) = 170.93; Prob > chi^2 = 0.0000
Number of obs = 162.
Number of groups = 27
Panel 2006, 2007, 2008, 2009, 2010, 2011
Hausman Test (RE vs FE):
Ho: difference in coefficients not systematic
chi^2(3) = (b−B)'[(V_b−V_B)^(−1)](b−B) = 20.75
Prob > chi^2 = 0.0001
H (alternative) accepted

Source: own elaboration.

Below I report data of the GLS model which are more appropriate with a greater number of variables than the OLS model.

This model, which should be analysed together with the correlation above, indicates that a higher CMI is caused by a higher EPL index (lower labour flexibility), and a lower level of temporary work and a lower lever of inequality. All the variables are very significant (most of them within 5 per cent levels), as one can see from the p-values. The signs and the magnitude in both regressions go in the same directions. Moreover, in the panel a random effect regression with dummy variables for each year was used, and the Hausman test proved the reliability of this effect.

These results call for reflection on the structure and situation of the labour market, and give suggestions for policy making in a specific direction. As regards to policy making, labour flexibility is a negative factor and contributed to deepening the effects of the crisis. At the same time, countries with higher shares of temporary work suffered more during the crisis and have lower CMIs. Inequality is also a negative factor that increased the negative effects of the crisis: in fact, countries with higher levels of inequality have lower CMI. From a Keynesian point of view this is quite obvious: societies with higher inequality have a middle class which suffers more in terms of consumption possibilities and income, and they consume less. This worsens the aggregate demand and consequently the level of activity of the economy decreases; therefore, in our model the CMI would decrease.

Labour flexibility was increasing everywhere in Europe in the last 10–15 years. However, some countries like Germany, Malta, Luxembourg and a few others still maintain rigid labour markets. These are the countries which managed to better cope with the current economic crisis, as we saw, along with Poland and Austria. Labour flexibility allows for the reduction of the labour costs and thus wage saving at the expense of wage earners, i.e. consumers. In such a situation inequality increases and also the aggregate demand could curb since consumption decreases. It is very interesting to note an inverse relation between inequality and the EPL index (labour flexibility): the lower the EPL (higher flexibility) the higher the inequality. As usual in this analysis, countries like Germany, and in general the rest of the top seven, performed better: they have higher EPL (lower flexibility) and lower inequality. On the opposite side, countries which suffered the most during the crisis (Estonia, Lithuania, Latvia, Ireland and Spain, followed by Portugal, Greece, Italy, the United Kingdom and some others) have higher inequality and lower EPL (higher flexibility) (see Figure 2.14).

The crisis itself proves that a coordinated (or corporative) market economy (CME), similar to the one that can be found in Germany, may do more to shape a new global governance and may be more appropriate to help prevent further crises (Pontusson 2005; EuroMemorandum 2010; Semmler and Young 2010). The CME would guarantee a more stable path of development and accumulation, mitigating the risk of boom and bust cycles illustrated by Minsky (1986). Examples of CME can be found in the EU and in particular among continental

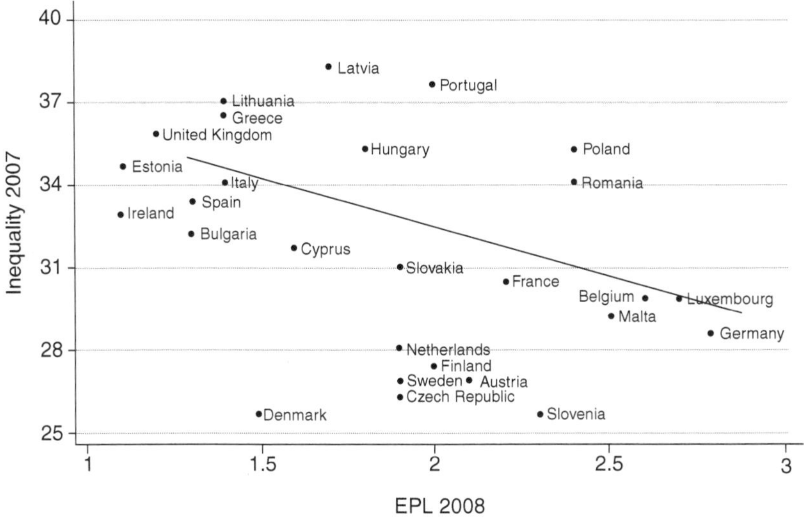

Figure 2.14 Correlation scatter inequality and EPL (source: own elaboration).

economies (Germany and Austria in particular), which combine interesting and functional elements of competitive market economies, such as competition and private investments, with useful market coordination systems such as financial regulation, public strategies of investments and welfare and important public goods (Rochon and Rossi 2010; Pitelis 2010; Whelan 2010).

In fact, countries like Poland, Malta and Luxemburg can be allocated in a type of socio-economic model similar to the one of Germany and Austria. These countries managed better in the crisis within all the dimensions analysed. On the contrary, countries which rely more on a liberal competitive market economy like Estonia, Lithuania, Latvia, Ireland and the United Kingdom suffered the most during the crisis. This was also the case of the Mediterranean economies (Greece, Spain, Portugal and Italy), which during the last 15–20 years liberalized strongly their labour markets, thus combining liberalized labour markets with inefficient social policies (Sapir 2005). On a different note, Scandinavian economies (such as Denmark, Sweden and Finland) suffered during the crisis, in particular in terms of employment reduction. Most of this reduction can be attributed to the very flexible labour market these economies have created during the last decade. This was coupled with an efficient security model and safety net in terms of income and employment security. However, during the crisis employment fell dramatically.

5 Conclusion

In this chapter I have argued that countries which performed relatively better during the economic crisis of 2007–11 are countries which do not have a strong flexible labour market and managed to keep stable employment levels. These countries combine a very good mix of economic policies and social institutions oriented to stabilize the level of consumption and the aggregate demand. Coordination mechanisms, higher levels of financial regulation and monitoring are also important features of these economies. These are Germany, Austria, Poland, Belgium, Netherlands, Malta and Luxembourg. On the contrary, along with a very strong flexible labour market, countries which performed the worst during the crisis also have a poor combination of: high inequality levels, higher exposure to foreign banks, a stronger reliance on the housing sector, less incisive labour market policies and expenditure, less trade union density, higher levels of private indebtedness, strong financialization and a lower level of savings. These countries are Latvia, Lithuania, Estonia, Spain, Ireland, Portugal and Greece, followed by Italy, the United Kingdom and other EU members.

Clearly, the first group of countries identifies better, in the EU, a coordinated or corporative market economy model, while the second group of countries identify better with a liberal (or hybrid) competitive market economy model. The regression model confirms such a result: the CMI is higher in the first group of countries and this is determined by higher levels of EPL (lower flexibility), lower levels of temporary work and lower levels of inequality.

Our suggestion is that rather than focusing on austerity measures, the EU should address other issues which are considered to be the main causes of the current crisis: these are the problems of the labour market, the uneven income distribution and the labour flexibility which weaken consumption and aggregate demand. Moreover, a strong financialization of the economy occurred in the last two decades in many EU countries and negatively affected economic growth. A finance-led regime of growth, driven by consumption and credit, is not sustainable in the long run, because investments and savings are needed. A stable economic growth path occurs when growth is driven by the aggregate demand and in particular by investments and consumption. The first may also be supported by finance and the second should be supported by wage increases, which should follow labour productivity growth. Such a type of growth is better identified in countries like Germany, Austria, Netherlands, Belgium, Poland, Malta and Luxembourg, which are in fact the best-performing countries of the current economic crisis.

Notes

1 A previous and different version of this chapter was published in the *International Labour Review* (Vol. 152(2) (2013)) with the title 'The impact of economic crisis on the EU labour markets: a comparative perspective' (see Tridico 2013).
2 The media pointed out how an election in the small Lander of Lower Saxon in Germany during the Greek crisis in Spring 2010 was enough to keep German chancellor Angela Merkel far away from an idea of integration and financial solidarity, which populists in Germany objected.
3 In this group we could have added most of the rest of the countries with very negative CMI (including Italy, Hungary, the United Kingdom, Bulgaria, etc.), but since we have

considered only seven countries at the top, for consistency we considered only seven countries at the bottom.

4 OECD Employment Outlook 2004, Chapter 2, *Employment Protection Regulation and Labour Market Performance*.

5 Such an exception about Luxembourg's higher level of financialization does not need further comment given the economy structure and the particular role and situation of the small economy of Luxembourg in the EU.

References

Barba, A. and Pivetti, M. (2009), 'Rising Household Debt: Its Causes and Macroeconomic Implications – Along-Period Analysis', *Cambridge Journal of Economics*, 33(1): 113–137.

Cesaratto, S. (2011), 'Europe, German Mercantilism and the Current Crisis', in Brancaccio, E. and Fontana, G. (eds), *The Global Economic Crisis: New Perspectives on the Critique of Economic Theory and Policy*, Routledge, London.

EuroMemorandum (2010), *Confronting the Crisis: Austerity Or Solidarity*. European Economists for an Alternative Economic Policy in Europe – EuroMemo Group 2010/11.

Fitoussi, J.P. and Saraceno, F. (2010), *Inequality and Macroeconomic Performance*, OFCE, Paris.

Fitoussi, J.P. and Stiglitz, J. (2009), *The Ways out of the Crisis and the Building of a More Cohesive World*, The Shadow GN, Chair's Summary, LUISS Guido Carli, Rome, 6–7 May.

Leon, P. and Realfonzo, R. (2008), 'A cura di', *L'Economia della Precarietà*, Manifestolibri.

Minsky, H.P. (1986), *Stabilizing an Unstable Economy*, Yale University Press, New Haven, CT.

OECD (2004) 'Employment Outlook, Chapter 2', *Employment Protection Regulation and Labour Market Performance*, OECD.

OECD (2010), *Employment Outlook* (online database).

Pitelis, C. (2010) 'From Bust to Boom: An Introduction', *Contribution To Political Economy*, 29: 1–8.

Pontusson, J. (2005), *Inequality and Prosperity: Social Europe vs. Liberal America*, Cornell University press, Ithaca, NY and London.

Posner, R.A. (2009), *A Failure of Capitalism*, Harvard University Press, Cambridge, MA.

Rochon, L.-P. and Rossi, S. (2010), 'Has "It" Happened Again?', *International Journal of Political Economy*, 39(2): 5–9.

Sapir, A. (2005), 'Globalization and the Reform of European Social Models', *Bruegel Policy Brief*, 1.

Semmler, W. and Young, B. (2010), 'Lost in Temptation of Risk: Financial Market Liberalization, Financial Market Meltdown and Regulatory Reforms', *Comparative European Politics*, 8(3): 327–353.

Stiglitz, J. (2010), *Recommendations by the Commission of Experts of the President of the General Assembly of United Nations on Reforms of the International Monetary and Financial System*, UN, New York.

Tridico, P. (2009), 'Flessibilità e Istituzioni nel Mercato del Lavoro: dagli Economisti Classici agli Economisti Istituzionalisti', *Lavoro&Economia*, 1: 113–139.

Tridico, P. (2011), 'Varieties of Capitalism and Responses to the Financial Crisis: The

European Social Model Versus the US Model', Working Paper no. 129, Dipartimento di Economia, Università Roma Tre.

Tridico, P. (2012), 'Financial Crisis and Global Imbalances: Its Labor Market Origins and the Aftermath', *Cambridge Journal of Economics*, 36(1): 17–42.

Tridico, P. (2013), 'The Impact of Economic Crisis on the EU Labour Markets: A Comparative Perspective', *International Labour Review*, 152(2): 175–190.

Whelan, K. (2010), *Global Imbalances and the Financial Crisis*, General Directorate for Internal Policies, European Parliament, Brussels.

Wolff, R. (2010), *Capitalism Hits the Fan: The Global Economic Meltdown and What to Do about It*, Pluto Press, New York.

Wray, L. Randall (2000), *The Neo-Chartalist Approach to Money*, Center for Full Employment and Price Stability. Available at: www.cfeps.org/pubs/wp/wp10.html (accessed 26 November 2013).

3 Aiding economic recovery after the financial crisis

Malcolm Sawyer[1]

1 Introduction

The North Atlantic financial crises which became evident in the second half of 2007 and intensified in late 2008 came after a long period of financialisation. In the aftermath of the financial crises much of the Western world (we focus on North America and countries of the European Union) has suffered from high and often rising unemployment alongside slow or negative economic growth.[2] It also appears that the capacity to produce (potential output) has diminished (or at least not grown at pre-2007 rates). The focus in this chapter with regard to some recovery in the economies is on the creation of something approaching full employment. As such this would imply at least most of the countries of the European Union more than returning to pre-crisis levels as those levels of unemployment were not those corresponding to full employment. Full employment is seen as a situation where there is a balance between those seeking work and job vacancies, with no-one who wishes to work being unemployed for more than six months. It would also require that the hours an individual worked matched their requirements. It can be readily recognised that the rate of employment (relative to the adult population) which corresponds to full employment will change over time as social norms and expectations change. Full employment is used as the benchmark for economic recovery rather than eliminating the output gap (that is, the difference between actual output and 'potential output') as 'potential output' is a slippery concept and one which has a tendency to adjust in line with actual output. The current estimates of potential output show signs of downward adjustments in the face of the recession. Economic recovery could be viewed in terms of restoration of economic growth at something like the pace experienced prior to the financial crisis. It is undoubtedly the case that economic recovery and falling unemployment would involve a relatively fast rise in GDP. But, for reasons indicated below, sustainable growth rates at pre-crisis levels may not be possible, and as such seeking a recovery in terms of full employment requires recognition of that. The key point here is that lower sustainable growth would involve lower investment requirements, and without compensating policy changes lower investment (relative to GDP) would involve lower employment.

In the years immediately prior to the financial crisis in many industrialised countries, demand was supported by a variety of factors which were themselves unsustainable. Consumer debt rose rapidly with household saving (as in the United Kingdom and United States) falling to virtually zero, and the rising debt was unsustainable. There were housing price and construction booms promoted by high volumes of lending which appeared to be only justifiable on the basis of continual rises in house prices. The rapid expansion of the financial sector with its high profits provided substantial tax revenues and lower than otherwise budget deficits.

In this chapter we focus on some aspects of a sustainable recovery which would involve something approaching full employment. Full employment of labour requires that there is a level of aggregate demand which is compatible with it, and a level of demand which is sustainable and is not reliant on unsustainable consumer debt nor on high rates of investment which would be unsustainable through rising capital:output ratio and/or involving a growth rate which was environmentally unsustainable. However, full employment of labour does require sufficient levels of productive capacity in the relevant locations consistent with full employment without inflationary pressures building up from a level of demand in excess of the productive capacity of the economy (what elsewhere we have described as an inflationary barrier (Arestis and Sawyer 2005)). Hence in the short term (a few years) higher rates of investment (as compared with present levels and with the average over the pre-crisis average) will be required to repair the damage of the financial crisis and to enable shifts in the composition of output. But in the longer term investment rates could be anticipated to be lower (at least as compared with pre-crisis norms) along with lower growth than experienced in the past.

2 Financialisation and the financial crisis

The financial crisis of 2007–09 was preceded by processes of financialisation during the previous three decades in many countries. The term financialisation is here used following that of Epstein (2005) Financialisation has been variously described and for our purpose that given by Epstein (2005) will serve: 'Financialization means the increasing role of financial motives, financial markets, financial actors and financial institutions in the operation of the domestic and international economies.' Financialisation is viewed here in terms of the growth of the scale and power of the financial sector with deregulation of the financial sector and changes in the structure of the financial sector and its operations, including securitisation. In this chapter we begin by a brief overview of some aspects of financialisation: it could perhaps be more accurately said to be some major changes in the capitalist system which have been widespread over the past three decades. Of particular relevance here is the growth of financial institutions, the shifts in their main areas of operation (relatively away from the clearing banks function) and the rise in the ratios of household debt to GDP and of financial assets to GDP. There have also tended to be changes in the flow of funds between households and firms.

There are four features to which we draw attention here as particularly rel-evant for our discussion, noting that those features are 'stylised facts' which relate to a greater or lesser extent across industrialised economies, but particu-larly the United Kingdom and United States. This is not to say that financialisa-tion broadly conceived has many other aspects. This does not deny that the economic, social and political power has been a continuing feature of capitalism. In the financialisation era (since 1980), in general, though varying from country to country, there have been a range of developments which are highly relevant for our discussion here.

First, there is the growth of the financial sector in scale and range of activ-ities. As argued in Sawyer (2010), this growth has not involved a substantial increase (relative to GDP) in saving nor in investment, and indeed in many coun-tries investment rates have been stable or declining. Thus, as the major role of the financial sector should be to link together savers with investors, the growth of the financial sector has not contributed to the fulfilment of that role in that the efficiency with which those linkages are made and the 'quality' of investment does not appear to have risen.

Second, there have been associated changes in the distribution of income both as between wages and profits (and rentier income of the financial sector) with shifts from wages to profits and in the personal distribution of income, in the dir-ection of increased inequality in the personal distribution of income with par-ticularly pronounced shifts towards the top 1 per cent. The financial sector itself has contributed to the shift in the personal distribution through being a relatively unequal sector and the growth of inequality within the sector. The profits and income of the financial sector have also tended to rise.

The literature on wage-led vs profit regimes[3] indicates that the income shares do have an impact on the level of demand, and for many countries and here sig-nificantly at the global level, higher profit share tends to depress demand.[4] But it is not just a matter of the direct effects on demand. The rise in profits and hence in the potential for retained earnings out of profits alongside a general lower investment climate can mean that some corporations move to a position of being net lenders rather than the traditional view of being net borrowers. If corpora-tions are net lenders then they have to lend to someone – and the options are lending to government, lending overseas (directly in the form of foreign direct investment or through acquisition of financial and other assets overseas) or lending to consumers. This lending may not be direct (though where corpora-tions establish finance arms to lend to consumers for the purchase of their own product it would be) and then flows through intermediaries: but the net sectoral flows would be in the direction from corporations to households.

Third, the overall effects on investment, and specifically investment in the non-financial sector, have been argued to be to lower rather than raise invest-ment. Hein (2011), for example, argues that

On the one hand, this [financialisation] has imposed short-termism on man-agement and has caused decreasing managements' animal spirits with respect to real investment in capital stock and long-run growth of the firm. On the other hand, it has drained internal means of finance for real investment purposes from the corporations, through increasing dividend payments and share buybacks in order to boost stock prices and thus shareholder value.

This depressing effect on investment would then be associated with slower growth of the capital stock and of output, as well as a depressing impact on aggregate demand.

Fourth, the growth of the financial sector has involved the development of a range of financial products such as derivatives, mortgage-backed securities and securitisation. But, as indicated above, this has not gone alongside any growth in savings or investment (relative to GDP). It has involved tiers of financial assets and liabilities in which the assets backing a financial asset are other financial assets (rather than backed by real assets). This raises two interesting questions. First, what forms the basis of the payment of returns on financial assets. When a financial asset is backed by a real asset, the simple answer would be that the payment of returns on financial assets (whether in form of interest payments or dividends) would be backed by the profits to be gained on the operation of the real asset (this may push the question back one stage – what is the source of the profits on real assets?). But the creation of a financial asset (such as a mortgage-backed security) poses the question of where the returns on the 'additional' financial asset arise from. Second, the expansion of the balance sheet of a single financial institution through expansion of both its assets and its liabilities generates enhanced risk of instability, simply because a change in the relative price of assets and liabilities (in an adverse direction) throws the financial institution into insolvency. Further, problems of contagion are exacerbated in that one institution's assets is another institution's liabilities, and the failure of one financial institution and its inability to meet its liabilities impacts on the value of the assets of another financial institution.

The processes of financialisation have placed many constraints on sustainable economic recovery with full employment. Here we highlight a few of those, without any claim that the list is complete, and to which we return. One comes from the power of the financial markets and credit-rating agencies in imposing constraints on the operations of fiscal policy in a range of countries. The allocation of saving and credit then lies in the hands of credit-rating agencies and other financial institutions. A second comes from the impacts of financialisation on aggregate demand (through higher inequality and depressing effects on investment). As argued below, these effects raise the need for budget deficits. Further, corporations have shifted to higher saving (out of profits) and lower investment and thereby shifted from being borrowers to lenders. The other side of that is some combination of government borrowing and household borrowing. The latter became evident with the fall of household saving to zero (or below) in the United Kingdom and United States around 2007. The reliance of demand on household borrowing and on rising asset (notably house) prices was unsustainable. The third is derived from the unstable nature of the financial sector, and with its growing role the greater impact which financial crises have on real activity. There are many processes of the financial sector which tend towards instability, and in Minsky's terminology the shift from hedge to speculative to Ponzi finance. In this chapter our focus is on the second of those constraints, but this should not be taken to mean that major reforms of the financial sector are not required. High on the list of reforms would be the adoption of policies and institutions which guide funds into social beneficial directions, including the fostering of the 'greening' of investment and of productive activities: these would include the development of publically and mutually owned development banks, requirements on the direction of bank funds (as for example in the American Community Reinvestment Act).

3 Revival of investment

Investment is an important component of demand (and hence in the determination of the level of economic activity and employment) and economic growth. Some basic statistics on investment in the past two decades in major European countries and the United States and Japan are displayed in Table 3.1. The pattern among these 'big six' economies is mixed, with a couple of notable falls in investment ratio between the 1990s and the 2000s up to the crisis (Germany, Japan), flat lining in the United Kingdom, and small increases in France, Italy and the United States. After the financial crisis, investment to GDP ratio is noticeably smaller (with the exception of France). The degree to which investment has to revive to return to the pre-crisis levels is, of course, somewhat understated by these figures since GDP has fallen post-crisis as well as investment. However, the major question which has to be addressed is whether a return (or beyond) to the levels of investment (relative to GDP) is feasible or desirable. The feasibility relates to the major question of the underlying sustainable rate of growth. We would postulate that the likely sustainable growth rate in many countries will be significantly below past rates. For a given capital–output ratio, a 1 per cent lower annual growth rate could well imply a net investment ratio which is 4–5 percentage points lower, assuming a capital–output ratio of that

Table 3.1 Investment record in past two decades

Country	Investment/GDP (%) average 1990–99	Investment/GDP (%) average 2000–08	Investment/GDP (%) average 2009–12
France	18.48	20.05	20.14
Germany	22.64	18.90	17.74
Italy	20.48	21.24	19.53
Japan	28.83	23.09	20.60
United Kingdom	17.29	17.33	15.03
United States	18.70	19.55	15.98

Source: calculated from World Bank Database.

magnitude. Comparisons with the investment ratios in Table 3.1 clearly indicate that such a reduction in investment would be substantial, and as we will point out below, would have significant implications for the future of budget deficits.

The willingness or otherwise of the financial system to provide funding for investment can also be raised. A pre-requisite for the revival of investment is often viewed as resting on the availability of funding for investment. It is then paradoxical that saving in most industrialised countries runs well ahead of investment – with the consequence that there are substantial budget deficits required to mop-up the saving. Some would this as 'crowding out' of private investment by the budget deficit. But the reality is that the saving would not be able to occur if there were not a budget deficit with the corresponding issue of financial assets. There is not a shortage of savings; indeed, there is a surplus of savings. The position on the relationship between private savings and investment prior to the financial crisis is illustrated in Table 3.2. It then becomes a trite observation to say that low levels of investment have to be ascribed to either a lack of willingness to undertake investment (low 'animal spirits' using Keynes' terminology) or a lack of initial finance to enable investment to occur. It is a basic post-Keynesian proposition that if investment occurs (through loan finance) then a corresponding amount of saving is generated, and that savings become available to fund the investment expenditure. This second case would then come from an unwillingness of banks to provide loans (or equivalently imposing more stringent conditions on loans). A higher level of savings and investment then crucially depends on an expansion of bank lending. In this perspective, the lending that is crucial is that by banks whose liabilities (bank deposits) count as money and hence are an addition to spending power. The present failings are partially related to the failure of 'quantitative easing' to stimulate lending by banks, and rather have contributed to boosting asset prices.

Within what is likely to be a lower rate of investment, the major challenge is to ensure that investment which is conducive to environmentally friendly production is funded. The market mechanisms cannot be relied upon to do this: and further it may be more readily accomplished through a bank-based financial system than a market-based system (see Pollin 1995 for a statement of this general argument). It may well require that a required proportion of lending by banks is directed towards 'green investment' (or at least to investment which is

Table 3.2 Private savings and private investment relative to GDP, 2002–07

	Private savings/GDP (%)	*Private investment/GDP (%)*
Germany	23.6	16.8
France	19.0	16.6
Italy	20.7	18.5
UK	15.3	15.3
Euro area	20.8	17.7

Sources: calculated from Eurostat, OECD Economic Outlook.

not environmentally unfriendly), and the establishment of publically sponsored banks specifically designed to support such investments.

Many have argued for 'green investment' as both necessary to address environmental and ecological concerns and as a means of stimulating employment.[5] In a recession situation, it is undoubtedly true that 'green investment' would increase employment (as indeed other forms of expenditure) and be socially useful. Some forms of 'green investment' (e.g. home insulation) is socially (and often privately) beneficial through reducing future consumption (in this case energy). Thus, with such forms of 'green investment', the level of future GDP would be diminished (though this is an illustration of the misleading nature of GDP as an indicator of human welfare). Other forms of 'green investment' (e.g. to enable use of solar energy) are in effect related to economic growth (as measured by GDP). In general we would then argue that a lower growth rate will be accompanied by a lower investment rate, even if there is a substantial shift in the direction of 'green investment'. However, a shift in the composition of investment (towards 'green investment') may enable a higher growth rate (than would have been the case). In Fontana and Sawyer (2012) we postulated that growth of GDP would be limited by the sustainable growth in the use of 'natural capital' ('ecological footprint'), but that the relationship between the growth of GDP and the sustainable use of 'natural capital' could be potentially changed through development of technology and through alterations in the productive structure; and a shift in the productive structure would have to be accompanied by a corresponding shift in the structure of investment.

From this brief discussion we draw the following thoughts. Investment cannot be said to be hampered by a shortage of saving, though there may well be an unwillingness of the banks to provide finance. The prospects of lower growth than previously experienced through environmental concerns and the pact of technical change means lower investment (relative to GDP) than previously. In macroeconomic terms, adjustments have to be made (as argued below through budget deficits) to the prospects of lower investment in the face of saving maintained at previous levels (or higher). Within the funding of investment, there are requirements that it is directed in the socially relevant directions.

4 Creating the conditions for full employment

The title of the chapter refers to economic recovery and most would interpret it in terms of a restoration of economic growth at the type of rates observed prior to the crisis. The recessions and slow growth in other periods have meant that in mid-2013 GDP remains below its level of 2008. If judged by the pre-crisis growth rates, then (in 2013) output is of the order of 15 per cent below what would have been the trend value. Recovery from the depths of the recession will involve higher output and the appearance of relatively rapid growth. Falling unemployment would accompany that relatively rapid growth, though the availability of productive capacity becomes a significant issue, particularly in areas of high unemployment, as the financial crisis and subsequent lower levels of investment have depressed productive capacity.

We would argue for full employment as the key objective to be achieved following a recovery. In saying this, we have to recognise that full employment has rarely been achieved, and that the creation and sustenance of full employment requires a whole gamut of policy measures, including demand management and macroeconomic policies, regional and industrial policies and the appropriate institutional arrangements.

One rationale for full employment is often seen in terms that unemployment (of labour) means that a society is not producing all that it is capable of, and goods and services which would be of value to people are not being produced. It has overtones of seeking to maximise output (given the resources available). This is not a rationale on which we rely here, in that higher levels of output require higher natural resource use. It is rather to view full employment as a right to employment and to participate in society.

We would measure economic recovery in terms of the degree to which employment rises and unemployment falls. This would, of course, bring higher output and what would be reported as growth in that output would indeed grow, and during a recovery could usually be expected to grow faster than the trend rate of growth. Our perspective, as indicated above, is that over the longer haul the rate of growth will be significantly lower than in the past (as far as industrialised countries are concerned). The lower investment rate would lead to higher unemployment unless it is compensated by higher demand elsewhere, which would need to come from some combination of budget deficits and lower savings (through a re-distribution of income). Lower growth (of output) would need to be accompanied by a lower growth of hours worked (to the extent to which growth of output differs from productivity growth) if rising unemployment is not to result.

5 The need for budget deficits

The financial crises and their aftermath have, of course, been associated with rising budget deficits as the automatic stabilisers of fiscal policy kicked in with some discretionary policies against recession before the forces of austerity struck. It has also been associated with lower rates of investment expenditure as growth slowed or went negative, and to some degree a cause of the slower growth. But in general domestic savings did not slow to the same degree: since $S + FA = I + BD$ (where S is domestic savings, I private investment, BD budget deficit and FA financial account inflow = current account deficit = imports minus exports and net income). Indeed in the face of decline in investment, it is the budget deficit which enables the savings to be realised and the sale of government bonds provides the financial assets which can be acquired through savings.

A return to high levels of employment will require appropriate fiscal policy (in the direction of significant budget deficits) and the abandonment of the target of balanced budgets. The 'fiscal compact' of the Economic and Monetary Union is a major obstacle for the restoration of high levels of employment. The 'fiscal compact' has as its central theme the achievement of a balanced structural budget. A structural budget position is that which would be achieved if the economy were operating at 'potential output'. We have pointed out elsewhere (Arestis and Sawyer 2014) the ambiguities of the notions of 'potential output', which is not as its name suggests the output which the economy is capable of producing, but rather the level of output which would be consistent with constant inflation. Ambiguities over the meaning and measurement of potential output and of structural budget position are significant for the formulation of economic policy – there is little point in saying that the objective is to balance the structural budget if that budget position cannot be estimated in an agreed manner. The major point, though, to be made here is that a balanced budget, particularly one balanced at 'potential output' (however that is defined) is unlikely to be achievable. The mainstream economics view has in effect been that there can readily be a balanced budget since from the equation mentioned above, when savings and investment are equal in a closed economy then the budget deficit will be zero. Then saving intentions and investment intentions can be brought into equality through setting the interest rate at the 'natural rate of interest' (cf. Wicksell 1936). The view here is that saving and investment decisions are made by different groups (though there is some overlap in that corporations make decisions on retained earnings, that is their savings out of profits). Since saving and investment decisions are undertaken by different people (households and firms in the case of the former, firms in the case of the latter) and the forces influencing those decisions are quite different, there is little reason to think that the general tendencies to save and to invest will be in alignment. Let us illustrate this as follows. The purpose of investment is to make additions to the capital stock in order to produce and sell a higher output (and make more profits). Investment is to enable the capital stock to grow broadly in line with growth of expected demand, and the underlying growth rate of the economy (which itself will be moulded by investment). If the trend growth of expected demand is g, and the capital–output ratio is v, then the growth of the capital stock required would be $g.v$. To illustrate an expected rate of growth of 2.5 per cent and a capital–output ratio of 4 would imply the net investment to GDP ratio of 10 per cent. Gross investment would be larger as it covers depreciation. Saving by households may be largely related to the level of income; saving by firms would be retentions out of profits. It may be expected that the savings propensity of households out of wages would be rather lower than the savings propensity of firms out of profits. The saving function can be written as $swW + spP$ where W is wages and P profits, with sw and sp propensities to save out of wages and profits, respectively. The average propensity to save $S/Y = sw(W/Y) + sp(P/Y)$. One feature to note is that the average propensity to save depends on the distribution of income between wages and profits, and is expected to be higher with a larger share of profits in national income.

A lower growth and investment rate that, as suggested above, may be the future prospect, has some significant implications for budget deficits. The obvious point which would follow from the equation above is that a lower investment regime would likely involve lower rates of employment and capacity utilisation. The growth rate would also, of course, be lower. There are, in effect, two ways to respond. A further way, that of net export promotion, can be readily ruled out as a general solution as not all countries (or even most) can boost net exports. The two ways to be considered are the use of budget deficits and changing savings behaviour.

In a slower-growth world, a budget deficit permits savings to occur which does not flow into investment. It also acts as a pension arrangement. Pension schemes can be funded or unfunded, and the latter is a mechanism by which the present working-age generation pays taxation and social security contributions which pay the retired generation's pensions. In return, it receives a 'promise' that when the present working-age generation are in retirement the same arrangements will benefit them. A similar mechanism works for funded schemes: the present working age generation saves, which enables the retired population to dissave (as the pension received is a combination of returns on savings plus rundown of saving this is not immediately apparent). The budget deficits and the debt which is then issued, and acquired by the present working-age population (or more usually by pension funds on their behalf), form the basis of a pension arrangement. In the absence of investment opportunities, budget deficits are required.

From this we may conclude that one of the conditions for recovery is the acceptance of the need for budget deficits on a long-term basis and that the chase for balanced budgets threatens to be MAD (mutually assured destruction). From the situation as of mid-2013 in industrialised countries a recovery of investment (for example) will bring a reduction of the budget deficit (cf. national income accounts equation given at the beginning of this section). However, the central question is what the budget deficit would look like if investment (and saving and net exports) was at some 'normal' level. Let us first mention net exports: the net export position of any country has to be consistent with the net export positions of the rest of the world – that is, globally net exports sum to zero. Further, a country with a net export deficit has to borrow from abroad; a country with a net export surplus has to lend to the rest of the world (and hence other countries willing to borrow). At the present time it is the 'normal' rate of investment which is particularly difficult to discern. The post-Keynesian analysis, following Keynes, stresses that we live in a world of fundamental uncertainty and that investment expenditure decisions by firms depends on their perceptions of the future; but the future is inherently unknowable. As the future is inherently unknowable for firms, so it is for analysts! We have suggested above that in light of the recent record on productivity rises (since the crisis), the continuing credit constraint on financial investment, the possibility of the drawing to an end of an information technology-inspired boom (which was particularly stimulating in the 1990s and the dot.com bubble) and the looming environmental and ecological concerns lowering the sustainable rate of growth, the 'normal' level of investment (relative to GDP) is likely to be lower in the future. But it is not possible to put a precise number on this, and hence not possible to calculate with any precision the budget deficit which would be required to underpin a high level of employment. What is required is a recognition that budget deficits are likely to be required and that the scale of the budget deficit has to be gradually adjusted as experience evolves (which is not to say that we would ever be sure as to what the 'normal' rate of investment is).

6 Inequality

It is widely acknowledged that there has been widespread increases in inequality, often focused on the increasing income of the top 1 per cent, and that there has been a shift away from wages towards profits (the extent of which varies between countries).[6] There are many reasons to decry the large changes in inequality in the past three decades or so, and here we have a narrow focus on the impact on demand and employment. The rise in inequality was widely viewed as feeding into financial instability through the pressures on low-income groups encouraging unsustainable lending and stimulated by easy but expensive credit and sub-prime mortgage availability.[7]

A downward shift in income inequality would, as argued by Sawyer (2011), be a 'progressive way' to reduce budget deficits since such a shift would raise average propensity to consume and lower saving rates. A shift to a more progressive tax regime could similarly be used in that in effect post-tax income is shifted from rich to poor. A more progressive tax regime also has the side benefit of enhancing fiscal policy as an automatic stabiliser, and indeed one of the effects of increased inequality and the general shift from direct to indirect taxation has been to reduce the automatic stabilisers.

The policy measures designed to shift the distribution of income can be easily listed, but the issues of implementation are inversely related with the ease of listing them! Significant increases in minimum wages where such exist and their introduction elsewhere, adoption of 'living wage' ordinances, structuring wage awards in the public sector to increase lower wages faster than higher wages, enhancing the power of trade unions. Making the tax system progressive through, for example, capital gains treated as income for tax purpose, removing caps on earnings limits for social security contributions (with no commensurate changes to social security benefits), enhanced property taxation.

A reduction in the propensity to save implies a rise in the propensity to consume, and encouraging higher consumption sounds a paradoxical response to environmental concerns. However, in terms of impact on the environment we are postulating a lower rate of investment and the production of investment goods will have environmental impacts. The rearrangement within GDP between investment and consumption may have a limited impact on the environment – depending on the relative environment intensity of consumer goods and investment goods.

7 Concluding remarks

The 'Great Depression' of the 1930s only came to an end in broad terms around the start of the Second World War; and the post-war period opened up into the 'golden age' of capitalism, with high levels of economic growth and something approaching full employment in many Western industrialised countries. The 'Great Recession' of the past five years has not involved in general the scale of unemployment seen in the 1930s, though of course some have experienced unemployment on a mass scale (at the time of writing Greece and Spain have over 25 per cent, for example). Output, if judged relative to trend, has fallen more sharply. The post-war boom can be variously ascribed, but it undoubtedly involved high levels of investment (as compared with prior experience (Matthews 1968)), government expenditure on a much enhanced scale (again as compared with the pre-war situation (e.g. Peacock and Wiseman 1961), the repairs of war damage and reconstruction and degrees of commitment to the achievement of full employment and a tendency for income inequalities to decline. The thrust of the argument in this chapter is first to reassert the centrality of full employment as a major objective of economic policy. It recognises the damage which has been done by the financial crisis to the productive potential, and the damaging consequences of financialisation. Some degree of reconstruction is required, and this is most evident in the South European countries suffering from austerity and the euro crisis.

An economic recovery with full employment and a growth rate which is environmentally sustainable would require adjustments to lower rates of investment, and above we have focused on the role of budget deficits in this regard. It also requires that the investment which does take place is well directed in terms of being environmentally sensitive and ensuring that productive capacity is in the right place in the relevant quantities consistent with full employment. This will require some social direction of the flows of finance.

But, as Kalecki (1943) argued, the major constraints on the achievement of full employment are not economic, but come from political and social forces which will so strongly resist the greater roles ascribed to government, enhanced power of labour and the direction of finance.

Notes

1 This chapter reflects research being conducted within the project Financialisation, Economy, Society and Sustainable Development (FESSUD) (www.fessud.eu) which is a five-year project funded by the European Commission Framework Programme 7 (contract number 266800).
2 For example, the Eurozone growth figures were negative in three years out of the five, 2009–13, and output in 2013 (OECD forecast) would be 2.2 per cent below the level in 2008. Unemployment for the Eurozone rose from 7.7 per cent in 2008 to 11.4 per cent in 2012 (from OECD Economic Outlook June 2013).
3 See, for example, Onaran and Galanis (2012).
4 Small open economies are seen as more likely to be profit led in that a reduction in wages and hence in unit labour costs, treated as a sign of competitiveness, would stimulate export demand, and this could then offset the depressing effects of lower wages on domestic demand. At the global level there is no export demand!

5 See, for example, Pollin *et al.* (2008).
6 See, for example, OECD (2011); and OECD database on income distribution www. oecd.org/els/soc/income-distribution-database.htm.
7 See van Treeck and Sturn (2012) for a review of the arguments.

References

Arestis, P. and Sawyer, M. (2005) 'Aggregate demand, conflict and capacity in the inflationary process', *Cambridge Journal of Economics*, vol. 29, no. 6, pp. 959–974.

Arestis, P. and Sawyer, M. (2014), 'On the sustainability of budget deficits and public debts with reference to the UK', in P. Arestis and M. Sawyer (eds), *Fiscal and Debt Policies for the Future*, Palgrave Macmillan, Basingstoke.

Epstein, G.A. (ed.) (2005), *Financialization and the World Economy*, Edward Elgar, Cheltenham.

Fontana, G. and Sawyer, M. (2012), 'Towards Post Keynesian ecological macroeconomics', University of Leeds, mimeo.

Fontana, G. and Sawyer, M. (2013), 'Post-Keynesian and Kaleckian thoughts on ecological macroeconomics', *European Journal of Economics and Economic Policies: Intervention*, vol. 10, no. 2, pp. 256–267.

Hein, E. (2011), *The Macroeconomics of Finance-dominated Capitalism: And Its Crisis*, Edward Elgar, Aldershot.

Kalecki, M. (1943), 'Political aspects of full employment', *Political Quarterly*, vol. 14, pp. 322–330.

Matthews, R. (1968), 'Why has Britain had full employment since the war?', *Economic Journal*, vol. 78, pp. 555–569.

OECD (2011), 'An overview of growing income inequalities in OECD countries: main findings', available at www.oecd.org/els/soc/49499779.pdf (accessed May 2013).

Onaran, O. and Galanis, G. (2012), *Is Aggregate Demand Wage-led or Profit-led? National and Global Effects*, ILO, Geneva. Available at: www.ilo.org/wcmsp5/groups/public/-ed_protect/-protrav/-travail/documents/publication/wcms_192121.pdf (accessed May 2013).

Peacock, A.T. and Wiseman, J. (1961), *The Growth of Public Expenditure in the United Kingdom*, Princeton University Press, Princeton, NJ.

Pollin, R. (1995), 'Financial structures and egalitarian economic policy', *International Papers in Political Economy*, December.

Pollin, R., Garrett-Peltier, H., Heintz, J. and Scharber, H. (2008), 'Green recovery: a program to create good jobs and start building a low-carbon economy', available at www.peri.umass.edu/green_recovery (accessed May 2013).

Sawyer, M. (2010), 'Re-structuring the financial sector to reduce its burden on the economy', in P. Arestis, R. Sobreira and Jose Luis Oreiro (eds), *The Recent Financial Crisis, Financial Regulation and Global Impact: Volume 1: The Financial Crisis: Origins and Implications*, Palgrave Macmillan, Basingstoke, pp. 114–136.

Sawyer, M. (2011) 'Progressive approaches to budget deficits', in O. Onaran, T. Niechoj, E. Stockhammer, A. Truger and T. van Treeck (eds), *Stabilising an Unequal Economy? Public Debt, Financial Regulation, and Income Distribution*, Metropolis Verlag, Marburg, pp. 143–159.

van Treeck, T. and Sturn, S. (2012), *Income Inequality as a Cause of the Great Recession? A Survey of Current Debates*, ILO, Geneva.

Wicksell, K. (1936), *Interest and Prices*, London: Macmillan, 1936, translation of 1898 edition by R.F. Kahn.

4 Could more flexibility of labour markets help to resume growth?

Lessons of an amended Kaleckian model

Amitava Krishna Dutt, Sébastien Charles and Dany Lang

1 Introduction

The conventional wisdom shared by policy makers in many parts of the world is that 'structural' reforms are needed in order to increase growth and employment, and a major aspect of these reforms is increasing labour market flexibility. In Europe, although this view is not new, the aftermath of the 'debt crisis' of 2009 has witnessed renewed calls for greater labour market flexibility. For instance, when Mario Draghi, the President of the European Central Bank, called for a 'growth pact' in Europe (on 3 May 2012), he declared: 'We have to put growth back at the centre of the agenda.… You have to reform the product markets and the labour markets together, because you have to have more competition in both.' Mario Monti, the former Italian Prime Minister, implementing labour market reforms, declared that 'It's a labour market reform for growth and employment' (4 April 2012) and a key aim was to eliminate the 'dualism' of Italy's current labour market. Angela Merkel, the German prime minister, also declared, in mid-May 2012: 'To promote growth … [one] … does not necessarily have to spend money', but 'to reduce unemployment through structural reform' through measures 'to improve labour market flexibility'. The French, Greek, Italian, Portuguese and Spanish governments have actually chosen this path. In France, for example, the labour relation law passed in April 2013 increases employment flexibility dramatically.[1]

These statements and actions of political leaders reflect the views of many mainstream economists. Since the publication of the seminal paper by Giersch (1985), it has been claimed that the alleged lack of employment flexibility in Europe has contributed to the European disease called 'eurosclerosis'. In this view, 'generous unemployment benefits, restrictions on hiring and firing, and restrained wage competition have led to rigid, "eurosclerotic" … economies, which could not cope with the big shocks of the 1970s' (Bentolila and Bertola 1990). 'Eurosclerotic' economies would be mainly characterized by high unemployment and low mobility.[2]

The kind of flexibility that has attracted the most attention has been referred to as *external numerical flexibility*. This flexibility involves changing employment protection legislation (EPL) that can be defined as 'in essence restrictions (whether specified in general legislation or in standard employment contracts) on firing: severance payments, mandatory notice periods, administrative procedures and delays' (Young 2003, p. 9). Increasing this kind of flexibility allows employers to fire and hire employees more easily (that is, by decreasing the time of notice, as well as the money costs of hiring and firing, for example severance pay) and relaxes the laws and regulations covering temporary work or fixed-term contracts.[3] In what follows we will refer to this form of flexibility as 'employment flexibility' for the sake of brevity.

Proponents of employment flexibility argue that EPL reduces the demand for labour. This happens because firms have a reduced incentive to hire workers who they will find difficult to fire in case they need to, so they substitute capital for labour and adopt labour-saving technological change. The lower level and growth of labour demand and employment, they argue, has the effect of reducing wages. Moreover, they argue that such employment restriction reduce profitability (by making it necessary to continue employing workers no longer required and by reducing the productivity of workers who do not fear the threat of being fired), and therefore reduce investment and the growth of output in the economy. Furthermore, they argue that employment inflexibility hinders structural change needed for the transition to an innovation-based economy (see Saint-Paul 2000). Thus, not only do government restrictions on firing workers (and the closing of firms which imply large-scale firing of workers) result in poor economic performance in terms of efficiency, profitability, investment, technological change and growth, but it also hurts those it intends to help, by reducing the growth of employment and wages.

Discussions of the effects of EPL sometimes focus on the dual labour market approach, which sees labour markets as separated into a 'primary' and a 'secondary' sector. Related to the idea of the dual economy in less-developed countries (see Lewis 1954) and to the work on Doeringer and Piore (1971) on internal labour markets within firms in advanced capitalist countries, the approach distinguishes between employees in the *primary sector* who have rather stable jobs, relatively high pay and status, good working conditions and opportunities for promotion through a developed internal labour market on the one hand, and employees in the *secondary sector* who have poorer working conditions and salaries, little job security and virtually no promotion or training opportunities.

The argument in favour of increasing employment flexibility (and in weakening EPL) is usually made in terms of the neoclassical theory of labour markets. In this approach, EPL creates a distortion in the economy, resulting in an inefficient outcome. The actual outcome will be a lower level of employment and its growth: profit-maximizing firms will take into account the fact that if they hire more workers, they will be costly to fire (which firms will want to do if there are negative expected or actual future shocks) because of EPL, so the incentive to hire new workers will be reduced. Moreover, there may be an effect on the productivity of workers who, because they are difficult to fire, would not work as hard as they would if they could be fired more easily. If there is EPL which requires firms to pay some minimum wages and benefits to more regular workers, but not casual workers (or workers hired by firms with whom they sub-contract), then firms will respond to laws about firing by replacing regular workers with casual workers and outsourcing to subcontractors who may use casual labour. In matching models *a la* Saint-Paul (2000), the lack of external numerical flexibility is a major explanatory factor of the higher unemployment rates for women, the low-skilled, the young and the senior workers. As argued in terms of insider–outside models of labour markets (see Lindbeck and Snower 2001), employment protection gives too much power to the 'insiders' who have been employed for a long time, at the expense of the 'outsiders' who are excluded from employment

One issue that is neglected in the neoclassical analysis of labour markets is the fact that even without laws that restrict firing, there is a considerable degree of labour hoarding by firms that takes the form of holding on to labour when they face declines in the demand for their products. This phenomena, however, is not difficult to reconcile with the neoclassical optimizing approach without distortions if one takes into account the hiring and training costs of workers required to augment the firm-specific skills of workers (see Oi 1962). In the presence of these costs, profit-maximizing firms may not reduce their workforce by much when there is a fall in the demand for their product because the costs they would save by doing so may be less than the costs of hiring and training new workers when they need to expand their workforce when there is a rise in demand. Taking this into account does not negate the neoclassical view of employment legislation, however, since such legislation, if it is binding, creates additional restrictions to what firms can do in terms of how much excess labour they will carry (see also Bentolila and Bertola 1990).

Given the emphasis currently placed among the political and mainstream economics elites on the view that the labour market should be deregulated, it is a bit surprising that the empirical literature supporting these views (over the past four years) is small. One of the reasons explaining this may be that, if the theoretical case in favour of a more flexible labour market has been well articulated, the empirical evidence showing that there is a positive effect of increased flexibility on the labour market is at best weak. As Freeman (2005, p. 105) points out,

> there are two reasons for inconclusive debate over the claim that labour institutions impair aggregate performance. The first reason is that many adherents to the claim hold strong priors that labour markets operate nearly perfectly in the absence of institutions and let their priors dictate their modelling choices and interpretation of empirical results. The second reason is that the cross-country aggregate data at issue is weak, too weak to decisively reject strong prior views or to convince those with weaker priors.

This chapter examines whether even the theoretical case based on the neo-classical approach is justified, not by criticizing the neoclassical approach – which is open to criticism for its neglect of issues related to uncertainty, power and institutions,[4] and its neglect of aggregate demand – but by examining alternative models of growth and distribution that take important aspects of real economies that are neglected in that approach. In particular, this chapter uses the Kaleckian approach to examine the issues of employment flexibility and labour market dualism.

A problem here is that existing Kaleckian models assume that workers are hired according to the needs of production so that as output increases and falls, the employment of labour rises and falls in line with it. This treatment of labour in these models is in sharp contrast to the treatment of capital in some models, especially, those in which firms are assumed to hold excess capital. To be sure, some models do allow for the existence of overhead labour, the employment of which does not change with output, that either takes the form of supervisory or managerial labour, or guard or technical labour, or some other form of fixed labour, sometimes called 'unproductive labour'.[5] But production labour is taken to be a variable factor. In the discussion on employment flexibility and dual labour markets, at least a part of such labour should be taken to be a fixed factor, at least for the short run because of the existence of long-term contracts, not only because of employment legislation but also because of hiring and firing costs due to the costs of firm-specific training and morale issues which induce them to provide greater stability to those they hire by offering long-term contracts.

The purpose of this chapter is to overcome this problem by developing models that extend a standard heterodox model of growth and distribution in which growth is determined by aggregate demand following the Kaleckian approach, to allow for the existence of long-term labour contracts and for the coexistence of formal labour with long-term contracts and informal labour which does not have such contracts, and can be fired at will.

The rest of this chapter proceeds as follows. Section 2 describes the basic structure of the model. Section 3 examines the consequences of increased employment flexibility. Section 4 concludes.

2 Structure of the model

We use a simple framework that makes the following assumptions. First, the economy produces a single good, which can be both consumed and invested. Second, the economy is a closed one that has no economic relations with the rest of the world. Third, the government does not undertake any fiscal activity. Fourth, the good is produced with two basic factors of production, labour and capital which is physically the same as the good produced. Fifth, production takes place with given fixed coefficients of production, which show the maximum amounts that can be produced with each input. Sixth, the economy has two classes, workers who work for wages and capitalists who own the capital and receive profits. Seventh, firms hold all the capital that they own and in the relevant equilibrium firms always hold excess capital. Eighth, capital does not depreciate. Ninth, workers consume their entire wage while capitalists save a constant fraction of their profits, and consume the rest of it. Tenth, all firms are identical which will allow us to examine firms by focusing on one (representative) firm. Many of these assumptions are made for simplicity and can be removed to incorporate additional elements into the model. Finally, and this is the new feature of the model, there are two kinds of workers, those with long-term labour contracts who cannot be fired instantly even if they are not needed for production, and those without such contracts who can be hired and fired at will.

Given these assumptions, total income is distributed among the two kinds of workers and profits according to:

$$PY = W_l L_l + W_s L_s + rPK,\tag{1}$$

where P is the price of the good, Y is real income and output, W_i is the money wage for workers of type i, where the subscript l denotes long-term labour and s denotes short term labour, L_i is the amount of labour employed of type i, r is the rate of profit defined as a ratio of total profits divided by the value of capital at replacement cost and K is the real stock of capital.

The major difference between long-term and short-term labour is that in the short run, at a point in time, the amount of long-term labour, L_l, is fixed, whereas the amount of short-term labour, L_s, can be freely altered and even be driven to zero. We assume that the amount of labour required per unit of output for each type of labour is fixed at b_i, and that the long-term labour is more productive than short-term labour, so that $b_l < b_s$. This assumption can be defended on the grounds that they have more firm-specific knowledge compared to short-term workers, have more motivation because they are feel more secure and because, as we shall see below, they have higher wages. It is possible that short-term workers may be driven to work harder because they are more concerned about losing their jobs, but we assume that the effects discussed earlier dominate, given that long-term workers are not guaranteed jobs, and can be fired after the passage of time. As we shall see later, this productivity advantage is not essential for our results. We are assuming, for simplicity, that apart from this productivity differential, long- and short-term workers are perfect substitutes in production, although there may be other differences between them. We denote the maximum output than can be produced by long-term workers as

$$Y_l = \frac{L_l}{b_l}.\tag{2}$$

If actual output, $Y \leq Y_l$, actual employment will be given by L_l and $L_s = 0$. If $Y > Y_l$, short-run labour is employed and:

$$L_s = b_s(Y - Y_l),\tag{3}$$

which, using equation (2) implies

$$L_s = b_s\left(Y - \frac{L_l}{b_l}\right).\tag{4}$$

Money wages for both kinds of workers are fixed. We assume that long-term workers are paid a higher wage, and the long-term wage premium, $\sigma > 1$, is given by

$$\sigma = \frac{W_l}{W_s}. \tag{5}$$

We will also assume that

$$\sigma \geq \frac{b_s}{b_l}, \tag{6}$$

that is, the wage premium is no less than the productivity differential between long-term and short-term workers. In a world with uncertainty and social norms, firms are assumed to work with long-term workers, although from a strict cost-minimization perspective (at least in production activity) it would seem that short-term workers are more profitable.

In terms of pricing, we assume that firms set their price as a fixed mark-up on unit long-term labour costs assuming that long-term labour will be fully utilized, so that

$$P = (1+z)b_l W_l, \tag{7}$$

where z is the fixed mark-up set by firms, which depends on the degree of monopoly *a la* Kalecki (1971). It is being assumed that long-term labour is used as a basis of the price because they consist of the bulk of labour, and short-term labour is used, if at all, as a way of producing what cannot be produced with long-term labour.[6] Thus, firms, in setting the price of the product, ignore short-term labour's contribution to unit costs. It is being assumed that $b_l W_l$ is used as a basis of pricing rather than actual average costs when the firm holds excess long-term labour because average costs are not constant but depend on actual output, which goes against the Kaleckian notion of the price being fixed by labour cost and independent of output. As noted earlier, firms are always assumed to hold excess capital and are never constrained by available capital.

Savings is given by

$$S = srK, \tag{8}$$

where S is real saving and s the fixed saving rate of capitalists out of profit income. Real consumption is, obviously, given by

$$C = Y - S. \tag{9}$$

We assume that firms make investment plans based on expected profitability and the buoyancy of aggregate demand, among other factors. More specifically, and as is assumed in some Kaleckian models (see Rowthorn 1981; Dutt 1984), we take planned investment to depend on the rate of capacity utilization and the rate of profit. We will make one of two assumptions. One is to assume that the investment–capital ratio, g, is given by

$$g = \gamma_0 + \gamma_r r + \gamma_u u, \tag{10}$$

where the parameters γ_i are positive. The other is to assume that firms make capital investment plans, which are given at a point in time. More specifically, we assume that

$$\frac{I}{K} = g,$$

where g is given at a point in time. Over time, investment changes according to the gap between actual investment and desired investment plans, so that we have

$$\dot{g} = \theta[g^d - g], \tag{11}$$

where $\theta > 0$ is a speed-of-adjustment parameter. Desired investment is assumed to depend positively on the rate of profit and on the level of capacity utilization, which we formalize with the linear investment function

$$g^d = \gamma_0 + \gamma_r r + \gamma_u u, \tag{12}$$

where we measure the degree of capacity utilization with $u = \dfrac{Y}{K}$ and where

γ_i are positive investment parameters: γ_0 represents exogenous investment; γ_r the positive effect of the rate of profit; and γ_u the positive effect of capacity utilization on the investment–capital ratio. In addition to the rate of profit and the rate of capacity utilization we will take into account, in what follows, that firms are also affected by others factors which depend on the extent of labour market flexibility.

Regarding the dynamics of long-term labour, L_l, we make the assumption that the rate of growth of long-term labour, l_l, is equal to the rate of growth of the stock of capital minus the rate of growth of the productivity of long-term labour, so that we have

$$l_l = g - \hat{b}_l. \tag{13}$$

This provides a simple formalization of the idea of labour flexibility. If we define

$$\lambda = \frac{Y_l}{K} = \frac{\dfrac{L_l}{b_l}}{K}, \text{ we have}$$

$$\hat{\lambda} = l_l - \hat{b}_l - g, \tag{14}$$

and equation (13) implies that λ becomes a constant. We assume that the level of

$\bar{\lambda}$, which is taken to be exogenous, measures the extent of employment flexibility. One way of interpreting this is to assume that firms are required by the government to maintain a given long-term labour–capital ratio, and choose to hold no more of it. Of course, firms may have good reasons to employ more long-term labour to encourage loyalty, to reduce the costs of hiring and firing and to speed up technological change. These factors can therefore also have a role in determining the size of $\bar{\lambda}$. However, it is likely that firms will not hire enough long-term labour left to their own devices because they may know that there are benefits of hiring long-term workers, but may not do enough of it because they feel that they reduce their flexibility. Thus, government regulations are likely to increase $\bar{\lambda}$.

Finally, we assume, as in standard Kaleckian models, that the goods market clears through variations in capacity utilization. Goods market equilibrium requires that

$$Y = C + I. \tag{15}$$

Using equation (9), this implies that in short-run equilibrium the standard saving–investment equality holds, so that

$$\frac{S}{K} = \frac{I}{K}. \tag{16}$$

It should be noted that the rate of profit will depend on whether only long-term labour is used or both long-term and short-term labour is used. In the former case, in which $Y \leq \dfrac{L_l}{b_l}$, the rate of profit is given, using equations (1), (2), (5) and (7), by

$$r = u - \frac{\lambda}{1+z} \tag{17}$$

where $u = Y/K$ is a measure of the rate of capacity utilization.

In the latter case, when both types of labour are used, we have $Y > \dfrac{L_l}{b_l}$, and the rate of profit is given, using equations (1) through (5) and (7), by

$$r = \left(1 - \frac{b_s}{(1+z)b_l\sigma}\right)u - \frac{\lambda}{(1+z)}\left(1 - \frac{b_s}{b_l\sigma}\right). \tag{18}$$

3 The consequences of increased flexibility

In our model we assume that investment is based on equation (10). We also take into account the fact that investment is affected by λ. Since λ is taken to be a measure of employment flexibility, it is possible that an increase in employment flexibility or a fall in λ will have a positive effect on hiring long-term labour, which implies a rise in g. This, a rise in λ, or a fall in employment flexibility, can be assumed to reduce g. However, a rise in λ can also be taken to imply an increase in productivity growth, since it can be assumed that long-term labour increases the knowledge base of the firm and increases productivity growth by increasing the motivation of workers to increase productivity at a higher rate, which in turn increases investment, given a positive relation between technological change and investment (see, for instance, Storm and Naastepad 2012). This contribution of long-term labour to productivity growth can provide an explanation of why firms may wish to hire long-term employees, who are less flexible in terms of hiring and firing than short-term labour, at a possibly higher cost. The contribution of a higher rate of technological change on investment is a standard feature of a number of Kaleckian models, including those in Rowthorn (1981), Dutt (1990) and Storm and Naastepad (2012). We therefore modify equation (10) with the formulation

$$g = \gamma_0 + \gamma_r r + \gamma_u u + \gamma_\lambda \lambda. \tag{19}$$

The sign of γ_λ can be positive or negative depending on whether the positive technological change effect or the negative disincentive effect of employment rigidity is dominant.

   We will assume that labour productivity growth caused by a higher level of λ increases the productivity of both long-term and short-term labour, and that the wage of each type of labour increases proportionately with productivity growth. This implies, from equations (5) and (7), that changes in λ leave z and σ, that is, the mark-up and the long-term wage premium, unchanged.

   For this model, using equations (8), (16) and (19), we obtain

$$(s - \gamma_r)r - \gamma_u u = \gamma_0 + \gamma_\lambda. \tag{20}$$

We now distinguish between the two cases, one in which only long-term labour is used, and the other in which both kinds of labour are used. In the first case, in which we have $Y \leq \dfrac{L_l}{b_l}$, which implies that $u \leq \lambda$; substituting from equation (17) in equation (20) we obtain

$$u = \frac{\gamma_0 + \left(\dfrac{s - \gamma_r}{1+z} + \gamma_\lambda\right)\lambda}{s - \gamma_r - \gamma_u}. \tag{21}$$

Substituting into the investment or saving function this implies that the rate of capital accumulation (and output growth, since u is a constant) is given by

$$g = s\,\frac{\gamma_0 + \left(\dfrac{\gamma_u}{1+z} + \gamma_\lambda\right)\lambda}{s - \gamma_r - \gamma_u}. \tag{22}$$

In the second case, in which we have $Y > \dfrac{L_l}{b_l}$, which implies that $u > \lambda$, substituting from (18) into equation (20) we get

$$u = \frac{\gamma_0 + \left(\dfrac{s - \gamma_r}{1 + z} \left(1 - \dfrac{b_s}{\sigma b_l} \right) + \gamma_\lambda \right) \lambda}{(s - \gamma_r) \left(1 - \dfrac{1}{(1 + z)} \dfrac{b_s}{\sigma b_s} \right) - \gamma_u}. \tag{23}$$

The rates of growth of capital and output are given by

$$g = s = \frac{[(\gamma)_0 + \gamma_\lambda \lambda] \left(1 - \dfrac{b_s}{(1 + z) b_l \sigma} \right) + \dfrac{\gamma_u}{1 + z} \left(1 - \dfrac{b_s}{\sigma b_l} \right) \lambda}{(s - \gamma_r) \left(1 - \dfrac{1}{(1 + z)} \dfrac{b_s}{\sigma b_l} \right) - \gamma_u}. \tag{24}$$

The model and its four equations (21) through (23) have the following properties. First, since λ is exogenously given and all the other symbols in the right-hand side of equations (21) through (24) are parameters (which therefore do not change over time), the values of u shown in equations (21) and (23) clear the goods markets and those of g in equations (22) and (24) show the rate of growth of output and capital consistent with those values and implied rates of profit. In other words, they are equilibrium values of the rates of capacity utilization and growth, and they do not change over time.

Second, since we have assumed that output and the rate of capacity utilization adjust to clear the goods market, the stability of equilibrium requires that the response of saving to the rate of capacity utilization is greater than the responsiveness of investment. This requires that the denominators of the right-hand sides of equations (21) and (23) are positive. In the case in which only long-term labour is used, the stability condition is $s - \gamma_r > \gamma_u$, while in the case in which both

kinds of labour are used it is $(s - \gamma_r) \left(1 - \dfrac{1}{(1 + z)} \dfrac{b_s}{\sigma b_l} \right) > \gamma_u$. Since we have

assumed that the inequality given by (6) is satisfied, $\dfrac{1}{(1 + z)} \dfrac{b_s}{\sigma b_l} < 1$, if $s > \gamma_r$,

which we assume, the first stability condition is more easily satisfied than the second condition: if the second is satisfied the first is necessarily satisfied, but the first may be satisfied without the second being satisfied. Thus, the stability of equilibrium is more likely to be satisfied if only long-term labour is used than when both are used. The reason for this is as follows. When only long-term labour is employed, an increase in capacity utilization results in an increase in output and profits without any increase in wage costs, since all labour costs are fixed, so that all of the increase in output results in an increase in profits. When both types of labour are employed, an increase in output requires an increase in the employment of short-term labour, which reduces the increase in profits. Thus, in the second case the increase in investment due to an increase in capacity utilization is larger in comparison to the effects on an implied increase in profits, which affects saving and investment, than in the first case.

Third, we examine the effect of an increase in λ on u and g, assuming that the stability conditions in both cases are satisfied. The effects of a rise in λ on capacity utilization and the rate of growth are seen to be affected by the sign of γ_λ, that is, the effect of λ on investment. Recall that the sign of this depends on whether the positive effect of λ on labour productivity growth, and through it, on investment, is stronger or weaker than the negative disincentive effect of employment rigidity on the rates of long-term labour and capital accumulation (which, in the model, are assumed to be equal). If $\gamma_\lambda > 0$ it follows from equations (21) through (24) that an increase in λ implies an increase in u and in g in both cases. In the case in which only long-term labour is used, an increase in λ increases aggregate demand by increasing wage income at the expense of profits, since there is saving out of profits but not out of wages. Therefore the overall effect of an increase in λ on u and g is positive even if γ_λ is negligible, and may even be positive if γ_λ is slightly negative. In the case in which both kinds of labour are used, if the condition given in (6) is satisfied as a strict inequality, a rise in λ increases u and g by increasing aggregate demand since long-term labour, which generates a higher level of income than short-term labour, substitutes for short-term labour. Thus, the overall effect on u and g can be positive even with γ_λ slightly negative. If (6) is satisfied as an equality, and there is no positive effect on labour income by substituting from short-term labour to long-term labour, the only effect of an increase in λ is through the effect on investment. If we assume that γ_λ is positive but small, the relation between λ and u can be shown in Figure 4.1. The bold line shows the relation. The line is seen to be steeper in case I, in which $\lambda \geq u$ and only long-term labour is used, than in case II where both types of labour are used, since, comparing the two slopes, we find that

$$\frac{\left(\dfrac{s-\gamma_r}{1+z}+\gamma_\lambda\right)}{s-\gamma_r-\gamma_u} > \frac{\left(\dfrac{s-\gamma_r}{1+z}\left(1-\dfrac{b_s}{\sigma b_l}\right)+\gamma_\lambda\right)}{(s-\gamma_r)\left(1-\dfrac{1}{(1+z)}\dfrac{b_s}{\sigma b_l}\right)-\gamma_u}.$$

The two segments of the line meet on the 45° line at the value

$$u = \frac{\gamma_0}{(s-\gamma_r)\dfrac{z}{1+z}-\gamma_u-\gamma_\lambda}$$

as shown in Figure 4.1. Since λ is exogenously given in this model, we can find the value of u from the bold lines in the figure, as well as the case in which the economy finds itself. The relation between g and λ can be shown in an analogous manner.

Fourth, the effects of the shifts in the parameters of the model other than λ can be seen in terms of a shift in the bold u schedule. For instance, an increase in z, the mark-up rate charged by firms, is seen to shift the point of intersection of

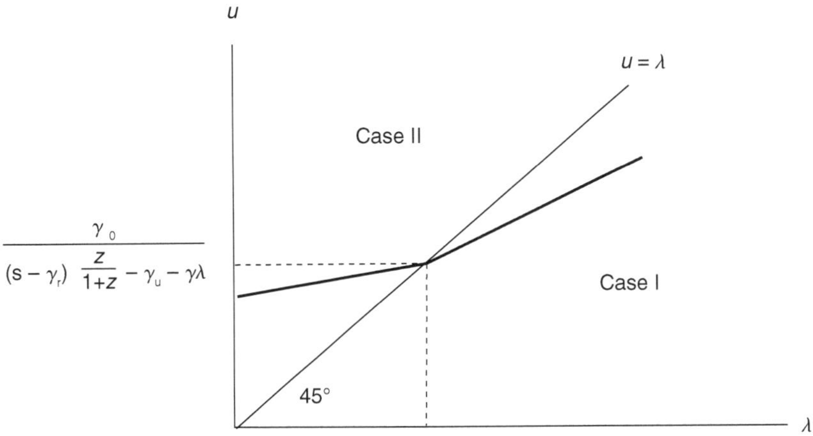

Figure 4.1 Effects of an increase in λ on u in a model with exogenous λ.

the u line and the 45° line downwards, and reduce the slope of both segments of the line. Given our assumptions, the effect is to reduce u at all levels of λ. The increase in the mark-up rate redistributes income from workers of both kinds to profit recipients who have a higher propensity to save, which reduces consumption demand and aggregate demand, reducing capacity utilization. To examine the effect on g, we need to consider separately the two cases. For case I, it follows from an inspection of equation (22) that an increase in z reduces g. For case II, when both types of workers are in use, equation (24) shows that

$$\frac{\mathrm{d}g}{\mathrm{d}z} = -s\gamma_u \frac{\left[\left(1-\dfrac{b_s}{\sigma b_l}\right)(s-\gamma_r-\gamma_u)\lambda + \dfrac{[(\gamma]_0 + \gamma_\lambda \lambda)b_s}{\sigma b_l}\right]}{\left[(s-\gamma_r)\left(1-\dfrac{1}{(1+z)}\dfrac{b_s}{\sigma b_l}\right)-\gamma_u\right]^2 (1+z)^2}$$

which, given our assumptions, is seen to be negative if $\gamma_\lambda \geq 0$ or small if negative. In both cases, an increase in the mark-up shifts income from workers to capitalists, decreases consumption and aggregate demand, capacity utilization, and investment, despite the positive effect the mark-up has on the rate of profit, as shown in equation (18).

Finally, we can summarize the effects on an increase in employment flexibility by examining the various effects at work. A high level of employment flexibility, by implying a low level of λ, has a number of consequences on the performance of the economy:

1   A low level of λ results, as we saw, in the greater likelihood of goods market instability. If the economy is subjected to shocks, there may be a tendency

for greater variability rather than stable adjustment. This result is due to the fact that when aggregate demand changes, variations in employment are likely to be greater when there is more labour market flexibility, which is likely to imply greater variations in profits and output. Long-term labour is more difficult to adjust over time, while short-term labour is freely adjustable.

2   A lower level of use of long-term labour can have a negative level effect on aggregate demand if the long-term wage premium exceeds the productivity gap between long-term and short-term labour. The wage premium may be due to norms, but also to the fact that long-run workers are more likely to be unionized. It may be reinforced by the fact that long-term workers result in higher levels of productivity growth.

3   A lower level of long-term labour can have a negative effect on the rate of technological change since long-term workers are more loyal to the firm and are more involved in bringing about and accepting productivity increases, and result in the accumulation of firm-specific knowledge. This can provide a boost to investment spending.

4   A lower level of long-term labour use can be seen by firms to reduce the flexibility of labour and reduce costs, and this can spur investment, other things constant. We have included these effects into our model by making λ affect the profit rate and by allowing the possibility of a negative effect of λ on investment. The latter has been assumed to be weak, given that the empirical evidence on this is not very clear, with some studies showing positive employment and growth effects and others showing negligible or negative effects of greater employment flexibility.[7]

5   A higher level of employment flexibility implies that the bargaining power of all workers is likely to fall: for long-term workers because they are more susceptible to dismissal; and for short-term workers because it reduces solidarity between workers of different types. Layoffs of long-term workers can also increase the ranks of the short-term labour force – or what can be called the reserve army – and this can exert downward pressure on all wages. We can examine the consequences of this by allowing z to increase, raising the profit share. There is a fair amount of empirical evidence that supports this conclusion. We have already examined the consequences of an increase in z and shown that it is, in addition to shifting the income distribution away from workers, growth retarding.

6   Changes in employment flexibility can also be expected to have an effect on σ, the long-term labour wage premium, which can be examined in terms of our model. If greater employment flexibility reduces the wage premium by reducing the bargaining power of long-term workers more than it does that of short-term workers, σ will fall. The examination of the implications of this, and possible feedback effects on λ, which can be endogenized, is left for future work.

4 Conclusion

This chapter has attempted to introduce long-term labour into the Kaleckian model of growth and distribution.

In terms of theoretical innovations, although it makes one change in the basic model – allowing for two kinds of employment conditions – this introduces a number of new issues. First, it provides a clear distinction between long- and short-term labour based on what kind of labour is held constant and what kind is variable in the short run. This difference can be related to other differences as well, including differences in wages and hence effect on aggregate demand, and implications for technological change, which have been analysed in our models. Second, the model allows for dual labour markets. This is not a necessary result of introducing long-term contracts, but is an important feature of many economies. Third, the model makes assumptions about the effect of changes in the composition of employment on aggregate demand. While productivity differentials may favour long-term workers, wage differentials more than offset this. Nevertheless, firms have the norm of conducting regular operations with long-term labour, perhaps because other firms do.

Armed with these innovations, this chapter has analysed the effects of increased flexibility. Our analysis allows us to examine the mainstream or neo-liberal case for greater employment flexibility in terms of a fall in the long-term labour to capital ratio, which, as claimed in the neoliberal approach, can increase employment growth and hence aggregate growth and even have a favourable distributional effect in terms of increasing the use of long-term labour. However, it has also been able to show the limits of this result.

The analysis of this chapter suggests avenues for future research. On the theoretical front, our model can be extended in various directions. It can take into account the implications of saving by workers – especially by long-term workers – and consumer debt. It can also introduce different kinds of investment functions, which allow for the possibility that investment depends positively on the profit share, wage and relative wage flexibility. The dynamics of flexibility (as represented by the parameter λ) could and should also be endogenized. This could be achieved by introducing an explicit labour accumulation function into the model. Another extension of the model could be to introduce open economy considerations, which would allow the economy to be subject to external shocks and international competitiveness issues. On the empirical front, the analysis points to the need for the political economy analysis of factors which result in changes in institutions and policies that bring about greater employment flexibility.

Notes

1 The French Parliament adopted this law, called 'Accord National Interprofessionnel' (ANI), on 9 April 2013. It formalizes an agreement signed on 11 January 2013 by an employers' union (MEDEF, representing mostly the firms listed on the French stock market) and three minor employees' unions (CFDT, CFTC and CFE-CGC). It allows

employers to fire employees more easily (external flexibility) and prevents employees from refusing a change in their workplace. It also allows employers to choose when an employee works and is paid, and does not work and consequently does not get paid (internal flexibility). On 12 January 2013 the French Minister of Industrial Relations, Michel Sapin, declared that in this agreement 'one can find the methods and the tools for employment, fighting unemployment, and invert the unemployment curve'.

2   Whether the European economies are still 'eurosclerotic' today is an open question, even among the proponents of the concept. For Boeri and Garibaldi (2009, p. 411), 'the sickness of Europe is no longer jobless growth. If anything, the symptoms are those typical of "growthless job creation", a very different pathology from Eurosclerosis.'

3   There are three other forms of 'flexibility' that are usually not dealt with in the literature about structural reforms of changes in EPL: wage flexibility, functional flexibility and internal numerical flexibility (see Atkinson 1984). Wage flexibility (sometimes also called 'financial' flexibility) refers to the degree to which wages can adapt to the level of economic activity and the differences between 'labour supply' and 'labour demand'. Functional flexibility (or 'organizational' flexibility) refers to how easy it is to transfer employees to various tasks within the firm. Internal numerical flexibility (or 'working time' flexibility) consists of adjusting working hours or schedules of employees already hired by a firm. Usually, these three kinds of flexibility are not stressed in these calls for 'more flexibility'.

4   See, for instance, Dutt (2012).

5   See, for instance, Rowthorn (1981), Dutt (1992) and Lavoie (2009).

6   This assumption is not essential to most of our analysis because it assumes that the wage differential and productivity differential between the two kinds of workers is constant.

7   See, for instance, Howell *et al.* (2007), and Storm and Naastepad (2012) for a review of the literature and some recent econometrics results for OECD countries.

References

Atkinson, J. (1984). 'Flexibility, Uncertainty and Manpower Management', *IMS Report*, No. 89, Brighton, Institute of Manpower Studies.

Bentolila, S. and Bertola, G. (1990). 'Firing Costs and Labour Demand: How Bad is Eurosclerosis?', *Review of Economic Studies*, 57 (3), 381–402.

Boeri, T. and Garibaldi, P. (2009). 'Beyond eurosclerosis', *Economic Policy*, 24 (59), 409–461.

Doeringer, P. and Piore, M. (1971). *Internal Labor Markets and Manpower Analysis*, Lexington, MA: D.C. Heath and Company.

Dutt, A. (1984). 'Stagnation, Income Distribution and Monopoly Power', *Cambridge Journal of Economics*, 8 (1), 25–40.

Dutt, A. (1990). *Growth, Distribution and Uneven Development*, Cambridge: Cambridge University Press.

Dutt, A. (1992). 'Stagnation, Growth and Unproductive Activity', in J.B. Davis (ed.), *The Economic Surplus in Advanced Economies*, Aldershot: Edward Elgar.

Dutt, A. (2012). 'Uncertainty, Power, Institutions and Crisis: Implications for Economic Analysis and the Future of Capitalism', in Bourgnine, H. and Rochon, L.P. (eds), *Capitalism and Crisis: Causes and Solutions*, Edward Elgar, forthcoming.

Freeman, R. (2005). 'Labour Market Institutions Without Blinders: The Debate Over Flexibility and Labour Market Performance', *International Economic Journal*, 19 (2), 129–45.

Giersch, H. (1985). 'Eurosclerosis', *Kiel Discussion Paper*, No. 112, Institut fur Weltwirtschaft, Universitat Kiel.

Howell, D., Baker, D., Glyn, A. and Schmidt, J. (2007). 'Are Protective Labour Market Institutions Really at the Root of Unemployment? A Critical Perspective of the Statistical Evidence', *Capitalism and Society*, 2 (1), 1–71.

Kalecki, M. (1971). *Selected Essays on the Dynamics of the Capitalist Economy*, Cambridge: Cambridge University Press.

Lavoie, M. (2009). '*Cadrisme* Within a Post-Keynesian Model of Growth and Distribution', *Review of Political Economy*, 21 (3), 369–91.

Lewis, W.A. (1954). 'Economic Development with Unlimited Supplies of Labour', *Manchester School*, 22, 139–91.

Lindbeck, A. and Snower, D. (2001). 'Insiders versus Outsiders', *Journal of Economic Perspectives*, 15 (1), 165–188.

Oi, W. (1962). 'Labor as a Quasi-fixed Factor', *Journal of Political Economy*, 70 (6), 538–55.

Rowthorn, R. (1981). 'Demand, Real Wages and Economic Growth', *Thames Papers in Political Economy*, Autumn, 1–39.

Saint-Paul, G. (2000). *The Political Economy of Labour Market Institutions*, Oxford: Oxford University Press.

Storm, S. and Naastepad, C. (2012). *Macroeconomics Beyond the NAIRU*, Cambridge, MA: Harvard University Press.

Young, D. (2003). *Employment Protection Legislation: Its Economic Impact and the Case for Reform*, Directorate General of Economic and Financial Affairs, European Commission.

5 Institutions and youth labour markets in Europe during the crisis

Niall O'Higgins

1 Overview of changes since 2007

This is not an easy time to be a young European seeking to enter the labour market. It is regularly argued that young people have been particularly hard hit by the recession, but more often than not, in order to justify this assertion, recourse is had to the changes occurring in youth unemployment rates. This is misleading; although youth unemployment rates increased significantly during the recession, the main way in which young people may be said to have suffered disproportionately is not directly related to unemployment rates per se. Figure 5.1 illustrates the percentage change in the major labour market indicators for young people between 2007 and 2012. Between 2007 and 2012 unemployment among young people (aged 15–24) in the EU increased by 33.6 per cent, while the number of unemployed 'prime-age' adults (aged 25–49) in the EU increased by 53.7 per cent (Figure 5.1).[1] Consequently, the ratio of youth/adult unemployment rates actually fell over the same period. True, the percentage *point* increase in youth unemployment rates (7.3 percentage points) was a little over double that of prime-age adults (3.5 percentage points), but this is due simply to the tendency for unemployment rates to be higher for young people than adults irrespective of the state of the economy. The reasons for this are well known and will not be entered into here,[2] but the obvious consequence is that a given *percentage point variation* will correspond to a much smaller *percentage variation* for young people than for adults – thus the percentage point variations are likely to be higher for young people than adults as a consequence of both positive and negative demand shocks.

Of more relevance, over the same period the prevalence of long-term unemployment[3] among young people increased by nearly 25 per cent (compared to an increase of 1.4 per cent for adults); youth employment fell by 17.4 per cent (compared to a fall of 4.4 per cent for adults); and the prevalence of temporary and part-time employment among young people also increased.

None of these changes can have been particularly welcome to young people; however, the increase in long-term unemployment is of particular concern. Following a period in which long-term unemployment had been persistently, albeit gradually, falling among young people, the recession precipitated a rapid and sustained growth in the indicator (Figure 5.2).

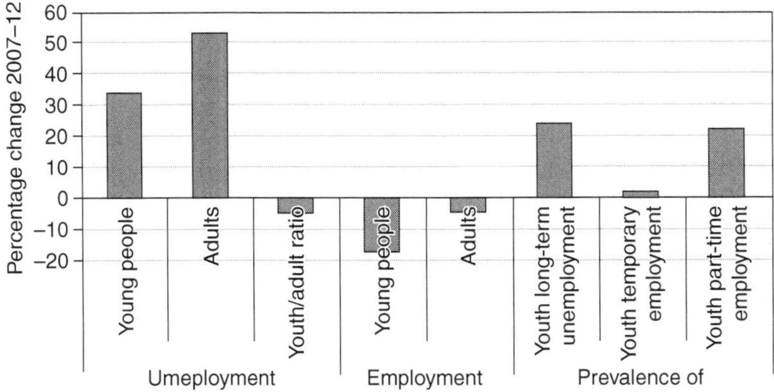

Figure 5.1 Percentage changes in labour market indicators in the EU, 2007–12 (source: calculated from Eurostat data (http://epp.eurostat.ec.europa.eu)).

Notes
1 For unemployment and employment, the percentage variation is calculated on absolute numbers while the change in the ratio reports the percentage variation in the ratio of youth (15–24) and adult (25–49) unemployment rates.
2 The final three figures reports the percentage change in the prevalence of the phenomena calculated as a percentage of the young unemployed (for long-term unemployment) or young employees (temporary and part-time employment).

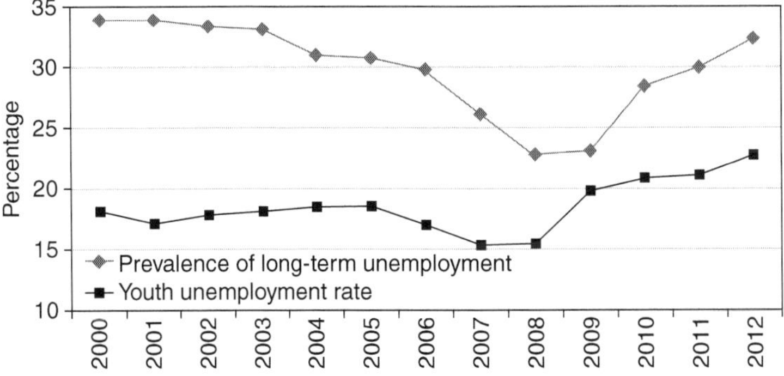

Figure 5.2 Youth unemployment rates and the prevalence of long-term unemployment among young people 2000–12 (source: calculated from Eurostat data (http://epp.eurostat.ec.europa.eu)).

Note
The prevalence of youth long-term unemployment is calculated as a percentage of the young unemployed.

The EU youth unemployment rate, following a big jump between 2008 and 2009, has since levelled off, although it is still rising gradually. The prevalence of long-term unemployment, however, continues to increase at a much faster rate. A number of papers over the years have noted that the effects of unemployment and/or joblessness early in one's 'working' career are likely to have long-term effects on employment prospects and wages (e.g. Gregg 2001; Gregg and Tominey 2005).[4] Methodological difficulties with separating individual heterogeneity from 'true' duration dependence cast some doubt on the causal influence of early unemployment on later careers identified by early studies. However, the regularity with which such scarring has been found, at least in the European context, as well as more recent attempts to control for these selectivity effects, suggest that there really is a scarring effect that goes beyond unobserved individual heterogeneity (e.g. Cockx and Picchio, 2011). The implication is that extended difficulties in the search for work early on are likely to have long-term negative consequences.[5] In the context of the current prolonged recession, this creates the spectre of a lost generation of young people who become permanently excluded from productive employment (Scarpetta *et al.* 2010). This is a real problem, and one which has prompted the recent resurgence of interest in youth guarantee schemes in the EU.

The overall picture presented above also conceals much cross-country variation. For example, between 2008 and 2011 the prevalence of long-term unemployment among the young unemployed more than trebled in Spain and more than doubled in Ireland, Latvia and Sweden, while it actually fell in the Czech Republic, Germany and Romania – in the case of Germany, by nearly 20 per cent.

Although the increase of 2.2 per cent in the prevalence of temporary employment at the EU level is rather moderate,[6] this too hides substantial cross-country variation. For example, Figure 5.3 compares trends in the prevalence of temporary employment in the EU as a whole with those in Italy. Whereas in the EU as a whole, the variations in temporary employment among young people have been relatively small since the turn of the millennium, in Italy the recession has reinforced an ongoing trend in increasing 'flexibility at the margin' initiated with

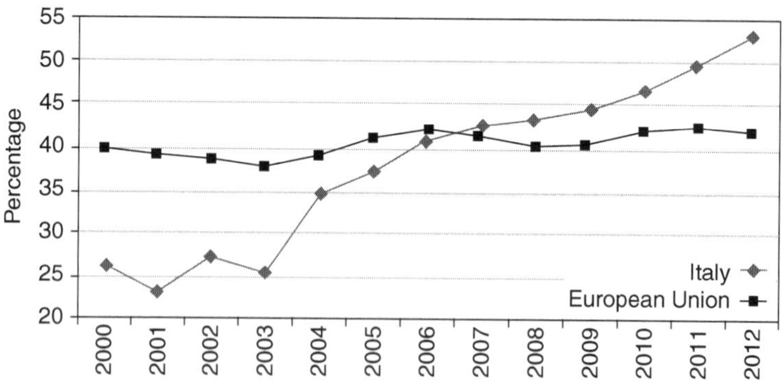

Figure 5.3 Prevalence of temporary employment in the EU and Italy, 2000–12 (source: calculated from Eurostat data (http://epp.eurostat.ec.europa.eu)).

Note

The prevalence of temporary employment among young people is calculated as a percentage of the young employed.

major labour market reforms in 1997 and 2003; so much so that, given the overall contraction in labour demand, practically all new employment of young people in Italy is on the basis of temporary contracts (O'Higgins 2011).

In contrast, the prevalence of part-time employment among the employed rose significantly, by 22.3 per cent between 2007 and 2012, as well as in absolute terms (by 2.2 per cent). Clearly a significant part of the fall in aggregate labour demand was translated into reduced working time.

2 Empirical analysis

2.1 Previous work in this area

A number of recent and some not so recent papers have looked at the factors driving youth employment and unemployment, in recent years focusing on the role of labour market institutions. Throughout this literature, from its beginnings in the 1980s, studies have unanimously found a major role for aggregate demand in determining youth labour market outcomes with a more variable role played by demographic and, above all, institutional factors.[7] Jimeno and Rodriguez-Palenzuela (2002) and Bertola *et al.* (2007) find a role for unionization rates in reducing youth employment; the former attribute this to wage compression, while the latter argue rather more convincingly that unions bargain to protect their core members, prime-age males, and are more willing to accept employment losses among more peripheral groups such as young people and women. Neither study finds a significant role for employment protection legislation (EPL) *per se*. The comprehensive study of the role of institutions on employment patterns undertaken by Bassanini and Duval (2006), on the other hand, finds a role for EPL in depressing youth employment rates, but, in contrast to Jimeno and Rodriguez-Palenzuela (2002), they also find a positive impact of youth minimum wages on youth employment.

In the context of the current recession, a number of papers have started to look at the role of recessions, as opposed to fluctuations in aggregate demand *per se*, in determining aggregate and/or youth labour market outcomes. Choudhry *et al.* (2012) find a consistently positive impact of financial crises on youth unemployment over and above that attributable to variations in aggregate demand, while Bernal-Verdugo *et al.* (2012) find, *inter alia*, that more flexible labour markets tend to exacerbate the initial negative employment effects of financial crises but that the negative effects of crises last longer in countries with more protected labour markets, particularly so in the case of youth labour markets.

Finally, a recent companion paper to this chapter (O'Higgins 2012), applying both cross-section and time-series rolling regressions to European countries, found that the aggregate demand-induced youth employment loss arising from the recession was reduced in countries with stronger, not weaker, EPL. Moreover, the analysis of the country-specific coefficients in the rolling regressions for the period prior to the recession further suggests that the strongly negative adjustment of youth employment in countries with relatively flexible labour markets prompted by the recession was not counterbalanced by a strong positive adjustment of youth employment to the growth in aggregate labour demand in the period of expansion prior to the downturn. Here I seek to investigate further developments in the youth labour market over the recession period, using a slightly different approach, but most significantly expanding the analysis to consider developments in a range of youth labour market indicators.

2.2 A simple framework for interpretation

In order to look at some of the factors underlying developments in the youth labour market during the recession, I adopt here a simple Okun law-inspired framework which looks at the relationship between a series of (primarily) youth labour market outcomes and real GDP over the period 2001–12. In particular, the analysis allows the relationship between GDP and outcome to vary across differing institutional regimes present in Europe. Thirty European countries (the 27 EU Member States plus Iceland, Norway and Switzerland) are grouped into one of four regimes on the basis of the cluster analysis developed by Eichhorst *et al.* (2009).

To be a little more specific, log differenced equations are estimated for a series of labour market outcomes (*X*) of the form:

$$\ln(X_{it}) - \ln(X_{it-1}) = \alpha_j + \beta_j[\ln(Y_{it}) - \ln(Y_{it-1})] + \varepsilon_{it} \tag{1}$$

Where ln stands for natural logarithm, Y is real GDP and subscript i stands for country ($i = 1, \ldots, 30$), j for country group ($j = 1, \ldots, 4$) and t for year. Differencing is intended to attenuate the rather obvious first-order autocorrelation in the error terms while maintaining the simple interpretation of β as the elasticity of the outcome with respect to real GDP. The α term picks up a linear time trend if present – that is, recalling that $\ln(1+c) \approx c - \alpha$ can be interpreted as the secular (i.e. not associated with variations in the growth rate of GDP) growth rate in X over time.

The analysis thus allows variations in the (positive or negative) growth rates of labour market outcomes to be decomposed into a constant time trend and an elasticity with respect to variations in real GDP. Two basic specifications are estimated: a base specification, constraining the two key coefficients to be constant across country groupings; and one in which both the time trends and the association with GDP are allowed to vary across institutional regimes. The main purpose is to see whether there are statistically significant differences in the reaction of labour market outcomes across countries according to their labour market institutions. Both specifications are estimated for three time periods. First, for the period 2001–12 as a whole; second, for the period 2001–06, characterized by moderate growth; and third, for the recession-dominated period 2007–12.[8] This allows one to look at differences in the differing reactions of country groups in periods of broadly moderate growth on the one hand, and recession on the other. This general framework is applied to a series of labour market outcomes and I seek to draw some meaningful conclusions from the associations and their variation across outcome indicators and regimes. I hasten to add, however, that the analysis is not intended to provide a causal analysis. Rather, the differences in the associations are used to draw implications about the differing labour market institutional regimes. Thus, the analysis lies somewhere between an examination of purely descriptive statistics and one which purports to identify structural parameters on the basis of strong, and questionable, underlying assumptions.

With the exception of the employment rate, each regression is run using two different denominators. This is important to distinguish, for example, labour market participation effects in the variations in unemployment.

The analysis of Eichhorst *et al.* (2009), which provides the basis for the identification of country groupings, distinguishes between internal (to companies) and external (labour market level) flexibility, and between numerical (variation of the workload) and functional (organizational adaptability) flexibility; finally, wage flexibility is considered as a separate category. The country groupings employed here are based on the external and wage flexibility criteria. Specifically:

1   *external numerical flexibility* concerns the ability to adapt the number of employees to economic circumstances through layoffs and hirings;
2   *external functional flexibility* concerns the adaptability of the labour force to structural change; and
3   *wage flexibility* refers to the ability to adjust wages to external shocks.

Based on these criteria, four clusters were identified by Eichhorst *et al.* which are the basis for the four country groups used here:[9]

1   'Education-based' systems comprising Scandinavian and Continental European countries characterized by low external numerical and wage flexibility and high external functional flexibility (i.e. Austria, Belgium, Denmark, Finland, Germany, Iceland, Luxembourg, the Netherlands, Norway, Sweden and Switzerland).
2   'Market-Oriented I' systems comprising Anglo-Saxon countries combining high external numerical and wage flexibility with intermediate functional flexibility (i.e. Ireland and the United Kingdom);
3   'Market-Oriented II' systems including the countries from Central and Eastern Europe characterized by high external numerical and wage flexibility but very low external functional flexibility (i.e. Bulgaria, the Czech Republic, Estonia, Hungary, Latvia, Lithuania, Poland, Romania, Slovakia and Slovenia); and
4   'Low flexibility' systems including the Mediterranean countries with low flexibility on all three dimensions (i.e. Cyprus, France, Greece, Italy, Malta, Portugal and Spain).

2.3 Results

As noted above, I report the results of six regressions for each labour market outcome indicator. For each indicator two core specifications are reported; (1) a specification constraining the coefficients to equality across country groupings; and (2) a specification which allows the coefficients to vary across labour market regimes as indicated in equation (1) above. For each of these specifications, regressions are run for the whole period (2001–12) and on the sub-periods 2001–06 and 2007–12 separately.

Tables 5.1 and 5.2 report the results of estimating the model for perhaps the key labour market indicator: the employment–population ratio[10] – for young people and prime-age adults, respectively. The results suggest first that variations in real GDP growth rates are associated with very different responses in the employment rate across country groupings; and second, comparing youths and adults, the pattern of response is fairly similar across country groupings and time, although the employment elasticities, the secular trends and the cross-country variation are all more pronounced for young people. Also of significance, estimation of the model in the second, 'recession-dominated' period provides a much closer fit to the data.

In principle, the results are more or less in line with what one would expect; the employment elasticities are less pronounced in the 'education-based' systems which are characterized by low external flexibility. The results suggest an important role for external functional flexibility, particularly in the later recession period; Continental European countries have a much lower employment elasticity with respect to GDP than do Mediterranean countries (0.7 as opposed to 1.8 for youths, and 0.3 as opposed to 0.6 for adults). The main difference between these two types of country is the degree of external functional flexibility, which is high in the Continent and low in Mediterranean countries. One may also observe that young people fared particularly badly – in terms of the elasticity of employment to GDP – also in Anglo-Saxon countries (1.6 compared to 0.7), although here the difference is only weakly statistically significant.

Important differences also emerge regarding the two periods examined. In general, employment elasticities and the differences in them across country groupings are both larger in the latter recession-dominated period. This is consistent with the results reported in O'Higgins (2012) based on rolling regressions, and which suggested that young people in countries with lower external flexibility, or greater employment protection, fared rather better than in more flexible labour markets, in that in the former, youth–adult employment elasticities fell during the recession period, while they increased in the more flexible market-oriented economies. In general, youth (and to a lesser extent also adult) employment was more responsive to variations in GDP growth during the recession period than during the earlier period of moderate, or in some countries, strong growth.

The analysis here also identifies the poor performance of Mediterranean countries, which although characterized by low flexibility on all counts, have

Table 5.1 Equation (1) estimated for the youth employment–population ratio

	2001–12		2001–06		2007–12	
	Base	*With interactions*	*Base*	*With interactions*	*Base*	*With interactions*
Intercept	*–0.04****	*–0.02****	*–0.03****	*–0.02**	*–0.03****	*–0.01**
• Market I		*–0.04****		0.00		*–0.05****
• Market II		*–0.03****		–0.06**		*–0.02***
• Low flexibility		*–0.03****		0.00		*–0.04****
GDP	*0.93****	0.56**	*0.48****	0.52	*1.10****	*0.68****
• Market I		0.96**		0.13		*0.96**
• Market II		0.35		0.71		*0.40**
• Low flexibility		*1.10****		0.30		*1.03****
R^2	0.27	0.31	0.03	0.05	0.43	0.50
N	360	360	180	180	180	180

Notes

1 In the varying coefficient specifications, the default coefficients are those for the 'education-based' country group; the other coefficients are additional to the default, so that, for example, the elasticity of the youth employment rate to GDP for the whole period (2001–12) in 'low flexibility' countries is estimated as 1.66 (0.56+1.10).

2 In order to facilitate ease of interpretation, the coefficient standard errors are not reported. Statistical significance of the coefficients is, however, indicated as follows: $p<0.01$ is indicated by ***; $p<0.05$ is indicated by **; and, $p<0.10$ is indicated by *.

Table 5.2 Equation (1) estimated for the adult employment–population ratio

	2001–12		2001–06		2007–12	
	Base	*With interactions*	*Base*	*With interactions*	*Base*	*With interactions*
Intercept	–0.01***	0.00**	0.00*	0.00	–0.01***	0.00
• Market I		–0.01**		0.00		–0.01*
• Market II		–0.01***		–0.01***		–0.01*
• Low flexibility		0.00		0.00		–0.01*
GDP	0.34***	0.22***	0.22***	0.18*	0.38***	0.26***
• Market I		0.21**		0.26**		0.27*
• Market II		0.12**		0.13		0.10
• Low flexibility		0.35***		0.00		0.34***
R^2	0.42	0.46	0.13	0.21	0.50	0.53
N	360	360	180	180	180	180

Note
See notes to Table 5.1.

progressively introduced 'flexibility at the margin' affecting, in particular, the young and females of all ages.

Tables 5.3 and 5.4 report the results of regressions run on the youth unemployment–population ratio and the youth unemployment rate, respectively. The difference between the two estimates concerns the denominator. Somewhat surprisingly, there is relatively little difference between the results reported in the two tables. This suggests that net movements from employment to non-labour force states were much less reactive to GDP than movements from employment to unemployment. The fact that the estimated elasticity of unemployment with respect to GDP is larger for the unemployment rate than for the unemployment–population ratio in the recession-dominated period (2007–12) implies the presence of a recession-induced movement out of the labour force, but the fact that the GDP coefficient values are close for the two models suggests that this labour force participation effect was small. The small participation effect may also reflect, to some extent a counter-cyclical induced labour force participation effect arising from the expansion of active, but also passive, labour market policy as a consequence of the recession. This appears to be particularly marked in the 'market oriented' countries and provides a plausible explanation for the marked secular growth in unemployment rates over the period 2007–12, which is much weaker for the unemployment population ratio.

One may also observe that, as with employment, the unemployment–GDP elasticity is much larger in the later recession period as well as being nearly four times as large as the employment–GDP elasticity reported above. The latter result is in line with the overall descriptive data reported in Figure 5.1, and, apart from reflecting the larger absolute size of employment compared to unemployment, it also indirectly supports the notion that falling GDP affected principally movements between employment and unemployment, rather than between employment and non-labour-force states.

Finally, it is worth observing that, perhaps in part because of the differing extent of the use of counter-cyclical expansion labour market policy measures and in contrast to the secular growth in unemployment, there is little variation – and no statistically significant differences – in the responsiveness of unemployment to GDP across the country groupings used here.

Tables 5.5 and 5.6 report the results of similar estimates for long-term unemployment, again distinguishing between long-term unemployment rate and ratio.[11] As one would expect, the coefficient values are much larger for the long-term unemployment population ratio than the long-term unemployment rate, the difference being explained by the substantial GDP-induced variations (as well as the 'secular' increases) in unemployment. The fact that the elasticity of the long-term unemployment rate remains statistically significant – as does the correspondingly larger coefficient on GDP in the 'ratio' equation in Table 5.5 compared to Table 5.3 – confirm that the GDP-induced increases in long-term unemployment were proportionately larger than the corresponding increases in unemployment as a whole.

Table 5.3 Equation (1) estimated for the youth unemployment–population ratio

	2001–12		2001–06		2007–12	
	Base	*With interactions*	*Base*	*With interactions*	*Base*	*With interactions*
Intercept	*0.09****	*0.08****	*0.10****	*0.15****	*0.08****	0.04**
• Market I		0.05		–0.17		*0.07**
• Market II		0.03		–0.10		*0.07****
• Low flexibility		0.00		–0.08		0.04
GDP	–3.27***	–2.97***	–2.92***	–4.01***	–3.67***	–3.39***
• Market I		0.25		5.67		–0.81
• Market II		–0.54		1.84		–0.42
• Low flexibility		–0.44		0.62		0.11
R^2	0.35	0.35	0.11	0.11	0.58	0.59
N	360	360	180	180	180	180

Note
See notes to Table 5.1.

Table 5.4 Equation (1) estimated for the youth unemployment rate

	2001–12		2001–06		2007–12	
	Base	*With interactions*	*Base*	*With interactions*	*Base*	*With interactions*
Intercept	*0.10****	*0.09****	*0.11****	*0.15****	*0.09****	*0.05****
• Market I		*0.07**		−0.16		*0.10***
• Market II		*0.04**		−0.05		*0.07****
• Low flexibility		0.00		−0.07		*0.05***
GDP	−3.35***	−3.09***	−2.90***	−4.11***	−3.83***	−3.53***
• Market I		−0.38		5.11		−1.31
• Market II		−0.46		1.33		−0.39
• Low flexibility		−0.51		0.51		0.12
R^2	0.40	0.40	0.13	0.13	0.62	0.63
N	360	360	180	180	180	180

Notes
1 See notes to Table 5.1.
2 The denominator of the unemployment rate is of course the (ILO definition) labour force.

Table 5.5 Equation (1) estimated for the youth long-term unemployment–population ratio

	2001–12		2001–06		2007–12	
	Base	*With interactions*	*Base*	*With interactions*	*Base*	*With interactions*
Intercept	*0.12****	0.09**	0.14***	0.10	*0.11****	*0.26****
• Market I		*0.15**		–0.13		–0.31
• Market II		0.04		0.05		–0.08
• Low flexibility		–0.01		–0.09		*–0.22**
GDP	*–4.26****	–3.27**	*–4.21****	–1.11	*–4.56****	*–7.32***
• Market I		–1.52		2.00		9.87
• Market II		–0.97		–2.07		2.50
• Low flexibility		–2.23		–1.42		3.41
R^2	0.24	0.27	0.10	0.12	0.32	0.32
N	294	294	137	137	157	157

Notes
1 See notes to Table 5.1.
2 The long-term unemployed are defined as persons with uncompleted unemployment durations of more than one year.

Table 5.6 Equation (1) estimated for the youth long-term unemployment rate

	2001–12		2001–06		2007–12	
	Base	*With interactions*	*Base*	*With interactions*	*Base*	*With interactions*
Intercept	0.04**	0.03	0.07**	0.10	*0.03*	0.00
• Market I		0.08		−0.13		*0.13**
• Market II		−0.01		0.05		0.02
• Low flexibility		0.01		−0.09		0.07
GDP	*−1.08***	−0.04	−2.07**	−1.11	*−0.85**	−0.42
• Market I		−2.04		2.00		−1.27
• Market II		−0.80		−2.07		−0.12
• Low flexibility		−2.39		−1.42		−1.21
R^2	0.03	0.02	0.03	0.04	0.02	0.01
N	294	294	137	137	157	157

Notes
1 See notes to Table 5.1.
2 The long-term unemployed are defined as persons with uncompleted unemployment durations of more than one year.
3 The denominator for the long-term unemployment rate is the number of unemployed.

Comparing the two periods, 2001–06 and 2007–12, one may observe that the elasticity of the long-term unemployment–population ratio with respect to GDP has increased slightly, although less than the increase in the elasticity of the unemployment rate and ratio; in consequence, the difference between the two corresponding estimated elasticities in Tables 5.5 and 5.6 has widened considerably (from just over 2 to nearly 4). That is, although as with unemployment, the recession period (2007–12) has led to a more than proportionate increase in long-term unemployment, the *increase* in the elasticity of long-term unemployment has been smaller than for unemployment as a whole. In other words, the recession has produced a GDP-induced worsening of both unemployment and long-term unemployment; however, things have got 'less worse' for long-term unemployment than for unemployment as a whole. This may in part reflect concerted action on the part of governments to target active labour market policies (ALMPs) towards the longer-term unemployed.

With the exception of the substantial 'secular' increase of around 16 per cent per year in the long-term unemployment rate registered in Anglo-Saxon (Market I) countries in the 2007–12 period, the estimated differences across labour market regimes are not statistically significant in this case.

Turning to the estimates for broadly defined unemployment (Tables 5.7 and 5.8), the smaller estimated elasticities with respect to GDP reported here compared to those in Tables 5.3 and 5.4 for unemployment, support the contention that GDP-induced variations in non-employment were primarily operating through movements within the ILO-defined labour market, rather than through movements out of the labour force. However, there are some curious exceptions worth noting. In the recession period (2007–12) the estimated elasticity of broad unemployment with respect to GDP is very substantial in the Anglo-Saxon (Market I) countries. This implies that in these countries the reaction to falls in GDP manifested itself – more or less – equally in terms of increased unemployment and increased discouragement from the labour market.

Moreover, the almost identical coefficients obtained using either the population or labour force (broadly defined) suggest that such movements out of the ILO-defined labour force induced by the recession were still within the broadly defined labour market. That is, recession-induced movements from employment to non-employment were largely confined to movements to ILO-defined unemployment or discouraged workers who wish to work but have given up searching. *Inter alia*, this provides some support for those of us who have been arguing in favour of the usefulness of a broader definition of unemployment for some time now.[12]

Estimates are also included here for so-called atypical forms of employment. As noted above, temporary and part-time employment are, at least in some countries, becoming a ubiquitous feature of young people's labour market experiences – supposing that they are fortunate enough to find a job. Tables 5.9 and 5.10 report estimates for temporary employment – again expressed in terms of rates and ratios. Here the outstanding feature is the large degree of variation in the reactivity – and, to a lesser extent, in secular time trends – across labour

Table 5.7 Equation (1) estimated for the youth broad unemployment–population ratio

	2001–12		2001–06		2007–12	
	Base	*With interactions*	*Base*	*With interactions*	*Base*	*With interactions*
Intercept	*0.05***	*0.05****	*0.09****	0.13**	*0.03****	*0.03**
• Market I		0.04		−0.11		0.05
• Market II		−0.01		−0.01		−0.02
• Low flexibility		−0.01		−0.13*		0.01
GDP	−2.15***	−2.06***	−2.61***	−4.61***	−2.36***	−1.73***
• Market I		−0.82		3.78		−2.11*
• Market II		0.04		1.99		−0.74
• Low flexibility		−0.05		4.51*		−0.84
R^2	0.23	0.21	0.10	0.09	0.40	0.40
N	231	231	107	107	124	124

Notes

1 See notes to Table 5.1.

2 The broad definition of unemployment includes discouraged workers; that is, in addition to the 'ILO unemployed', broad unemployment includes also persons who wish to work but who do not fulfil all the ILO criteria for unemployment.

Table 5.8 Equation (1) estimated for the youth broad unemployment rate

	2001–12		2001–06		2007–12	
	Base	*With interactions*	*Base*	*With interactions*	*Base*	*With interactions*
Intercept	*0.06****	*0.06****	*0.09****	*0.13****	*0.05****	*0.03****
• Market I		*0.05**		−0.09		*0.07***
• Market II		0.00		0.04		0.00
• Low flexibility		0.00		*−0.13****		0.02
GDP	*−2.21****	*−2.22****	*−2.57****	*−4.39****	*−2.40****	*−1.99****
• Market I		−1.08		3.20		*−2.16****
• Market II		0.18		1.13		−0.33
• Low flexibility		0.01		4.16**		−0.57
R^2	0.31	0.31	0.14	0.17	0.48	0.50
N	231	231	107	107	124	124

Notes
1 See notes to Table 5.1.
2 The broad definition of unemployment includes discouraged workers; that is, in addition to the 'ILO unemployed', broad unemployment includes also persons who wish to work but who do not fulfil all the ILO criteria for unemployment.
3 The denominator here is the enlarged labour force, including also discouraged workers.

Table 5.9 Equation (1) estimated for the youth temporary employment–population ratio

	2001–12		2001–06		2007–12	
	Base	*With interactions*	*Base*	*With interactions*	*Base*	*With interactions*
Intercept	−0.01	−0.01	0.01	−0.07	−0.02*	0.02
• Market I		0.00		0.00		0.03
• Market II		0.02		0.23**		0.00
• Low flexibility		−0.02		0.10		−0.02
GDP	0.88***	1.32**	0.35	3.82**	0.93***	0.53
• Market I		−0.14		−1.83		2.34*
• Market II		−0.84		−6.04***		0.14
• Low flexibility		0.42		−4.80*		1.93*
R^2	0.03	0.02	0.00	0.01	0.08	0.10
N	354	354	174	174	180	180

Note
1 See notes to Table 5.1.

Table 5.10 Equation (1) estimated for the youth temporary employment rate

	2001–12		2001–06		2007–12	
	Base	*With interactions*	*Base*	*With interactions*	*Base*	*With interactions*
Intercept	0.03**	0.00	0.04	−0.04	*0.02**	0.00
• Market I		0.04		0.00		0.08**
• Market II		*0.05**		0.29***		0.02
• Low flexibility		0.01		0.10		0.03
GDP	−0.05	0.76	−0.10	3.30**	−0.20	−0.15
• Market I		−0.82		−1.96		1.39
• Market II		*−1.19**		*−6.73***		−0.27
• Low flexibility		−0.68		*−5.10***		0.89
R^2	0.00	0.00	0.00	0.04	0.00	0.01
N	354	354	174	174	180	180

Notes
1 See notes to Table 5.1.
2 The denominator here is the number of young employees.

market regimes. On average, the estimated elasticity of temporary employment with respect to GDP is moderately positive; however, this hides very substantial variation across country groups, and to some extent, periods. During the earlier period when the expansion of temporary employment forms was more pronounced,[13] the elasticity of the temporary employment rate with respect to GDP varied between over +3 in the education-based systems to less than −3 in the Market II systems of Central and Eastern Europe.

In the later recession period, the overall positive elasticity of the temporary employment ratio with respect to GDP is clearly driven by a moderately strong positive elasticity observable in both the Anglo-Saxon countries, and above all (in terms of statistical significance) in the low flexibility Mediterranean countries. In the latter, temporary contracts have proved important as a mechanism to accommodate falling labour demand in the presence of strong restrictions on external (and in practice also internal) numerical flexibility.[14]

Finally, Tables 5.11 and 5.12 report the results for part-time employment. Overall, particularly in the second period (2007–12), there is a moderate positive secular growth in part-time employment, both as a percentage of the employed and as a percentage of the population, which does not vary greatly across labour market regime. Although, for the most part, the reported estimates are not very well defined, two major points emerge. First, with the exception of Mediterranean countries, variations in the part-time employment rate are negatively associated with variations in GDP growth. On the other hand, however, in the low flexibility Mediterranean countries, part-time employment is positively correlated with economic growth.

A plausible explanation for these patterns of response in the different country groupings during the recession period is as follows: whereas in the first three country groupings, part-time employment was used directly as an adjustment mechanism in response to falling employment demand, in Mediterranean countries characterized by low flexibility on all dimensions, the expansion of temporary and part-time employment in concomitance with falling GDP may be the result of the increasing dominance of these forms of employment for any new employment opportunities arising during this period. In a recent study of Italy (O'Higgins 2011), case studies of firm strategies suggested that employers were using temporary and part-time contracts on any new hires so as to insure against future product demand uncertainty. One reason for this is that such contracts typically provide much more limited employment protection. For both temporary and part-time employment this positive correlation between GDP and these types of employment shows up in ratios rather than in rates since, of course, youth employment (the denominator of the rates) is also strongly positively correlated with GDP, as we have seen. Certainly these phenomena would bear further investigation.

3 Concluding remarks

In this chapter I have looked at the role of differing institutional regimes in moderating the reactions of a series of youth labour market indicators to variations in

Table 5.11 Equation (1) estimated for the youth part-time employment–population ratio

	2001–12		2001–06		2007–12	
	Base	*With interactions*	*Base*	*With interactions*	*Base*	*With interactions*
Intercept	0.03**	0.03	0.03	0.04	0.04***	0.04**
• Market I		−0.01		0.15		−0.02
• Market II		0.01		0.03		0.02
• Low flexibility		−0.01		0.04		−0.02
GDP	−0.06	−0.49	−0.45	0.01	0.20	−0.46
• Market I		0.12		−3.81		0.50
• Market II		0.28		−0.58		0.56
• Low flexibility		*1.80**		0.44		2.01**
R^2	0.00	0.00	0.00	0.00	0.00	0.00
N	354	354	174	174	180	180

Notes
1 See notes to Table 5.1.

Table 5.12 Equation (1) estimated for the youth part-time employment rate

	2001–12		2001–06		2007–12	
	Base	*With interactions*	*Base*	*With interactions*	*Base*	*With interactions*
Intercept	*0.07****	0.05**	*0.06**	0.03	*0.07****	*0.05****
• Market I		0.03		0.15		0.02
• Market II		0.04		0.09		0.04
• Low flexibility		0.03		0.04		0.03
GDP	−0.99***	−1.05	−0.89	−0.49	−0.94***	−1.14**
• Market I		−0.85		−3.94		−0.46
• Market II		−0.06		−1.28		0.15
• Low flexibility		0.70		0.14		0.98
R^2	0.04	0.03	0.00	0.00	0.08	0.06
N	354	354	174	174	180	180

Notes
1 See notes to Table 5.1.
2 The denominator here is the number of young employees.

aggregate demand. The chapter built on previous work which suggested that in countries with strong employment protection, young people suffered less in terms of the recession-induced employment losses. The more detailed analysis of different indicators and the slightly different approach adopted allows a more nuanced picture to emerge. There is clear evidence of significant differences in the response of youth labour markets to variations in GDP across institutional regimes. Moreover, the analysis confirms the basic finding of O'Higgins (2012), at least concerning the education-based systems of Continental Europe; however, in Mediterranean countries characterized by very low flexibility on all the dimensions considered here, young people suffered more than in other countries both in terms of the overall reactivity of youth employment to aggregate demand, but also in terms of the substitution of full-time permanent employment with temporary and/or part-time employment forms. That these should come to dominate – so much so that, in the case of part-time employment, they were actually increasing in absolute terms and not just as a percentage of the employed – certainly does little to suggest that these contractual forms are being used as a stepping stone to long-term secure employment. It is hoped that the findings here provide a basis for further investigation.

Notes

1 All the figures and calculations reported here are based on the Eurostat database, as is the econometric analysis.
2 See, for example, O'Higgins (2001) and Ryan (2001) for a discussion.
3 The prevalence of long-term unemployment is defined here as the percentage of the unemployed of a specific age-group who have been so for one year or more.
4 The cited paper provides perhaps the strongest case for duration dependence, looking at the effects of early unemployment on career prospects some 10–15 years later, controlling for observed heterogeneity.
5 Gregg and Tominey (2005) identify a scarring effect on wages more than 20 years after unemployment episodes experienced during youth.
6 Indeed, in absolute terms, it fell by 15.4 per cent over this period, a little less than the fall in employment – hence the slight rise in prevalence.
7 Early examples here are Clark and Summers (1982) on the United States and Rice (1986) on the United Kingdom.
8 On (unweighted) average, real GDP grew by 21 per cent in EU countries between 2001 and 2006 and fell by 1 per cent between 2007 and 2012. Of course, there was much variation across countries. Between 2001 and 2006 growth ranged from 3 per cent in Portugal to 53 per cent in Latvia, while between 2007 and 2012 growth ranged between –20 per cent in Greece and +18 per cent in Poland.
9 The 'Eichhorst *et al.*' grouping of countries does not actually differ greatly from several other possible classifications; however, it has the advantage of being based on a formalized statistical procedure (cluster analysis) in order to identify the groupings. Note that, for the analysis here, additional European countries are added to those identified in Eichhorst *et al.* (2009) – Iceland and Luxembourg are added to the 'education-based' group; Bulgaria, Estonia, Latvia, Lithuania, Romania and Slovenia are added to the CEE 'Market-Oriented II' group; and Cyprus and Malta are included in the Mediterranean 'low flexibility' group.
10 While, these days, it is more common to refer to this indicator as the employment rate, in what follows the convention used is that 'rates' refer to indicators which use the (youth) labour force, employment or unemployment as denominators, while 'ratios'

refer to indicators which use the (youth) population as the denominator. Thus, for consistency here the term employment–population ratio refers to the proportion of the age-specific population which is employed; the employment rate in usual parlance.

11 The former is, of course, the prevalence of long-term unemployment among the unemployed as used in Figure 5.1 and the latter its prevalence in the population.

12 See, for example, O'Higgins (2001, 2010).

13 During the period 2001–06, temporary employment among young people grew by a little over 14 per cent, both in absolute terms and in terms of its prevalence among the employed.

14 See, for example, O'Higgins (2011) and the references therein on Italy.

References

Bassanini, A. and Duval, R., 2006: Employment patterns in OECD countries: Reassessing the role of policies and institutions. *OECD Social, Employment and Migration Working Papers*, no. 35.

Bernal-Verdugo, L.E., Furceri, D. and Guillame, D., 2012: Crises, labor market policy, and unemployment. *IMF Working Paper*, no. 12/65.

Bertola, G., Blau, F.D. and Kahn, L.M. 2007: Labor market institutions and demographic employment patterns. *Journal of Population Economics* 20: 833–867.

Choudhry, M., Marelli, E. and Signorelli, M., 2012: Youth unemployment and the impact of financial crises. *International Journal of Manpower* 33: 76–95.

Clark, K.B. and Summers, L.H., 1982: The dynamics of youth unemployment, *NBER Working Paper Series*, no. 0274.

Cockx, B. and Picchio, M., 2011: Scarring effects of remaining unemployed for long-term unemployed school-leavers. *Institute de Recherches Économiques et Sociale de L'Université catholique de Louvain, Discussion Paper*, no. 2011-32.

Eichhorst, W., Marx, P. and Tobsch, V., 2009: Institutional arrangements, employment performance and the quality of work. *IZA Discussion Paper*, No. 459.

Gregg, P., 2001: The impact of youth unemployment on adult unemployment in the NCDS. *Economic Journal* 111: 626–653.

Gregg, P. and Tominey, E., 2005: The wage scar from male youth unemployment. *Labour Economics* 12: 487–509.

Jimeno, J.F. and Rodriguez-Palenzuela, D., 2002: Youth unemployment in the OECD: Demographic shifts, labour market institutions, and macroeconomic shocks. *ECB Working Paper*, no. 155.

O'Higgins, N., 2001. *Youth Unemployment and Employment Policy: A Global Perspective*. ILO, Geneva.

O'Higgins, N., 2010: Youth labour markets in Europe and Central Asia. *IZA Discussion Paper*, no. 5094.

O'Higgins, N., 2011: Italy: limited policy responses and industrial relations in flux, leading to aggravated inequalities, in D. Vaughan-Whitehead (ed.), *Inequalities in the World of Work: The Effects of the Crisis*. Edward Elgar: Cheltenham.

O'Higgins, N., 2012: This time its different? Youth labour markets during 'The Great Recession', *Comparative Economic Studies* 54, 2: 395–412.

Rice, P., 1986: Juvenile unemployment, relative wages and social security in Great Britain. *Economic Journal* 96: 352–374.

Scarpetta, S., Sonnet, A. and Manfredi, T., 2010: Rising youth unemployment during the crisis: how to prevent negative long-term consequences on a generation?, *OECD Social, Employment and Migration Working Papers*, no. 106.

Part II

Financial regulations for better economic stability

6 Financial regulations for minimizing economic and social crises

An evolutionary developmental analysis reckoning with unequally rational individuals

Pavel Pelikan

1 Introduction

This chapter has two objectives: to produce new arguments for an actual policy issue, and thus demonstrate the fruitfulness of a new theory. The theory is the generalization of Darwinism termed "evolutionary-developmental economics" ("evo-devo economics") presented by Pelikan (2011, 2012), which differs on several important points from the previously proposed generalization by Hodgson and Knudsen (2006, 2010). Why a generalization of Darwinism needs to demonstrate its usefulness is that many economists, even some evolutionary ones, have for a long time been claiming that none of its forms might have fruitful economic applications, and could support this claim by pointing to the lack of such applications for the Hodgson–Knudsen form (see, e.g., Cordes 2006; Witt 2006; Schubert 2013). Demonstrating that a different form of generalized Darwinism *can* be fruitful is therefore important: this may stop economists from throwing all of Darwinism into a wastebasket, and thus missing many of its principles which, when suitably generalized, may throw valuable new light on several important economic issues.

Some hints that evo-devo economics may be more fruitful than the purely abstract top-down generalization of Darwinism by Hodgson and Knudsen may be seen in its building bottom-up on principles that already helped understand certain concrete issues – for example, how to compare capitalism with socialism for the abilities to generate, and adapt to, innovations (Pelikan 1988), or how to transform a failed socialist economy into a more successful one (Pelikan 1992). But all those issues are now rather dated, which makes it necessary to demonstrate its usefulness, to address another, more actual one.

It is for this purpose that the issue of government financial regulations appears particularly suitable. While it allows the demonstration to be relatively easy, the recent financial crises with their disastrous impact on entire economies and societies have also made it highly actual. It may be stated as follows: By what government regulations, if any, could financial crises be prevented, or at least mitigated, and what regulations would, or actually did, make the crises even worse?

But the present dealing with this issue will be limited in two ways. First, it will not produce any new financial regulations, and for a good reason: All of their possible and imaginable forms appear to have already been extensively debated, which makes it virtually impossible to invent any brand-new ones. It is only that many of the known ones still make even the most respected economists disagree. What can be produced are thus only some additional arguments that strengthen the already existing support of some and/or the opposition to other known regulations, and in this way help settle such disagreements.

Second, the dealing is limited in space. On the few pages that a chapter in a collective book is allowed to take, it is not possible to elaborate the arguments in all relevant details. But I hope the main ideas will be presented clearly enough to allow interested readers to elaborate the details themselves.

The rest of the chapter is organized as follows. Section 2 will present the main idea of evo-devo economics, with particular attention to its reckoning with rationality inequalities. Section 3 will summarize its perspective on the financial sector, centered on the role of this sector in rationality allocation. Section 4 will recall and summarize the main finding of rationality allocation analysis by Pelikan (2010): *markets have the potential for selecting far better entrepreneurs and investors than government, but need certain government regulations to realize it.* Using examples from the recent financial crises, Section 5 will show why in the case of financial markets this potential may indeed remain far from realized, and how these markets, when left alone, may develop in the wrong way and lead to deep economic and social crises. Considering some of the often debated financial regulations, Section 6 will indicate which of them evo-devo analysis finds helpful, or even urgently needed, and which of them it finds ineffective or harmful. Section 7 will conclude by briefly considering the possible obstacles to the implementation of the needed regulations, due in part to government and in part to private investors, and by pointing out the evolutionary sanctions bound to hit the economies where these obstacles will not be overcome.

2 Evo-devo economics: main principles

As indicated by its name, evo-devo economics decomposes economic change into two interconnected, but to a large extent separately analyzable layers: (1) developmental processes that take place under given institutional rules; and (2) evolutionary processes that change these rules.[1]

It thus combines parts of the neo-Schumpeterian economics following Nelson and Winter (1982) with the new institutional economics following North (1990), but with two terminological adjustments. The first is that neo-Schumpeterian economists like to call their field "evolutionary," while the evo-devo economics terms it, in agreement with their grandfather's classical work, "developmental" (cf. Schumpeter 1912/1934).

The second adjustment is that what North defines as "institutions" is called more explicitly "institutional rules." The reason is that despite North's efforts to provide the term "institutions" with a clear operational meaning – namely the one of "the rules of the game," such as formal laws and informal socio-cultural norms – this term still remains highly ambiguous. It is still widely used in many other and not always well-defined meanings – including routines, language, money, large firms, banks, universities and government agencies. This ambiguity is particularly disturbing in applications to financial economics, where the term "institutions" usually denotes large banks and investment firms, which, according to North's definition, are "organizations." It appears therefore safest to avoid this term altogether, and use the more explicit term "institutional rules" for referring to "institutions" in the sense of North, while following him by referring to banks, other firms and government agencies as "organizations."

The terminology of new institutional economics is moreover complemented in two ways. First, the term "institutional framework" is defined to denote the set of all the formal and information institutional rules that belong to a given organization, or a given economy. Second, institutional rules and frameworks are admitted to be of several interrelated organizational levels – such as the one of the entire economy and the one of its firms and other organizations. An important example is the corporate law that constrains the permissible variety of forms of corporate governance of a large category of firms by prescribing some of the governance rules and/or prohibiting others.

This terminology makes it possible to relate in a well-defined way "institutional rules" to "regulations," and clearly distinguish the different meanings in which this term has been used. This may be useful, as proponents and opponents of financial regulations sometimes appear to disagree simply because they differ, without realizing it, in their understanding of this term. Two distinctions are of particular importance.

One is between *general regulations* that are themselves institutional rules, designed and implemented by the legislative branch of government, and *specific controls* that intervene in the course of selected transactions and/or the management of selected firms, possibly including their ownership, which is conducted by the executive branch of government. The key relationship is that the latter can be conducted only to the extent allowed by the former. Note that this solves the apparent paradox that weakening the state may require strengthening it, which confused many ideological controversies between proponents and opponents of government activities. The solution simply is that the state may have to be strengthened as legislator, to be able to limit, against the usually powerful opposition of its employees, the extent of its executive decision making.[2]

The second important distinction is between general regulations concerning *inter-firm relationships* and those concerning *intra-firm governance*. This distinction is particularly important when searching for remedies against inefficiently behaving firms – such as too risk-loving banks. It usefully structures this search by dividing the great number of possible regulations between those accepting the firms as they are and trying to stop their inefficient behaviors by disincentives and interdictions from outside, and those trying to make the firms themselves behave more efficiently by changing them from inside – for instance, by enforcing rules that better align the incentives of their managers with their long-term performance. Note that such regulations, if successful, would make most of the outside disincentives and interdictions – known never to be precise and often do more harm then good – largely superfluous.

It has been necessary to make all this clear to avoid the terminological fuzziness and misunderstandings by which the debate about financial regulations has often been scourged. For making a meaningful contribution to this debate, however, it is necessary to bring into it another feature of evo-devo economics, on which it most markedly departs from existing economic theories, namely its recognition that human rationality – in the empirical sense of cognitive abilities (skills, competence, intelligence, talents) – is not only bounded, but moreover unequally so across individuals. This recognition ranges rationality among the scarce resources that pose the problem of their efficient allocation in society, and makes it play a central role in both the development of economies and the evolution of their institutional rules.

In its entirety, the problem of rationality allocation is difficult to solve. As explained by Pelikan (2010), it involves what Hofstadter (1979) terms "tangled hierarchies," which puts it outside the reach of straightforward analysis. For present purposes, however, it suffices to view it as a trial-and-error experimental process of job-designing and job-assigning, of which we only need to consider two relatively simple aspects: (1) the relevant rationality of the individuals selected for top entrepreneurial, managerial and investment jobs; and (2) the losses from what Heiner (1983) calls "competence–difficulty gaps" ("c–d gaps"), caused by individuals that are, or have become, insufficiently rational (competent) for their jobs, and/or by jobs that are, or have become, too difficult for their individuals.

What leads to the present issue of financial regulations is that the outcomes of rationality allocation, including the two indicators, strongly depend on the prevailing institutional rules related to financial regulations in the above-clarified ways.

3 The perspective of evo-devo economics on the financial sector

As usual, the financial sector is seen composed of financial markets and financial agents, which may be individuals or organizations, including private firms and specialized government agencies. All organizations are seen to consist of interrelated decision-making individuals – such as capital owners, managers, other employees, politicians and government bureaucrats. The sector's forming, operating and reforming (restructuring) are constrained and shaped by specialized institutional rules, a subset of the economy's institutional framework.

The main task of the financial sector is seen to be transforming concrete savings into concrete investments. As opposed to the Keynesians, who assume this automatically done by the equation $I = S$, this transformation is recognized to require a complex network of incompletely informed, and therefore full of trials and errors, organizational and allocational processes, shaped by the prevailing institutional framework, and far from guaranteed to work well.

In this context, the key step of evo-devo economics is to enlarge attention from the usually studied allocation of investments to *the selection of the investors*. While investment decisions are always risky and cannot avoid errors, some investors are more relevantly rational, able better to observe, perceive and process available information, and thus also *likely* to commit fewer and less serious errors, than others. As is well known, some investors have indeed proved better able to distinguish, among actual and potential entrepreneurs, future winners from future losers. An institutional framework that leads the selection to promote relevantly highly rational investors, and demote the poorly rational ones, makes the economy more efficient than an alternative framework that prevents potentially excellent investors from entering and/or protects little-competent incumbent investors from exiting.

This does not mean to neglect the sector's other tasks, in particular the usually studied provision of *stability*, *liquidity* and *risk-spreading*. Although perfect stability, because of both exogenous and endogenous disturbances, can never be achieved, the institutional framework, to be evolutionarily sustainable, must be able to keep the unavoidable fluctuations from falling into too deep, institutionally disruptive crises. Liquidity remains important, but only as an extra incentive for short-term savers, to increase the amount of the savings available for investment above the one offered by the long-term savers – although this increase may often be decisive. Risk-spreading also remains important, but is not the only risk-related task that the sector is seen to perform.

How evo-devo analysis modifies the usual views of these tasks can be summarized in three points. One is a slight lowering of the status of liquidity from "most important" to "important." The top importance is here accorded to the efficiency of allocation of investments to entrepreneurs, and therefore to the selection of investors. This makes room for trade-offs in which some liquidity may prove worth sacrificing as a means of improving the efficiency of the allocation and/or the selection.

Second, the selection of investors, to be efficient, must favor highly rational *fundamentalists*, to the detriment of highly rational trend-traders (noise-traders). For the efficiency of the financial sector, as explained below, trend-traders are not very helpful, and may even be highly harmful as sources of important disturbances and market failures. But how to direct the selection to make it promote fundamentalists, and not trend-traders, is a difficult problem for which no known institutional framework appears to have a fully satisfactory solution. Financial regulations that could help solve this problem would thus be of a particularly high social value.

Third, the financial sector is seen to have an extra task in dealing with investment risks. Instead of assuming them exogenously given and limiting attention to their spreading, as is usual to do, their sum is seen to a large extent endogenous, significantly depending on the relevant rationality of the investors: the higher this is, the lower the sum will be. This enlarges the risk-related tasks of the financial sector from risk-spreading to risk-minimizing, and thus further enhances the importance of the selection of investors.

4 Markets have the potential to select far better entrepreneurs and investors than government, but may fail to realize it

This is, in essence, the main finding of the comparative rationality allocation analysis presented by Pelikan (2010). This means that, in whatever ways the financial sector might fail, government selection of entrepreneurs and investors cannot be the right remedy. The only hopeful strategy is therefore to search for ways in which the failures could be alleviated, and the markets could thus realize their greatly superior potential. This finding implies a few lessons which may help start this search.

Lesson 1: market competition has a higher social value than usually recognized. In addition to being important for the efficiency of prices and quantities of the transactions among given market participants, it is even more important for the efficiency of the *selection* of these participants – especially of efficient producers, and of such producers finding investors. This is indeed a key point of the entire finding: for top *economic* jobs, the *politico-administrative* selection run by governments – democratic or not – cannot, *on average*, do much better than select individuals of only slightly above-average *relevant* rationality (talents, competence), but is unlikely to find and keep any of the exceptional entrepreneurial champions, without whom no economic development can be very successful.

Lesson 2: The limits of socially efficient sizes of firms are lower than usually recognized. The drop is particularly great compared to transaction-costs economics, by which the old classical limits, due to concerns with inefficient pricing and monopoly rents, were substantially lifted (Williamson 1985). In contrast, evo-devo economics lowers them again, for three reasons.

First, the high importance of market competition for firm selection and rationality allocation increases the importance of keeping it going. No current winner must therefore be allowed to grow so big as to become a serious obstacle to its continuation, and especially not "too big to fail."

Second, the recognition of the possibility that individuals in any firm, however large and previously successful, may commit errors which cause the firm to decline or even collapse, leads to the problem of the safety of the entire economy. It is this safety that requires the sizes of the economy's firms to be kept relatively low, to prevent the collapse of any of them from seriously damaging the rest.

Third, as noted, rationality allocation involves the problem of c–d gaps, which implies yet another constraint on the sizes of firms. To avoid such gaps, no firm can be larger and/or more diversified than the individuals selected for its management, given their relevant rationality (competencies, talents), can handle. If market selection worked well, of course, such gaps would be rather easily discovered and corrected: the individuals causing them would be demoted or their firms would be forced to shrink, or both. But there is rich empirical evidence showing that market selection is often far from working so well. Many firms appear to have grown, or even been purposefully made, so big that they can hinder the selection, and thus allow wasteful gaps between the difficulties of managing them and the relevant rationality of their managers to last for quite a long time.

Lesson 3: Evo-devo analysis makes it possible to assess and compare institutional frameworks of economies in a value-free way, independent of the ideologies or political preferences of the analysts. Instead of letting these choose some social welfare function according to their subjective values – depending, for instance, on their preferred efficiency–equity trade-off – evo-devo assesses institutional frameworks according to their evolutionary *sustainability* (maintenance, "survival"). This depends on their success in two selection tests: (A) for *economic efficiency* and (B) for *political acceptability*.

Test (A) depends on the harshness and the variability of the natural and economic environments, which imply a certain minimum of efficiency, both allocative and adaptive, to which a successful institutional framework must lead. Test (B) depends on the values and preferences of the population, which imply certain criteria of perceived justice, both procedural and substantive, that a successful institutional framework must meet. Note that many institutional frameworks that succeed in (A) may fail in (B), and vice versa. Note also that values do play a role, but they are those of the population considered, and not the ones of the analyst.

What matters most here is that this evolutionary value-free way of assessing institutional frameworks implies a value-free definition of the notion of "failure": this refers to any of the ways in which they may fail in any of the two tests.

5 Why may financial markets fail to realize their potential?

In general, the failures of any part of an economy can always be ascribed to some "misbehaving" individuals, who – because of their wrong incentives and/ or insufficient or misleading information and/or insufficient competence (bounded rationality) for using the information available – don't do what they should and/or do what they shouldn't.

In the case of the financial sector, the misbehaving individuals may be private investors, or government agents, or both. The recent financial crises can indeed be shown as due to both. The failures of governments were enormous indeed, but are rather obvious. In part, as pointed out by public choice and rent-seeking theories, all governments tend to grow and overspend, which in many cases, both in Europe and the United States, resulted in enormous public debts. In part, though this was mainly the case of the US government, it was the wrong regulations that limited the possibilities of private investors behaving efficiently – such as the anti-discrimination laws that importantly contributed to the growth of subprime mortgages. Moreover, the US government may also be blamed for underestimating the possibilities of market failures, and consequently allowing private investors to behave inefficiently by mistaken deregulations – such as the one that abolished the Dodd–Frank Act, and thus allowed fusions of low-risk commercial banking with high-risk investment banking. But this blame, in fact, leads to market failures: without them, all deregulations would be efficient.

The failures of financial market due to the (mis-)behavior of private investors may be divided into six types. All of them can be shown theoretically possible and – according to the wisdom of engineers that if something *may* go wrong, sooner or later it *will* – must therefore be considered practically inevitable if nothing is done to prevent them. In fact, all can be found to have played a non-negligible role in causing the recent financial crises.

Failure 1: Financial firms that irrationally misuse market freedoms (to the great surprise of the market-efficiency-expecting deregulators) for taking excessive risks and consequently suffering excessive losses. Note that this does not necessarily concern the rationality of the individuals within the firms. Although many of them may have also been far from perfectly rational, faulty corporate governance – such as the one that fails to make managers responsible for the losses caused – would suffice to make even perfectly rational individuals form an irrationally (inefficiently) behaving firm.

Failure 2: Overgrown financial firms that become "too big to fail" – or in other words, attain the blackmailer status. They become able to blackmail the taxpayers, demanding these pay for their losses under the threat that their fall would be even more socially costly. This failure puts the valuable market selection out of work, allowing underperforming financial firms, together with their – from c–d gaps likely suffering – management to eschew it and stay put.

Failure 3: Developing increasingly complex, for buyers insufficiently described, financial instruments, which amplify information asymmetries and make financial firms increasingly interdependent. Errors committed by one can thus seriously damage in not fully understood ways many others. The growing complexity is also an important source of costly c–d gaps. It increasingly challenges even the best investors, as many of them sincerely admitted that they no longer knew very well what they were trading with.[3]

Failure 4: Excessive market volatility, exaggerating the amplitude of market fluctuations, and thus the depth of the recurrent crises, far beyond what appears to be, given the complexity of an advanced capitalist market economy and the chaotic character of the fluctuations, inevitable. The prime suspects are trend-trading investors, traditionally known for their flock behavior causing excessive market volatility, and speculative bubbles followed by deep crises. More recently, advances of mathematical modeling and developments of information technologies have increased their opportunities for making private gains by destabilizing the markets – for instance, by various tricks in high-frequency trading. This is one of the ways in which they are harmful.

Failure 5: Trend-traders cause an even more serious market failure, which appears to need evo-devo analysis to be clearly seen. When their number exceeds some relatively low threshold – which now appears to be always the case – they distort the very selection criteria of financial markets. This in turn distorts the incentives for all investors, who will find it most rewarding to become trend-traders themselves, and will therefore spend most of their efforts on guessing how other investors will act, rather than on the socially more useful learning about the real abilities and future possibilities of producers.[4] This market failure may thus be seen as a new variant of the old public-goods market failure: in both cases the markets fail to provide the right individual incentives for socially efficient behavior, including socially efficient learning.

Failure 6: An important overgrowth of the entire financial sector, observable in the growing volume of transactions on financial markets. This was growing much faster than the useful output of the sector in terms of the capital supplied to producers and consumers – estimated to have grown since 1998 up to six times as large (cf. Blundell-Wignall 2011, figure 1). Intuitively, such a financial sector might be compared to a highly inefficient motor that uses more and more energy just for running itself, or to a cancerous growth that threatens to kill the entire organism.

All of these failures are both economically wasteful and – because of the many growing and to a large extent perceived as undeserved wealth and income inequalities – also politically explosive. This is a serious double threat to the evolutionary sustainability of capitalist institutional frameworks, so much more serious that for large society needing innovations, capitalism has no good substitute (cf., e.g., Pelikan 1988).

6 What financial regulations might help?

In general, referring to the above classification of government regulations, evo-devo analysis strengthens the advocacy of certain institutional rules and the objections to virtually all specific controls. The objections directly follow from Lesson 1 of Section 3. As governments are unlikely to select the best relevant rationality for complex economic decision making, they cannot be relied upon to choose the right indicators, calculate for them the right values and effectively coerce the individuals within financial firms, most likely far more competent than themselves, into the desired behaviors. Their situation may be compared to the one of Soviet planners facing the managers of socialist firms: These always found ways of formally fulfilling the plan without really doing what the planners wanted them to do – to which all the Basel capital and liquidity requirements appear increasingly to resemble.

The advocacy of regulations by institutional rules needs more elaboration. First of all, it must be admitted that government is unlikely to have the best relevant rationality even for this task. But it must then also be recognized that this task is significantly less demanding than most of specific controls. Intuition may be helped by comparing this task to the organizing of chess tournaments, for which there are good explicit theories and which even average-talented people can do reasonably well; and specific controls to actually playing top chess, for which talents are much scarcer and cannot be properly discovered other than just by competition in well-organized tournaments (cf. Pelikan 2010).

The regulations by institutional rules that evo-devo analysis helps to advocate are of four main types. They may be surveyed and their expected effects on the above-listed market failures briefly mentioned as follows.

1   The rules of corporate law constraining the design of corporate governance within financial firms which help minimize the rent-seeking opportunities of the firms' managers and better align the incentives of all employees with the firms' long-term performance. This type of regulation is needed for alleviating Failure 1, and may also help alleviate Failure 2, to the extent that the excessive growth of financial firms is also due to distorted incentives of their managers.

2   Antitrust legislation that cuts down growing financial firms into smaller parts in good time, before they could reach the "too big to fail" level, and stops all the mergers and acquisitions that could lead to it. The cuts may be into smaller firms competing on the same market, or specializing in different markets (e.g., as required by the Dodd–Frank Act, separating investment banking from retail banking).

    It is, of course, hardly possible to determine with precision what this critical level should be. Only some imperfect guesses and rules of thumb may be used, possibly combined with some experimental learning process. Evo-devo analysis, by pointing to the high social value of keeping market competition and selection working, adds an argument for cutting more than what standard analysis may indicate. This type of regulation is mainly needed for preventing Failure 2, but may also alleviate Failure 6, to the extent that the inefficient overgrowth of the entire financial sector is also due to the excessive growth of some of its firms.

3   Rules constraining the complexity of financial instruments, demanding full buyers' information on their contents, and excluding those that interconnect financial firms too tightly. This type of regulation is directly required by Failure 3. It is, of course, again impossible to precisely determine the limits of admissible complexity and admissible interconnectedness. Some imperfect guesses and rules of thumb are therefore again necessary. But, given the large losses that Failure 3 demonstrated to be capable of causing, setting the limits a little too low appears again safer than setting them too high.

4   A small tax on financial transactions ("Tobin tax"). Evo-devo analysis plays down its often quoted redistributive effects as secondary, and objects to labeling it "Robin Hood," as this can make people mistakenly believe that it is only a kind of enforced charity. In contrast, evo-devo analysis finds it efficiency improving, alleviating Failures 4 and 5. In other words, this analysis finds its main task not in helping the poor, but in calming down the rich and inducing them to compete for excellence in the socially valuable art of fundamental investing, rather than in the much less valuable and possibly even harmful one of over-smarting each other thousands of times per

second. If the tax is so small that it discourages only high-frequency trading, but not the investing by fundamentalists, it may indeed alleviate both of these failures. Intuitively, its effects on Failure 4 may be compared to those of an oscillation-dampening resistance inserted into the feedback loop of a too jumpily overreacting servomechanism. Its effects on Failure 5 may be compared to those of a pesticide limiting the spread of noxious organisms. If so small, the inevitable loss of liquidity may be quite negligible, largely compensated for by lower volatility and more relevant criteria for the market selection of investors.

7 Political obstacles and evolutionary consequences

It is essential to avoid wishful illusions about both markets and government. While markets, especially the financial ones, may seriously fail, government may be far from doing any better. Instead of designing and implementing the right regulation, it may implement the wrong ones that make the markets fail even more, and/or fail to implement the right ones, and thus let the market failures fully develop into a deep crisis.[5]

The reasons why government may, and often indeed does, fail are of two types, nicely summarized a long time ago by Mill (1861/1972):

> The positive evils and dangers of the representative, as of every other form of government, may be reduced to two heads: first, general ignorance and incapacity, or, to speak more moderately, insufficient mental qualifications, in the controlling body; secondly, the danger of its being under the influence of interests not identical with the general welfare of the community.[6]

Since then, however, most economic analysis has been built on the assumption that everyone is perfectly rational, able to find optimal solutions to all economic problems, which made it blind to the possibilities of "insufficient mental qualifications" and narrowed its attention to the second head. This has perhaps most thoroughly been examined in the original version of public choice economics.[7] Important obstacles to efficient economic policies, and therefore also to efficient financial regulations, were there discovered in the vested interests of government policy makers, or the private investors on which these may depend, or both.

Most policy makers must indeed be expected to be opposed to limiting their powers, as this would threaten their jobs, and to shrinking the size of the financial sector, as this would decrease, in the short term to which their horizon is often limited, the economy's GNP and their tax revenues. To oppose such shrinking is also in the interest of private investors and their employees, who are moreover likely to oppose all sharpening of market competition and selection, for few of them can be sure of remaining the winners. In addition, managers of financial firms must be expected to oppose all reforms of corporate governance that would limit their opportunities for rent-seeking at the owners' expense.

In this context, the advantage of evo-devo economics is that it can clearly see and fruitfully analyze what Mill listed as the first head. Thanks to its recognition of rationality inequalities, it can estimate the expected rationality bounds of politicians and civil servants, and compare them to those of private entrepreneurs and investors, by exploring the selection processes by which the former and the latter, respectively, are being chosen for their jobs (cf. Pelikan 2010).

In fact, most of the above arguments about financial regulations may be seen as partial results of this exploration. But one point may need an additional clarification. This is the distinction between (1) the relevant rationality needed for top business entrepreneurship and investment, and (2) the one needed for designing efficient institutional rules, including financial regulations. While government is likely to suffer from some "insufficient mental qualifications" for both, the two cases substantially differ in their policy implications.

In case (1), the rationality needed is scarcer, more difficult to recognize, and more sophisticated in tacit, non-communicable ways, which limits the possibilities for obtaining it from explicit theories. Of this kind of rationality, as noted above, government is unlikely to possess enough to make its firms and investment banks lastingly efficient. But this is not a very serious problem, as there is an alternative way of finding and keeping enough of it: market competition and selection. The policy implication is that government should not try to own, organize and manage firms – and especially not the financial ones – but leave all this to the private sector.

Case (2) differs in two ways. First, the needed rationality is less exceptional and less tacit, and may therefore also be more extensively helped by theories – such as new institutional economics, constitutional economics and law and economics. Intuitively, as noted, this difference can be compared to the one between the highly exceptional abilities for playing top chess and the less exceptional ones for organizing chess tournaments. But, and this is the second difference, there is no alternative way to putting this kind of rationality to work than by means of political selection, democratic or not, of the legislators. The policy implication is that for the markets that are prone to developing serious failures unless shaped by suitable institutional rules (regulations) *and* unable to evolve such rules spontaneously themselves, there is no other solution than to ask the imperfect legislators to do their best and try to design and implement such rules, and ask the imperfect theoretical economists to do their best and try to build *and communicate* theories that could be helpful, and not misleading, for this task.

Thus, although the theories may be insufficient or even wrong – as the past crises have so many times revealed – and the legislators can make costly mistakes by missing the right regulations and/or implementing the wrong ones, there is simply no alternative. The favorite argument of the opponents to government regulations that government should do nothing because it cannot know what the optimal regulations are does not hold: Many markets, and especially the financial ones, if unregulated by any formal institutional rules, would be far from optimal, too.

In evo-devo economics, however, the notion of "optimality" is not even very important. As explained in Lesson 3 above, the main success criterion is the evolutionary sustainability of institutional frameworks of economies, to which financial regulations directly belong and/or by which they are indirectly constrained. The inquiry into these regulations, including non-regulation, is thus led to their evolutionary consequences. Particularly important ones are the crises that different regulations and non-regulation may sooner or later cause, or fail to prevent. These may be economical, due to a too low economic performance with a too high unemployment, and/or political, due to too high income inequalities, especially if a large part of the highest incomes is perceived, according to prevailing values, as undeserved, acquired in too unethical ways.

Of course, such an evolutionary inquiry is far from easy. It needs tools from several new fields of economic research and must take into account the variability of many parameters. For instance, cultural evolution may change the prevailing values in different directions, and thus make large income inequalities politically more explosive, or less explosive.

But the inquiry is definitely worth conducting, for its findings promise to be of a great social value. The knowledge that certain financial regulations have a chance to be evolutionarily sustainable, whereas others are bound to lead to a painful, institutionally disruptive crisis, would doubly facilitate policy making: it would help to make generally beneficial choices; and it would lower the political obstacles to such choices by enlightening the different opposing self-interests. That the knowledge is expected only to lower the obstacles, and not to efface them entirely, deserves emphasis, to avoid the suspicion of a naive wishful thinking. Even so, however, its social value is great enough to put the search for it high on the economists' agenda, much higher than it is now.

Both objectives of this chapter may now be considered met. Evo-devo analysis did produce some new arguments for an important policy issue, and thus did demonstrate its fruitfulness.

Notes

1 The readers who understand biology may like to compare the two layers of economic change to the two layers of biological change: (1) the development of organisms shaped by their genome (ontogeny); and (2) the evolution of genomes (phylogeny). The proposed evo-devo economics may then also be compared to the relatively new field of evo-devo biology. But these comparisons have important factual limits that must be carefully taken into account (Pelikan 2011). While they may inspire economists with a good understanding of biology, they may confuse the others, who should therefore disregard them.

2 This distinction closely corresponds to the one made by Hayek (1973) between "general rules" and "particular measures."

3 This failure is nicely described with many concrete examples by Harford (2011).

4 This distortion was pointed out by many investors, including J.M. Keynes and G. Soros. With some imagination, the situation may be compared to an absurd search for the best chess players in which only winners in poker tournaments could participate.

5 An example of government simultaneously failing in both ways can be found in the recent history of the Czech economy. After the sophisticated and arguably successful

coupon privatization in the beginning of the 1990s, intended to start the working of financial markets, the government failed to provide the standard regulations for protecting minority owners, which allowed widespread and greatly harmful asset-stripping – the so-called "tunneling" – and instead protected old socialist managers by forbidding investment funds to acquire more than 30 per cent shares in one enterprise. The harm was triple: (1) economic, as for several following years many international investors avoided Prague; (2) political, as a large part of the Czech electorate lost the initial enthusiasm for the market economy and started to vote for economically irresponsible leftist parties, including the old communists; and (3) long-term social, as these two failures seriously distorted the criteria for the selection of top entrepreneurs and investors, causing a large part of the Czech economic elite to be selected from ethical bottom.

6 I am grateful for this reference to Niclas Berggren.

7 For a clear, concise presentation of the main ideas of this version of public choice economics, see Buchanan (2003).

References

Blundell-Wignall, A. and P. Atkinson (2011), "Global SIFIs, Derivatives, and Financial Stability," *OECD Journal, Financial Market Trends*, Vol. 1, www.oecd.org/dataoecd/62/10/48299884.pdf.

Buchanan, J.M. (2003), *Public Choice: On the Origins and Development of a Research Program*, Fairfax: Virginia.

Cordes, Christian (2006) "Darwinism in Economics: From Analogy to Continuity," *Journal of Evolutionary Economics* 16: 529–541.

Harford, T. (2011), *Adapt: Why Success Always Starts with Failure*. Little, Brown: London.

Hayek, F.A. (1973), *Law, Legislation and Liberty, Vol. 1: Rules and Order*, University of Chicago Press: Chicago, IL and London.

Heiner, R. (1983), "The Origins of Predictable Behavior," *American Economic Review* 73: 560–595.

Hodgson, G. and T. Knudsen (2006), "Dismantling Lamarckism: Why Descriptions of Socio-Economic Evolution as Lamarckian are Misleading," *Journal of Evolutionary Economics* 16: 343–366.

Hodgson, G. and T. Knudsen (2010), "Generative Replication and the Evolution of Complexity," *Journal of Economic Behavior and Organization* 75: 12–24.

Mill, J.S. (1861/1972), "Considerations on representative government," in H.B. Acton, (ed.), *Utilitarism: On Liberty and Considerations on Representative Government*, J.M. Dent & Sons: London.

Nelson, R.R. and S. Winter (1982), *An Evolutionary Theory of Economic Change*, Harvard University Press: Cambridge, MA.

North, D.C. (1990), *Institutions, Institutional Change, and Economic Performance*, Cambridge University Press: Cambridge and New York.

Pelikan, P. (1988), "Can the Imperfect Innovation System of Capitalism be Outperformed?" in G. Dosi, C. Freeman, R. Nelson G. Silverberg and L.L. Soete (eds.), *Technical Change and Economic Theory*, Pinter Publishers: London and New York.

Pelikan, P. (1992), "The Dynamics of Economic Systems, or How to Transform a Failed Socialist Economy," *Journal of Evolutionary Economics* 2, 39–63; reprinted in H.J. Wagener (ed.), *On the Theory and Policy of Systemic Change*, Physica-Verlag: Heidelberg; and Springer-Verlag: New York.

Pelikan, P. (2010), "The Government Economic Agenda in a Society of Unequally Rational Individuals," *Kyklos* 63: 231–255.

Pelikan, P. (2011), "Evolutionary Developmental Economics: How to Generalize Darwinism Fruitfully to Help Comprehend Economic Change," *Journal of Evolutionary Economics* 21: 341–366.

Pelikan, P. (2012), "Agreeing on Generalized Darwinism: A Response to Geoffrey Hodgson and Thorbjørn Knudsen," *Journal of Evolutionary Economics* 22: 1–8.

Schubert, C. (2013), " 'Generalized Darwinism' and the Quest for an Evolutionary Theory of policy-making," *Journal of Evolutionary Economics*: February, online.

Schumpeter, J.A. (1912/1934), *The Theory of Economic Development*, Harvard University Press: Cambridge, MA.

Williamson, O.E. (1985), *The Economic Institutions of Capitalism*, The Free Press: New York.

Witt, U. (2006) "Evolutionary Concepts in Economics and Biology," *Journal of Evolutionary Economics* 16: 473–476.

7 'Liquidity' in light of the shadow banking system

Lessons from the two crises

Anastasia Nesvetailova

1 'Liquidity' in capitalism: some lessons from 1930s–40s

At first view, the idea of liquidity is straightforward and quite intuitive. Liquidity describes the convertibility of an asset into a form of money (most commonly, cash), and thus is often likened to an asset's 'money-ness'. At the same time, liquidity also describes a state of the (financial) market where transactions can be executed within the prevailing price levels. Although seemingly comprehensive and uncontroversial, this two-fold perspective on liquidity opens up several analytical hurdles. On the one hand, it is difficult to disentangle the two aspects of liquidity, since assets are only tradable if the institution facilitating such a trade – a market – is functional. On the other hand, however, the market mechanism, especially the financial market mechanism, is a complex socio-political construction embedded in a specific legal, socio-economic and political context. It is therefore prone to its own problems of operation which can, in turn, affect the nature of asset liquidity and the liquidity and solvency of individual financial institutions.

It is perhaps not surprising that a similar set of dilemmas and questions arose in the context of the last devastating crisis when liquidity disappeared: the Great Depression of 1929–36. At the time, there was a small number of scholars including, most famously, J.M. Keynes, who pondered the same conceptual problem. Their published ideas amount to two systemic approaches to the problem of liquidity: Berle and Pederson (1934) examine the mechanisms that underlie newly liquid wealth in the US economy at the time; Courtney Brown (1940) analyses the consequences of changes in aggregate desires for liquidity in a society. Both studies are built on the authors' critique of two alternative schools of thought on liquidity. One current was called the *classical* school of liquidity (and banking). It is premised on the belief that real liquidity is based on consumption: a truly liquid claim is one upon goods which are moving towards a final market. The other current, which later would become dominant (we are most familiar with it because it is intuitive and we are accustomed to it), is the so-called *shiftability s*chool (Brown 1940). It regards liquidity as the ability to sell or shift an asset on relatively short notice.

The 1934 volume *Liquid Claims and National Wealth* was a research exploration by Adolf Berle and his wife, Victoria Pederson, and has come out of Berle's much larger and more definitive work on the nature of private property and the nature of US corporations at the turn of the century.[1] If *Modern Corporation and Private Property* deals with the increase in size of corporations and the implications of the new political economic divide – the separation of management and ownership with the resulting effect upon the individual (Williams 1935: 165), *Liquid Claims* is a research commentary examining some of the financial consequences of this shift.

The second volume of interest, C. Brown's *Liquidity and Instability*, published in 1940, deals with the consequences of cumulative changes in the 'desires for liquidity' from the point of view of banking stability. In contrast to Berle's focused and empirically led research, Brown offers a more academic format of engagement with existing scholarly works on liquidity, banking and wealth. Notwithstanding the differences in scope and certain disagreements between the authors, the two volumes present the most systematic to date, and certainly definitive for the time, theoretical examination of liquidity. Their original research and few elaborations on it that exist (Mueller 1953; Hicks 1962) suggest that liquidity is as important in the analyses of political economy as, for instance, are capital, money or value.

From the perspective of early twenty-first-century financial capitalism, when the types and quantities of liquidities have become abundant, Berle and Pederson's study offers something of great interest. It is their argument that any investigation of liquidity in the context of an economic system is 'a study of the mechanisms which make particular forms of wealth acceptable' (Berle and Pederson 1934). Chapter 10 of the monograph charts a comparative history of two types of negotiable instruments: instruments representing mercantile transactions, and shiftable instruments representing capital values. The historical evolution of the second type of instrument goes back to 1909, a period during which liquidity began to expand in the United States. Berle's key insight here is that throughout history the law has followed the finance:

> In America the common law looked not to the underlying agencies of the transaction but for the form. So by judicial interpretation public and corporate bonds, which of course have entirely different economic content from commercial paper, were declared negotiable; and the law so stands today.
>
> (Berle and Pedersen 1934: 175).

Berle's conclusion from this is instructive if idealistic. Although he does sense the underlying conflict between real and artificial (financial) liquidity, he sees the banking system as serving the real cycle of economic turnover:

> To complete the logic of Senator Glass ... it would seem necessary to have a separate banking system paralleling the commercial banking system, whose primary objective was to act as purveyor of liquidity to investment transactions and to the investment market, replacing the speculator pure and simple by the soberer and more calculable mechanism of loans.... Such a

banking system could, among other things, determine how far speculation is necessary, and if so, how far it should be financed, and to reduce the necessity of such speculation, since a holder of securities who wished to reduce them to cash but feared the effect on immediate sale might delay the time element by borrowing on his security.

(Williams 1935: 192)

The second contemporary investigation of liquidity, also focused on the destabilising role of new liquid claims in the general state of the banking system, was offered in 1940 by Courtney Brown, a professor at Columbia University. The author was concerned with the stability/solvency of the banking system in the era of liquid wealth, and placed his analysis of liquidity in the debates between currency and the banking school of commercial banking. Brown's general thesis is that changes in liquidity desires, while not an initiating cause of booms and depressions, contribute in an important way to the cumulative movements which make such crises severe (Millikan 1941: 359).

Brown's study is framed around a distinction between the problems with the maintenance of liquidity of owned assets, on the one hand, and the problems of the maintenance of *value*, on the other. Concerned with the cumulative changes in the desires for liquidity, conceptually Brown situates his research in the context of the banking controversy of the time: namely, a debate about the doctrine of bank lending. Brown also focuses on what place the *desire for liquidity* occupies in economic life in general. Here, he attempts to describe the institutional organisation of wealth and titles to wealth, and makes some interesting observations about the relationship between liquidity, price and value.

Brown's closer engagement with earlier theories of banking and liquidity proves useful. For instance, we learn that in contemporary (1930s) application of orthodox theory of banking, there was already a recognition that as a concept, 'liquidity' was applicable not only to assets and persons, but to the whole community as well. It therefore means more than convertibility of assets into money:

> The liquidity of a community does not necessarily depend upon ability to convert into coin or into anything else.... Liquidity consists of the ability to meet claims in full when they are presented for payment – but such payments may consist in the presentation of similar, or offsetting claims of simultaneous maturity.

(Willis 1936: 32)

According to Brown's own definition, the liquidity of assets applies to 'the ease or difficulty of exchanging them for money ... but *not* for a specific amount of money'. The liquidity of persons, corporations, etc., on the other hand, is closely related to solvency; liquidity in this sense relates to 'the nature and amount of assets owned relative to the 'nature and amount of debt owned' (Brown 1940: 22). Saleability of assets is therefore the final test of liquidity, with money regarded as the most liquid of all assets. In accord with these definitions, a change in liquidity desires is reflected not only by the desire to hold more or less money, but also by the desire to shift to other assets possessing varying degrees of liquidity, interest rate, in the case of persons, by the desire to alter the nature and amount of assets in relation to debts (Brown 1940: 31–32; Watkins 1942: 477).

Brown makes an attempt to provide an index of liquidity desires and a check-up on the main outlines of the theory by utilising differentials between yields of commercial paper and high-grade corporate bonds corrected by reserve changes, though like in Berle's study, this part of the work remained underdeveloped. There are also echoes between Berle's insight into the nature of property and types of liquidity, and Brown's analysis of liquidity-driven instability. Unlike John Commons, he distinguishes between corporeal (real physical), intangible (financial) and token (legal titles to wealth) wealth, observing that the use of tokens

> has permitted an organisation of wealth-titles which has in part divorced the liquidity characteristics of ownership from the liquidity characteristics of the associated real wealth. The divorce has been far from complete. It is, nevertheless, a highly significant derivative of the institutional development of society.
>
> (Millikan 1941: 360)

Just like Berle and Pederson's 1934 research study, *Liquidity and Instability* was found interesting but wanting at the time. It was commended for its insight into the importance of a systemic social context, for its critical reading of Keynes' liquidity preference (it is the *desire* for liquidity and not the transaction demand for money that matters, according to Brown). Yet it was criticised for many suggestive yet unfinished conceptual proposals (no conclusive definition of liquidity, raw statistical illustration), and for the rather simplistic understanding of the economic cycle (Millikan 1941: 360).

Probably reflecting the weaknesses of the two research pieces, as well as the nature of the economic times, these early theorisations of liquidity remained forgotten in the general evolution of economic and financial ideas. The immediate post-war research on finance discussed liquidity in the international context, mainly from the point of view of international monetary stability (e.g. Kindleberger 1966; Willett 1983). The onset of the financial revolution of the 1970s meant that liquidity has been increasingly understood, theorised and modelled as a feature of the financial markets (e.g. Tobin 1958; Diamond and Dybvig 1983; Diamond and Rajan 1999).

Conceptual elaborations of the 1930s–1940s scholarship on liquidity remain scant. Muller (1953) examines the nature of liquidity in the general capital turnover and builds upon Berle's distinction between real and artificial liquidity, by identifying *structural* and *organic* liquidity. The concept of structural liquidity stretched from the notion of artificial liquidity, meaning that 'assets may be liquid because there is some device which insures that to the extent that conversion of them into cash is asked the cash will be forthcoming' (Mueller 1953: 171). Organic liquidity, on the other hand, derives from the assumption that liquidity as such 'does not imply the preparation for liquidation. On the contrary, liquidity means the preparation for the avoidance of liquidation.' In Mueller's vision, therefore, the mission of an economy is to provide a mechanism for the provision and exchange of goods. The heart of liquidity, he argues, 'is found to be a function of want satisfaction, the source of which is inextricably bound to and dependent on human appetites and freedom of choice' (Mueller 1953: 172).

John Hicks (1962) summarises various ideas about and definitions of liquid assets, discussing them mainly in the framework of Keynesian liquidity preference. It was only Hyman Minsky (1986) who, without any direct reference to the 1930s scholars, placed liquidity at the heart of his own theory of financial innovation and financial crisis:

> In a world with a wide variety of financial markets and in which capital assets can be sold piecemeal or as collected in firms, all financial and capital assets have two cash-flow attributes. One is the money that will accrue as the contract is fulfilled or as capital asset is used in production; the second is the cash that can be received if the asset is sold or pledged. The ability of an asset to yield cash when needed and with slight variation in the amount is called its liquidity.
>
> (Minsky 1986: 202)

It was Minsky (1982) again, who would attempt to analyse the role of systemic liquidity – and more accurately, illiquidity, in the dynamic context of the financial system as a whole (Nesvetailova 2007).

It follows from this brief survey of early theorisations of liquidity, which from early on, the controversy around the concept and definitions of liquidity, was paradigmatic. The divide centred on the methodological emphasis given to the role of the (financial) market and legal mechanisms in facilitating liquidity. For the adherents of the shiftability school, liquidity is a market-related phenomenon and thus is an external property that assets acquire. In the classical approach, liquidity is an inherent quality of assets and at a wider level, an (organic) characteristic of the economy as such. Importantly, notwithstanding methodological differences of the two schools of thought, in both paradigms it is *prospective* liquidity that is being conceptualised. Both in historical and current studies of liquidity, just like in biology – an intellectual forefather of modern economics and social sciences – liquidity denotes a continuity of flows, both between various nodes of the system (Weston 2013) and, crucially, between the present and the future. It is the way that the continuity of flows is being conceptualised at the *level of a system* that remains to be the dividing line between orthodox studies of liquidity and heterodox approaches.

2 The challenge of shadow banking

The crisis of 2007–09 was by many accounts a crisis of shadow liquidity. In fact, it can be argued that it was the shadow banking system that in a matter of days in August 2007 transformed what Ben Bernanke (2005) described as a global savings or liquidity glut into a liquidity crunch, and facilitated its international-isation. The crisis that started off as a money and interbank market liquidity seizure was transformed into an international credit crunch and, ultimately, a crisis of the global banking system whose lingering effects on the real economies made it the worst general economic crisis since the Great Depression. The disappearance of liquidity and its underlying causes have many dimensions, but one of them is theoretical: what exactly is 'liquidity' that is able to change its nature so quickly and with such destructive consequences?

On the one hand, as the first section of this chapter implies, this question does not seem to have a clear answer. It was J.M. Keynes who observed that plainly, there is no such thing as liquidity for a system as a whole. At best, therefore, scholars, analysts and policy makers can aim to examine the dynamics of liquidity at the level of individual markets and institutions, correlate these with other estimations of risk, and hope that a focus on market developments will suffice in preventing a systemic outbreak of a financial crisis. On the other hand, however, this approach evidently did not work in the attempts to foresee the 2007–09 financial meltdown; nor was it sufficient in preventing any of the earlier financial crises. Understanding liquidity in a systemic context, and its relationship to the political-economic context, thus remains a critical unresolved dilemma in the age of financial innovation.

Addressing the liquidity conundrum requires a closer engagement with the phenomenon of shadow banking, or more accurately, financial innovation through shadow banking. The complex and still not well understood system of shadow banks, financial-legal entities and their connections, is one of the most challenging results of the endogenous financial process. Narrow definitions of this phenomenon describe shadow banking as market-based (as opposed to bank-based) ways of funding financial transactions, or in other words, 'money market funding of capital market lending' (Mehrling *et al.* 2012). More inclusive definitions suggest that shadow banking is simply, 'credit extension outside of the banking system' (FSB 2012). Recent estimates from the FSB suggest that the global size of the shadow banking system is $67 trillion, or what is roughly one-third of the world financial system. Shadow banking has played a major role in the recent crisis, though debates continue as to whether the shadow banking system has played a leading (McCulley 2007, 2009) or merely an amplifying role in the banking crisis (Lysandrou 2012).

Both sides of the debate do acknowledge, however, that the ability to create apparently liquid instruments (and therefore, credit) outside the regulated realm of banking has enlarged the de facto size of banks and financial institutions. There are three main ways through which this process, largely undetected until 2007–08, has impacted on the financial system. First, the shadow web of financial transactions that connect a regulated bank with a myriad of complex and opaque financial and legal structures widens the actual economic size of the bank. Access to market-based funding and alternative financial channels may help a single institution be more adept in a competitive environment, realise economies of scale and manage its risks more efficiently. At the aggregate level of the system, however, a complex web of undetected financial links through the shadow banking system has made individual institutions like Lehman Brothers, Bear Sterns or Northern Rock illiquid and insolvent, putting the financial system as a whole on the brink of a collapse.

Second, shadow banking operations have the capacity to transform a group of non-bank financial entities, such as hedge funds, money market funds, special purpose vehicles, into a bank-like structure, the financial activity of which is unregulated. Both processes raise prudential and systemic risk concerns for the tasks of financial regulation and stability, a matter currently forming a central part of the international financial regulatory reform. Third, the size of banks and financial institutions is related to the problem of financial fragility and has political ramifications, both overtly and covertly. The funding models of banks and other financial institutions relied on complex schemes of financial ownership that generated liquid instruments or held financial products or operations that could only function as long as the 'music' of financial boom (or the market mechanisms for pricing these instruments) functioned (Langley 2013).

With the onset of the crisis in the summer of 2007, this pricing mechanism ceased to function, and it became impossible to price complex financial products or execute individual transactions to get access to funding in the wholesale financial market. Instruments that were assumed to be liquid and marketable have lost their value and were impossible to sell. As a result of this cumulative process, the viability of major banking and financial institutions came into question. The exposed failures of individual institutions pointed to the fragility of the system as a whole, which in turn centred on the problems of progressive illiquidity of innovative financial schemes. The situation, caused by a massive illusion of liquidity (Nesvetailova 2010), was exacerbated by the micro-prudential approach to financial regulation that had informed national and international financial policies up to 2007, most prominently in the Anglo-Saxon countries, but also in Europe.

In the wake of the crisis, most of the illiquid conduits were rolled back onto banks' balance sheets; the reforms of OTC trading and bank capital requirements are designed to prevent a similar crisis of systemic illiquidity happening in the future. Yet since the technique of loan securitisation and the very process of financial innovation have not ceased to evolve in financialised capitalism, important and unresolved questions about the nature of liquidity and its role in financial stability continue to linger. In the political debate about the costs and lessons of the crisis, the role of shadow banking is inextricably linked to the role and function of liquidity in capitalism. The problem centres on the fact that the financial values created out of private liquidity through complex mechanisms of financial and legal innovation needed to be validated by a massive injection of public (or outside) liquidity during the management of the financial crisis. The ultimate dependence of private financial innovation on outside liquidity support that was so vividly illustrated by the global financial crisis makes the question about the nature and role of liquidity in economic stability particularly relevant today.

3 'Liquidity' in light of the crisis

At present, when debates about finance are dominated by references to shadow banking, securitisation and financialisation, distinctions between 'real' and 'artificial' liquidity seem obsolete. The advance of the financial markets across the global economy, as well as the 'financialisation' of the many aspects of economic life, has meant that any asset, be that an item of real estate or even an expectation, can be made into a liquid security by the magic of financial innovation. Indeed, since the 1970s through to 2008, securitisation, the essence of which is precisely to transform previously untradeable assets into liquid securities, has brought profits and economic benefits to various participants of the economic system.

At the same time, however, the global credit crunch, like many earlier financial crises, has revealed that the (financial) liquidity of many newly invented securities was presumed, or even performed (Langley 2010), but not guaranteed. The controversial bailouts of failed banks and the size of the so-called shadow banking system have cast questions over the social utility of many channels and products of financial innovation today. Understanding of liquidity before 2007, and in light of the lessons of the crisis, is central to the post-crisis financial architecture.

Current mainstream approaches to liquidity descend from the shiftability school: they prioritise the role of the market mechanism in ensuring the liquidity of assets. Here, for instance, post-crisis academic and policy research has made distinctions between funding and market liquidity (Brunnermeir and Pedersen 2009), between inside and outside liquidity or between private and public liquidity provision (Holstrom and Tirole 1998, 2011). The few critical insights into the theory of liquidity made in recent years are intellectually closer to the economic circuit school; they prioritise the 'public good' aspect of liquidity and its systemic role in tying together the various segments of the economic system and ensuring financial stability. Carruthers and Stinchcombe, for instance, have defined liquidity 'as the degree to which an asset is a fungible, generalized resource' (1999: 375). Policy makers, commenting on the dangers of private liquidity creation, argue that

> the strong growth in global liquidity before and even after the [global financial crisis] has revealed the endogenous nature of private credit. Bank credit has been fuelling the growth of the shadow banking system, based on a combination of repo lending, securities lending, and rehypothecation. The market growth is so strong that many are questioning the wisdom of central banks unconditionally backstopping the system.
>
> (Moe 2012: 69)

The dichotomies between global and official, economic vs financial or real and artificial liquidity lead us to consider another analytical problem of the liquidity concept: namely, its multi-dimensionality. Indeed, the singular term 'liquidity' comprises at least five dimensions: spatiality, quality, quantity, probability and legality, a typology recognised back in the 1930s by both the shiftability and the classical schools of thought.

Liquidity is a spatial notion to the extent that it can be a characteristic of various parts of the economic system, including individual assets and persons, portfolios of financial actors or an economic community more generally. Liquidity is a qualitative notion because it describes either an inherent characteristic of an asset or a property that is attributed to it by the operation of some financial mechanism. Liquidity is a quantitative notion because it can be a measure of a certain reservoir of funds, such as reserves, or at a broader level a pool of available credit or money in given circumstances. Finally, liquidity is an intertemporal notion: although the concept implies currentness of operations or flows, it is *prospective* liquidity that determines an asset's marketability and price (the shiftability school), or its socio-economic function (classical school). This fourfold complexity makes any generalisations and simplified definitions of liquidity analytically problematic.

The *spatial* dimension of liquidity describes a state of an economic unit. In this case, liquidity is defined as an ability to meet existing obligations without incurring huge losses or disruptions. Liquidity of a national economy, as in the case of an emerging market country, can be understood as an ability to meet obligations related to the present value of its currency. In other words, definitions of liquidity ultimately depend on the part of the economic system that is being characterised. Here, the key challenge in generalising individual meanings of liquidity lies in the method by which analyses of individual parts of the economic system are being aggregated into a holistic vision, since the shiftability and the economic circuit theories of liquidity identified above each suggest different paradigms of aggregation, leading in turn, to contrasting policy implications.

Liquidity is most often conceived as being synonymous with the tradability of assets, and more narrowly with an asset's proximity to a form of money. For instance, a 1931 definition suggested that 'liquid or cash assets are those assets of any kind which may readily be converted into cash' (Special Committee on Terminology 1931). The idea of proximity to a form of money implies that different types of assets possess various degrees of liquidity, with high-earning and riskier assets assumed to be less liquid, and with cash and high-quality governmental securities such as US Treasury bills to be most liquid. This vision is based on an inverse relationship between an asset's liquidity and its earning potential. There are, however, three major problems with approximating liquidity to 'money' and cash. First, the convertibility of an asset into 'cash', while a useful gauge of an asset's money-ness (and thus safety) in most circumstances, does not work as a universal criterion. Economic history provides many examples of situations where cash was non-functional as a means of payment, either because of specific political and historical factors or due to hyperinflation and related problems of currency credibility (Mueller 1953).

Second, the advance of financial innovation over the past few decades has crowded cash out to the margins of the daily life of the modern credit system. In response, and by way of an alternative, analysts suggested distinguishing between *funding liquidity* (the ability of financial institutions to perform their intermediation functions) and *market liquidity* (the ability to undertake transactions in such a way as to adjust portfolios and risk profiles without disturbing underlying prices) (e.g. Brunnermeier and Pedersen 2009; Crockett 2008). At the same time, in a real-life context, it is increasingly difficult to separate the two concepts. As Borio (2000: 38–39; 2004) stressed, the nexus of cash and market liquidity remains crucial for determining the robustness of financial markets, because the mechanisms that lead to the disappearance of cash liquidity under stress can be similar to those that lead to the evaporation of market liquidity.

Third, although many studies have argued recently that financial innovation has stretched the frontier of liquidity, the major problem with classifying assets along a liquidity spectrum is that it assumes that the liquidity of an asset is fundamentally a question of market equilibrium and a right price. Essentially, therefore, the problem of liquidity is deemed solvable by the operation of the market mechanism. The problem with this classification is that it conflates liquidity with marketability. Fundamentally, this vision presumes the existence of an unallocated fund waiting upon the demands of those possessing particular assets. In reality, however, there is no such reservoir of funds, as the phenomenon of shadow banking has illustrated. While individual members of the aggregate may at one time be 'liquid', it is not true for all members (Keynes 1936: 155, cited in Mueller 1953).

Thus, in terms of qualitative analysis of liquidity, we again encounter the problem of aggregation: convertibility of an asset into money or cash provides a gauge of liquidity only as long as analysis remains confined to individual practices; at the level of the system, this understanding simply does not work. The *quantitative* facet of liquidity, in turn, describes a financial 'cushion' – either in a form of reserve capital held by a financial institution or as a stock of global credit more broadly. For example, the most widely accepted notion of international liquidity refers to 'those assets available to the authorities of a country for the purpose of stabilising the external value of its domestic currency' (Genberg and Swoboda 1993: 271).

IMF studies distinguished several indicators of liquidity, including central bank liquidity (base money), household and corporate liquidity (monetary aggregates) and an economy's liquidity (measured as all of the above plus currency liabilities of the central bank). There also exist more complex composite measures of liquidity as a general financial climate. Most popular among these is the so-called financial conditions index, first suggested by Goldman Sachs. It is a weighted combination of the real three-month interbank lending rate, the interest rate on corporate bonds, the market capitalisation of equities in relation to GDP, and the real effective exchange rate. Finally, in 2005 the IMF suggested a more refined definition of global liquidity as holdings of a financial asset that represents a claim on a foreigner that could be turned readily into foreign exchange, which can be held by the private or the public sector (IMF 2005, Box 2.1: 14–15).

Elaborate quantitative measures notwithstanding, in the international sphere liquidity, while quantifiable, is not reducible to a single formula or concept. More problematically, the validity of the definition of an economy's liquidity (and indeed, global liquidity), is highly questionable in an era when the 'visible' balance sheets of banks represent only a fraction of the complex web of financial institutions, many of which constitute the 'shadow banking system' and therefore operate with shadow liquidity. While this problem may not be acute in times of economic stability, it came to the fore in October 2008, when the viability of basic banking services was threatened by the seizure of the shadow banking system precipitated by the failure of Lehman Brothers (Nesvetailova 2008).

From the above it can be inferred that liquidity also denotes a *probability* of completing a transaction in given circumstances at certain speed. At a broader level, liquidity implies the viability of maintaining financial flows over time and during different stages of an economic cycle more generally. Correspondingly, economic examinations of liquidity tend to focus on various problems that arise in the operation of the price mechanism, efficiency and transparency of the financial market, typically aiming to find a quantitative solution to these problems. For instance, the look of the bid–ask spread curve is what determines market liquidity. The smoother the curve the more liquid the market is considered to be. If the curve is erratic, it means that it is difficult to match bid and ask prices for a particular asset, and thus market liquidity is impaired.

Liquidity, in other words, also denotes a probability of executing a particular transaction (be that a simple sale of an asset, a rollover of debt or a complex restructuring of a deal in the financial markets). The probability aspect of liquidity resonated to its prospective character noted by the scholars of the 1930s–1940s, and highlights that it is an inter-temporal notion: a specific stage of a business cycle does affect the nature of liquidity, because 'liquidity' in good times is not the same as liquidity in bad times. In this instance, Crockett (2008) refined the four dimensions of market liquidity: market 'depth' (or the ability to execute large transactions without influencing prices unduly); 'tightness' (or the gap between bid and offer prices); 'immediacy' (or the speed with which transactions can be executed); and 'resilience' (or the speed with which underlying prices are restored after a disturbance).

Finally, and perhaps most importantly, liquidity is a *legal* notion. As Berle noted in 1934, it should be understood as a legal concept: historically, customary use of various negotiable instruments between parties was routinely legalised by US courts. 'Securities which are somewhat like stocks and bonds have been legislated into negotiability whenever a doubt as to their ready transmissibility has troubled the commercial world' (Berle 1934: 175–176). This legal treatment has underpinned the evolution of American finance during the twentieth century, contributed to the erosion of the Glass–Steagall Act of 1933 and lay at the heart of structural and institutional transformation of US banking. Liquidity, and acceptability of certain forms of liquidity, has been central to both.

The conceptual conundrum of liquidity, as well as its role in the 2007–09 crisis, has prompted many observers to consider alternative definitions and approaches to liquidity. Here, three notable attempts are worth mentioning. One comes from a market participant. Paul McCulley, then of PIMCO, acknowledging the ever-elusive nature of liquidity, which he defined simply as 'appetite for risk' (McCulley 2008). Kevin Warsh, one of the governors of the Federal Reserve, suggested that market liquidity is synonymous with confidence (Warsh 2007). Andrew Crockett (2008), elaborating on the concept in a more comprehensive manner, and echoing some of the conceptual insights of the 1930s–1940s, proposed that the essence of liquidity lies in the ease with which value can be extracted from assets. Value extraction, in turn, can be possible either on the basis of an asset's creditworthiness or through its sale.

These definitions seem fairly inclusive, and attempt to reconcile liquidity as a quality of the moment, and liquidity as a quality of an asset. Both appetite for risk and general confidence in the economy depend on the publically available knowledge about economic assets and how best to discount future outcomes into today's present value. At a glance, therefore, the idea of 'liquidity as confidence' does accommodate economic agents' expectations and knowledge about the future.

The problem, however, is that definitions based on the factor of confidence (and hence risk), ultimately locate liquidity in the realm of the *financial market*, rather than the economy as a whole. As a result, these views do take into account the issue of the fungibility of an asset, yet only within the limits of the financial market. As a consequence, analytical dilemmas of aggregation and in this specific case of the role of liquidity in economic stability, are not resolved. One key question that remains open goes back to the dilemma noted by Berle and Pederson in 1934: does liquidity imply extracting value from the assets because such an extraction is facilitated by some intermediating mechanism, or is value extraction possible because value is inherent in an asset? This question, in turn, relates to a much more controversial issue of financial vis-à-vis social (or economic) value and to the wider questions about the place and function of the financial market in the socio-economic system picked up by Brown and Mueller.

The wide spectrum of dilemmas arising from the notion of complexity in finance is ultimately derivative of one underlying fact: today, the financial system is as much a 'credit' system as it is a debt system. The current phenomenon of shadow banking, a giant web of cells and channels that transform loans into apparently liquid securities, has illustrated this most vividly. The historical origins of this problem go back to 1971, when key financial processes were removed from state controls, the financial system had transformed itself from a service industry that connects savers and borrowers in space and time (if indeed it was ever that), to an industry of mining, trading and multiplying risk (Kurtzman 1993). This shift only served to amplify a much longer historical trend beautifully captured by John Commons, who analysed the legal foundations of a capitalism in which 'mere expectations of money are converted into money itself' (1989: 393).

Writing in 1934, Commons noted in his monumental history of the discipline that 'political economy [is] not a science of individual liberty, but a science of the creation, negotiability, release, and scarcity of debt' (Commons 1989 [1934]: 390). A more recent study has argued that 'a debt is just a perversion of a promise. It is a promise corrupted by both math and violence' (Graeber 2011: 391). In the context of risk-based financial capitalism, the old distinctions between credit and debt are of limited use: both credit and debt are essential 'economic quantities', in the terminology of McLeod and Commons; credit offers a valorised access to the future, while debt is a valorised promise of a future. The trouble is, both of these quantities, and their special characteristics, are now tradable market instruments (Wigan 2009).

In financialised capitalism, financial innovation is best seen as a set of techniques, products and institutions aiming to mine the future. Liquidity – due to its inherently prospective nature – is a key instrument in this mining exercise. The core function of financial innovation is to employ debt in the economic circuit in new, transformed and enhanced liquid forms. Securitisation, in turn – the central artery of the shadow banking system – is a set of mechanisms of assigning property titles to debt and recycling these titles as negotiable and liquid instruments. Shadow banking provides the infrastructure for (mining), marketing, trading and recycling the debt and its related products. From the viewpoint of the financial system, this means that the frontier of liquidity is being continually stretched by private financial innovation. As a result, a cloud of apparently liquid financial instruments has assumed money-like characteristics for a select but important group of economic agents (Gerding 2012), and thus expanded the credit system through private means of financial innovation. Yet lacking official monetary support, this chain could only serve as 'money' during (good) economic times, as Minsky warned (Mehrling 2010).

Increasingly, today's regulators seem to recognise the importance of control over private financial innovation and the need to draw a line between official (high powered, or state money) vs. global (privately created) liquidity (Moe 2012; Turner 2012, 2013). A great deal of technical effort on both sides of the Atlantic is dedicated towards modelling and testing the boundaries between private and official liquidity, and between socially useful and speculative financial activities. There are provisions to separate commercial from casino-type banking, impose higher capital and liquidity requirements on individual banks, move over-the-counter (OTC) trades onto organised platforms and tax financial transactions.

The historical record of financial regulation and financial innovation leads to a rather sceptical prognosis of the efficacy of these newly devised rules. Perhaps by way of an alternative we can go back to another time of structural crisis of capitalism and take a note of some policy measures that Berle suggested back in 1934, after he observed a worrying (!) 40 per cent mismatch between liquid claims to wealth and actual wealth produced in the US economy:

1   the reorganisation of the banking system so that the stream of 'real' liquidity and the stream of 'artificial' liquidity shall not be confused;
2   the creation of a central bank analogous to a mortgage rediscount bank, or some similar device, to stand as underpinning for the assumed liquidity of our security mechanisms;

3   possibly, a frank attempt to bring the business of stock exchanges more nearly in line with the procedure in bond markets – that is, to diminish their reliance on purely speculative elements;

4   a *laissez-faire* policy relying on a change in public opinion or technical developments in industry to force the bankers to be more cautious in granting loans, especially on claims having only the quality of 'artificial' liquidity;

5   a diminishing of the necessary area of liquidity, which would involve an endeavor to switch a certain amount of the savings of the country from investment in savings banks, or in withdrawable life insurance, towards social insurance based on stated contingencies. (Berle and Pederson 1934).

Berle's second suggestion was fulfilled in the current crisis by national central banks. It may be too late and too unfeasible to think of a modern-day implementation of points 1 or 4, but perhaps it is time to consider seriously a version of Berle's fifth point.

4 Conclusion

The aim of this chapter has been to revisit the early (and ultimately unfinished) theorisations of liquidity published in the 1930s and early 1940s in light of the lessons we draw from the financial crisis of 2007–09, and the phenomenon of shadow banking more specifically. Early theories of liquidity distinguish between two major schools of thought – classical and shiftability approaches. The work of early institutionalists also helps us disentangle the various dimensions of liquidity (spatial, quantitative, temporal, qualitative and legal), putting the category of liquidity on par with more established and classical concepts of political economy, such as capital, prices and value. Early theories of liquidity also suggest that liquidity in any aggregate meaning is only partly related to the operation of the financial markets as such. This insight contradicts the major views on liquidity that have informed financial theory and policy prior to 2007. At a time when academics and policy makers confront the changes of regulating shadow banking, a major insight from the 1930s–1940s work suggests that any study of liquidity is a study of the ways through which various types of wealth, and therefore titles to wealth, become accepted and acceptable in a society, and what are the ultimate costs and benefits of this process.

Note

1 Berle and Means' *The Modern Corporation and Private Property* has 12,218 Google Scholar citations, while their *Liquid Claims and National Wealth* scores a mere 12.

References

Berle, A. and V. Pederson, 1934, *Liquid Claims and National Wealth*, New York: Macmillan.

Bernanke, B., 2005, 'The Global Saving Glut and the U.S. Current Account Deficit', Remarks at the Sandridge Lecture, Virginia Association of Economics, Richmond, Virginia, 10 March.

Borio, C., 2000, 'Market Liquidity and Stress: Selected Issues and Policy Implications', *BIS Quarterly Review*, November.

Borio, C., 2004, 'Market Distress and Vanishing Liquidity: Anatomy and Policy Options', *BIS Working Paper*, no. 158, Bank for International Settlements.

Brown, C., 1940, *Liquidity and Instability*, New York: Columbia University Press.

Brunnermeier, M.K. and L.H. Pederson, 2009, 'Market Liquidity and Funding Liquidity', *Review of Financial Studies*, 22 (6), doi: 10.1093/rfs/hhn098.

Carruthers, B. and A. Stinchcombe, 1999, 'The Social Structure of Liquidity: Flexibility, Markets, and States', *Theory and Society*, 28: 353–382.

Commons, J.R., 1989 [1934], *Institutional Economics: Its Place in Political economy, Vol. 1*, New Brunswick, NJ: Transactions Publishers.

Crockett, A., 2008, 'Market Liquidity and Financial Stability', *Financial Stability Review (Special Issue on Liquidity)*, Bank of France, February.

Deloitte, 2012, *The Deloitte Shadow Banking Index: Shedding Light on Banking's Shadows*, New York: The Deloitte Center for Financial Services.

Diamond, D. and P. Dybvig, 1983, 'Bank Runs, Deposit Insurance, and Liquidity', *Journal of Political Economy*, 91(3): 401–419.

Diamond, D. and R. Rajan, 1999, 'Liquidity Risk, Liquidity Creation and Financial Fragility: A Theory of Banking', *NBER Working Paper*, no. 7430.

FSB (Financial Stability Board), 2012, *Shadow Banking: Scoping the Issues*, Background Note of the FSB.

Genberg, H. and A. Swoboda, 1993, 'The Provision of Liquidity in the Bretton Woods System', in M. Bordo and B. Eichengreen, eds, *A Retrospective on the Bretton Woods System*, Chicago, IL: University of Chicago Press.

Gerding, E., 2012, 'The Shadow Banking System and its Legal Origins', University of Colorado Law School, August.

Graeber, D., 2011, *Debt: The First 5000 Years*, Brooklyn, NY: Melville Publishers.

Hicks, J., 1962, 'Liquidity', *The Economic Journal*, 72: 288.

Holmstrom, B. and J. Tirole, 1998. 'Private and Public Supply of Liquidity', *Journal of Political Economy*, 106(1): 1–40.

Holmstrom, B. and J. Tirole, 2011, *Inside ad Outside Liquidity*, Cambridge, MA: MIT Press.

IMF, 2005, 'Gauging Global Liquidity Conditions', *World Economic Outlook*, Washington, DC: International Monetary Fund.

Keynes, J.M., 1936, *General Theory of Employment, Interest and Money*, New York: Harcourt, Brace & Co.

Kindleberger, Ch., with Emile Despres and Walter S. Salant, 1966, 'The Dollar and World Liquidity: A Minority View', *Brookings Institution Reprint*, no. 115.

Kurtzman, J., 1993, *The Death of Money*, New York and London: Little, Brown and Co.

Langley, P., 2010, 'The Performance of Liquidity in the Subprime Mortgage Crisis', *New Political Economy*, 15: 71–89.

Langley, P., 2013, 'Toxic Assets, Turbulence and Biopolitical Security: Governing the Crisis of Global Financial Circulation', *Security Dialogue*, 44(2): 111–126.

Lysandrou, P., 2012, 'The Primacy of Hedge Funds in the Subprime Crisis', *Journal of Post Keynesian Economics*, 34: 225–254.

McCulley, P., 2007, 'Teton Reflections', *PIMCO Global Central Bank Focus*, No. 2.

McCulley, P., 2008, 'The Liquidity Conundrum,' *CFA Institute Conference Proceedings Quarterly*, March.

McCulley, P., 2009, 'The Shadow Banking System and Hyman Minsky's Economic Journey', *Insights into the Global Financial Crisis*, Charlottesville, VA: Research Foundation of CFA Institute.

Mehrling, P., 2010, *The New Lombard Street: How the Fed Became the Dealer of Last Resort*, Princeton, NJ: Princeton University Press.

Mehrling, P., Z. Pozsar, J. Sweeney and D. Neilson, 2012, *Shadow banking, Central banking, and the Future of Global Finance*, City University London, November.

Millikan, M., 1941, '*Liquidity and Instability*: By Courtney Brown', book review, *American Economic Review*, June: 359–361.

Minsky, H., 1982, *Can 'It' Happen Again?*, New York: M.E. Sharpe.

Minsky, H., 1986, *Stabilizing an Unstable Economy*, New York: McGraw-Hill.

Moe, T., 2012, 'Shadow Banking and the Limits of Central Bank Liquidity Support: How to Achieve a Better Balance between Global and Official Liquidity', *Levy Working Paper*, No. 712.

Mueller, F., 1953, 'Corporate Working Capital and Liquidity,' *The Journal of Business of the University of Chicago*, 26(3): 157–172.

Nesvetailova, A., 2007, *Fragile Finance, Debt, Speculation and Crisis in the Age of Global Credit*, New York: Palgrave Macmillan.

Nesvetailova, A., 2008, 'Three Facets of Liquidity Illusion: Financial Innovation and the Credit Crunch', *German Policy Studies*, 4(3): 83–132.

Nesvetailova, A., 2010, *Financial Alchemy in Crisis: The Great Liquidity Illusion*, London: Pluto.

Special Committee on Terminology, 1931, *A Preliminary Report*, New York: Century Co.

Tobin, J., 1958, 'Liquidity Preference as Behaviour Towards Risk', *The Review of Economic Studies*, 25(2): 65–86.

Turner, A., 2012, *Shadow Banking and Financial Instability*, London: Financial Services Authority.

Turner, A., 2013, 'Debt, Money and Mephistopheles: How Do We Get Out of This Mess?', Cass Business School annual lecture, 6 February.

Warsh, K., 2007, 'Market Liquidity: Definitions and Implications', Remarks at the Institute of International Bankers Annual Washington Conference, Washington, DC, 5 March.

Watkins, L., 1942, 'Liquidity and Instability by Courtney C. Brown', book review, *Journal of Political economy*, 50(3): 476–478.

Weston, K., 2013, 'Lifeblood, Liquidity, and Cash Transfusions: Beyond Metaphor in the Cultural Study of Finance', *Journal of the Royal Anthropological Society*, 19: S21–S43.

Wigan, D., 2009, 'Financialisation and Derivatives: Constructing an Artifice of Indifference', *Competition and Change*, 13(2): 157–172.

Willett, T., 1983, 'U.S. Monetary Policy and World Liquidity', *The American Economic Review*, 73(2), 43–47.

Williams, A., 1935, 'Liquid Claims and National Wealth, by A.A. Berle, Jr. and Victoria J. Pederson', book review, *Marquette Law Review*, 19(4): n.p.

Willis, H., 1936, *The Theory and Practice of Central Banking: With Special Reference to American Experience, 1913–1935*, New York: Harper.

8 Financial instability and functional finance

A Lerner–Minsky perspective

Faruk Ülgen

In the last three decades the implementation of the neoliberal agenda all around the world resulted in a new accumulation regime that rested on speculative finance and submitted economies to the caprices of myopic markets behavior. In the "consensual" vein, money-neutralization policies (independent central banks) and anti public-deficit policies (sound finance) let the public debt be mainly financed on speculation-oriented financial markets and gave rise to a kind of *dysfunctional finance*. After several crises in emerging economies in the 1990s, the neoliberal wave of globalized capitalism reached its sustainability shore and threw itself into a worldwide financial crisis in 2007–08, when markets suddenly froze and trapped the advanced economies.

To mitigate the subsequent depression, public authorities have massively intervened through monetary quantitative easing policies and large budget deficits. Public spending policies have been implemented in several countries to support the economic activity damaged by the effects of the crisis without being able to stop the rapid descent into the abyss. These policies sought to reduce depressive pressures in liberalized markets without any long-term restructuring and recovery plan, while the nervousness of markets and the rise of unemployment have not been calmed. Such a disarray involved governments in large deficits that prevented public policies from using sustainable growth-oriented functional finance as public expenditures were caught up in the rescue of market failures. After the subsequent increase of budget deficits and public debt beyond what is considered an acceptable level as regards the power of speculative flows, financial markets put pressure on the financing of public debts and incited numerous European countries to reduce their stimulus measures to regain market confidence without having strengthened fragile financial structures. The search for new macroeconomic policy principles in order to guarantee a sustainable and stable accumulation regime seems to be lost in transition from the ongoing crisis to the (yet unreached) recovery.

Such a situation gives economists and policy makers a dilemma: implementing reflationary policies to revive the economic activity by taking on more and more deficits on an unknown horizon or returning to conservative policies that feed unemployment by hoping that markets could find suitable means to catch up as fast as possible by the "magic" of liberal mechanisms. Therefore, the question which worries economists is to know whether it is necessary to support economic activity by means of public deficits (and steadier interventionism) or whether it would be more suitable to let markets "invent" spontaneous solutions (without recalling the principles of liberalism). Yet this debate does not seem relevant as its "original sin" lies in the implicit assumption that public spending is harmful to economic activity in the long run. Furthermore, this assumption does not provide consistent analysis of the malfunctioning of financialized and weakened economies.

Another alternative, which is suggested in this chapter, is to consider the arguments of the functional finance (FF) of Abba Lerner and the financial instability hypothesis (FIH) of Hyman Minsky for an integrated analysis of relevant public interventions. It then seeks to bring together FF and FIH in order to point to some principles of an alternative macroeconomic stabilization framework able to support job-creating productive activities and to prevent disequilibria-fueling speculative finance.

The first section points to major theoretical and policy stakes in the aftermath of the ongoing worldwide crisis. The second section states the common theoretical grounds of FF and FIH which underline the weaknesses of free markets' self-adjustment mechanisms and call for public intervention. The third section presents the general principles of a financially stable anti-austerity policy framework and sheds light on the links between public finance and financial stability in the process of macroeconomic stabilization. The last section concludes that economic policies must aim at preventing growth-reducing financial crises and sustaining employment-creating activities.

1 What is at stake in the aftermath of the 2007–08 crisis?

The 2007–08 turmoil has provoked massive public interventions to mitigate the negative impact of cumulated financial disequilibria and subsequent bank failures on the demand side and supply side of market economies. Governments paused (or rather put on standby) previously self-imposed deficit or debt (sound finance) constraints. However, as Arestis and Sawyer (2010: 331) note

> it is rather doubtful whether a paradigm shift has occurred. We may cite as an example of this argument the European governments, which have dealt with this crisis as a crass exception that makes extraordinary measures necessary, only to return to normal once the crisis seems to have evaporated.

Unfortunately, unconventional and supportive monetary/public spending policies implemented in major capitalist economies did not succeed in calming down negative effects of the crisis while public deficits reached exceptionally high levels six years after the first signs of the ongoing crisis. The central policy debate now focuses on how to stabilize growing public debt/GDP ratios, given that a "semblance" of recovery is not yet achieved and post-crisis growth remains fragile all around the world. Therefore, in the face of persistent cumulating disequilibria, more conservative policies are advocated in order to reduce budget deficits and public spending and the emphasis is again put on the opposition between "fiscal prudence" and "fiscal profligacy" (Mauro *et al.* 2013), usually referring to the theoretical foundations of neoliberal orthodoxy through the so-called Barro–Ricardo equivalence theorem (ambiguous relation between the government tax and debt policy and aggregate activity),[1] to the supply-side economics assertions (positive incentives of decreasing marginal tax rates on economic activity)[2] and to the depressive effects of public debt on growth (public debt overhang episodes are assumed to be associated with lower growth and the cumulative shortfall in output from debt overhang is assumed to be potentially massive).[3] In this vein, according to the International Monetary Fund (IMF 2012), in 2012 fiscal policy became more contractionary in the advanced economies but much less contractionary in the emerging market and developing economies, where the fiscal deficit is expected to be about 1.5 percent of GDP (much lower than the 6 percent of GDP level projected for the advanced economies) as before the crisis, emerging market and developing economies were running surpluses:

> Over the medium term, many should strengthen their fiscal positions to rebuild room for policy maneuvering. The main challenges with respect to deficit reduction lie, however, in the advanced economies, where public debt is in excess of 100 percent of GDP and rising.
>
> (IMF 2012: 6, figure 1.4)

However, the long-lasting character of the current crisis leads some researchers to point to the negative impacts of austerity policies on growth and public debt. Cherif and Hasanov (2012) argue that even if, in the medium term, austerity may reduce the debt ratio on average, there is large uncertainty about the projected debt impulse response, especially in a weak economic environment:

> Reducing debt via austerity in the 2011 environment may lead to the opposite outcome with the debt ratio barely changing or even increasing. The policy regime in place will affect the response of debt to higher inflation. Our findings suggest that given the economic dynamics of the recent past, an inflation shock, for example due to a hike in crude oil price, would in fact increase the debt ratio after only a few quarters. Finally, we find that a positive growth shock can substantially reduce debt with none of the pain associated with austerity.
>
> (Cherif and Hasanov 2012: 13)

A recent work of the IMF (2013) argues that macroeconomic risks will weigh on both the supply and the demand for credit, and then while monetary policy can help, fiscal and financial regulatory policies are also important. In the same vein, Romer (2011, p. 3) puts the emphasis on discretionary fiscal stimulus as part of the macroeconomic toolkit for short-run stabilization and on the mistake of the conventional wisdom which maintained that short-run stabilization was almost exclusively the province of monetary policy:

> Given the magnitude and persistence of the demand shortfall in a major crisis and the limited possibilities for policies that shift intertemporal incentives, much of discretionary fiscal stimulus is likely to take largely conventional forms, such as broad-based income tax cuts, increased transfers, and higher government purchases. My second lesson is that the evidence that has come out of the crisis has made the case that such conventional fiscal actions stimulate the macroeconomy even more compelling than it was before.

Janet Yellen, Vice Chair of the Board of Governors of the Federal Reserve System, then argues that history shows that fiscal policy often helps to support an economic recovery. But Yellen (2013) remarks that

> instead of contributing to growth thereafter, discretionary fiscal policy this time has actually acted to restrain the recovery. State and local governments were cutting spending and, in some cases, raising taxes for much of this period to deal with revenue shortfalls. At the federal level, policymakers have reduced purchases of goods and services, allowed stimulus-related spending to decline, and have put in place further policy actions to reduce deficits.

However, these statements do not give information about the weaknesses of markets behind the 2007–08 crisis. Indeed, Taylor points to two major characteristics of modern capitalism. The first is the "Great Leveraging," i.e., the high financialization of economies and the return to frequent bank and financial crises, as from the 1970s "we entered what might be called the 'Age of Credit'" (Taylor 2012: 10). That means the decoupling of loans from broad money, reflecting the rise of non-monetary liabilities on bank balance sheets, such as wholesale funding, and faster expansion of bank assets with a diminishing weight of safe assets (government securities "which was down to virtually zero in the 2000s, after starting at 60%–70% in 1950" (ibid.)) in banks' asset mix. The second characteristic is that financial crises can be traced back to developments in the financial sector (excess credit). Taylor argues that the idea that financial crises have their roots in fiscal problems is not supported over the long sweep of history: "Over 140 years there has been no systematic correlation of financial crises with either prior current account deficits or prior growth in public debt levels. Private credit has always been the only useful and reliable predictive factor" (ibid.: 27). Taylor then maintains that even after substantial post-crisis increases in average public debt in advanced countries, it is private debts on bank balance sheets that far outweigh public debts on sovereign balance sheets. It is also worth noting that the policy responses to the current financial crisis have involved governments to engage in bailouts that have led to a substantial increase in public debt. Arestis and Sawyer (2010: 328) report that the nationalization of Northern Rock and other relatively small financial institutions in the United Kingdom would increase public-sector debt by nearly one-quarter. As Minsky reminds us, the essential effect of economic policies in the post-World War II period was to sustain profits even when private demand fell in the aftermath of financial crunches and crises: "This is the hidden fact of the big government and high deficits of the past fifteen years; they have sustained and then increased profits in the recession" (Minsky 1982b: 16).

To deal with this two-fold issue (employment-growth-oriented economic policies and financial stabilization) unorthodox works developed major ideas of some non-orthodox economists like Keynes, Lerner and Minsky, to name a few, to suggest alternative approaches to combat neoliberal conservative policies which have fueled the roots of the recent crisis. Seccareccia (2011–12) points to the Keynesian principle of socialization of investment – in conceptual relation with Lerner's FF – to combat the conservative sound finance approach. Nersisyan and Wray (2010) criticize the mainstream assumptions on the relationship between debt, finance and growth and remind us of major alternative analytical arguments developed by Lerner and Minsky as regards the meaning of the public debt and expenditures and the crucial role played by (financial) instability concerns in economic evolution. In a similar vein, Arestis and De Antoni (2007) argue that even if Minsky is well known through his works on the financial instability issues, he also developed relevant analysis on fiscal and employment policies (that he (Minsky 1965) called "an efficient program – the war – against poverty through the use of expansionary monetary and fiscal policy") and maintained that government intervention must be oriented toward two aims: containing capitalism's instability and preventing financial disaster and reaching and maintaining full employment such that "The effect of fiscal policy is not only to underpin and stabilize aggregate demand, income and employment. It can also protect the robustness of the financial system by stabilizing profits and by issuing government bonds" (Arestis and De Antoni 2007: 2).

Whatever the policy orientation of alternative works in this area, it is commonly asserted that in a capitalist economy, public interventions are of the greatest importance to sustain economic evolution as decentralized markets often are unable to ensure a coherent systemic evolution. In this, central banks and governments implement rescue policies even in liberalized markets, the former through, for instance, quantitative easing-like interventions and lower interest rates, and the latter through increasing spending and budget deficits and debt. In the current crisis, central banks are expanding dramatically their traditional role as lenders-of last-resort to provide liquidity on money and financial markets. But they also became market makers of last resort as financial turmoil sharply affects the interconnected funding and derivatives markets. At the same time, fiscal rules and public spending have to play a crucial role by combining high consumption and employer of last resort as essential ingredients of a coherent strategy for achieving macro-stability and poverty diminution (Kaboub 2007;

Nell 2003; Wray 2007). The common theoretical grounds of such arguments can be found in the works offered by Lerner and Minsky, who maintained that the free market-based capitalist economy is unable to adjust cumulated disequilibria without consistent public intervention.

2 Common theoretical grounds: the inability of markets' self-adjustment mechanisms to stabilize the economy

The main issue behind the economic instability concern is indeed a coordination problem in a decentralized market economy in which interactions of heterogeneous agents lead to some results that may give multiple equilibria or disequilibria without any obvious presumption of global optimality of the final situation reached and any relevant assertion about the existence of endogenous market adjustment mechanisms. Facing this central issue, Lerner and Minsky both have rejected the neoclassical assertion of full-employment equilibrium – assumed to be reached by market mechanisms – and tried to show how a decentralized capitalist economy can function and what consistent economic policies might be designed in order to dampen the endogenous instability and to support job-creating profitable activities. In *The Economics of Social Control* (1944) where "control does not necessarily mean collectivism" (p. 1), Lerner states that "The economics of control is contrasted with the attitude which would have the government leave things alone just because it is the government and as such has no right to interfere with business" (ibid.). In search of economic and social efficiency, Lerner maintains that a controlled economy "would make use of all the available resources and in particular of all men who seek work" (ibid.: 3). From the same perspective, Minsky (1965: 193–194) states that "The function of intervention in a free enterprise economy is to make the economy behave so as to achieve the best of attainable situations."

Lerner and Minsky argue that public interventions are strategic parts of the social coherence as individuals' reactions faced with difficulties in decentralized markets (e.g., markets' self-adjustment mechanisms according to micro-rationality assumption) result in perverse behavior and systemic imbalances (pointing to the macro-instability concern). *They both go against the tide: micro-rational behavior is not system compatible (e.g., macro-consistent) without external public intervention.* Lerner assumes that individual-based market mechanisms fail to result in full-employment equilibrium when unemployment increases and real or financial difficulties increase. He then advocates for public intervention with the aim of attaining a desired level of employment: "reactions of individuals are perverse. Instead of correcting an excess or an insufficiency in total spending, they rather tend to aggravate the situation.... Whenever the individual reactions in any situation are perverse, what is needed is social action" (Lerner 1951: 125). This "perverse" behavior of markets may result in collective panic and prolonged recessive tendencies because of coordination failures among private actors. Lerner (1943) then maintains that the most important task facing society (at the time of his writing, in the 1940s) is the elimination of economic insecurity, e.g., unemployment and lack of growth. It is worth noting that this task still remains the major concern of our present free-market economies.

Developing the same perspective, especially regarding the financial system's behavior, Minsky (1982a: 132) states that

> We should expect the privative, profit-maximizing, risk-averting commercial banks to behave perversely, in that with a decrease in uncertainty they are willing and eager to increase the money supply and with an increase in uncertainty they act to contract the money supply.

In his FIH stance Minsky (1992, 2008a) maintains that business cycles are due to the financial attributes that are essential and endogenous to capitalism (Ülgen 2013). Minsky (1985) then asserts that free-market-mechanisms-based financial systems are not able to result in a stable evolution, thus the major macroeconomic concerns (unemployment and inflation) call for permanent public intervention and regulation to achieve a "semblance of coherence" by preventing costly and growth-reducing crises. We then have to "build a structure of policy that is based upon a modern understanding of how our type of economy generates financial fragility, unemployment, and inflation" (Minsky 2008a: 323). Minsky, as an eminent "Financial Keynesian" (Wray 2007), endorses an institutionalist approach as he puts the emphasis on the effects of policies on individuals and institutions: "The war against poverty must not depend solely, or even primarily, upon changing people, but it must be directed toward changing the system" (Minsky 1965: 176) through a commitment to the maintenance of tight full employment and the adjustment of institutions.

Those views are now widely supported also by various analyses. As the IMF (2013) notes, financial markets became impaired for several reasons. One of these reasons is the classical problem of rational runs, in which the market can coordinate on a "bad" equilibrium in which it is rational for investors to run on a bank, sovereign or market. Another reason is the self-reinforcing amplification of asset price cycles and borrowing constraints (or other financial frictions). In this setting, lower asset prices weaken balance sheets and lead to tighter borrowing constraints and higher funding costs, requiring further asset sales. These, in turn, further depress asset prices and amplify the credit contraction. Then there is no automatic market self-adjusting mechanism which would bring the economy back to a consistent equilibrium. King *et al.* (2012: 11) bring forward the crisis-prone character of financialized capitalism which "have outpaced the capacity to be supervised and regulated" and the negative impact of this evolution on real economy, "causing a collapse in effective demand as debt-laden consumers, and others fearful of the future, cut spending" (ibid.). King *et al.* then maintain that the austerity policies aiming at cutting subsequent budget deficits in response to a burgeoning sovereign debt crisis would have substantial and long-lasting effects on the whole economy: "In recessions, the fiscal intentions of austerity are overwhelmed by the tax and social welfare consequences of the economic downturn, so the ratio of public sector debt can be expected to rise sharply" (ibid.: 9). Boyer (2012: 310) states that current austerity policies implemented "whatever the causes of the public deficits and regardless of the structural and institutional configurations of each national economy – without any distinction – repeats the error of the Washington consensus, namely the 'one size fits all' approach."

Authorities run some so-called unconventional anti-crisis policies in times of crisis – without leaving the consensual wisdom – and let the fiscal and financial breaches subsist on markets (Colander 2002; Minsky 1982a). Seccareccia (2011–12: 64) remarks that there was a "Keynes moment" during 2009–10 when governments implemented fiscal stimulus packages and ran budget deficits to tackle the subsequent recession. But "policy makers seem to have reverted to the pre-2008 policy position on the need for an 'exit strategy' and a return to balanced budgets" (ibid.: 65). This reversal, publically announced at the Toronto Summit of the G20 in June 2010, places deficit reduction as a central aim of a sound recovery plan. All governments in the EU are now involved in deficit reduction programs and call implicitly or explicitly for fiscal austerity. For instance, to support such austerity policies, the UK government "played much more on doomsday scenarios of the reactions of credit rating agencies and financial markets if actual and planned deficit reduction measures were not introduced" (Fontana and Sawyer 2012: 29). Financial instability, regulatory weaknesses and unemployment-prone market mechanisms are no longer on the scene of the political debate and to date we witness once more the prevalence of sound finance beliefs upon policy makers' decisions.

In search of consistent alternative policies, Lerner's FF seems to be able to offer some relevant reflections to prevent economic policies from remaining prisoners of markets' vicissitudes, especially in times of crisis. FF is a set of principles that seek to guide public spending, but also its financing in order to obtain a desired level of employment when markets working cannot result in full-employment equilibrium. However, the consistency of FF-based policies cannot be reached without a real change in the monetary and financial environment of capitalist economies. FF is closely linked to a stable financial environment, at least through the financing needs of the public debt.

3 Principles of financially stable anti-austerity policy framework

The FF is a vanguard approach opposed to the conventional wisdom, 40 years before this latter was coined by economic literature as "Consensual macro-economics." Colander (2002: 2) remarks that Lerner's purpose is

> to shift thinking about government finance from principle of sound finance that make sense for individuals – such as a balanced budget – to sound finance principles (now designed as functional finance) that make sense for the aggregate economy in which government spending and taxing decisions

affect levels of economic activity. These two differed because the secondary effects of spending decisions and savings decisions – what Lerner and I called macro externalities – had to be taken into account in the aggregate economy.

FF is a specific mix of fiscal, budget and monetary policy implemented in order to control (if not to prevent) markets malfunctioning:

> government fiscal policy, its spending and taxing, its borrowing and repayment of loans, its issue of new money and its withdrawal of money, shall all be undertaken with an eye only to the results of these actions on the economy and not to any established traditional doctrine about what is sound or unsound.... The principle of judging fiscal measures by the way they work or function in the economy we may call *Functional Finance*.
>
> (Lerner 1943: 39)

As Lerner assumes that the market economy is not a full-employment economy, the public intervention must use economic policies to increase (decrease) total spending by spending more (less) itself or by reducing (raising) taxes so that the taxpayers have more (less) money left to spend. FF rests on two simple "laws." The first is the regulation of economic activity through government spending and taxation. Public spending can be financed through the "monetary financing" and the raising of taxes. The choice will depend on whether it would be desirable that the taxpayers should have less money to spend (in order to prevent inflation) or it would be desirable that the public should have less money and more government bonds. The second law of functional finance states, therefore, that the public borrowing can be used to regulate the rate of interest, the investment and the level of inflation. Lerner argues that the monetary expansion does not increase the money supply of private agents as it is used to modify the level of interest and of government bonds to balance the level of production (the supply side) and the level of consumption (the demand side). The relevant economic policy consists of keeping the equality between the aggregate (domestic) demand and the aggregate (domestic) supply. The keystone of the macro-equilibrium is the total spending, and the government spending constitutes the main adjustment tool for this (Lerner 1951). Lerner (1943: 41) then suggests three policy orientations: (1) adjustment of total spending to eliminate unemployment (and also inflation) through the use of government expenditures;[4] (2) modification of money and government bonds held by markets through government borrowing or debt repayment in order to affect the interest rate according to the desirable level of investment; and (3) use of monetary policy (monetary expansion or contraction) to support previous prescriptions.

As functional finance aims at maintaining the equality between the level of total demand and the current output, it would be, *ceteris paribus*, a long-run balancing of the budget. But such a balancing does not rest on the principle of sound finance: "As long as the public is willing to keep on lending to the government there is no difficulty, no matter how many zeros are added to the national debt" (Lerner 1943: 42). In the opposite case, the public must either hoard money or spend it. If individuals hoard, the government prints money to meet its obligations, such that private agents hold money instead of government bonds. If total spending increases through individual expenditures, the government has to spend more (and then to borrow more). If the rate of spending of economic agents becomes too high regarding the level of aggregate supply, the government can increase taxes to prevent inflation. The public spending is thought of as a contribution to provide full employment when private spending is insufficient. In this schema, the unemployment comes from insufficient demand as in the Keynesian effective demand model. The leading figure in economic stabilization when things go wrong is the public power (Lerner 1947). To support this view, Lerner (1943) argues that, following the deficit-spending multiplier, the public spending increases the real national income by several times the amount spent by the government and that taxes will be levied only in the social interest to prevent excessive spending or excessive investment which would bring about inflation. Functional finance does not imply continuous increasing of the national debt because "The guarantee of permanent full employment will make private investment much more attractive, once investors have got over their suspicions of the new procedure. The greater investment will diminish the need for deficit spending" (ibid.: 48). The greater investment will then diminish the need for more deficit spending. The national debt increases, and with it the sum of private wealth. There will be no fiscal crowding out effect as there will be an increasing yield from taxes on higher incomes and inheritances.

From this perspective, Arestis and Sawyer (2010: 339) remark that the principles of FF advocate budget deficits when there is inadequate demand and hence FF does not lead to any crowding out as it does not generate any upward pressure on the interest rate on government bonds.[5] As regards the positive effects of public spending on private activities, developed also by Forstater (1999) in an insightful analysis, Mastromatteo (2011: 8) argues that:

> One should not overlook the fact that public works may in fact increase the productivity of the private sector ... through reduction of the costs for firms, because there are numerous social services and services of collective interest that are not adequately provided by the private sector and which have beneficial effects for the economy and for society.

From a similar point of view, Seccareccia (2010) maintains that

> what the G20 leaders and their economic advisors fail to understand is an elementary accounting fact that what is a spending for one sector (say, the government sector) is necessarily a receipt or income for another sector (say, the private sector) and that what is a net spending (or a budgetary deficit) of one sector must inevitably be a positive net saving (or a financial

surplus) of another sector. Hence it follows that, regardless of how they are financed, expenditures generate income, and private sector saving is merely the pecuniary accountancy of public sector deficits.

However, the implementation of FF calls for "big" government able to frame the behavior of financial markets to prevent the accumulation of short-sighted speculative positions, especially on public debt as active employment policies involve changes in public spending, interest rate, public deficit funding and financing conditions of private investments. Minsky (1982a) argues that the behavior of capitalism as a monetary economy cannot be understood without integrating financial relations into an explanation of employment, income and prices. In a capitalist economy where money and monetary institutions play a first-order role, government interventions like public spending and fiscal policies have strong effects on interest rates, private agents' portfolio arbitrages and behavior of financial markets. Once markets are liberalized and financial needs provided through market transactions, government spending falls under the power of speculative financial operations. The financing of public debt then becomes prisoner of the willingness of banks and other financial institutions to fund them with the aim of making higher profits. From this perspective, the financial structure of the economy is one of the major variables that determine the extent to which functional finance can effectively be implemented. Consistent employment policies call for consistent macro environments that should be framed by government according to a set of desired targets without increasing the likelihood of a deep depression. That means that macro stabilization policies must be thought of as an integrated fiscal–budgetary–monetary–financial structural and policy design: "The recovery rests on big government. An attempt to reduce government deficits before the private financial system is robust will soon lead to a resumption of the decline and increase the likelihood that the financial time-bombs will detonate" (Minsky 1975: 5). To Minsky, while "the policy problem is to develop a strategy for full employment that does not lead to instability, inflation, and unemployment" (2008a: 343), the expansion of capitalism endogenously generates instabilities: "As high investment and high profits depend upon and induce speculation with respect to liability structures, the expansions become increasingly difficult to control" (Minsky 2008b: 164). Furthermore, one may obviously notice that in an open economy there can be market pressures on public debt (flight from government debt, increasing interest rates on the debt, etc.) (Minsky 2008a).[6] Therefore, a given functional finance policy needs a debt monetization framework which must be accompanied by a high degree of coordination between fiscal and monetary authorities (Palacio-Vera 2011) and by consistent financial market structure that could enable government to be financed without speculative attacks:

> The history of capitalism is punctuated by deep depressions that are associated with financial panics and crashes.... In a Big Government capitalist economy with an activist central bank, debt deflations and deep depressions

can be contained. Furthermore, central bank administrative actions and legislation can attempt to control and guide the evolution of the financial structure in order to constrain cyclical instability.

(Minsky 2008a: 349)

As in Lerner's FF laws, Minsky maintains that a major portion of the profit-stabilizing deficits and the inflation-controlling surpluses has to come from variations in the tax take. But the implementation of such a policy needs a robust financial structure of which the key element is

> the quality of the best available short-term asset – short-term government debt. An in-place tax structure that yields a surplus when the economy either does well on the income and employment front or poorly on the inflation front is a necessary condition for maintaining the quality of government debt.

(Minsky 2008a: 340)

The monetary and financial authorities need to guide the evolution of financial institutions by favoring stability-enhancing institutions and practices and by discouraging instability-augmenting behavior. Minsky (1982b: 21) then advocates financial conservatism and business profitability-supportive public deficit: "Stabilization policy will do better only as it is recognized that the policy objectives are to sustain profits and constraint liability experimentation by bankers and businessmen by removing the safety net of premature lender of last resort interventions."

In a monetary capitalist economy engagements are founded on debt-financing relations through individuals' expectations about what the evolution could be ahead. Then a debt is validated when maturing commitments to pay are fulfilled and expectations are sustained that future remaining commitments will be fulfilled.[7] The financial instability hypothesis is related to the impact of debt on system behavior and incorporates the manner in which debt is validated (Minsky 1992). Private debt, the source of the monetary creation in the economy, is founded on private expectations as asserted by Lerner and Minsky. However, as the efficiency of public deficits cannot rest on the expected private profits criterion, their financing cannot rely on free market mechanisms but on their social utility. Therefore, the market evaluation (rating) throughout the financing of public debt on markets (increase/decrease of interest rates and risk premium paid on debt) has no meaning. Private spending units and public spending units have not the same aim and cannot be guided according to the same principles since the efficiency of public debt is not the economic efficiency (maximizing profit).

4 Concluding remarks

This chapter sought to show the relevance of an anti-austerity but financially conservative economic policy framework that uses Lerner's FF and Minsky's

FIH stance as regards the theoretical and policy-related stakes in the aftermath of the 2007–08 crisis. It is argued that FF should be accompanied by financial stability in order to sustain economic growth and employment policies and to direct markets' behavior toward long-term productive activities. The analysis presented here points out two major conclusions. The first is that the public spending and related fiscal, budget and monetary policies aim at responding to the weaknesses and incapacities of the market mechanism to bear economic evolution in time. Therefore, their effects on the economy cannot be assessed through the same lenses that one uses to evaluate the efficiency of private decisions, but according to social aims like employment, poverty reduction, etc. The second conclusion is that the financing of the public debt and public spending should not be left to the vicissitudes of markets and the power of speculative funding operations. While beyond the scope of this chapter, these conclusions obviously bring to the fore the fact that a relevant regulatory framework must be implemented (macro-prudential regulatory mechanisms) to replace the dominant free-market-based financial systems. Consequently, the functioning of our financial systems and the regulatory mechanisms that should guide them must be designed according to the objective of stable and sustainable growth in order to keep markets from collapsing. As the free market mechanisms do not seem to be able to ensure sustainable growth and development, non-conformist public spending policies in order to restore full employment are required. With this aim, the brief synthesis of the main principles developed by Lerner about the public spending and related monetary policies and by Minsky about the unstable character of financialized economies seems to offer a fruitful and promising research agenda.

Notes

1 See Barro 1979; Elmendorf and Mankiw 1998.
2 See Prescott 2002.
3 See Reinhart *et al.* 2012.
4 Increase of public spending (of taxes) when total spending is too low (too high) regarding the equality level of domestic aggregate supply and aggregate demand.
5 But this condition rests on the consistency of financial structures. In a financialized economy, without tight regulation, pressures can appear and prevent budget deficits from generating expected positive effects, as it will be argued below.
6 While beyond the scope of this chapter, it can be noticed that the balance-of-payment constraints when they may exist are not specific to fiscal policy but they are "rather constraints on the economy in achieving through whatever means a high level of income and output" (Arestis and Sawyer 2010: 343).
7 By extension,

> a debt structure, either in total or for various subdivisions of the economy, is validated when on the whole maturing commitments to pay are fulfilled and when expectations are that future receipts by debtors will enable payment commitments that extend over time to be fulfilled.
>
> (Minsky 1982a: 34)

References

Arestis, P. and De Antoni, E. (2007) "Rediscovering Fiscal Policy Through Minskyan Eyes," *Departimento Di Economia Discussion Paper*, No. 31, Universita Degli Studi Di Trento.

Arestis, P. and Sawyer, M. (2010) "The Return of Fiscal Policy," *Journal of Post Keynesian Economics*, Vol. 32, No. 3: 327–346.

Barro, R.J. (1979) "Determination of the Public Debt," *The Journal of Political Economy*, Vol. 87, No. 5: 940–971.

Boyer, R. (2012) "The Four Fallacies of Contemporary Austerity Policies: The Lost Keynesian Legacy," *Cambridge Journal of Economics*, Vol. 36, No. 1: 283–312.

Cherif, R. and Hasanov, F. (2012) "Public Debt Dynamics: The Effects of Austerity, Inflation, and Growth Shocks," *IMF Working Paper*, No. 12/230.

Colander, D. (2002) "Functional Finance, New Classical Economics and Great Great Grandsons," *Middlebury College Economics Discussion Paper*, No. 02-34.

Elmendorf, D.W. and Mankiw, G.N. (1998) "Government Debt," *NBER Working Papers Series*, No. 6470.

Fontana, G. and Sawyer, M. (2012) "Setting the Wrong Guidelines for Fiscal Policy," *International Journal of Political Economy*, Vol. 41, No. 2: 27–41.

Forstater, M. (1999) "Functional Finance and Full Employment: Lessons from Lerner for Today," *Journal of Economic Issues*, Vol. 33, No. 2: 475–482.

IMF (International Monetary Fund) (2012) "World Economic Outlook: Coping with High Debt and Sluggish Growth," International Monetary Fund.

IMF (International Monetary Fund) (2013) "Unconventional Monetary Policies: Recent Experience and Prospects," International Monetary Fund.

Kaboub, F. (2007) "Employment Guarantee Programs: A Survey of Theories and Policy Experiences," *The Levy Economics Institute of Bard College Working Paper*, No. 498.

King, L., Kitson, M., Konzelmann, S. and Wilkinson, F. (2012) "Making the Same Mistake Again: Or is *This Time* Different?" *Cambridge Journal of Economics*, Vol. 36, No. 1: 1–15.

Lerner, A.P. (1943) "Functional Finance and the Federal Debt," *Social Research*, Vol. 10, No. 1/4: 38–51.

Lerner, A.P. (1944 [1947]) *The Economics of Social Control: Principles of Welfare Economics*, New York: Macmillan.

Lerner, A.P. (1947) "Money as a Creature of the State," *American Economic Review, Papers and Proceedings*, Vol. 37, No. 2: 312–317.

Lerner, A.P. (1951) *Economics of Employment*, New York: McGraw-Hill.

Mastromatteo, G. (2011) "The Debate on the Crisis: Recent Reappraisals of the Concept of Functional Finance," *Universita' Cattolica del Sacro Cuore, Quaderni dell'Istituto di Economia e Finanza*, no. 105.

Mauro, P., Romeu, R., Binder, A. and Zaman, A. (2013) "Modern History of Fiscal Prudence and Profligacy," *IMF Working Paper*, No. 13/5.

Minsky, H.P. (1965) "The Role of Employment Policy," in M.S. Gordon (ed.), *Poverty in America*, San Francisco, CA: Chandler Publishing Company, pp. 175–200.

Minsky, H.P. (1975) "Our Financial Heritage and the Prospects for '76," prepared remarks for the 23rd Annual Conference on the Economic Outlook, 12 December.

Minsky, H.P. (1982a) *Can "It" happen again?* Armonk, NY: M.E. Sharp, Inc.

Minsky, H.P. (1982b) "Policy Pitfalls in a Financially Fragile Economy," *Hyman P. Minsky Archive*, http://digitalcommons.bard.edu/hm_archive/66 (accessed 21 May 2013).

Minsky, H.P. (1985) "Efficiencies, Institutions and the Contained Instability of Capitalist Economies," *Hyman P. Minsky Archive*, http://digitalcommons.bard.edu/hm_archive/205 (accessed 25 November 2012).

Minsky, H.P. (1992) "The Financial Instability Hypothesis," *The Jerome Levy Economics Institute of Bard College Working Paper*, No. 74.

Minsky, H.P. (2008a [1986]) *Stabilizing an Unstable Economy*, McGraw Hill: New York.

Minsky, H.P. (2008b [1975]) *John Maynard Keynes*, New York: McGraw Hill.

Nell, E.J. (2003), "Short-run Macroeconomic Stabilization by an Employer of Last Resort," in E.J. Nell and M. Forstater (eds.), *Reinventing Functional Finance: Transformational Growth and Full Employment*, Cheltenham: Edward Elgar, pp. 299–318.

Nersisyan, Y. and Wray, L.R. (2010) "Does Excessive Sovereign Debt Really Hurt Growth? A Critique of *This Time Is Different*, by Reinhart and Rogoff," *Levy Economics Institute of Bard College Working Paper*, No. 603.

Palacio-Vera, A. (2011) "Quantitative Easing, Functional Finance, and the 'Neutral' Interest Rate," *Levy Economics Institute of Bard College Working Paper*, No. 685.

Prescott, E.C. (2002) "Prosperity and Depression," *AEA Papers and Proceedings*, Vol. 92, No. 2: 1–15.

Reinhart, C.M., Reinhart, V.R. and Rogoff, K.S. (2012) "Public Debt Overhangs: Advanced-Economy Episodes Since 1800," *Journal of Economic Perspectives*, Vol. 26, No. 3: 69–86.

Romer, D. (2011) "What Have We Learned about Fiscal Policy from the Crisis?" *IMF Conference on Macro and Growth Policies in the Wake of the Crisis*, March 2011

Seccareccia, M. (2010) "No to Fiscal Austerity: The Perils of Deflation and the Case for Functional Finance," *Economia e Politica: Rivista on line di critica della politica economica*, 19 Luglio. Available at: www.economiaepolitica.it/index.php/europa-e-mondo/no-to-fiscal-austerity-the-perils-of-deflation-and-the-case-for-functional-finance (20 October 2012).

Seccareccia, M. (2011–12) "The Role of Public Investment as Principal Macroeconomic Tool to Promote Long-Term Growth: Keynes's Legacy," *International Journal of Political Economy*, Vol. 40, No. 4: 62–82.

Taylor, A.M. (2012) "The Great Leveraging," *BIS Working Papers*, No. 398.

Ülgen, F. (2013) "Institutions and Liberalized Finance: Is Financial Stability of Capitalism a Pipedream?" *Journal of Economic Issues*, Vol. 47, No. 2: 495–504.

Wray, L.R. (2007) "Minsky's Approach to Employment Policy and Poverty: Employer of Last Resort and the War on Poverty," *The Levy Economics Institute Working Paper*, No. 515.

Yellen, J.L. (2013) "A Painfully Slow Recovery for America's Workers: Causes, Implications, and the Federal Reserve's Response," Remarks at "A Trans-Atlantic Agenda for Shared Prosperity," Conference Sponsored by the AFL-CIO, Friedrich Ebert Stiftung, and the IMK Macroeconomic Policy Institute, Washington, DC, 11 February 2013.

9 Fiscal consolidation and sovereign debt risk in balance-sheet recessions

An agent-based approach

Marco Raberto, Andrea Teglio and Silvano Cincotti

The commonly accepted policy hypothesis is that austerity might have expansionary effects, because the expectations that today's sacrifices will translate into tax reductions and higher disposable income in the future might induce economic agents to increase consumption and investment in the short term. Another common defense of current austerity programs is the risk that bond markets, whenever a government is not sufficiently committed to budget balance, may demand huge spreads for sovereign debt and possibly push a nation into default.

The question of whether fiscal consolidation may have expansionary effects is a relevant policy issue as the emerging empirical evidence is actually contradicting the tale of expansionary austerity. Economies under austerity programs are experiencing a second severe contraction of economic activity, following the one that already occurred in 2008–09; in addition, bond yields of peripheral Eurozone countries, which, unlike the United Kingdom, cannot devaluate their currency, are at levels which are not sustainable at the present negative growth rates. Indeed, historical evidence tells us that expansionary effects of austerity measures are rarely observed (Guajardo *et al.* 2011); in particular, they occurred only when austerity measures were implemented in an international setting where trade partners were flourishing. Fiscal austerity was typically combined with a mix of internal and external devaluation that resulted in sinking real wages and prices with respect to the trade partners. Due to lower relative prices, the competitive position of these countries in international trade became better, the current account position increased and, due to increased exports and/or decreased imports, both the economy and the government budget recovered. On the contrary, in the current situation, where government spending decreases and/ or taxes rise, i.e., demand from the government and disposable private income decrease, none of the major centers of economic activity – Europe, the United States and China – is willing to accept substantially lower exports and/or higher imports. As all current accounts must sum up to zero by definition, the attempt to improve, e.g. by external devaluation, all current accounts simultaneously just gives rise to a beggar-thy-neighbor policy in which no one will eventually be able to attain this goal. The same logic also holds of course for the economies within the Eurozone, where indeed internal devaluation is the main policy available. Furthermore, following the asset bubble burst, most European economies (as well as the United Kingdom and United States) are now in an economic scenario where the over-indebted private sector is trying to deleverage its balance sheets and financial institutions are unwilling to lend because they also need to strengthen their balance sheets and face a shortage of willing and creditworthy borrowers. This deleveraging of the private sector reduces aggregate demand, due to both lower consumption and investments, and throws the economy into a very special type of recession which has been named as balance-sheet recession (Koo 2009, 2011). In such a scenario, monetary policy, the traditional remedy to recessions, is ineffective because the private sector is unwilling to increase borrowing, even at very low interest rates; and unconventional monetary measures boosting base money, like quantitative easing, are scarcely effective to increase the broad money supply and then sustain the economy. The money supply may actually contract, because the private sector collectively draws down bank deposits to repay debts. In the absence of new economic players borrowing and spending money, the economy enters a deflationary spiral where demand is continuously reduced by net debt repayments. In such a scenario, it is argued that the public sector should actually move in the opposite direction to offset private sector deleveraging, i.e., perform a deficit-financed fiscal stimulus aimed to maintain incomes of businesses and households and allow balance-sheet repair without forcing the economy into depression. Government borrowing should not encounter much difficulty in a balance-sheet recession, unlike in a dysfunctional monetary union (Wolf 2012), due to the availability of savings in excess from the private sector, low interest rates and high risk aversion. Moreover, recent studies (see, e.g., DeLong and Summers 2012) have provided convincing theoretical and empirical evidence about the efficacy of temporary expansionary fiscal policy in severely depressed economies. First, the absence of supply constraints and low interest rates makes the fiscal multiplier substantially greater than in normal times. Second, preventing prolonged output shortfalls though a deficit-financed fiscal stimulus may ease rather than jeopardize the long-run government budget constraint because of hysteresis effects of present output drops on the economy's future potential, through the decrease of investments and the increase of structural unemployment. In a balance-sheet recession as well as in a severe depression scenario, like the one faced now by most Western economies, fiscal stimulus could actually turn out to be expansionary and self-financing while fiscal austerity may turn out to be depressive and self-defeating.

The research questions we aim to address concern the role of fiscal policy combined with monetary expansion (quantitative easing) in different economic scenarios, characterized by a higher or lower vulnerability to balance-sheet recessions. In previous works (see Raberto *et al.* 2012; Teglio *et al.* 2012) we have shown that the economic system is more vulnerable when the amount of credit money injected in the system becomes too high. We have shown that excessive banks' leverage, due to permissive banking regulation, significantly reduces economic stability, increasing the probability of financial crises and economic recessions. In this chapter we investigate the effect of a combination of fiscal and monetary policy according to different fragility levels of the economic system. In particular, we aim to understand whether a regime of quantitative easing mixed with fiscal expansion (tax reduction) can be successful in weakening the impact of economic crises without deteriorating deficit and debt of the public sector in the medium to long run.

1 Methodology

The study of the economy by means of agent-based computational models is a relatively new field and dates back to the 1990s, when the increasing availability of cheap computing power made it possible to undertake the computationally expensive experiments required to model the interactions of large numbers of bounded rational, heterogeneous agents (see Tesfatsion and Judd 2006 for a review). Agent-based models (ABMs) allow simulations of large numbers of agents and encourage bottom-up approaches, allowing the modeler to study the emergent aggregate statistical regularities in the economy, which cannot be originated by the behavior of a "representative" individual (Kirman 1992), but are the result of agents' behavior and interaction.

The pre-crisis research agenda of macroeconomics was to improve the consensus among macroeconomists and to further refine the DSGE model paradigm (Smets and Wouters 2002). The crisis has, however, modified this agenda and has led to an intense debate about the modeling tools currently available (Caballero 2010). As Jean-Claude Trichet put it:

> the atomistic, optimizing agents underlying existing models do not capture behaviour during a crisis period. We need to deal better with heterogeneity across agents and the interaction among those heterogeneous agents. Agent-based modelling dispenses with the optimisation assumption and allows for more complex interactions between agents.
>
> (Trichet 2010)

ABMs have the advantages of flexibility and modularity in model building and dispense with theoretical consistency requirements. The ABM approach avoids the lack of realism of the optimizing agent assumption by relying on a more realistic description of agents' behavior, which is based on heuristics and behavioral patterns instead of perfect rationality, as pointed out by the increasing literature on behavioral economics (Kahneman and Tversky 2000; Gigerenzer and Selten 2002). ABMs also easily allow for adaptive rules and learning (Kirman 2011). Policy makers could be more willing to trust insights obtained in models with "realistic" economic structures rather than in abstract mathematical models (see Dawid and Fagiolo 2008).

During the last decade, a number of research papers using agent-based computational economics (ACE) methodology has appeared, focusing on different fields of economic theory, such as finance (see, e.g., LeBaron 2006; Ussher 2008), industrial organization (Kutschinski *et al.* 2003), labor markets (Tassier and Menczer 2001), innovation (Dawid 2006) and the relationship between financial fragility of firms and business cycles (Delli Gatti *et al.* 2005). Generally speaking, these studies are able to drop the unrealistic assumptions of general equilibrium theory, i.e., perfect competition, centralized exchange and full information. The outcome of market failures, which may depend on asymmetric information among agents, imperfect competition and coordination failures, are then easily observed and investigated. Furthermore, the agent-based approach offers a realistic environment that is well suited for studying the out-of-equilibrium transitory dynamics of the economy caused by changes of policy parameters. A number of studies have in fact appeared recently on the issue of policy analysis (see, e.g., two special issues: Dawid and Fagiolo 2008; LeBaron and Winker 2008). Some studies are focused on the design of regulatory policies for financial markets (Mannaro *et al.* 2008; Pellizzari and Westerhoof 2009), others on the design of appropriate fiscal and monetary policies (Russo *et al.* 2007; Cincotti *et al.* 2010).

While several agent-based models have been developed so far regarding single sectors of the economy, the development of models of a multiple-market economy as a whole is still at the beginning phase. In particular, the agent-based approach seems better suited to take into account the complex pattern of agents' behavior and interactions that take place in financial markets, like herding behavior and information cascades, and in credit markets, like network effects, credit rationing and bankruptcy waves, and to figure out their influences on the real side of the economy. Part of mainstream research in economics, usually named as new-Keynesian economics, showed how the financial and liability structure of the economy may influence aggregate economic activity and amplify business cycles. The credit channel, i.e., the financing of business investment, has been pointed out as the main linkage between finance and the real economy. The seminal papers by Stiglitz and Weiss (1981) and Myers and Majluf (1984) showed that informational asymmetries in the credit markets may prevent firms, even ones with good investment projects, obtaining credit. Further research highlighted the so-called financial accelerator mechanism, i.e., a balance sheet channel through which monetary policy has real effects in the economy (Bernanke and Gertler 1990, 1995; Greenwald and Stiglitz 1993). The credit channel regards both the balance sheet of banks and firms. The balance sheet of credit institutions conditions the potential supply of loans due to the capital adequacy ratios, while firms' net worth influences the willingness of banks to lend to highly leveraged firms. Furthermore, Kiyotaki and Moore (2002) stressed the importance of asset prices and the role of net worth as collateral. It is worth noting, however, that in the new-Keynesian literature the investment–finance linkage is considered as a propagator mechanism of shocks which are exogenous with respect to the economy. On the contrary, the agent-based approach is able to emphasize the role of the investment–finance link not just as a propagator of exogenous shocks, but as the main source of financial instability and business cycles, in line with Minsky's financial instability hypothesis (Minsky 1986; Fazzari 2008).

The agent-based model and simulator Eurace (Cincotti *et al.* 2010; Raberto *et al.* 2012; Teglio *et al.* 2012) is currently one of the most complete models in the field. We will address the research question of the chapter by designing a computational experiment based on the Eurace model. Further details of the experiment and the model are given in the next sections.

2 The model

In the following, we will present a brief outline of the Eurace model. For further details, we recommend the reader consult the following references: Cincotti *et al.* (2012a, 2012b); Raberto *et al.* (2012); Teglio *et al.* (2012).

Eurace is an agent-based model and simulator of an artificial economy populated by different types of agents that interact through different types of markets. The model includes households that have the multiple role of consumers, workers and financial investors, consumption goods producers (CGPs), a capital goods producer, banks, a government and a central bank (CB). Agents interact through different types of markets, namely a market for consumption goods and one for capital goods, a labor market, a credit market and a financial market for stocks and government bonds. Market interactions are decentralized and pairwise, prices are set by agents on the supply side, except for the financial market and the labor market. The financial market is characterized by a central Walrasian auction that sets asset prices so as to equate aggregate demand and supply. In the labor market, the exchange is decentralized but wages are set by the demand side, i.e., CGPs, while workers have a reservation wage.

Agents are myopic, have limited information and scarce computational capabilities. In particular, CGPs decide their production plans based on past sales and present inventory stock, according to the literature on firms' inventory management (Hillier and Lieberman 1986), then try to maximize short-term profits following mark-up pricing (see, e.g., Plott 1982), i.e., by setting prices at a fixed mark-up on their costs (wages and interests on their debt). The production plan determines the labor demand and capital goods demand by CGPs.

Households' saving–consumption decision is modeled according to the theory of buffer-stock saving behavior (Carroll 2001; Deaton 1992), which states that households' consumption depends on a precautionary saving motive, determined by a target level of wealth to income ratio. Households can invest their savings in the asset market by buying and selling equity shares or government bonds. Households' portfolio allocation is modeled according to a preference structure designed to take into account the psychological findings that emerged in the framework of behavioral finance, and in particular of prospect theory (Kahneman and Tversky 1979).

Households' behavior in the financial market has been thoroughly described by Raberto *et al.* (2008) and Teglio *et al.* (2009). It is worth noting, however, that only the equity shares of CGPs are exchanged among households in the stock market and only CGPs are allowed to issue new equity shares to be sold to households.

Each agent has been modeled according to a rigorous balance-sheet approach, which allows stock flow consistency checks both at the single agent and at the aggregate level. The balance-sheet variables can be regarded as the state variables of any agent and, along with wages, interest and prices, are endogenously determined within the system. In particular, wages and consumption goods prices are heterogeneous and fixed by any consumption goods producers according to labor market conditions and costs, interest rates are fixed by banks and are heterogeneous as well, because they depend on the creditworthiness of the borrower as well as on the CB rate. The CB rate is endogenously determined via a Taylor rule. The government collects taxes both on income and consumption, while government expenses are made by unemployment benefits, general transfers to households and interests on debt. Deficit is covered by issuing new government bond and by adjusting tax rates adaptively to pursue a predetermined deficit target. The central bank may perform quantitative easing, i.e., buy government debt on the bond market.

The choice of time scales for the agents' decision making has been made in order to reflect the real time scales in economic activities. The agents' financial decisions are made on a shorter time scale (day) than the economic decision making, for example, consumption and production, where the proper time horizon can be a week, a month or a quarter. Interactions are asynchronous. We model this asynchronous decision making by letting agents have different activation days. This means that on a single market different agents are active on different days. Thus, who interacts with whom changes from day to day. Some activities, however, are synchronized. In particular, this is the case when activities are institutionally initiated as, for instance, yearly tax payments or monthly wage payments.

The Eurace model has been implemented in FLAME[1] (Flexible Large-scale Agent-based Modelling Environment). The FLAME framework is specifically designed to provide a formal and very flexible approach to ABM and enables the creation of ABMs that can be run on high-performance computers. The framework is based on the logical communicating extended finite state machine theory (Xmachine) which gives modellers more power to enable the writing of complex models for large complex systems. The agents are modeled as X-machines which communicate through messages being sent to each other as designed by the modeler. This information is automatically read by the FLAME framework and generates a simulation program that enables these models to be parallelized efficiently over different computers.

3 Results

We performed a computational experiment based on repeated simulations of the Eurace model, with the following setting: 3,000 households, 50 CGPs, three banks, one investment goods producer (IGP), one government and one CB.

We compare two scenarios for the fiscal and monetary policy. In the first scenario, henceforth "fiscal consolidation" (FC), fiscal policy targets a 3 percent deficit/GDP ratio irrespective of the conditions of the economy, thus performing fiscal consolidation by raising tax rates, in particular during economic downturns. In the second policy scenario, fiscal policy still targets a 3 percent deficit/GDP ratio in normal economic conditions, except during economic downturns when the unemployment rate goes above 20 percent. In the latter case, tax rates are not increased despite a growing deficit to GDP ratio, while government financing in the bond market is helped by quantitative easing operations by the CB. We call this second scenario "fiscal and monetary accommodation" (FMA).

The two fiscal and monetary policy scenarios have been performed considering three different values of the capital adequacy ratio (CAR) of banks, therefore considering a total of six (2*3) possible cases. The choice of the CAR as a control parameter is due to the fact that previous studies have shown a higher instability of the economic system associated with low values of the CAR (see Teglio *et al.* 2012) generating a credit bubble. Therefore, varying the CAR we can have more stable or less stable economic scenarios. For each of the six cases we performed ten simulation runs using ten corresponding different seeds for the pseudo-random number generator.

Results of the simulations are presented both in the form of plots and tables. Figures 9.1–9.4 show the dynamic trajectories of several economic indicators for a specific seed. All the plots include three trajectories. The first one represents the FC scenario, while the other two trajectories are associated to a more accommodative fiscal policy for high unemployment rates (FMA), where the government does not raise taxes but finances its spending mostly by selling bonds in the secondary market (where the central banks acts as a buyer, then avoiding a bond price collapse). The first two trajectories correspond to a ratio between banks' weighted assets and equity capital (henceforth banks' leverage, i.e., the inverse of CAR) $\alpha=10$ while the last trajectory corresponds to $\alpha=20$. Tables 9.1–9.4 present the aggregation of several economic indicators over different simulation runs, considering the average value of all the available random seeds.

Figure 9.1 shows the real and nominal output in the three considered scenarios. The fiscal consolidation policy performs poorly with respect to the fiscal and monetary accommodation policy. When banks' leverage is low, i.e., $\alpha=10$, the output growth is higher in the case of an FMA policy but it seems to be slightly more unstable too. The higher growth and instability are even more evident if we look at the case of $\alpha=20$, where banks' leverage is greater.

These results are confirmed in Table 9.1, showing the yearly growth rate of output averaged over different random seeds. Irrespectively of α, the growth rate is higher when the fiscal and monetary accommodation policy is active. The higher investments and the lower unemployment rate corroborate the positive impact of this policy on the real economy. Please note that the model has not been calibrated on empirical data, and the high values of the unemployment rate should not be considered alone but should be compared in the different cases in order to identify a potential trend.

Let us analyze more in detail the output instability that seems to emerge in Figure 9.1 in the FMA case. In order to do this, it is useful to look at Figure 9.4,

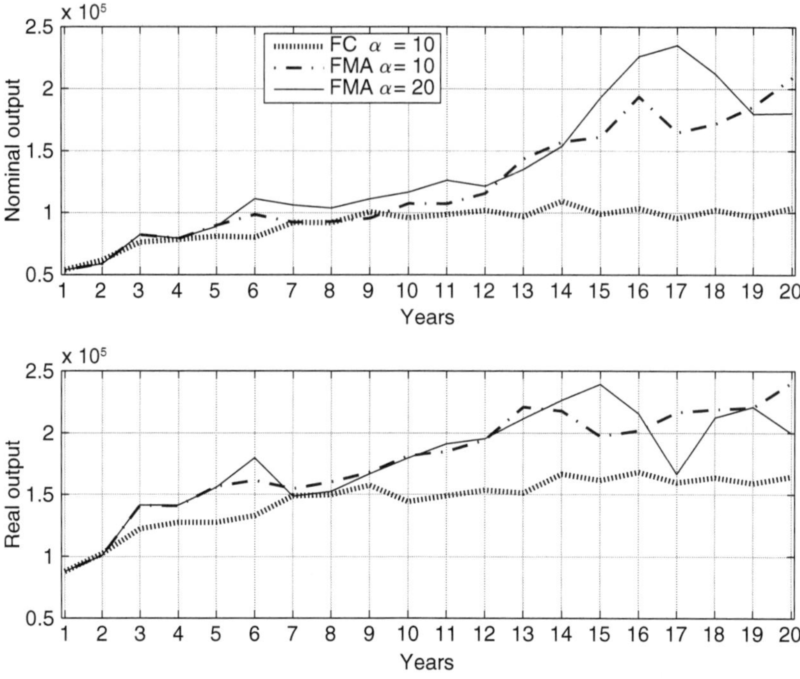

Figure 9.1 Nominal and real output in the case of fiscal consolidation policy (FC) or fiscal and monetary accomodation (FMA). Two different banks' leverage α (ratio between banks' weighted assets and equity capital) are considered.

Table 9.1 Average values of output and capital yearly growth rates (%) and unemployment rate (%) in the case of fiscal consolidation policy (FC) or fiscal and monetary accommodation (FMA)

	Policy	Output	Unemployment	Capital
$\alpha=10$	FC	3.60 (0.27)	36.7 (1.2)	8.7 (0.1)
	FMA	5.89 (0.23)	17.5 (2.2)	11.4 (0.3)
$\alpha=15$	FC	3.80 (0.20)	35.5 (1.1)	38.8 (0.1)
	FMA	5.79 (0.17)	16.4 (1.2)	11.3 (0.3)
$\alpha=20$	FC	3.63 (0.15)	36.3 (1.2)	8.9 (0.2)
	FMA	6.95 (1.12)	19.6 (2.4)	11.2 (0.4)

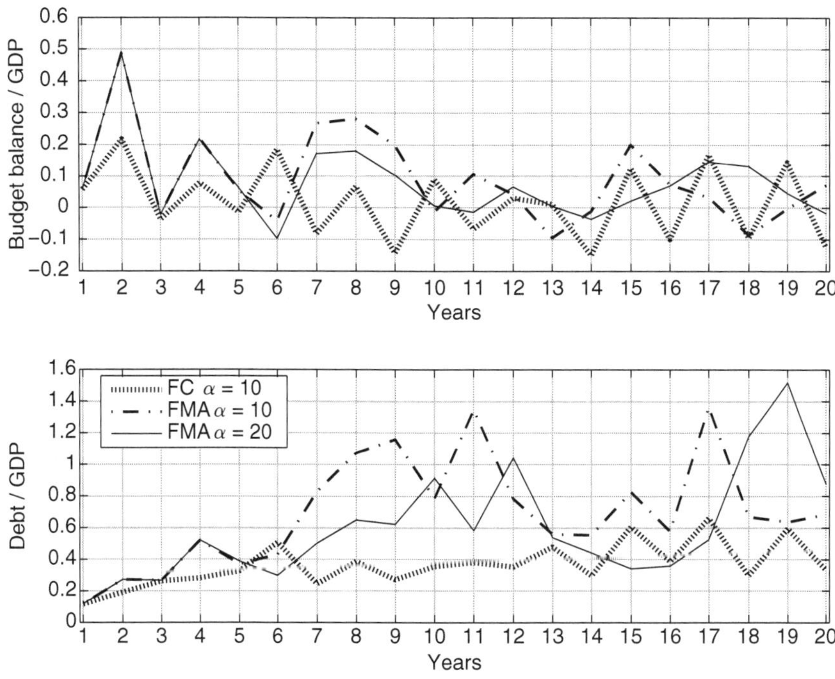

Figure 9.2 Government deficit and debt over nominal GDP in the case of fiscal consolidation policy (FC) or fiscal and monetary accommodation (FMA). Two different banks' leverage α (ratio between banks' weighted assets and equity capital) are considered.

Table 9.2 Average values of credit yearly growth rate, inflation and loan rates (%) and in the case of fiscal consolidation policy (FC) or fiscal and monetary accommodation (FMA)

	Policy	Credit	Inflation	Loan rate
$\alpha=10$	FC	3.83 (0.23)	0.87 (0.23)	1.93 (0.61)
	FMA	7.49 (0.55)	2.86 (0.35)	3.77 (1.19)
$\alpha=15$	FC	4.07 (0.28)	0.87 (0.11)	1.95 (0.62)
	FMA	7.43 (0.46)	2.87 (0.36)	3.47 (1.10)
$\alpha=20$	FC	4.25 (0.28)	1.01 (0.07)	2.00 (0.63)
	FMA	7.06 (0.71)	3.07 (0.43)	3.89 (1.23)

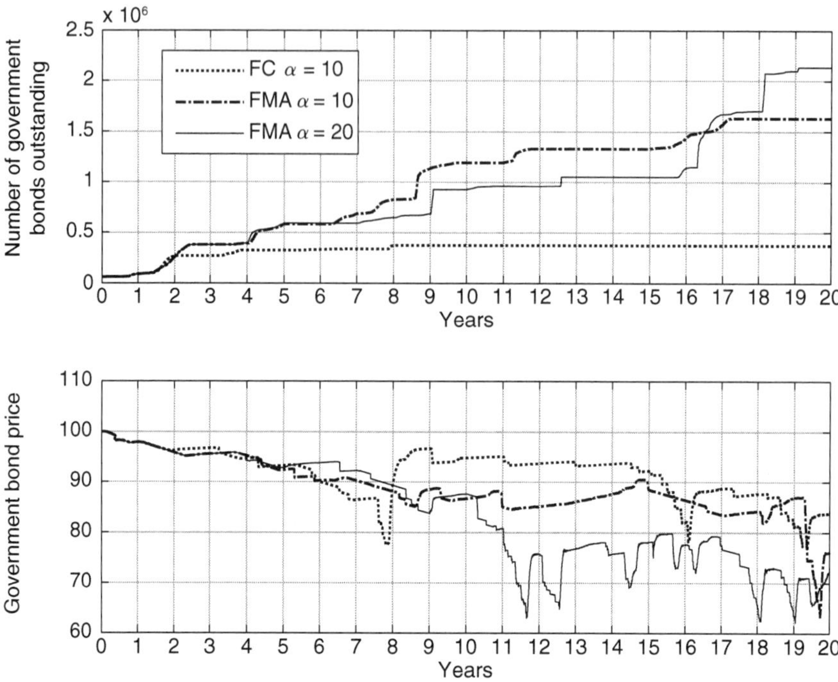

Figure 9.3 Price and number of outstanding government bonds in the case of fiscal consolidation policy (FC) or fiscal and monetary accommodation (FMA). Two different banks' α leverage (ratio between banks' weighted assets and equity capital) are considered.

Table 9.3 Average values of firms' leverage (debt over equity capital) and firms' number of bankruptcies in the case of fiscal consolidation policy (FC) or fiscal and monetary accommodation (FMA)

	Policy	Firms leverage	Illiquidity bankruptcies	Insolvency bankruptcies
$\alpha=10$	FC	2.5 (0.1)	21.0 (2.6)	6.6 (1.0)
	FMA	2.5 (0.1)	55.9 (5.5)	3.6 (1.0)
$\alpha=15$	FC	3.3 (0.4)	18.7 (1.5)	6.9 (1.1)
	FMA	3.2 (0.4)	32.4 (7.0)	7.4 (2.3)
$\alpha=20$	FC	3.1 (0.2)	17.2 (1.5)	9.8 (1.4)
	FMA	3.3 (0.2)	41.8 (10.9)	9.7 (2.4)

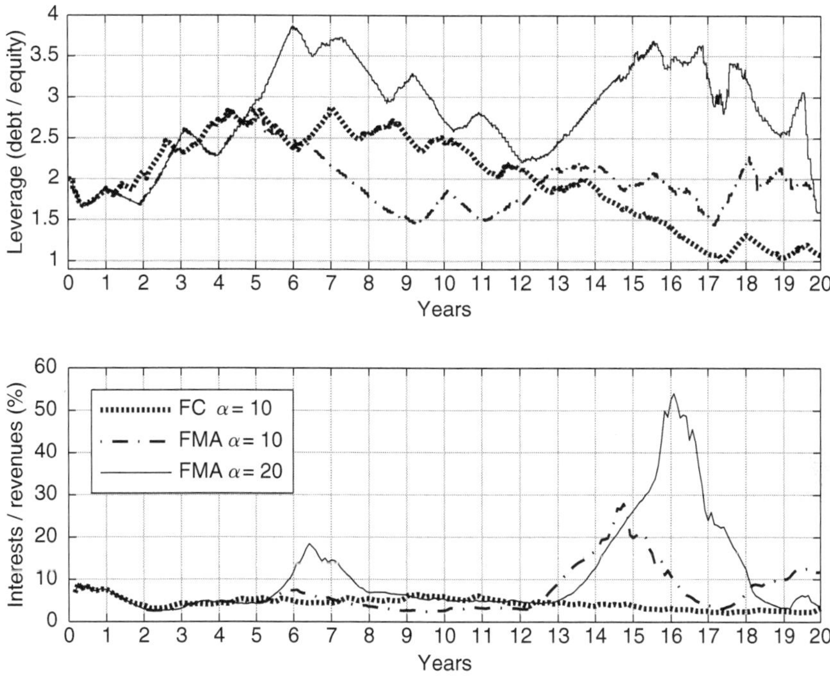

Figure 9.4 Firms' financial fragility indicators in the case of fiscal consolidation policy (FC) or fiscal and monetary accommodation (FMA). Two different banks' leverage   (ratio between banks' weighted assets and equity capital) are considered.

Table 9.4 Average values of tax rate and government surplus and debt over GDP in the case of fiscal consolidation policy (FC) or fiscal and monetary accommodation (FMA)

	Policy	*Balance/GDP*	*Debt/GDP*	*Tax rate*
$\alpha=10$	FC	−3.4 (0.5)	44.5 (3.1)	26.9 (8.5)
	FMA	−7.9 (0.3)	61.8 (2.2)	16.6 (5.2)
$\alpha=15$	FC	−2.6 (0.3)	40.9 (2.9)	26.3 (8.3)
	FMA	−8.9 (0.6)	64.1 (3.7)	16.4 (5.2)
$\alpha=20$	FC	−2.3 (0.5)	40.2 (3.1)	26.4 (8.4)
	FMA	−10.1 (1.1)	72.9 (6.3)	16.8 (5.3)

where two indicators of firms' financial fragility are plotted (firms' interest payment over revenues and firms' debt over equity capital, commonly known as firms' leverage). When the quantitative easing by the CB is active, firms' leverage tends to be higher and the resulting amount of debt generates a higher interest bill for firms. At some point, this interest flow is no longer manageable and some firms go bankrupt. If the system is fragile enough, these events can cause a chain of bankruptcies with a resulting deleveraging process and a balance-sheet recession. This phenomenon can be observed after year 16 in the case of FMA and $\alpha=20$ or after year 14 in the case of $\alpha=10$.

The cost of a higher output growth rate in terms of a higher instability can be observed in Table 9.3 looking at the average number of bankruptcies during the 20 years of the simulation run. We can also see in Table 9.2 how a higher amount of money in the economic system leads to a higher level of inflation. Nevertheless, from this first part of the analysis, the FMA policy seems to be beneficial with respect to fiscal austerity, especially in the case of lower credit leverage, i.e., $\alpha=10$.

Another aspect we should look at is the impact of the two policies on the public balance. Figure 9.2 shows the government deficit (at the top) and the government debt (at the bottom), both divided by the GDP. The number of government bonds outstanding and their price, expressed as centimes of their face value, can be found in Figure 9.4.

Public deficit and debt look relatively under control in the three considered scenarios. We mean that there is no evidence for a path leading to an unsustainable or explosive government debt. The deficit is unsurprisingly generally higher in the FMA case, and obviously tends to grow during a crisis in order to finance unemployment benefits and transfers. However, the higher level of output and its capacity to recover after recessions keep the deficit over GDP level under control. In the case of fiscal austerity, government finances are surely in order but the cost is represented by a production path that stays quite far away from the potential output, with a resulting higher level of unemployment.

Table 9.4 confirms the narrative of the plots. The government manages to keep its deficit around 3 percent by conducting a tight fiscal policy, with public debt at very reasonable levels. In the case of a loose fiscal policy with monetary accommodation, public finances are less controlled and the government runs an averagely higher budget deficit; however, as noted before, there is no explosive trend. The volatility of deficit and debt is higher because public finances act as a buffer for the real economy, absorbing shocks relying on both fiscal and monetary policy. On the other hand, in the case of fiscal austerity, the only adjustment is through taxation (look at Table 9.4 for the average tax rate) and the aggregated demand turns out to be almost always depressed.

We can finally point out a potential warning concerned with the so-called FMA policy. The difference among different levels of banks' leverage α becomes clear by looking at Table 9.2, where the growth rate of total credit in the economy is described. Without quantitative easing, the amount of credit money in the system grows significantly with the leverage, i.e., the ratio between banks' weighted assets and equity capital. When the quantitative easing mechanism is active, the growth rate of credit becomes higher, accompanied by higher inflation and interest rate. The warning is related to the combination of an expansionary monetary policy and loose banking regulation. On one hand we can affirm that credit money deriving from banks' loans and CB's money used for buying government bonds do not sum up; they spread into the economic system through different channels, having a different economic impact. On the other hand we can warn about a potentially excessive instability related to the case of FMA associated with loose banking regulation. We observe a higher rate of significant output drops in our simulations (like the one at years 6 and 15 in Figure 9.1), which tell us to be cautious with the risk of overloading the different channels of monetary expansion. In this respect, what emerges from our computational experiments is that stricter banking regulation combined with monetary accommodation has better results than fiscal consolidation combined with high banks' leverage. Nevertheless, we plan to examine in depth this issue with further simulations and statistical analysis in order to reach more robust and definitive results.

4 Concluding remarks

This chapter presented a computational experiment addressing the issue of comparing two different fiscal policy approaches in times of recession. The first one is the currently adopted approach in the European economies, which is commonly known as an austerity program or fiscal consolidation. The second approach relaxes the fiscal tightening during recession, relying on monetary accommodation and on the CB acting as a lender of last resort.

The computational experiment shows that fiscal consolidation tends to depress the aggregated demand with negative consequences on the output, which stays far away from its potential level. On the other hand, under an FMA policy, the output growth is more significant and the unemployment rate is reduced. The results then confirm a previous study investigating the effect of the quantitative easing policy in the Eurace simulator, yet in a different experimental setting (Cincotti *et al.* 2010, 2012b).

Some caution is necessary when the credit leverage is very high and the private debt load is considerable. In this case an expansive monetary policy might amplify the economic instability, leading to potential depressions.

The results we present have to be considered as preliminary results of a wider investigation project which will be enhanced in the near future.

Acknowledgments

A.T. acknowledges project GV/2012/045 of the Generalitat Valenciana, project UJI-Bancaja P11A2010-17, and the Spanish national project ECO2011-23634. M.R. and S.C. acknowledge financial support by the University of Genoa under project PRA 2011. The authors acknowledge EU-FP7 collaborative project SYMPHONY (www.projectsymphony.eu) under grant no. 611875.

Note

1 www.flame.ac.uk.

References

Bernanke, B. and Gertler, M. (1990), Financial fragility and economic performance, *Quarterly Journal of Economics*, 105, 87–114.

Bernanke, B. and Gertler, M. (1995), Inside the black box: the credit channel of monetary policy transmission, *Journal of Economic Perspectives*, 9, 27–48.

Caballero, R.J. (2010), Macroeconomics after the crisis: time to deal with the pretense-of-knowledge syndrome. *Journal of Economic Perspectives*, 24, 85–102.

Carroll, C.D. (2001), A theory of the consumption function, with and without liquidity constraints. *Journal of Economic Perspectives*, 15(3), 23–45.

Cincotti, S., Raberto, M. and Teglio, A. (2010), Credit money and macroeconomic instability in the agent-based model and simulator Eurace. *Economics: The Open-Access, Open-Assessment E-Journal*, 4, 2010–26.

Cincotti, S., Raberto, M. and Teglio, A. (2012a), The Eurace macroeconomic model and simulator. In *Agent-based Dynamics, Norms, and Corporate Governance. The proceedings of the 16th World Congress of the International Economic Association*, volume 2, Palgrave.

Cincotti, S., Raberto, M. and Teglio, A. (2012b), Macroprudential policy in an agent-based artificial economy. *Review de l'OFCE*, 124, 205–234.

Dawid, H. (2006), Agent-based models of innovation and technological change, in L. Tesfatsion and K.L. Judd (eds.), *Handbook of Computational Economics, Vol. 2: Agent-Based Computational Economics*, North-Holland/Elsevier, Amsterdam.

Dawid, H. and Fagiolo, G. (2008), Agent-based models for economic policy design: Introduction to the special issue. *Journal of Economic Behavior and Organization*, 67, 351–354.

Deaton, A. (1992), Household saving in LDCs: credit markets, insurance and welfare. *The Scandinavian Journal of Economics*, 94(2), 253–273.

Delli Gatti, D., Di Guilmi, C., Gaffeo, E., Giulioni, G., Gallegati, M. and Palestrini, A. (2005), A new approach to business fluctuations: heterogeneous interacting agents, scaling laws and financial fragility. *Journal of Economic Behavior and Organization*, 56, 489–512.

DeLong, J.B. and Summers, L.H. (2012), Fiscal policy in a depressed economy. *Brookings Panel on Economic Activity*, 1, 233–297.

Fazzari, S., Ferri, P. and Greenberg, E. (2008), Cash flow, investment, and Keynes–Minsky cycles. *Journal of Economic Behavior & Organization*, 65, 555–572.

Gigerenzer, G. and Selten, R. (2002), *Bounded Rationality*. Cambridge, MA: MIT Press.

Greenwald, B.C. and Stiglitz, J.E. (1993), Financial market imperfections and business cycles. *Quarterly Journal of Economics*, 108, 77–114.

Guajardo, J., Leigh, D. and Pescatori, A. (2011), Expansionary austerity: new international evidence. *IMF Working Paper WP/11/158*.

Hillier, F. and Lieberman, G. (1986), *Introduction to Operations Research*, Boston, MA: McGraw-Hill.

Kahneman, D. and Tversky, A. (1979), Prospect theory: an analysis of decision under risk. *Econometrica*, 47, 263–292.

Kahneman, D. and Tversky, A. (eds.) (2000), *Choices, Values and Frames*, New York: Cambridge University Press.

Kirman, A. (2011), Learning in agent-based models. *Eastern Economic Journal*, 37(1), 20–27.

Kiyotaki, N. and Moore, J. (2002), Balance-sheet contagion. *American Economic Review* 85, 46–50.

Koo, R.C. (2009), *The Holy Grail of Macroeconomics: Lessons from Japan's Great Recession*, Hoboken, NJ: Wiley.

Koo, R.C. (2011), The world in balance sheet recession: causes, cure, and politics. *Real-World Economics Review*, 58, 19–37.

Kutschinski, E., Uthmann T. and Polani, D. (2003), Learning competitive pricing strategies by multiagent reinforcement learning. *Journal of Economic Dynamics and Control*, 27, 2207–2218.

LeBaron, B. (2006), Agent-based computational finance, in L. Tesfatsion and K.L. Judd (eds.), *Handbook of Computational Economics, Vol. 2: Agent-Based Computational Economics*, North-Holland/Elsevier, Amsterdam.

LeBaron, B. and Winker, P. (eds.) (2008), Agent-based models for economic policy advice. *Journal of Economics and Statistics*, special issue, 228.

Mannaro, K., Marchesi, M. and Setzu, A. (2008), Using an artificial financial market for assessing the impact of Tobin-like transaction taxes. *Journal of Economic Behavior & Organization*, 67, 445–462.

Minsky, H. (1986), *Stabilizing an Unstable Economy*, New Haven, CT: Yale University Press.

Myers, S. and Majluf, N. (1984), Corporate financing and investment decisions when firms have information that investors do not have. *Journal of Financial Economics* 13, 187–221.

Pellizzari, P. and Westeroff, F. (2009), Some effects of transaction taxes under different microstructures. *Journal of Economic Behavior & Organization*, 72, 850–863.

Plott, C. (1982), Industrial organization theory and experimental economics. *Journal of Economic Literature*, 20, 1485–1527.

Raberto, M., Teglio, A. and Cincotti, S. (2008), Prospect theory behavioral assumptions in an artificial financial economy, *Lecture Notes in Economics and Mathematical Systems*, vol. 614, New York: Springer, 55–66.

Raberto, M., Teglio, A. and Cincotti, S. (2012), Debt, deleveraging and business cycles: an agent-based perspective. *Economics – The Open-Access, Open-Assessment E-Journal*, 6(27), n.p.

Russo, A., Catalano, M., Gallegati, M., Gaffeo, E. and Napoletano, M. (2007), Industrial dynamics, fiscal policy and R&D: evidence from a computational experiment. *Journal of Economic Behavior and Organization*, 64, 426–447.

Smets, F.,Wouters, R. and Europeo, B.C. (2002), *An Estimated Stochastic Dynamic General Equilibrium Model of the Euro Area*, Brussels: European Central Bank.

Stiglitz, J.E. and Weiss, A. (1981), Credit rationing in markets with imperfect information. *American Economic Review*, 71, 393–410.

Tassier, T. and Menczer, F. (2001), Emerging small-world referral networks in evolutionary labor markets. *IEEE Transactions on Evolutionary Computation*, 5, 482–492.

Teglio, A., Raberto, M. and Cincotti, S. (2009), Explaining equity excess return by means of an agent-based financial market, Lecture Notes in Economics and Mathematical Systems, vol. 631, New York: Springer, ch. 12, 145–156.

Teglio, A., Raberto, M. and Cincotti, S. (2012), The impact of banks' capital adequacy regulation on the economic system: an agent-based approach. *Advances in Complex Systems*, 15(2): n.p.

Tesfatsion, L. and Judd, K. (2006), *Handbook of Computational Economics, Vol. 2: Agent-Based Computational Economics*, Amsterdam: Elsevier.

Trichet, J.-C. (2010), Reflections on the nature of monetary policy non-standard measures and finance theory. Opening address at the ECB Central Banking Conference in Frankfurt, 18 November 2010. Available at: www.ecb.int/press/key/date/2010/html/sp101118.en.html (accessed 23 November 2013).

Ussher, L. (2008), A speculative futures market with zero-intelligence. *Eastern Economics Journal*, 34, 518–549.

Wolf, M. (2012) Why is the eurozone different? Part 3. *Financial Times*, 23 May.

Part III

Competitiveness and sustainability in time of crisis

10 Leading factors for catching-up by developing economies
Conclusions from the time of crisis

Tomasz Geodecki

1 Invention, innovation and entrepreneurship in J.A. Schumpeter's theory

The perception of innovation as an activity that, in principle, consists of the implementation in economic practice of new inventions must have had a long tradition, since in 1911 J.A. Schumpeter (1960) attempted to prove that equating innovation with invention was unjustified. He introduced the distinction between the concepts of invention (inventiveness) and innovation. If an invention has not found its application in business practice, it has no economic significance, regardless of its potential (Schumpeter 1960, p. 141). Innovation is thus a broader phenomenon that may include invention, though it does not constitute its prerequisite, while identifying one with the other plays down the fundamental role that, in Schumpeter's view, innovations play in the process of economic growth (Schumpeter 1939, p. 85). Entrepreneurs motivated by future profits use both new and already existing knowledge in order to introduce innovation which, as defined by Schumpeter in his *Business Cycles*, means a shift in the production function without the increase in the amount of labour and capital, i.e. a change that makes it possible to combine these factors more effectively.[1]

Innovations also have a decisive impact on the occurrence of business cycles, and these phenomena tend to be treated as inseparable. An economic boom consists of the creation of new purchasing power by financing the acquisition of resources in order to start new production using credit lines. As soon as a newly developed product appears on the market, prices increase in the entire economy more slowly because of increased supply as pioneers begin to pay off their debts. Its inevitable consequence, once a critical point has been reached through reduced demand, is depression. For innovations in Schumpeter's sense, the period of depression constitutes a process of resorption and liquidation of innovator's profit (1960, p. 375). However, at the same time, a new development phase is initiated, since economic processes are now carried out by entrepreneurs in a more economical manner. Older, less effective methods and means of production or products are eliminated, owing to the increased costs borne by old enterprises during a boom, followed by the elimination of their income, since at this stage consumer demand is directed at the newly developed products.

This chapter draws on all three of Schumpeter's concepts: first, his clear distinction between research-and-development (R&D) activities and broadly conceived innovation activities, of which R&D constitute only one part. This distinction helps to explain why technical change occurs not only in highly developed countries, but is also a feature of economies trying to bridge the development gap. Second, this is linked with the postulate that innovation in an economy should be measured using parameters of economic effects, not, for example, R&D expenditure. Recognising the factors that contribute to different economic growth rates and improving labour productivity in highly developed and less developed countries (LDCs) is a factor of special importance for policies oriented towards long-term economic growth. Third, the analysed determinants of labour productivity include the influence of public institutions on entrepreneurs' profit construed in two ways – as the extent of entrepreneurs' control over profit, which, according to Schumpeter's intuition (1960, p. 24) has a key significance for his motivation, and hence his inclination to pursue innovation, as well as 'legislative, administrative and legal practice' (Schumpeter 1995, p. 193) that influences the likelihood of companies achieving their economic objectives.

2 R&D activity as the basis for innovation: implications for measuring innovation

The idea of describing macroeconomic impacts of innovation by shifting the function of production once the influence of changes in amount of factors of production has been deducted was used, among others, by Solow, who in this way estimated the share of technical change in GDP. However, although it has a crucial impact on increased productivity of factors of production and constitutes the main growth factor, technical progress in Solow's model is treated as something external with respect to the model – it is neither explained, nor is it subject to shaping by economic policy. Consequently, as D. Romer claims, 'the pattern of the variable identified as the driving force of growth – constitutes input data in the model' (D. Romer 2000, p. 43).[2] This observation, combined with the convergence hypothesis contested by a number of researchers, became one of the reasons behind the search for the causes of different economic growth rates in various countries.

The 1950s and 1960s saw a more comprehensive analysis of R&D activity as the main 'contribution' to innovation. The question of why they became a matter of interest was indirectly answered by Blaug, who finds fault with traditional theories in that they 'limited themselves to innovation rather than invention' (Blaug 2000, p. 484). In such an approach, entrepreneurs choose a given solution from the register of available inventions to achieve their own innovation; however, the way in which such a register is developed and new inventions are added

> is an issue that was always handed over to economic historians and industrial sociologists. But an analysis of the rate at which techniques improve in

an economy cannot really ignore the pace and scope of inventive activity. Economists, however, have rarely addressed themselves to the analysis of what Kaldor has aptly called 'the degree of technical dynamism' in an economy. Instead, they have been almost exclusively concerned with the actual pattern of technical change in economies that are known to be technically dynamic.

(Ibid. pp. 484–485)

It may be assumed that the focus on reasons, conditions and outcomes of R&D activity constitutes a response to the absence of explanation of the qualitative factor responsible for more than 80 per cent productivity increase in Solow's model (1957). This move towards analysing invention contributed to the development in the 1960s of the Frascati methodology for collecting and analysing statistics on R&D activity of enterprises to facilitate their comparison internationally.

One of the implications of Solow's contribution (1956) is the hypothesis of convergence that stipulates faster development of poorer economies than richer ones based on the assumption of decreasing capital productivity as its resources increase. A critical look at Solow's model became the basis for the formulation in the 1980s of a new theory of economic growth, later called the endogenous growth theory. In P. Romer's model (1986), new knowledge is produced not only as a result of investment in research technologies, but also by the accumulation of knowledge resulting from increased material capital. According to Romer, the inclusion of this factor permits entrepreneurs to achieve non-diminishing returns to scale. As a result of the positive exogenous effect of spreading knowledge, one may observe increasing returns to scale in the entire economy.

Romer's model offers far-reaching insights into economic growth processes worldwide. Owing to increasing returns to scale, GDP may grow without limit. This may mean that convergence of per capita income will not occur, since rich economies can develop faster than the poorer ones. The implications for the economic policy are also important: it is possible to sustain increasing growth rates in an economy by improving its knowledge production rate, which can be achieved by increasing the resources of human capital and investment expenditure in the sphere of science and technology.

3 Non-linear models of the innovation process and their implications for research into innovation

The contemporary approach to the sources and nature of the innovation process, at least as conceived in the international methodology for research into innovation (the Oslo methodology), clearly indicates a considerably narrower sphere of R&D activity, as compared with innovation. This approach seems to draw on Schumpeter's achievements rather than clarify technological dynamism in terms of R&D.

The development of this approach resulted from research into the links among individual elements of the innovation process carried out, among others, by Mowery and Rosenberg (1979) and Kline and Rosenberg (1986), who underscore limited usefulness of previous linear models of the innovation process, in which market demand, invention and innovation succeeded one another in more or less clearly delineated chronological stages.

In this perspective, R&D is not so much a basic source of ideas for innovation, but rather a form of problem solving, which can be consulted at every stage of the innovation process. Research activity becomes an additional, not always indispensable element, because the knowledge necessary for effective implementation of innovation is dispersed throughout the enterprise.

Indirect indicators of innovation based on R&D activity turned out to be insufficient, because, as the authors of the Oslo Manual remarked:

> First, R&D is an input. Although it is obviously related to technical change, it does not measure it. Second, R&D does not encompass all the efforts of companies and governments in this area, as there are other sources of technical change… which escape this narrow definition.
>
> (OECD and Eurostat 1999, p. 12)

Hence the later attempts to capture the variety of innovation (e.g. staff training, marketing research and, especially, the factors that facilitate the interactive learning process) in research based on the Oslo Manual as the Community Innovation Survey (CIS).

This research into innovation has confirmed, among other things, that expenditure on R&D constitutes a very important, but only a part of expenditure on innovation. A significant proportion of this expenditure comprises purchases of capital assets, especially machinery and equipment. Figure 10.1, based on CIS findings of 2010, corroborates the observation that expenditure on machinery and equipment constitutes a significant group of outlays on innovation.

What is especially striking is the difference between the technologically advanced countries and those that are trying to bridge the development gap. It may be explained by specialisation that consists of a division of labour that prevents enterprises from undertaking activities whose outcomes can be acquired from others in a more cost-effective manner. Hence entrepreneurs from the LDCs have a stronger incentive to acquire R&D results in the form of licences and advanced production equipment rather than undertake such activities themselves. Taking into account the concept of technology embodied in the purchased capital equipment, we can explain why the absence of R&D expenditure does not significantly discriminate against firms that do not undertake such activities in the LDCs (cf. Ahn and Hemmings 2000; Smith 2004). Besides, this allows us to observe that certain kinds of investment have a much greater impact on economic growth than others, especially in terms of capital assets (production equipment) (DeLong and Summers 1991, 1993). It is also clear that the impact of investment on capital assets is more pronounced in the LDCs. Their spending

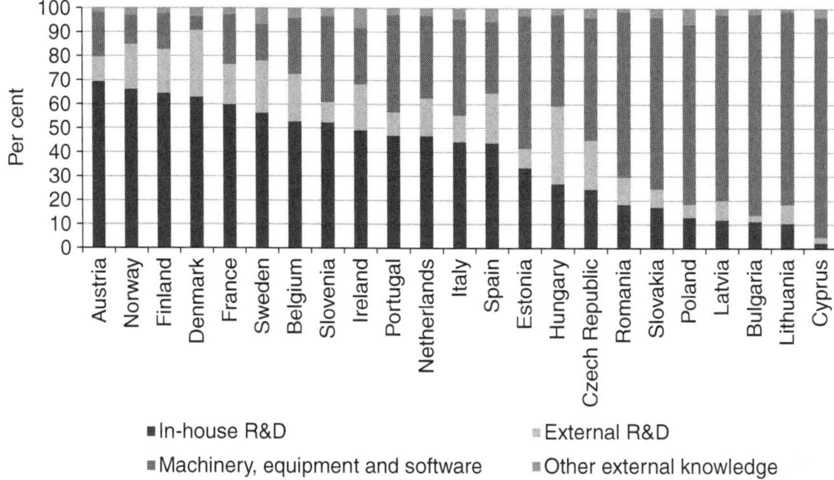

Figure 10.1 Share of individual categories of outlays in total expenditure on innovation of enterprises implementing product and process innovations in 2010 (source: author's own calculations based on Eurostat data (CIS)).

tends to be dominated by outlays on machines and equipment, which can be explained by the fact that they constitute a channel for technology transfer (Gomułka 1998; Ahn and Hemmings 2000). In wealthier countries, the transfer of non-material technology is more significant for the process of diffusion.

4 R&D activity and technology transfer in the convergence process

4.1 Knowledge transfer and quality of institutions as the factors enabling countries to bridge the development gap

In Barro and Sala-i-Martin's model (1997), although the worldwide growth rate is determined principally by inventions made in the technologically advanced countries (technological frontier areas – TFAs),[3] diffusion is a significant source of growth in the LDCs. After all, copying is usually less expensive than developing new technological knowledge, so most countries representing the latter group tend to imitate rather than invent. Moreover, fairly low costs of copying enable relatively backward countries to achieve higher growth rates than the leaders in the field, and thus gradually bridge the development gap (catch-up with the best).

As the catching-up process continues, the ratio of imitation costs to innovation costs increases due to the fact that innovation costs do not increase to scale, since it is assumed that the number of potential inventions is infinite, while the imitation costs increase, because as the number of copied and adapted solutions grows, their accessible pool shrinks, with the most effective solutions having been implemented at the very beginning. The cost of imitation gradually approaches the cost of developing the country's own technological solution. In this way, the catching-up countries, as long as their growth rate permits them to adopt more advanced solutions quickly enough, experience an ever-growing motivation to undertake their own research efforts, since imitation itself will not allow them to match the productivity level of the leader. At the same time, as the number of copied technologies grows, such spectacular increases in productivity are no longer possible.

This explanation appears to be attractive, but in accordance with the criticism levied against Solow's model, it does not by itself explain why technological knowledge flows into some countries while leaving out others, i.e. why only in certain countries the costs of innovation diminish with respect to the costs of imitation. For this reason, Barro and Sala-i-Martin supplement their model with the aspect of quality of institutional environment. Apart from the cost of innovation, an important factor that makes a difference in technological terms (measured by the number of available technological solutions) is also the level of economic effectiveness, which, in this approach, depends mainly on the institutions and the quality of public policies such as infrastructure, taxation, observance of property rights, rule of law, etc. One country may outdo another in the technological race, first of all thanks to improvements in the quality of its institutional environment. Thus, the cost of implementing new technological solutions is explained both in terms of relative backwardness and the quality of institutions.

4.2 Increased productivity of the factors of production as the basis for measuring the outcomes of innovation activities

The results of the above-referenced technological race are usually assessed with the aid of measuring the GDP growth ratio, or its derivatives.

Quite popular are analyses of factors that influence the Solow residual (TFP) as a technological factor, although a significant number of analysts of technical change seem to prefer labour productivity, which is not calculated as a residual and can be obtained directly using easily accessible data. In this way, errors that may appear during TFP estimation can be avoided. Similar conclusions concerning the usefulness of the labour productivity index are offered by Gomułka (2005), although at the same time he points to a certain difficulty related to isolating the influence of technological progress on economic growth from, for example, the influence of institutional changes or education, we do know the magnitude of the joint influence of all these factors. Accordingly, we should use this measure of 'innovation' or, more generally, 'qualitative change'.

4.3 Technological determinants of development duality in the world and of labour productivity convergence

This measure is worth adopting in the context of the rich and varied literature devoted to different models of innovation activity, in which the dynamics of the technological gap are explained in terms of the increasing labour productivity rate. An important work that combines the issues of catching-up processes as the result of technology transfer with the features of the institutional environment of an economy is the article by M. Abramovitz of 1986, in which he shows labour productivity convergence in 1870–1979 that occurred in a group of a dozen or so industrialised economies.

B. Verspagen (1991) offered an interesting explanation of the convergence process influenced by the development of a country's own potential and the use of foreign technology resources supported by empirical analysis. The starting point for his analysis is the observation that the sometimes adopted premise of automatic diffusion of technology is unrealistic. According to Verspagen the actual *catching-up phase* must be preceded by a vitally important phase of building the country's inherent capacity to absorb the know-how (Verspagen 1991, p. 366), consisting of an adequately developed educational system, infrastructure, etc. As a vast majority of those factors at least to some extent happens to be in the domain of public activities, it might be reasonably expected of a government to assume a clearly proactive role within the actual *pre-catching-up* phase.

In the *actual catching-up phase* by way of absorbing technological know-how from the TFAs a particular economy may well reduce the technological gap with the leaders without actually expanding much its own research infrastructure up to a certain point, whereupon this process would be bound to slow down perceptively. Full convergence does not therefore happen within the actual *catching-up phase* only. This may happen only when a particular catching-up economy has gone through yet another phase, called by Verspagen a *post-catching-up* phase, which occurs when their own research endeavours have reached such a level that they equalise with the research expenditure incurred by a technological leader.

A natural consequence of such a development model should therefore consist first and foremost of a higher propensity to invest in R&D, after a certain development phase has been attained; and second a consequence of the lack of absorptive powers in some LDCs is the distinct dualism of the world economy indicated by Gomułka (2006). One of its symptoms is the division into the rich (TFAs) and the less advanced ones (LDCs). Between these kinds of economies 'differences are so fundamental that it is necessary to apply two distinct theories of the economic growth' (Gomułka 2006, p. 5). The sources of technological progress in the technologically advanced countries are the size and the growth rate of the domestic R&D sector and innovation activity.[4] In the LDCs, growth acceleration is influenced to a greater extent by such factors as institutions, economic policy and the formation of human capital, which collectively determine its absorptive power (among others, the propensity to save and invest in machinery, existing technologies and the inflow of foreign investment).

This assumption is reflected in numerous empirical analyses. For example, in the Global Competitiveness Report, it was determined on the basis of econometric analysis of productivity determinants that depending on the actual extent of advancement of a particular economy, the respective components of a country's overall potential determine differently its overall competitiveness. The countries classified in the ranking were split-up into the three groups in which competitiveness was determined by similar factors, although of different intensity. For the development of factor-driven economies it is vital to comply with the basic requirements, e.g. basic infrastructure, efficient public institutions, proper macroeconomic environment and education. In the case of the efficiency-driven economies, economic benefits are being achieved to the largest extent through making use of the efficiency-enhancing factors (efficiency enhancers), e.g. higher education and training, efficiency of goods, labour and financial markets, technological readiness and market size. In the innovation-driven economies development is determined by innovation and sophistication factors, and also to a much larger extent than in the countries of lower GDP per capita.

5 Hypotheses concerning innovation factors and a model for their verification

In the LDCs the most important questions arising from such an approach to the dynamics of development of the catching-up countries appear to be those that underlie the formulation of hypotheses that (1) labour productivity convergence factors in both groups are different – in TFAs they are determined by the R&D expenditure, which, in the LDCs does not influence the dependent variable, while in the latter group, technological change tends to be influenced by technology transfer; and (2) the role of complementary factors with respect to material investment, which include the absorbed technologies, is more noticeable in the LDCs than in the TFA countries.

In order to verify these hypotheses, the parameters in the labour productivity growth rate equation were estimated, taking into account the above-referenced factors that influence technological change. The model was based on Gomułka's proposal (2006), which was modified to a certain extent:

$$\Delta \ln \frac{Y}{L} = \beta_1 \frac{\Delta T}{T} + \beta_2 \frac{\Delta TRu}{TRu} + \beta_3 \frac{\Delta TRn}{TRn} + \beta_4 \frac{\Delta H}{H} + \beta_5 \frac{\Delta IN}{IN} + \beta_6 \frac{\Delta P}{P} + \beta_7 \frac{\Delta \frac{K}{Y}}{\frac{K}{Y}}.$$

(1)

In this approach, labour productivity growth per man-hour is influenced by the growth rates of the qualitative factors: R&D investment (T), transfer of technology embodied in machines (TRu) and technologies acquired in a non-embodied form (TRn), human capital (H), institutional order (IN) and appropriate economic policy (P), as well as the increase of capital resources in the economy with respect to the product (K/Y). Information concerning the design of variables used in the analysis is provided in the Appendix.

At the same time, we need to bear in mind that the assumption concerning constant returns on the factors of production could be wrong. Besides, we may be facing technological progress in Hicks-neutral technical change, that is, increased labour and capital productivity to a similar extent; consequently, the assumption about the constant K/Y ratio does not hold. Inclusion of these modifications (see Tokarski 2005, p. 138) results in the following adjustment to the formula:

$$\Delta \ln \frac{Y}{L} = \beta_1 \frac{\Delta T}{T} + \beta_2 \frac{\Delta TRu}{TRu} + \beta_3 \frac{\Delta TRn}{TRn} + \beta_4 \frac{\Delta H}{H} + \beta_5 \frac{\Delta IN}{IN} + \beta_6 \frac{\Delta P}{P} + \beta_7 \frac{\Delta \frac{K}{L}}{\frac{K}{L}}$$

$$+ \beta_8 \frac{\Delta L}{L}. \tag{2}$$

This means that, apart from the factors determining TFP growth, i.e. technological progress in Hicks' sense, all increase in labour productivity is also influenced by an increased K/L ratio (K/L) and production flexibility in relation to capital ($\beta_7 = \alpha$). It also depends on the growth in the number of workers (or hours worked) and on the extent of homogeneity of the production function θ, where $\beta_8 = \theta - 1$.

The data collected can be used to analyse selected economies from 1999 to 2005, i.e. involving a seven-year period. The selection was made on the grounds of data availability and includes a group of 28 countries – 15 TFAs and 13 LDCs, for which the available data reflect the entire time frame in question, 1999–2005. The analysis of diversity in innovation factors requires that these economies should be assigned to one of these two groups.[5] The classification was based on labour productivity levels (both US$ per hour and per person employed). They were subsequently divided on the basis of patenting intensity (supporting criterion).

In order to compare the actual impact of the same variables in the times of economic crisis, the 2006–10 period was also taken under consideration and subjected to an analysis. Singling out this particular period was well warranted by the fact that already in 2006 a clear slow-down was observed with regard to certain types of business activities, apparently in anticipation of the *bona fide* economic slow-down following 2007. The R^2 values seemed to imply, though, that the period under analysis should be reduced to the years 2007–10, despite offering a smaller body of data. This in turn might well imply that this particular period, covering the actual crisis years, was characterised by certain specifics, and therefore the years following 2007 should be taken under consideration separately, so as to ensure full viability of the adopted models.

It should also be noted at this point that the list of countries under analysis was altered in the wake of the realisation that South Korea in the new period complied with the two out of three eligibility criteria for the TFA group of countries. Availability of data made it possible to include Bulgaria and Romania in the analysis in the second period, although at the same time it effectively precluded the inclusion of Mexico.

6 Analysis of determinants of increase in labour productivity

6.1 Investment in knowledge creation vs knowledge transfer in technical change in 1999–2005

The basic difference between the models of innovation processes in both analysed groups of countries appears to be rooted in the role played in them by knowledge production and technology transfer. In the initial models (1L and 1T) three main variables were analysed: (1) knowledge resources accumulated as a result of the R&D outlays of companies; (2) the capital stock resulting from the resources invested in machinery and equipment, and (3) increase in assets spent on purchasing foreign licences and royalties. As in order to achieve the capital growth the investment rates are occasionally used as a proxy,[6] thus offering a viable alternative, it was analysed how the labour productivity growth rate was influenced not by the increased resources, but by the share in GDP of individual kinds of investment connected with technology production and transfer (*lnBERD/GDP, M&E/GDP, R&LF/imp*) (models 2L and 2T, 3L and 3T). Further analysis involved models that included this modification, because they were considerably better adjusted to the variables, which is supported by the coefficients of determination R^2. This feature is also characteristic of the less restrictive models, in which constant returns to scale were not assumed, but included the increased technical *K/L* ratio (*r K/L*) (3L and 3T).

In the LDCs we can perceive (Table 10.1) a strong positive and statistically significant correlation of increase in labour productivity and investment in machinery and equipment (*M&E/GDP*) (similar results were obtained by DeLong and Summers 1993). In the developed countries, this relationship is different. The higher the increase in the labour productivity rate, the lower the investment in production facilities. The opposite is the case with R&D investment. Here we note a strong and statistically significant negative correlation of BERD investment (*lnBERD/GDP*) and productivity growth in the LDCs, whereas in the TFAs the relationship is clear and positive.[7] In both groups, a relatively weaker positive correlation of licence fees (*R&LF/imp*) and the dependent variable is perceived, yet this relationship in the LDCs is not statistically significant, whereas in the TFAs it is statistically significant, but negative.

As far as the R&D expenditure is concerned, the observed results appear to confirm the hypothesis that increased innovativeness of the TFA countries is to a considerable extent due to the R&D expenditure, whereas in the LDCs it has little to do with growth. Quite possibly, the negative relationship perceived in the LDCs does not mean causality, i.e. more R&D spending is unlikely to adversely affect growth. The LDCs are less active in terms of research due to the so-called backwardness rent. In an attempt to catch-up, enterprises in the LDCs improve the efficiency of their operations by way of technology transfer embodied in machines, whereas such a transfer plays a considerably smaller role in the innovation growth in the developed economies. Characteristically, the countries which have achieved the greatest increases in efficiency are those where the joint

Table 10.1 Models including investment variables in knowledge production and transfer and with Hicks' and Harrod's technical progress in 1999–2005

Labour productivity growth rate	LDC	TFA	LDC	TFA	LDC	TFA
	1L LSM FE	*1T LSM FE*	*2L LSM PW*	*2T LSM FE*	*3L LSM PW*	*3T LSM FE*
Constant	3.505*** (0.267)	1.884*** (0.176)	−17.614*** (2.808)	8.404*** (1.598)	−17.46*** (2.516)	12.265*** (1.760)
r lnBERDstock Increase in business R&D capital	0.062 (0.076)	0.334 (0.479)	–	–	–	–
r M&Estock Increase in machinery and equipment capital	0.138 (0.126)	−0.096 (0.093)				
r R&LFstock Increase in knowledge stock purchased from abroad	0.041* (0.021)	0.071* (0.033)	–	–	–	–
r TertAtt1y Increase in higher education rate	0.022 (0.032)	−0.010 (0.020)	–	–	–	–
lnBERD/GDP Share of business R&D investment in GDP	–	–	−0.961*** (0.209)	0.216 (0.620)	−0.862*** (0.216)	2.057** (0.797)
M&E/GDP Share of investment in machinery and equipment in GDP	–	–	0.363*** (0.083)	0.026 (0.103)	0.333*** (0.080)	−0.278** (0.119)
R&LF/imp Share of licence and royalty payments in imports	–	–	0.016 (0.047)	−0.207** (0.080)	−0.035 (0.071)	−0.197** (0.080)
SchExpect1y School expectancy	–	–	1.126*** (0.139)	−0.301*** (0.082)	1.165*** (0.126)	−0.435*** (0.080)
r GERQRL Improvement in institutional indicators	0.224 (0.125)	−0.018 (0.069)	0.273*** (0.088)	0.041 (0.061)	0.315*** (0.081)	0.088 (0.060)
r GovExpend Increase in public expenditure in GDP	−0.050 (0.051)	−0.081* (0.048)	−0.109*** (0.035)	−0.024 (0.044)	−0.098*** (0.034)	−0.115*** (0.037)
r K/Y Increase in capital resources in GDP	–	–	−0.027 (0.046)	−0.285 (0.076)	–	–
r K/L Increase in *K/L* ratio	−0.002 (0.031)	0.025* (0.014)	–	–	0.011 (0.017)	0.021* (0.011)
r L Increase in man-hours	−0.008 (0.032)	0.009 (0.015)	–	–	−0.032 (0.022)	−0.021 (0.013)
R^2	0.80	0.79	0.83	0.84	0.85	0.85
Adjusted R^2	0.74	0.73	–	0.80	–	0.81
Number of observations/samples	84	105	84	105	84	105

Notes
Standard errors of estimates are given in parentheses. Levels of statistical significance of regression parameters (p) are marked as follows: *<10%, **<5%, ***<1%.
For explanation of acronyms LSM FE and LSM PW, see the Appendix.

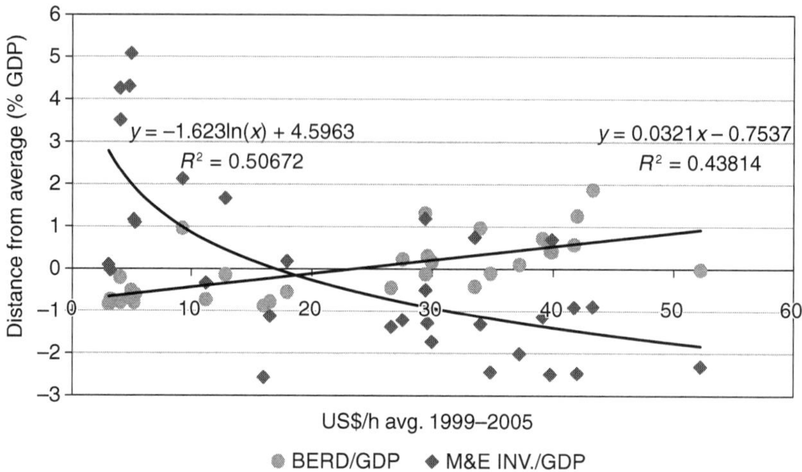

Figure 10.2 R&D intensity of enterprises and investment in machinery and equipment vs the productivity level in LDCs and TFAs collectively (average for 1999–2005) (source: OECD and Eurostat database).

share of all the above-referenced categories of spending on knowledge both in the LDCs and the TFA is the highest.

These observations can be interpreted to corroborate Verspagen's theory: in order to be able to develop more rapidly and to catch up with the best-developed economies, the LDCs must rely on knowledge transfer. However, in order to be able to increase relative productivity in the leading group, the economies must close the technological distance to the leader, which entails considerable R&D expenditure. Consequently, as was observed by Barro and Sala-i-Martin (1997), it seems that technology transfer and domestic inventiveness have a substitutive nature, while the volume of spending on R&D and machines depends on the development level of a particular economy (cf. Figure 10.2). As a result, innovation efforts of companies from poorer Central European countries do not differ significantly from the European average, but their structure is different.

6.2 Complementary factors to the investment in knowledge production and technology transfer

Since the variables of human capital, public R&D spending, institutional environment and economic policy, apart from their correlation with the dependent variable, also demonstrate a significant relationship with the variables adopted as the measures of knowledge production and transfer (cf. Table 10.2), they can be called technological change support factors (cf., e.g. Benhabib and Spiegel (1994) on the influence of human capital on technology transfer; Olson (1996), Verspagen (1991), Bassanini and Scarpetta (2001) on the interaction and impact of institutional environment with public expenditure on total investment and, in particular, on capital investment in equipment and R&D).

The analysis of estimated regression parameters of equation (2) reveals the absence of a statistically significant correlation between the labour force growth rate and higher education (*r TertAtt*) with changes in labour productivity. Alternatively, drawing on Benhabib and Spiegel's (1994) conclusions, instead of the increase in the educational status of population of economically productive age, we can use the expected duration of the entire process of education (*SchExpect* – models 2 and 3) construing this variable as a proxy for the influx of human capital into a particular economy. Now, school expectancy has a definitely stronger relationship with the dependent variable. There is a strong positive and statistically significant impact of the total duration of education on the LDCs' productivity. In the TFAs, however, the relationship is reverse – observations, for which the length of education indicators were higher, were characterised by lower increases in labour productivity.

The share of public R&D expenditure does not correlate directly with the labour productivity growth. Its likely positive influence may be revealed by stimulating research in enterprises, which is supported by the correlation of these categories (cf. Table 10.2). The impact comes to light first of all in the relationship with the formation of human capital, because a large part of the variable in question involves research undertaken by higher education institutions.

The impact of quality of public institutions on innovation in the period under review highlights yet another difference between the LDCs and the TFA countries. In the former ones, the estimated parameter value for the combined institutional variable (*r GERQRL*) shows statistical significance. In the TFAs, the impact of improvements in the quality of the institutional environment on growth was generally smaller and statistically insignificant (cf. Table 10.1).

Table 10.2 Linear correlation coefficients for investment in knowledge production and transfer in LDC and TFA economies, 1999–2005

	lnBERD/GDP	lnPubERD/GDP	M&E/GDP
LDC			
SchExpect	0.47***	0.69***	0.13
lnPubERD/GDP	0.56***	–	0.09
r RL	–0.20*	–0.23**	0.35***
r GovExpend	0.18	0.11	–0.22*
TFA			
SchExpect	–0.12	0.14	–0.00
ln PubERD/GDP	0.58***	–	–0.07
rRL	0.19*	0.16	–0.12
r GovExpend	0.06	0.06	–0.22**

Source: author's own analysis.

Notes
* statistically significant at 0.1, ** at 0.05, *** at 0.01.

As far as the impact of economic policy on labour productivity growth rate in the LDCs is concerned, the basic variable, i.e. the increase in public expenditure with respect to GDP (*r GovExpend*)[8] in model 3 shows a similar relationship with innovation in the LDCs and in the TFAs, both in terms of statistical power and significance.

6.3 Investment in innovation in 2007–10

In the years 2007–10, the key characteristics of the presented models were subjected to slight alterations. First, in the LDCs no negative correlation was observed between business expenditures in R&D (BERD) and the dependent variable, whereas in all the adopted models the regression coefficients for BERD were positive. In the TFA group of countries the impact of BERD on the increase of productivity was also positive as a rule, but much more appreciable and statistically significant.

This implies that in the case of those observations which were accompanied by lower labour productivity ratios, in both groups of countries under review this was also accompanied by smaller investments in the R&D activities. It should be noted at this juncture that although the economic crisis affected business innovation expenditure in both groups of countries, not all the countries experienced the attendant economic slow-down to the same extent. Duality of development mechanisms manifested itself in particular in this regard: in the LDCs (Czech Republic, Lithuania, Latvia, Slovakia), following a transient fall or a slow-down in the BERD investment (in relation to GDP), there was a rapid increase in the R&D investment, as compared to 2007. Unlike in the TFA countries – apart from Ireland, Italy and South Korea – the increase in R&D expenditure in relation to GDP was expressed by a single digit, whereas in 2010 in five countries relative BERD was lower than in 2007. In the period spanning 2007–10 the actual share of BERD in GDP grew in the LDCs by almost one-third, whereas in the TFA countries it was by 4 per cent (cf. Table 10.4).

It is quite interesting to make a comparison between the R&D investments and the expenditure incurred through the purchases of plant and machinery that stand for technological transfer. Very much like in the previous period under review, those investments exerted positive impact on the labour productivity growth rate. However, both in the case of LDCs and the TFA countries the share of actual investment in machinery and equipment in the GDP diminished significantly, although in the case of the TFA countries only by 15 per cent, whereas in the LDCs by as much as one-third (cf. Table 10.5).

Even a perfunctory look gives ample grounds for making a few observations on the nature of investments in the times of crisis.

- R&D expenditure seems to be far more resistant to an economic crisis than other types of investment, especially those in plant and machinery, which seem to be more responsive to the economic cycles. Since the R&D investments require a long-term approach and sustained protection of the research

Table 10.3 Models including investment variables in knowledge production and transfer and with Hicks' and Harrod's technical progress, 2007–10

Labour productivity growth rate	LDC	TFA	LDC	TFA	LDC	TFA
	4L LSM FE	4T LSM FE	5L LSM FE	5T LSM FE	6L LSM FE	6T LSM FE
Constant	2.610	0.506	2.808	−17.236	−12.402	13.184
	(2.216)	(1.417)	(18.185)	(21.227)	(17.835)	(23.259)
r lnBERDstock	3.037	18.946***	–	–	–	–
Increase in business R&D capital	(2.835)	(5.819)				
r M&Estock	0.243	−0.712*	–	–	–	–
Increase in machinery and equipment capital	(0.457)	(0.365)				
r R&LFstock	−0.044	−0.019	–	–	–	–
Increase in knowledge stock purchased from abroad	(0.046)	(0.014)				
r TertAtt1y	−0.066	−0.029	–	–	–	–
Increase in higher education rate	(0.174)	(0.099)				
lnBERD/GDP	–	–	2.570	7.945*	6.256*	−0.615
Share of business R&D in GDP			(3.295)	(4.118)	(3.086)	(4.655)
M&E/GDP	–	–	0.232	−1.013***	1.459***	0.174
Share of investment in machinery and equipment in GDP			(0.276)	(0.368)	(0.399)	(0.485)
R&LF/imp	–	–	−0.423	0.154	−0.001	0.051
Share of licence and royalty payments in imports			(0.565)	(0.135)	(0.568)	(0.140)
SchExpect	–	–	−0.562	−0.816	−1.197	−0.436
School expectancy			(0.880)	(0.803)	(0.856)	(0.821)
r GERQRL	−0.263	−0.174*	−0.394*	−0.174	−0.249	−0.179
Improvement in institutional indicators	(0.271)	(0.102)	(0.225)	(0.111)	(0.229)	(0.112)
r GovExpend						
Increase in public expenditure in GDP	−0.263***	−0.296***	−0.073	−0.166***	−0.302***	−0.280***
	(0.090)	(0.040)	(0.086)	(0.046)	(0.069)	(0.038)
r K/Y						
Increase in capital in GDP	—	—	−0.236**	−0.253***	–	–
			(0.101)	(0.071)		
r K/L						
Increase in capital/labour ratio	−0.047	−0.505	–	–	−0.196	−1.311***
	(0.506)	(0.335)			(0.229)	(0.372)
r L						
Increase in man-hours	−0.093	−0.862**	–	–	−0.686*	−0.969***
	(0.627)	(0.345)			(0.357)	(0.296)
R^2	0.52	0.82	0.65	0.77	0.67	0.77
Adjusted R^2	0.21	0.71	0.45	0.64	0.46	0.63
Number of observations/samples	52	64	52	64	52	64

Notes
Standard errors of estimates are given in parentheses. Levels of statistical significance of regression parameters (p) are marked as follows: *<10%, **<5%, ***<1%.

Table 10.4 Unweighted averages of business expenditures on R&D/GDPs ratios (2007 = 100)

	2004	2005	2006	2007	2008	2009	2010
LDC average	89	93	107	100	102	110	131
TFA average	95	97	99	100	104	105	104

Source: author's own analysis.

Table 10.5 Unweighted averages of machinery and equipment investments/GDPs ratios (2007 = 100)

	2004	2005	2006	2007	2008	2009	2010
LDC average	91	94	95	100	94	70	67
TFA average	97	98	98	100	98	85	85

Source: author's own analysis.

> teams, business ventures tend to be rather unwilling to introduce any drastic cutbacks in this regard (cf. Hall 2011; OECD 2012).

- Although initially the LDCs experienced a slight fall in the R&D expenditure, in the period 2006–10 their share in GDP on average actually increased. On the one hand, this might be attributable to the demise of older, less innovative business ventures, whose resources and assets may still be utilised by the innovators in the expansion of their own enterprises, much in line with the creative destruction approach. Admittedly, the reduction of GDP in some LDCs reached almost the 10 per cent mark.
- An increase of BERD in both groups of countries was accompanied by a reduced propensity to invest in fixed assets, although in the LDCs the dynamics of attendant changes was much more appreciable. It is believed that in line with the above-referenced mechanism the expenditure incurred through the creation of know-how and its subsequent transfer in the form of purchased plant and machinery are partly of a substitutive character.

The impact of complementary factors in relation to the investments in the know-how in the years of crisis was demonstrably different than in 1999–2005. In the TFA countries group the countries boasting by far the highest educational capacity experienced a smaller growth in labour productivity, which might well imply that very much like in the case of fixed assets, the human capital may also be susceptible to decreasing marginal productivity. Furthermore, in the face of difficulties on the labour market a certain proportion of the young people tends to keep on studying, which may in turn cause pertinent educational indicators to 'improve' appreciably in times of economic downturn.

Among the LDCs economic slow-down affected all countries regardless of their respective educational standards, but also the most affluent ones boasted the longest educational cycles. Greece, Portugal and Slovenia were affected to a much larger extent. This resulted in the negative correlation of this variable with the dependent variable, but a positive one with the R&D expenditure, be that in the private or public sector. As far as an institutional variable was concerned, its growth was weakly correlated with an increase in labour productivity with regard to both groups of countries, which in the case of the LDCs makes a clear difference in comparison to the period actually preceding the crisis.

With regard to the government expenditure, the regression coefficients were statistically significant and negatively correlated with the dependent variable, with hardly any exceptions. A closer look would allow appreciation that this particular variable should by no means be construed exclusively as a proxy for facilitating the entrepreneurs' control over the profits. In modern economies government expenditure, as the one more rigidly structured than in the private sector, has a stabilising function and therefore its share in the GDP automatically goes up in times of economic slow-down or during a recession. The years within the period spanning 2007–10, in which labour productivity was acknowledged to fall, were characterised by a dynamic increase of government spending within the GDP.

Certain interpretative difficulties seem to consist of the fact that in both periods under study there was a clear convergence of GDP per man-hour and per person employed. The fading-out of the respective development patterns in the period spanning 2007–10 may not necessarily be due to the impact of the economic crisis and creative destruction only, but may well result from certain countries having reached such a GDP level, whereupon in order to achieve any further increase in overall efficiency it is necessary to compete in the actual quality and innovativeness of the products. A competitive edge through lower manufacturing costs no longer works in view of growing wages.

If we were to apply the classification of countries in line with the Global Competitiveness Report (GCR) (Schwab 2012), as many as eight out of 13 countries, as originally allocated to the LDC group back in 1999–2005, in the period spanning 2005–10 found their way to the innovation-driven economies group. As may be gleaned from the GCR analyses, different growth factors exert different impacts throughout the successive development stages; therefore those components of economic environment that are pivotal for the investments in the fixed assets may gradually lose significance to the benefit of those actually supporting the R&D expenditure. This assertion may be further corroborated by the fact that the LDC economies that had been allocated the innovation-driven status the earliest, i.e. the ones boasting in excess of US$17,000 per capita income, are in fact the very same ones in which the R&D expenditure reached the highest level (Figure 10.3).

If those economies effectively converged in terms of the actual growth factors to those of the TFA countries, then a weaker correlation of the factors complementary to the investments facilitating effective absorption of outsourced technologies, and a stronger one of those supporting the R&D investments should come as no surprise. It is for this very reason that a transition of a

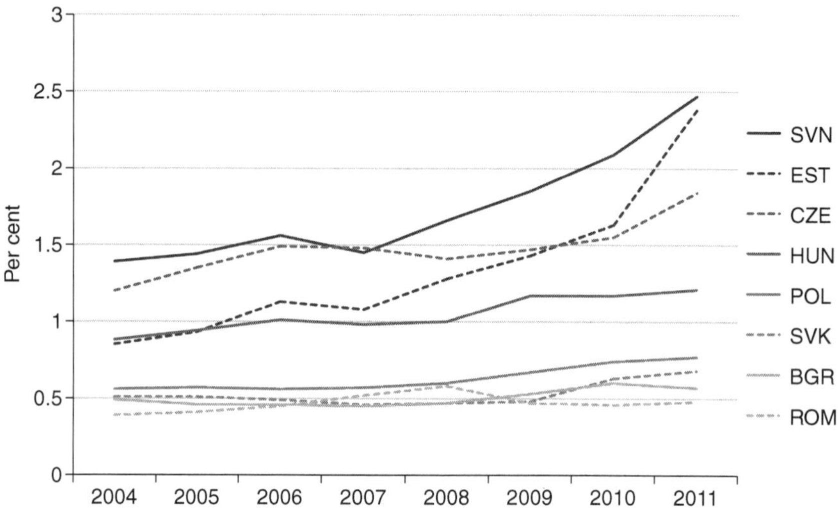

Figure 10.3 Gross expenditures on R&D relative to GDP in LDCs, 2004–11 (source: Eurostat database).

particular economy from one to another development phase should prompt the redefining of key objectives of a country's economic policy. This is not to say, however, that any deficits in terms of basic factors should be ignored. Despite the fact that institutional variables and government expenditure, irrespective of their actual level and growth, do not correlate directly with the labour productivity growth rate, their level significantly impacts the propensity to increase R&D expenditure (Table 10.6).

Rule of law and government expenditure were statistically significantly positively correlated with the R&D in the LDCs, but government effectiveness shows significant association with the outlays on research in both groups of countries. Since both in the TFA and the LDCs the economies of the lower GDP per hour levels were characterised by the higher spending on the technology transfer (*M&E*), better structured, more efficient institutions and higher public expenditure, typical for affluent countries, were negatively correlated with the expenditure incurred for machinery and equipment.

6.4 Conclusions and recommendations for further research

The evidence discussed above confirms the hypothesis that the labour productivity growth rate positively correlates with R&D spending in TFA investment, while in the LDCs it is rather the investment in machinery and equipment that determines the higher labour productivity growth rate. The LDCs with appropriate social infrastructure owe their rapid development to possibilities for technology transfer greater than in the TFA, which may constitute a major factor

Table 10.6 Linear correlation coefficients for investment in knowledge production and transfer in LDC and TFA economies, 2007–10

	lnBERD/GDP	lnPubERD/GDP	M&E/GDP
LDC (*N*=52)			
RL	**0.42***	**0.38***	**−0.42***
RQ	0.15	0.13	−0.25*
GE	**0.36***	0.31**	**−0.40***
GovExp	0.28**	0.25*	**−0.49***
TFA (*N*=64)			
RL	0.17	0.18	**−0.42***
RQ	−0.15	−0.14	**−0.45***
GE	0.30**	0.31**	−0.23*
GovExp	−0.10	−0.09	**−0.54***

Source: author's own analysis.

Notes
* statistically significant at 0.1, ** at 0.05, *** at 0.01 (in bold print).

behind the improved efficiency of their economies. Therefore, a further improvement in those components of social potential that promote the use of knowledge for economic ends by way of investment in new production methods (for companies) is of key significance, if these countries are to maintain powerful incentives to invest and promote entrepreneurial attitudes.

In times of crisis one could notice transient stagnation in the R&D expenditure in both groups of countries, even though they are commonly acknowledged to be far more resistant to an economic crisis than other types of investment. On the other hand, however, in 2007–10 the LDCs experienced a significant growth in the R&D expenditure. This was accompanied by a lesser propensity to invest in the fixed assets. Alteration of investment patterns in the LDCs may be of a more sustainable character, however. As convergence in GDP progresses, the successive LDCs join the TFA group. The first one to join the club was South Korea, although there are a number of other countries that already boast systematic growth in terms of R&D activities. This assertion may well be corroborated by the results yielded by the regression analysis which demonstrate the fading-out of the differences between the TFA and LDCs in terms of the actual impact of diverse factors upon the labour productivity growth rate. In general, it appears that irrespective of their level of economic development, the countries which were able to guarantee their own systems of innovation, an appropriate institutional environment and conditions conducive to improved education of their societies at large were characterised by considerable investment in technology production and transfer, as well as the quick pace of closing the technology gap measured in terms of the GDP growth rate per man-hour.

In times of crisis the economic geography of the world keeps on changing at a very rapid rate. Western countries demonstrably lose their share in the world GDP and exports, to the benefit of emergent economies. It is for this reason that the actual catching-up mechanisms merit confirmation. Future investigators should make all due allowances for the implications of the analyses comprised in the GCR, conducted on an annual basis, in line with the method put forward by Sala-I-Martin, according to which certain countries allocated to the LDC group should actually be regarded as within the TFA group. On the other hand, the LDC group should be duly augmented with the slightly less affluent countries from Latin America, Asia and Northern Africa. This would in turn require access to appreciably better statistical data, in particular those pertaining to the decomposition of capital outlays.

Appendix

Variables used in the analysis

The dependent variable

The explained variable is the increase in the logarithm of labour productivity, i.e. the values of the GDP stream per man-hour. Data on the GDP of the countries included in the analysis have been obtained from the United Nations database (United Nations Statistics Division)

The number of hours worked in a given economy was obtained from OECD, KLEMS and Eurostat data.[9]

The explanatory variables

Capital and knowledge transfer variables

In order to calculate the growth rate of various kinds of capital formation, first the capital resources in the individual economies were calculated using the perpetual inventory method (cf. OECD 1998, formula 3.1). Next, the previous gross capital formation was calculated using Coe and Helpman's proposal (1995).

In this way the capital formation and then the dynamics of capital formation were calculated for the following five variables:

- share of capital in the product (K/Y) and the technical K/L ratio (K/L) (assumed annual depreciation rate of fixed assets: 5 per cent),
- machines and equipment stock (*M&Estock*) (10 per cent),
- fixed assets resulting from R&D investment (*lnBERDstock*) (15 per cent),
- intangible assets that derive from investment, royalty payments and licence fees (*R&LFstock*) (20 per cent).

It should be mentioned that R&D investment constitutes an indicator of inventiveness, while the indicators of investment in machinery and equipment, royalties and licence fees are the variables that represent the embodied and the non-embodied technology transfer, respectively.

Human capital indicators

In consideration of the advantages and disadvantages of different kinds of indicators of human capital (*HC*), two basic indicators of the parameter were selected: the percentage of population (aged 25–64) with university education and the expected total duration of education at all levels, including proportional increases of these variables.

Institutional indicators

Out of many possible institutional environment indicators, selected were the World Bank indicators collected within the framework of the *World Governance Indicators*. Fundamental conditions that influence economic activity, reduce environment uncertainty and significantly affect innovative activity include government effectiveness (administration) (*GE*), the quality of regulations (*RQ*) and rule of law (*RL*). The basic explanatory variable in this area is the average *GERQRL*.

Macroeconomic policy indicators

Contemporary understanding of appropriate economic policy can be based on the policy recommendations formulated by J. Williamson in 1989 as part of the so-called Washington Consensus (Williamson 1990). The basic indicator adopted as a macroeconomic policy variable is the increase in the share of public expenditure in GDP (*r GovExpend*), which reflects, among other things, the degree of control of the Schumpeterian entrepreneur over his profit.

Moreover, in models that take into account other than constant returns to scale, the labour force growth rate was adopted as the explanatory variable.

Using panel data in a regression analysis usually causes certain difficulties, which make it impossible to retain the principles of the classical least squares method (LSM). Many analysed models estimated with the LSM without accounting for individual effects are characterised by the lack of homogeneity of the random component (heteroscedasticity), as well as the lack of normality of residuals. Some of them are also affected by first-order autocorrelation. Thanks to the application of procedures used to estimate panel data, most of the problems resulting from the violation of the LSM principles were eliminated. In the cases where the introduction of individual effects would have been unjustified, despite heteroscedasticity and/or first-order autocorrelation of residuals, the Prais–Winsten estimation procedure was applied (LSM PW).

Notes

1 'The production function ... describes the way in which the quantity of product varies, if the quantities of the factors vary. If, instead of the quantities of factors, we vary the form of the function, we have an innovation' (Schumpeter 1939, p. 87).
2 Subsequently, Solow's residual was called total factor productivity (TFP) or multifactor productivity (MFP).

3 When talking about convergence, certain abbreviations proposed by S. Gomułka (1998) may be useful. They include TFA – technology frontier area, i.e. countries that rank among the best technologically and economically developed ones, while LDC stands for less developed countries.

4 Clearly, innovation activity thus understood refers to technological product and process (TPP) innovation innovation, or is outright identical with R&D activity.

5 TFA countries: Australia, Belgium, Finland, France, Spain, the Netherlands, Ireland, Japan, Canada, Germany, New Zealand, United States, Sweden, United Kingdom and Italy. LDC countries: Cyprus, Czech Republic, Estonia, Greece, South Korea, Lithuania, Latvia, Mexico, Poland, Portugal, Slovakia and Hungary.

6 Such an approach may help avoid the problems resultant from a simplified way of assuming specific depreciation rates for the capital assets.

7 The absence of a clear-cut relationship between *BERD/GDP* and the dependent variable in model 2T is likely due to the correlation of this variable with the increase in the share of capital in the product (K/Y). Once the latter is removed, a strong impact of BERD can be perceived. Although from the perspective of quality of the statistical model co-linearity is undesirable, the correlated variables have been preserved, since their elimination when analysing one of them informs about the nature of correlation that holds between them.

8 The indicator is the resource growth rate – the share of public expenditure in GDP or the share of public authorities in determining investment directions.

9 Population and labour force statistics, OECD.

References

Abramovitz, M. (1986), Catching Up, Forging Ahead, and Falling Behind, *Journal of Economic History*, vol. XLVI, no. 2, pp. 385–406.

Ahn, S. and P. Hemmings (2000), Policy Influences on Economic Growth in OECD Countries: An Evaluation of the Evidence, *OECD Economics Department Working Papers*, no. 246.

Barro, R.J. and X. Sala-i-Martin (1997), Technological Diffusion, Convergence, and Growth, *Journal of Economic Growth*, vol. 2, pp. 1–27.

Bassanini, A. and S. Scarpetta (2001), The Driving Forces of Economic Growth: Panel Data Evidence for the OECD Countries, *OECD Economic Studies*, no. 33/II.

Benhabib, J. and M.M. Spiegel (1994), The Role of Human Capital in Economic Development: Evidence from Aggregate Cross-country Data, *Journal of Monetary Economics*, vol. 34, pp. 143–173.

Blaug, M. (2000), *Teoria ekonomii; Ujęcie retrospektywne*, Wydawnictwo Naukowe PWN, Warszawa.

Coe, D.T. and E. Helpman (1995), International R&D Spillovers, *European Economic Review*, vol. 39, no. 5, pp. 859–887.

DeLong, J.B. and L.H. Summers (1991), The Equipment Investment and Economic Growth, *The Quarterly Journal of Economics*, vol. 106, no. 2, pp. 445–502.

DeLong, J.B. and L.H. Summers (1993), How Strongly Do Developing Economies Benefit from Equipment Investment?, *Journal of Monetary Economics*, vol. 32, pp. 395–415.

Gomułka, S. (1998), *Teoria innowacji i wzrostu gospodarczego*, Wydawnictwo CASE, Warszawa.

Gomułka, S. (2005), Innowacje a trwałość wzrostu polskiej gospodarki, in: *Procesy innowacyjne w polskiej gospodarce*, Raport nr 26 Rady Strategii Społeczno-Gospodarczej przy Radzie Ministrów, Warszawa.

Gomułka, S. (2006), Mechanizm i źródła wzrostu gospodarczego w świecie, in: R. Rapacki (ed.), *Wzrost gospodarczy w krajach transformacji: konwergencja czy dywergencja?*, Polskie Wydawnictwo Ekonomiczne, Warszawa.

Hall, B. (2011), *R&D and Innovation Expenditures in the Crisis*, OECD, Paris. Available at: http://elsa.berkeley.edu/~bhhall/papers/BHH11_OECD_RD_crisis.pdf (accessed 21 May 2013).

Kline, S.J. and N. Rosenberg (1986), An Overview of Innovation, in: R. Landau and N. Rosenberg (eds), *The Positive Sum Strategy: Harnessing Technology for Economic Growth*, Washington, DC, National Academy Press, pp. 275–305.

Mowery, D.C. and N. Rosenberg (1979), The Influence of Market Demand Upon Innovation: A Critical Review of Some Recent Empirical Studies, *Research Policy*, vol. 8, no. 2, pp. 102–153.

OECD (1998), *Perpetual Inventory Method*, Paris, OECD.

OECD (2012), *Science, Technology and Industry Outlook 2012*, Paris, OECD.

OECD and Eurostat (1999), *Podręcznik Oslo, Proponowane zasady gromadzenia i interpretacji danych dotyczących innowacji technologicznych, 1997*, Komitet Badań Naukowych, Warszawa.

Olson, M. (1996), Big Bills on the Sidewalk: Why Some Nations are Rich, and Others Poor, *Journal of Economic Perspectives*, vol. 10, no. 2, pp. 3–24.

Romer, D. (2000), *Makroekonomia dla zaawansowanych*, Wydawnictwo Naukowe PWN, Warszawa.

Romer, P.M. (1986), Increasing Returns and Long-Run Growth, *Journal of Political Economy*, vol. 94, no. 5, pp. 1002–1037.

Schumpeter, J.A. (1939), *Business Cycles: A Theoretical, Historical and Statistical Analysis of the Capitalist Process*, New York: McGraw-Hill.

Schumpeter, J.A. (1960), *Teoria rozwoju gospodarczego*, Państwowe Wydawnictwo Naukowe, Warszawa, (original: *Theorie der wirtschaftlichen Entwicklung*, Berlin, 1952).

Schumpeter, J.A. (1995), *Kapitalizm, socjalizm, demokracja*, Polskie Wydawnictwo Naukowe, Warszawa (original: *Capitalism, Socialism and Democracy*, Routledge, 1976).

Schwab, K. (ed.) (2012), *The Global Competitiveness Report 2012–2013*, Geneva, World Economic Forum.

Smith, K. (2004), Measuring Innovation, in: J. Fagerberg, D. Mowery and R. Nelson (eds), *The Oxford Handbook of Innovation*, Oxford, Oxford University Press.

Solow, R.M. (1956), A Contribution to the Theory of Economic Growth, *Quarterly Journal of Economics*, vol. 70, no. 1, pp. 65–94.

Solow, R.M. (1957), Technical Change and the Aggregate Production Function, *The Review of Economics and Statistics*, vol. 39, no. 3, pp. 312–320.

Tokarski, T. (2005), *Wybrane modele podażowych czynników wzrostu gospodarczego*, Wydawnictwo Uniwersytetu Jagiellońskiego, Kraków.

Verspagen, B. (1991), A New Empirical Approach to Catching Up or Falling Behind, *Structural Change and Economic Dynamics*, vol. 2, no. 2, pp. 359–380.

Williamson, J. (1990), What Washington Means by Policy Reform, in: J. Williamson (ed.), *Latin American Readjustment: How Much has Happened*, Washington, DC: Institute for International Economics.

11 Added value of design as a factor of firms' competitiveness in times of crises

Łukasz Mamica

The current economic and financial crisis generates strong pressure on public expenditures. Although public spending cuts are not a common response in a global sense, with the most well known example being the United States, who try to stimulate economic growth by increasing public spending (where the federal deficit as a percentage of GDP grew from over 1 per cent in 2007 to over 8 per cent for the last four years), many EU governments try to restructure and minimise budget deficits. Lower aggregated demand imposes a pressure on firms to be more competitive. At the same time, crises in banking systems have a negative impact on willingness of financial institutions to credit companies' investments.

The key issue of current economic policy is to find the balance between stabilising public finances and keeping the drivers of long-term growth, which, because of global markets, should be based mainly on innovativeness. Without strong, global-oriented firms, which are able to compete in global markets, stabilisation of public finances will have only a temporary effect. Innovation is a broad concept, which can have technological, organisational or a functional/design background. With limited financial resources for innovation, special attention should be given to relatively low-cost actions connected with design (mainly, but not only, in its industrial dimension).

This chapter presents data showing that the popularity of using design as a factor of firms' competitiveness during times of financial crisis is growing, while other more expensive actions are limited.

The global market exerts high pressure on the ability of firms to compete. Competition on price alone, because of the high level of production costs in developed countries, plays a limited role. There is the perpetual process of creating the value of products, which goes beyond price. One of the most important factors, which creates a product's added value, is its design.

Although it is difficult to measure what and at which level product design creates value for consumers, such knowledge has a key role for informed management decisions. There are two fundamental questions in this field. First, is there a correlation between the level of a firm's activity in design and the consumer opinion of this firm's products? Second, what is the added value of the design from the customer's perspective, and how much more are they ready to pay if the product has a high-quality design? In this chapter results are presented from questionnaire research in this field at both national and international levels.

1 Growth of the role of design compared to other factors of a firm's competitiveness during the financial crisis

From 2006 onwards we can observe the permanent decline of patent applications to the European Patent Office per million inhabitants in the European economy's 27 EU countries (Figure 11.1). While in 2006 the value of this indicator was over 116, in 2010 it was just under 109.

Because the result of innovation activity is difficult to predict, the level of support of venture capital investment has an important role in the process of creating new competitive firms. Unfortunately this indicator has also seen a strong decline in the last few years (Figure 11.2). While in 2007 the average value for venture capital investments in 15 EU countries was about 0.047 per cent of GDP, in 2011 it was only 0.03 per cent.

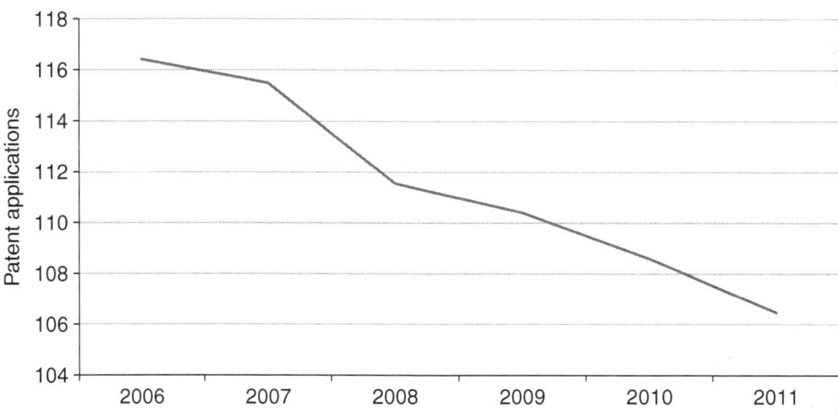

Figure 11.1 Patent applications to the EPO per million inhabitants in the EU27 (source: based on Eurostat database 2012).

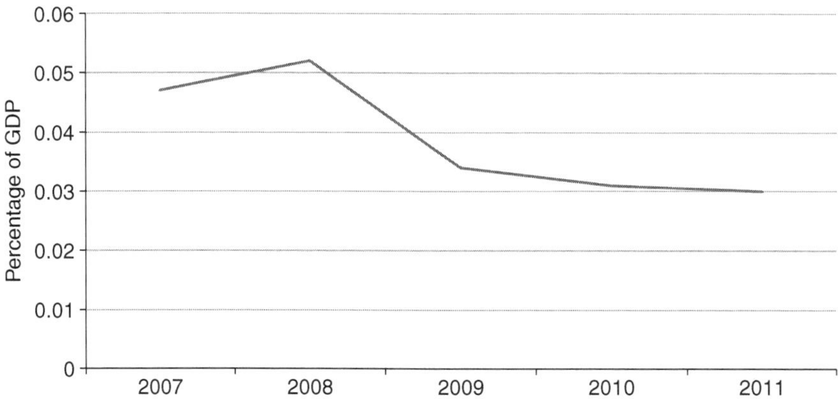

Figure 11.2 Venture capital investments as a percentage of GDP in 15 EU countries (source: based on Eurostat database 2012).

One of the explanations of lower activity within patent registration during the crises could be the relatively high cost of investment needed to achieve new solutions, which can be protected by patents, and also by the high costs of obtaining patents themselves. Supporting solutions for companies who do not have enough financial resources to maintain their patent activity could be a industrial design right, called a design patent in the United States or a community design, which covers the EU. As opposed to decline of patent applications, the activity of firms connected with community design registration is characterised by stable growth during the last few years, both in the EU (Figure 11.3) and on a global scale (Figure 11.4).

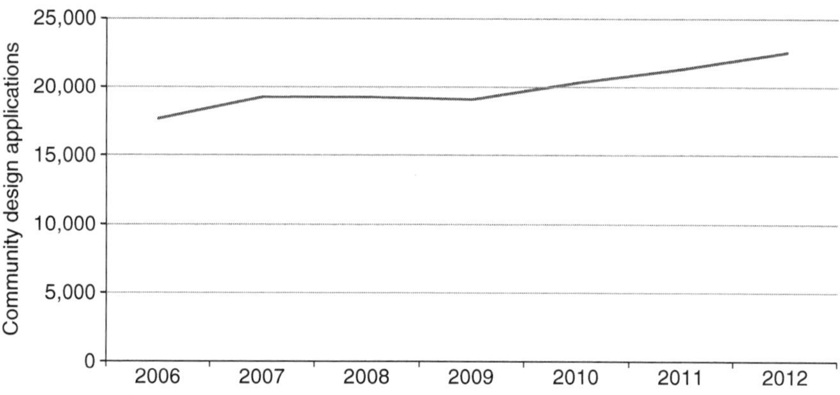

Figure 11.3 Community designs applications to the Office for Harmonization in the Internal Market (OHIM), 2006–11 (source: based on data delivered by the Office for Harmonization in the Internal Market 2012).

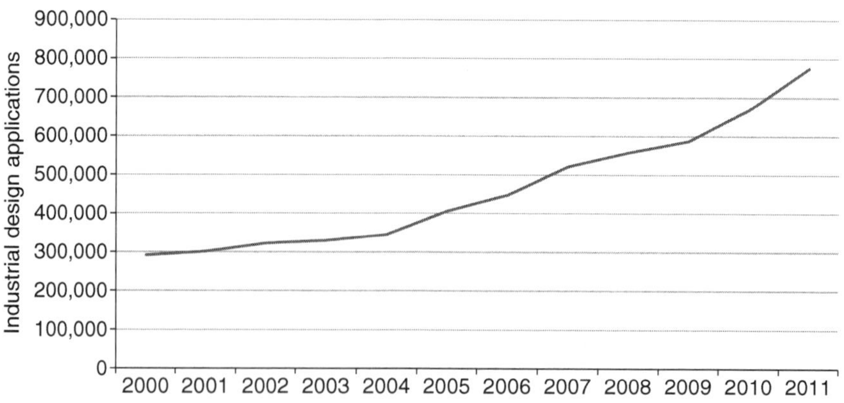

Figure 11.4 Trend in world total industrial design applications (source: WIPO statistic database, based on WIPO estimation covering around 130 offices received via international registrations through the Hague system, 2011).

2 Fields of added value created by design

The aim of design is the creation of added value to products and services from the perspective of clients, firms and society. Clients are ready to pay for design because it gives them the ability to demonstrate, through design, their tastes or social status. This phenomena was observed by T. Veblen, who pointed out that rich people often choose less useful goods, whose design is a sign of high price. In his 1899 book *The Theory of the Leisure Class*, Veblen described a demonstration effect also called the Veblen paradox, whereby the demand for certain goods increase despite their increasing prices, which he explained as a way people show their social status. The value of design for consumers is also connected with generating aesthetic feelings, and design is a factor of emotion creation. If users feel an emotional relation to any design product then they will be more open to its long-term use as well as to its renovation. This has a positive impact on the environment because of lower usage of raw materials. Design therefore plays an important role both for individual users and for society as a whole, resulting from ergonomic aspects of goods production, which increase users' quality of life and reduces healthcare expenditure through the reduction of postural defects.

Apart from the ability to sell at higher prices, as mentioned above, firms also benefit from design usage by minimising production costs and optimisation of the production process, and by the reduction in the amount of materials used.

Design, because of its permanent presence, effects everyday life and has a great cultural impact on society, as well as supporting the process of formation of aesthetics sensitivity. In countries where design achieves an extraordinarily high standard, it starts to play a positive role as a factor supporting exports. Such phenomena are now observed, for example, in Italy or in Scandinavian countries.[1] Firms that function in countries recognised as design leaders receive image benefits and achieve a premium in creation of added value for consumers. Goods which are designed in a way that allows for effective decomposition of used materials in recycling processes also have a positive impact on environmental protection (see Figure 11.5).

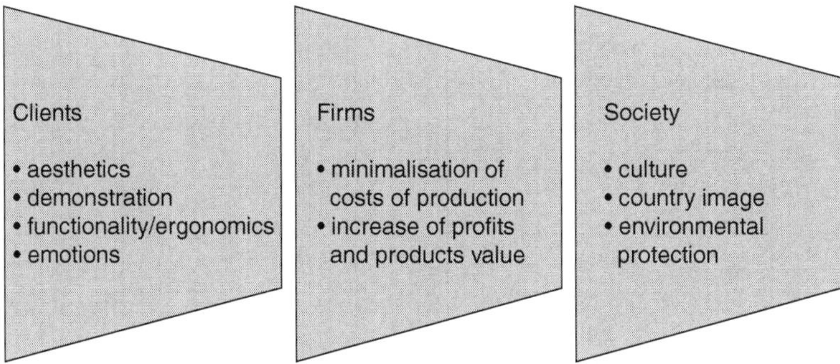

Figure 11.5 Fields of added value created by design.

3 Design as a determinant of product value

Design is an element of the whole process of product development, guaranteeing market success. A knowledge of client preferences is essential for the proper construction of this process. In one survey, marketing managers confirmed the leading role of design, where 60 per cent of respondents indicated design as the most important determinant of new product performance (Bruce and Whitehead 1988). The research of management of technology confirmed that communication among manufacturing, marketing, engineering, production and R&D provides the proper conditions for the economic success of the product (Hise *et al.* 1990). Cooper and Kleinschmidt (1987), after analysis of 203 new products (both commercial successes and failures), found synergy, both marketing and technical, to be crucial factors in sales success. According to them, product definition and early, pre-development activities are the most important steps in the new product's development process. Further, product design is an important determinant of commercial success. The relation between client and product is determined by many external factors. It has been shown that market segment tastes are determined by various groups or subcultures (Reingen *et al.* 1984). Design preferences are also impacted by design acumen (described as something with which certain people are born and who therefore have more sophisticated design preferences (Csikszentmihalyi and Robinson 1990)). In analysis of aesthetic experience, Mitias points out that the validity of the judgement would be determined by 'an examination of the correctness, richness, poverty, or adequacy of the experience, which the critic has had of the art work' (Mitias 1988, p. 47). Design, which can be called an applied art based on the interaction between client, object and perception, is highly determined by this psychological attitude. Interactions with professional design or interior magazines, exhibitions and publications shape the individual perception of design.

Furthermore, firms treat design as an important determinant of their competitiveness: 88 per cent of firms' representatives in Malopolska support and expect the establishment of a centre of design in Krakow (Mamica 2008). The research dedicated to measuring the impact of design on the economic performance of firms done by Hertenstein and Platt (2001) showed that firms whose design was evaluated as high quality have better economic conditions. Research in New Zealand showed that 67 per cent of exporters treated design as a key factor in achieving success in business and 80 per cent of firms claimed it supported the creation of their firm's added value (Walton and Duncan 2003). In firms where design is integral to operations, over three-quarters declared that they have increased their competitiveness and turnover through design (Design Council 2006). The research done in Denmark by the Danish Design Centre in 2003, covering 1,000 companies, showed that the increase in exports is double in firms that employ designers and purchase design externally (33.5 per cent) compared to companies that neither employ designers nor purchase design externally (17.6 per cent), (Danish Design Centre 2003).

Despite the fact that it is only a small part of design dimension, the shape of the product creates the most recognisable element of product recognition.

Berkowitz (1987) analysed product shape as an element of innovation strategy in food processing and treats it as an effective competitive company tool. He finds that good design encourages trading up and provides a basis for market segmentation. Temple and Swann have analysed the impact of British Design Awards on a firm's level of competitiveness. They found beneficial effects of the activities of the Design Council, connected with 'selecting products from industries which were good performers in international terms and which were exposed to the full rigours of international competition' (Temple and Swann 1995, p. 52). According to them the most important role of such a design award is in being a benchmark for successful design practices, this being an especially important function for smaller firms.

Knowledge concerning consumer preferences has a great impact on a firm's strategy development. The Quality Function Development is a total-quality-management process that supports the use of consumer preferences in the strategy of a company. The research done by Griffin and Hauser (1993) showed that if concepts of the product are created based on measured importance, then such products are preferred by consumers. The structure of consumer preferences described in this article holds a message to producers concerning client expectations.

Design is a wider term, covering the processes of product creation, appearance and functionality. These last two product features are particularly important from the client's point of view. The product design aspect also covers the package, playing an important informational role. The research of the role of the package in price expectancy (different bottles of wine were used for this research) showed dependences in this field (Orth *et al.* 2010). Most noticeably, they found that design plays a strong role in consumers' view of both product attractiveness and quality. Price expectation was, however, more strongly based on product attractiveness. Holbrook (1987) distinguishes non-visualising consumers from visualising consumers who appreciate visual design elements and use them as important determinants of their demand.

Decisions about buying a specific product are not only connected with the design preferences of the consumer, but are also determined by other objects that he possesses. This was described by Forty (1986), who noticed that clients compare the fitting of a new product with previously possessed goods. Product lines (for example, sets of furniture, which can be bought in pieces or all together) allow newly bought products to be matched to those already possessed. The concept that the possession of some products has an impact on newly bought products was developed as the concept of ensemble (Holbrook and Anand 1992). In this way the general overview of possessed goods (and harmony among them) plays a more important role than the aesthetic perception of some products.

Because of technological developments, differences in the field of quality and functionality among competitors are decreasing. Design gives an opportunity for firms to distinguish their product on the market. Jordan stresses the aesthetic aspect of design: 'the product should provide aesthetic pleasure to those for whom it is designed' (Jordan 2000, p. 85). The client's satisfaction level is determined by the kinds of relations between him and the product. 'Pleasurability, then, is not simply a property of a product but of the interaction between a product and a person' (Jordan 2000, p. 12). Design strengthens this relation and makes easier the identification of the client with specific products, thus losing their anonymity.

Products with much of their value connected with design are difficult to explain in terms of their structural value. Some similarities can be found in this matter with wine preferences, which have a great part of their customer value determined by difficult-to-measure parameters. The research concerning determinants of wine consumer preferences in New Mexico showed that price, reputation and origin significantly affect the demand for such goods (Alimova *et al.* 2008). Other research showed that reputation and origin have the greatest impact on wine choice (Lockshin *et al.* 2006). Reputation is a parameter connected not with the physical, individual product unit, but rather with the producer and its brand. Therefore, some similarities can be observed between the reputation of the firm in its design sphere and the new product being launched in the market by this firm. Clients can transfer the image of the firm onto a given individual product.

4 Correlation between the level of a firm's activity in design and consumer opinion of products produced by them

The research on which the analysis is presented here covered questionnaire interviews designed by the author and carried out in Poland with representatives of 232 firms (medium and large size, employing over ten staff) and 2,088 of their customers who expressed their opinions concerning the quality of their products from the design point of view. A total of 132 firms were categorised as 'passive' in the field of design and 100 as 'active'.[2] The questionnaire research was carried out in 2009 and 2010.

To check the correlation between the level of a firm's activity in the field of design and consumer opinion of their products, a logistic regression model was introduced. It included two independent variables for which the value of the test probability was lower that 0.05 (details in Table 11.1). A positive value of the parameter ('mark' in Table 11.1) means that a given variable has a significant impact on the opinion on its quality of design.

For the variable, '*Number of new products introduced to the market within the last 12 months*', the term of reference was '*Maximum of five products*'. The analysis of the calculations (Table 11.1) shows that the probability of a much higher mark of product design is almost three times higher (2.93) in firms that, within the last 12 months, introduced 6–10 products, than in firms which introduced fewer than five products in the same period of time.

For the variable, '*Percentage of expenditure on design out of all expenditure*', the term of reference was '*Level of expenditure lower than 5 per cent*'. The possibility for a much improved assessment of a firm's design is almost three times higher (2.95) in firms where the level of expenditure at design time was 5–10 per cent. This is compared with firms where such expenditure was lower than 5 per cent.

Table 11.1 Survey of parameters of logistic regression

	Constant B0	Introduction to market within last 12 months of 6–10 new products	Expenditure on design out of all expenditure, 5–10 per cent
Mark	−2.41	1.08	1.08
Standard error	0.29	0.51	0.42
p-value	0.00	0.04	0.01
Wald chi-square	69.12	4.42	6.71
p-value	0.00	0.04	0.01

Source: own calculation based on questionnaire research.

The logistic regression model used confirmed that the activity of a firm in the field of design has a positive impact on customer opinions on the design quality of their products. The first line in Table 11.1 (mark) covers the values of model parameters, which allow writing it in a logistic form.

5 The value of design and preferences connected with it in light of the international comparative questionnaire research

Price of the product is an evident determinant of client purchase decisions. Jun *et al.* (2005) found in their research that consumers' price expectations of a brand extension are affected by the price of the parent brand. It is important because the price expectation affects consumers' perceptions of the extension's quality and its value. By analogy, good design can be used by firms as a factor, which informs clients about its potentially higher price. The process of formulation by consumers of a product's price is common with reference prices (Winer 1988).

The research based on the questionnaire designed by this chapter's author was done with a group of people (mainly students) from the Czech Republic, Finland, France, Germany, Great Britain, Hungary, Norway, Poland, South Africa and Spain, from January to December 2010. Ultimately, 820 completed questionnaires were received. The age of participants ranged from 16 to 58 years (13 per cent were 18 or under, 52 per cent were 19–21, 17 per cent were 22–24 and 18 per cent were over 25). As the group had a majority of men (58 per cent), a weighting factor was used in statistic calculations.

The research confirmed that consumers do appreciate the role of design and are ready to pay more for it. The average amount of money said to be paid for a product characterised by a higher quality of design was about 27 per cent of its price. This is in comparison with other products having similar materials but with a lower quality of design.

The analysis of the data (Table 11.2) shows that the highest added value of design is stated by the citizens of South Africa, Hungary and Norway (32–34 per cent). Relative to this, the lowest increase of a product's value by its good design is declared by Frenchmen, Germans and Finns (but is still 20–21 per cent).

Table 11.2 Willingness to pay more for products (%) because of a higher quality of design according to gender (in national terms)

Nationality	Total	Gender	
		Men	*Women*
British	29.5	36.5	21.9
Czech	25.0	25.2	24.9
Finns	20.9	19.4	26.6
French	19.9	18.7	21.2
Spanish	26.6	24.8	30.7
German	20.6	20.1	21.3
Norwegian	31.6	33.7	30.0
Polish	27.2	28.2	26.3
South Africans	33.8	32.1	37.0
Hungarian	33.4	36.7	30.6

Source: own calculations based on questionnaire research.

For the purpose of determining whether these are significant statistical differences between different nations, an analysis of variance was used. Because of non-fulfilment of the expectations in the assumptions in this analysis, a non-parametric equivalent was used – the test of Kruskal Wallis. Most often, statistical differences were observed among Finns and South Africans ($p=0.00$), Spanish and Norwegians ($p=0.04$) and Poles ($p=0.01$). The differences were also observed between French, Hungarians and South Africans (in both cases $p=0.00$).

The added value of design for women was 27.4 per cent of a product's price, and for men just a little less (26.7 per cent). At the same time, differences in results within the group of women were lower (standard deviation of 20.7). No statistical differences were noticed among men and women in their willingness to pay more for a high quality of design. But if this analysis is done between the genders, taking into account nationality, more visible differences can be noticed. On average, British men are ready to pay more than British women for a high quality of design by almost 15 percentage points. In other nationalities, differences are at least two times smaller. Using the U Mann–Whitney test, it can be noticed that statistical differences in the willingness to pay for a high quality of design by men and women can be observed in people from Britain, Finland and Spain (in the two first cases $p=0.01$; in the third $p=0.00$).

6 Client's opinion about purchase decision determinants

In the research designed by the author for the Institute of Industrial Design in Warsaw, conducted between October 2009 and January 2010, 2,088 clients were interviewed in selected shops across the country. Clients were asked to give their opinion about selected parameters which determine their product-buying decisions. The importance of every parameter was estimated on a five-point scale, where 1 is not important at all and 5 is most important. The research showed that the most important product feature for the researched group of clients is the product's quality, with 57 per cent of those interviewed giving the answer 'very important'. In second place is 'materials quality', estimated by 56 per cent of customers as 'very important'. Almost the same high level (53 per cent) is given to reliability/durability. Almost half the group (49 per cent) gave product design the highest value. The lowest number of the highest mark ('very important') was given to 'product packaging' (22 per cent) and advertising (16 per cent). The low rank of the last feature of products could probably be explained by the unwillingness of clients to accept the fact that a firm's marketing activities can influence them.

Analysis of the average mark given by clients to product parameters impacting on their purchase decision (Table 11.3) confirms the most important role of the quality aspect of the goods. The highest average mark, 4.45, was given to product quality, and almost the same mark (4.44) to quality of materials. Very closely connected with quality is reliability/durability, and this parameter receiving an average mark of 4.37. Next came functionality (4.35), price (4.35) and design (4.31). The lowest declared marks given to product parameters impacting on purchase decisions are others' opinions (3.59), packaging (3.39) and advertising (3.11).

7 Impact of gender on consumer preferences

During the process of estimating the relation between gender and consumer preference, the statistical assumptions for the t-test were not fulfilled. Therefore, the non-parametric equivalent of this test was used: the U Mann–Whitney test. Calculations showed that the opinions of women and men differ in statistically important ways in the case of three product parameters: design ($p=0.03$), ease of product usage ($p=0.04$) and repair time ($p=0.01$) (Table 11.4). Despite these differences in preferences connected with design across the genders, it is clear that the populations of men and women are not homogeneous. The study of adolescent girls' website design preferences carried out by Agosto (2004) showed that such preferences vary widely, despite their shared biological sex.

The differences among men and women concerning their willingness to pay more for product design are not important from the statistical point of view ($p=0.23$, higher than 0.05), but Table 11.5 presents some important information. The number of women who are not at all ready to pay for design is 5 per cent lower than men. This means that addressing good design to women is more profitable from a firm's point of view.

Table 11.3 Average marks of selected products parameters, having an impact on clients' purchase decisions

Product parameters	1 – not important at all (%)	2 (%)	3 (%)	4 (%)	5 – very important (%)	Average mark
Product quality	0.2	1.3	8.9	32.3	57.4	4.45
Quality of materials	0.2	1.1	9.5	33.0	56.2	4.44
Reliability/durability	1.0	1.6	9.6	34.6	53.2	4.37
Functionality	0.4	2.4	11.2	33.9	52.1	4.35
Price	1.3	2.3	9.0	35.0	52.5	4.35
Design	0.9	2.3	10.7	37.2	49.0	4.31
Ease of usage	1.6	1.8	11.5	37.0	48.2	4.28
Accessibility	1.1	3.2	14.0	41.7	40.1	4.17
Repair time	5.9	4.6	14.6	35.0	40.0	3.99
Brand/producer	3.0	5.8	19.0	37.8	34.5	3.95
Others' opinion	8.1	9.1	22.8	35.6	24.4	3.59
Package	11.4	12.5	23.6	30.8	21.7	3.39
Advertising	16.0	15.7	25.9	26.2	16.3	3.11

Source: based on own calculation of questionnaire research results.

Notes:
Results from a five-point scale where 1 is not important at all and 5 is the most important)
$N = 2,088$.

Table 11.4 Average marks of selected product parameters, impacting on clients' decisions concerning the purchase.

Product parameters	Men	Women	Total
Functionality	4.36	4.34	4.35
Brand/producer	3.95	3.95	3.95
Accessibility	4.17	4.16	4.17
Quality of materials	4.43	4.44	4.44
Product quality	4.44	4.47	4.45
Design	4.25	4.36	4.31
Reliability/durability	4.40	4.36	4.70
Repair time	4.08	3.91	3.99
Ease of usage	4.31	4.26	4.28
Price	4.34	4.36	4.35
Package	3.36	3.41	3.39
Others' opinions	3.55	3.63	3.59
Advertising	3.07	3.15	3.11

Source: based on own calculation of questionnaire research results.

Notes:
Results from a five-point scale where 1 is not important at all and 5 is the most important
$N = 2,088$.

Table 11.5 Declared willingness to pay more for a product with a more attractive design compared to another product with similar quality but with a poorer level of design according to genders

Willingness to pay for design	Men (%)	Women (%)	Total (%)
nothing (0%)	21.4	16.4	18.6
Up to 5%	25.7	27.9	26.9
6–10%	20.6	23.5	22.2
11–15%	10.9	11.9	11.5
16–20%	10.9	9.9	10.3
21–25%	3.6	3.7	3.7
26–30%	3.8	3.6	3.7
31–40%	1.8	1.6	1.7
over 40%	1.3	1.7	1.5

Source: based on own calculation of questionnaire research results.

Note
$N = 2,088$.

8 Conclusions

During times of crises the role of design as a factor of competitiveness and growth from a firm's perspective is increasing. It is confirmed by design registration data, which are characterised by stable growth during the last few years, both in the EU and also on a global scale. At the same time the lack of financial resources has had a negative impact on patent activity. Also observed is a permanent decline in venture capital investment.

Investments in design are profitable for firms and this is confirmed by clients' opinions. The research on customers showed that the probability of receiving much higher marks for product design is remarkably higher for firms active in the field of design.

Design is an important determining factor in a client's purchase decision. Almost half of the researched group of over 2,000 clients in Poland (49 per cent) gave product design the highest value. Clients declared a willingness to pay for good design. For over 25 per cent of the research group the value of design is estimated at between 0 and 5 per cent of product price. Also, almost 25 per cent declared that the value of design is between 6 and 10 per cent of a good's price. One in ten interviewed clients is ready to pay 16–20 per cent of a product's price for good design. The research showed that the opinions of women and men differ in statistically important ways in the case of three product parameters: design, ease of product use and repair time.

The international research also confirmed that consumers are ready to pay for good-quality design. The average amount of money said to be paid for a product characterised by a higher quality of design was about 27 per cent of its price.

Notes

1 This position is changing with the passage of time. For example, for the top achievements of design in the twentieth century, particular countries are recognised at particular times: 1910–1920 is France; 1930–1940 is Germany; 1950s is Scandinavian countries and the United States; and Italy from 1960 to early 1970 (Bosoni 2008, p. 7).
2 Firms that design passively are those who fulfil at least one of the following requirements:

   1 They do not employ a designer with an education background in this field and do not cooperate with a firm that offers design-related services.
   2 The number of new products, in which a new design was used and found in the marketplace within the last three years, was not higher than two.
   3 The number of new products found in the marketplace during the last three years and which were prepared using a firm's own projects was fewer than two.
   4 All new products found in the marketplace within the last three years were only based on projects given by other firms or foreign partners. Firms that design actively are those who fulfil all of the following requirements:

   a They employ a designer who has an education background in this field or they cooperate with a firm which offers design-related services.
   b The number of new products in which a new design was used and found in the marketplace within the last three years was higher than two.
   c The number of new products found in the marketplace during the last three years which were prepared using a firm's own projects was higher than two.
   d All new products found in the marketplace within the last three years were only based on a firm's own projects.

References

Agosto, D.E. 2004. 'Design vs. Content: A Study of Adolescent Girls' Website Design Preferences', *International Journal of Technology and Design Education*, 14, pp. 245–260.

Alimova, N., Lillywhite, J.M., Hurd, B.H. and Hadjigeorgalis E. 2008. 'High Desert Wine: A Discrete Choice Analysis of Consumer Preferences for New Mexican Wine', *Journal of Food Products Marketing*, 14, 1, pp. 1–10.

Berkowitz, M. 1987. 'Product Shape as a Design Innovation Strategy', *Journal of Product Innovation Management*, 4, pp. 274–283.

Bosoni, G. 2008, *Italian Design*, Museum of Modern Art, New York.

Bruce, M. and Whitehead, M. 1988. 'Putting Design into the Picture: The Role of Product Design in Consumer Purchase Behavior', *Journal of the Market Research Society*, 30, 2, pp. 147–162.

Cooper, R.G. and Kleinschmidt, E. 1987. 'New Products: What Separates Winners from Losers?' *Journal of Product Innovation Management*, 4, pp. 169–184.

Csikszentmihalyi, M. and Robinson, R.E. 1990. *The Art of Seeing*, J. Paul Getty Museum, Malibu, CA.

Danish Design Centre. 2003. *Economic Effects of Design*, Report for National Agency for Enterprise & Housing, September, Copenhagen.

Design Council. 2006. *Design in Britain 2005–06*, Design Council, London.

Forty, A. 1986. *Objects of Desire: Design and Society 1750–1980*, Thames & Hudson, London.

Griffin, A. and Hauser, J.R. 1993. 'The Voice of the Consumer', *Marketing Science*, 12, 1, pp. 1–27.

Hertenstein, J.H. and Platt, M.B. 2001. 'Valuing Design: Enhancing Corporate Performance through Design Effectiveness', *Design Management Journal*, 12, 3, pp. 10–23.

Hise, R.T., O'Neal A., Parasuraman, A. and McNeal, J.U. 1990. 'Marketing/R&D Interaction in New Product Development: Implication for New Product Success Rates', *Journal of Product Innovation Management*, 7, 2, pp. 142–155.

Holbrook, M.B. 1987. 'Alms, Concepts, and Methods for the Representation of Individual Differences in Esthetic Responses to Design Features', *Journal of Consumer Research*, 13, pp. 337–347.

Holbrook, M.B. and Anand, P. 1992. 'The Effects of Situation, Sequence, and Features on Perceptual and Affective Responses to Product Designs: The Case of Aesthetic Consumption', *Empirical Studies of the Arts*, 10, 1, pp. 19–31.

Jordan, P.W. 2000. *Designing Pleasurable Products: An Introduction to the New Human Factors*, Taylor & Francis, London.

Jun, S.Y., MacInnis, D.J and Park, C.W. 2005. 'Formation of Price Expectation in Brand Extensions and Impact on Brand Extension Evaluation', *Advances in Consumer Research*, 32, pp. 137–142.

Lockshin, L., Wade, J., D'Hauteville, F. and Perrouty, J.P. 2006. 'Using Simulations from Discrete Choice Experiments to Measure Consumer Sensitivity to Brand, Region, Price, and Awards in Wine Choice', *Food Quality and Preference*, 17, 3–4, pp. 166–178.

Mamica, L. (ed.) 2008. *The Expectations of the Companies and Students from Malopolska Towards Industrial Design in this Region*, Krakow Technology Park, Krakow.

Mitias, M.H. 1988. *What Makes an Experience Aesthetic?*, Konigshausen & Neumann, Amsterdam; Rodopi, Wurzburg.

Orth, U.R., Campana, D. and Malkewitz, K. 2010. 'Formation of Consumer Price Expectation Based on Package Design: Attractive and Quality Routes', *Journal of Marketing Theory and Practice*, 18, 1, pp. 23–40.

Reingen, P.H., Foster, B.L. and Brown, J.J. 1984. 'Brand Congruence in Interpersonal Relations', *Journal of Consumer Research*, 11, pp. 771–783.

Temple, P. and Swann, P. 1995. 'Competitions and Competitiveness: The Case of British Design Awards', *Business Strategy Review*, 6, 2, pp. 41–52.

Veblen, T. 1899. *The Theory of the Leisure Class: An Economic Study in the Evolution of Institutions*, The Macmillan Company, New York.

Walton, M. and Duncan, I. 2003. *Building a Case for Added Value through Design: Report to Industry New Zealand*, NZ Institute of Economic Research, Wellington.

Winer, R.S. 1988. 'Behavioral Perspectives on Pricing: Buyers' Subjective Perceptions of Price Revisited', in Devinney, T. (ed.). *Issues in Pricing: Theory and Research*, Lexington Books, Lexington, MA.

12 The *decent work basic–relations–fairness* approach in a context of crisis in Italy

Martina Lavagnini and Antonella Mennella

1 Introduction

In recent years, there has been an intense debate on how to measure *decent work* around world regions and compare performances among countries and over years. This debate is still open and lively and the aim of this work is to take part in it by proposing a multidimensional approach to the *decent work* measure. It is an attempt to experiment with a connection between development and labour market analysis which could enrich the study of labour markets, focusing on the worker.

The concept of *decent work* was conceived by the ILO in 1999 as: 'opportunities for women and men to obtain decent and productive work, in conditions of freedom, equity, security and human dignity' (ILO 1999, p. 3). In this study it will be reinterpreted coherently with Sen's capability approach and a methodology to calculate it will be proposed.

The proposal of *decent work* is articulated into three profiles: *basic, relations* and *fairness*. These will be prioritized into two levels: *basic* is the fundamental one and concerns elements of the daily working conditions, *relations* and *fairness* are complementary and regroup indicators linked to the social aspect of working.

The approach will be tested by analysing the case of Italy and observing the impact of the crisis on *decent work*. The empirical analysis has been realized using data from different sources, among them the ISTAT labour force survey, statistics on accidents and diseases from INAIL, data from the INPS observatories on workers and the Eurostat database.

After this introduction which displays aims and steps of the work, in the second section the proposed approach of *decent work* is described in its sense, definition and methodology. In the third section the basic profile of the Italian labour market is analysed and the proposed approach is used to evaluate policies that can foster *decent work* in Italy. In the last section conclusions are drawn.

2 The *decent work basic–relations–fairness* proposal

In the lively debate on *decent work* there have been proposals of large dashboards of indicators, comprehensive of the social and economic conditions of the entire economy (e.g. Anker *et al.* 2002) and proposals of proxy numbers, which are much more concentrated on a few selected indicators of working conditions (e.g. the index of labour morale by Godfrey 2003).

A motivation to choose one or the other approach is the identity of the individual identified as the depositary of *decent work*. The first and official definition (ILO 1999) of *decent work* refers to 'women and men', so, coherently, analysis enlarged to the entire economy considers any kind of relationship between a person and work as part of the *decent work* analysis.

However, other more focused analyses suggest that different interpretations are possible. Analyses that take into account only characteristics of the labour market and the system of welfare provisions linked to work suggests the idea that the subject studied is the group or population who has or had an active relationship with the labour market (employed, unemployed, retired, etc.).

Furthermore, a study can be focused on working conditions, in this case is the worker to be entitled to aspire and experience *decent work*. In this sense the *decent work basic–relations–fairness* proposal is intended to focus on working conditions.

Peculiarities of an economy and characteristics of a labour market are obviously important as fields where work is created and takes place, but the aim of this interpretation of *decent work* is to investigate the individual and relational conditions of the person while working.

Even if work is such an important possibility in life that has social and personal effects also on non-working moments, still it is possible to analyse workers' and people's conditions separately: 'in the broad concept of decent work the main focus is on work *per se*' (Saith 2004, p. v).

Democratic states recognize a great and positive intrinsic value to labour in itself; for example, the first article of the Italian Constitution states that 'Italy is a democratic Republic, based on work'.

It is also commonly perceived that through work a person can find a way to express himself or herself, or at least to meet social respectability; furthermore, there are studies which show that when not working 'individuals suffer psychologically as well as socially (besides the obvious drop in income)' (Krauser 2011, p. 1).

Turned in this direction and harmoniously in line with the capability approach,[1] the proposed interpretation of *decent work* aims mainly to detect *labour unfreedoms*, in the belief that, if not under given constraints, labour, in its multifarious possibilities, can enlarge the range of human capabilities.

Being impossible and unnecessary to list the benefits that a person can achieve through labour, it is intended here that the identification and the removal of *labour unfreedoms* is sufficient to liberate the power of labour as a mean for people to 'lead the kind of lives they have reason to value' (Sen 1999).

Decent work, so intended, and, as said before, referring only to the worker (which is one of the possible functionings[2] that an individual can fulfil), is constitutive and instrumental of development.

Listing the positive contributions of work is considered here to be impossible because of the belief that the human creativity applied to changing market and socio-cultural circumstances can generate choices of infinite functionings.

This is to say that, as long as the persons involved in the labour relation are using their 'reasoned agency' (Sen 1999) to behave among fully available capabilities (whether taking choices of action or of non-action), functionings that will come out are impossibly unfree.

The destination of development – how the *capability approach* is here understood – is inside human beings and their personal, mutual relations; it is more an attitude to gain through the destruction of constraints than a condition to build up.[3]

Secondarily, the proposed approach aims to register some specific achievement that work can bring to a person; these have been chosen as markedly relevant in the current society.

The indicator proposed is composed of three parts, placed into two levels. The fundamental level concerns the basic profile, while the complementary one includes the other two (Table 12.1).

2.1 Fundamental level: basic profile

Basic profile regroups fundamental indicators, which are characterized as being the ones more intimately linked to daily working conditions. For these indicators it is possible to point out a chosen desired value, and the gap, whether positive or negative, between the actual and the desired value is recorded as a *decent work basic defect*.

Similarities with this part of the approach can be found in Bescond *et al.* (2003), where the aim of the methodology is to identify the percentage (in that case the average percentage) of workers that live with a decent work deficit.

Defects are to be intended as *labour unfreedoms*; the chosen desired value (or range) is where freedom lays.

The first basic physical and psychological indicator is *working hours*.

Table 12.1 Decent work basic–relation–fairness proposal

Fundamental level		Complementary level			
Basic profile		*Relations profile*		*Fairness profile*	
Working hours defect	WHD	Monetary sufficiency	MS	Irrelevance of private characteristics defect	IPCD
		Monetary enrichment	ME		
Physical safety defect	PSD	Educational enrichment	EE	Hanging work	HW
Legality of jobs defect	LJD	Freedom to voice	FV		
Unemployment rate pressure	URP				

The amount of personal time spent on working activities is the most important element of *decent work*. Time is a non-renewable personal resource and the opportunity cost[4] of working an hour more instead of interrupting market working activities after the working regular time – no matter how personally satisfying the job is – is doubtfully rewarded with the overtime hourly wage.

In every economy there is a different range for the formally accepted length of the working week; contract types available in the economy show the possibilities for people on how to share and organize work through time, both as employed and self-employed.

Once a range is detected, that range is the target for this basic aspect. For Italy the right amount of working hours is identified as between 20 and 40 hours per week, corresponding respectively to a part- and a full-time employee contract. Working more and working less than that are equally undesired.

The WHD (*working hours defect*) indicator shows the percentage of the employed population working an amount of weekly hours different from the ones within the working hours range.

Working too little is outside the target because of the importance of spending time at work once a person has made that choice. Working too little, in comparison to the expected amount in the society in question, can prevent a worker getting involved in what is happening in his/her organization, so he/she may feel excluded, detached, or may miss chances to advance his/her career. It can give the worker the perception that his/her contribution to society is of minor importance.

Working too much is unhealthy and stressful; it can increase the likelihood of work-related illnesses or of working accidents due to hazardous moments of poor concentration; it can interfere with the worker's familial and personal life.

The indicator on working hours is largely used in many other measurement proposals: Anker *et al.* (2002) place the indicator 'excessive (and extreme) hours of work'[5] under 4 out of 11 aspects of *decent work*: adequate earnings, decent hours, combining work and family life, safe work environment. They also analyse the insufficient amount of working hours with the indicator 'time-related underemployment rate'[6] which is part of three aspects of *decent work*: employment opportunities, adequate earnings, decent hours.

Anker *et al.* (2002) recognize a slightly different meaning of these two opposite ends of the 'correct' working hours, while in the *decent work basic–relations–fairness* proposal they are specular and eventually they are summed up to build the WHD indicator.

Bescond *et al.* (2003) use as well the indication of the effective amount of worked hours but, according to their proposal, a decent work deficit is identified only when this excess is not freely chosen for personal reasons. Such distinction is not used in this proposal: even if spontaneously chosen, an amount of weekly worked hours over the threshold constitutes a *working hours defect*. Even if 'a person has to take responsibility for his or her own preferences' (Sen 1999, p. 72), this is due to the interpretation that working too much or too little can only seem a free choice, but actually must be driven from some form of constraints, such as a confusion between self-identity and one's own profession, an exceptionally high conversion rate,[7] a disregard or unease about one's own job or workplace.

An individual should not be either working too much or too little, so as not to compromise his/her capability to be a 'fuller social person' (Sen 1999, p. 15).[8]

The second basic indicator is PSD (*physical safety defect*).

Another fundamental aspect of *decent work* is that a worker should not be in physical danger while staying in his/her working environment, so as not to compromise the capability to 'live long and have a good life' (Sen 1999, p. 14).

To run into an accident – which can possibly cause physical handicaps of various seriousness and length – is a possible source of extra adversity for the worker in converting income (or other resources) into functionings.

Assuming that annually no more than one accident or disease can be related to the same worker, PSD is obtained summing up working accidents and working diseases and dividing all by the number of employed people.

The percentage of workers involved in unsafe happenings should be nil; every percentage different from zero is a *physical safety defect.*

Ghai (2002) expresses the aspect 'working conditions' of *decent work* only through 'accidents and deaths at work in relation to the employed population', so PSD is similar to the indicator proposed there, except that in the present proposal work-related illnesses are added to accidents (fatal and not). In Anker *et al.* (2002) there is the indicator 'fatal injury rate' among indicators of 'safe work environment'.

The third basic indicator is LJD (*legality of jobs defect*). It shows the share of non-regular employees on the totality of employees (regular and non-regular) or the share of non-regular working hours on the total amount of regular and non-regular working hours.

In Sen's (1999) theory *transparency guarantees* are instrumental freedoms that are able to advance the general capability[9] of people; these are better assured when a labour relationship is managed under formal rules: working hours escaping formal rules constitute a *labour unfreedom.*

Anker *et al.* (2002) introduces an indicator on 'informal economy employment' under the aspect 'economic and social context for *decent work*'; in this proposal the idea is to approach this indicator among the basic aspects of *decent work*, in the belief that performing one's working activities non-regularly affects every other component in a non-predictable way.

The target of the LJD indicator is zero: in industrialized countries non-regular work should not exist.[10] The critique raised to many *decent work* approaches is that they are better applicable to market industrial countries. For this indicator proposed here the critique is valid, because, while it may be possible that in non-industrialized countries good working conditions can also be found in non-market productive situations, it is of crucial importance to record as an *unfreedom* non-regular work in industrialized countries, which tend to concentrate in the formal sector the most righteous linkages between people.

The fourth basic indicator is URP (*unemployment rate pressure*). This is meant to be a proxy of the *unfreedom* to change job that a worker has.

Due to the importance of obtaining the status of worker to interact within society, a worker can decide to leave a job for personal reasons only if the economic environment – in terms of employment, unemployment and job creation – shows real alternatives.

Since leaving a job for a worker actually means trying to change job, or maybe getting from the condition of employee to the one of self-employed, the target value for simplicity is no unemployment; this should indicate that a worker is free to leave his/her job without being subordinated to the hazard of unemployment. 'Having an x when there is no alternative may be sensibly distinguished from choosing x when substantial alternatives exist' (Sen 1999, p. 76).

This indicator is built by summing up discouraged people with workers unemployed from more than one year and dividing this sum by the labour force augmented with discouraged people.

The unemployment rate (or youth/female/wage-employment-specific unemployment rate) is taken into account in most of the proposals on *decent work*, but in terms of indication of the employment opportunities (Ghai 2002; Anker *et al.* 2002; Bescond *et al.* 2003) or gender discrimination (Ghai 2002).

2.2 Complementary level

2.2.1 Relations profile

The *relations profile* regroups indicators linked to the social aspect of working.

The remuneration of labour is influenced but hardly identified with its marginal productivity; on the contrary, it is much more influenced by social relations,[11] such as the bargaining power of social actors. The same job can be rewarded and perceived differently among societies. This is the reason why information about earnings is introduced in the part of the approach dedicated to relations. In other approaches wage information is managed in the sense of income-poverty analysis.[12]

The virtuosity of these kind of relations is vital because through wages workers can achieve many important functionings, and 'since income remains only instrumentally important, we cannot know how significant the income gaps are without actually considering the consequences of the income gaps' (Sen 1999, p. 84).

It is a concept largely endorsed in constitutional democracies that every job should give sustenance to the worker,[13] so this indicator is not intended to evaluate income-poverty or income-distribution, but is intended, on the one hand, to measure the difference in remuneration levels between actual monetary entitlements and perceived need for monetary credit, and on the other hand, the difference between a selected threshold and average wages.

Two indicators are proposed together in this section: *monetary sufficiency* (MS) and *monetary enrichment* (ME).

The first one compares labourers' personal judgements of an earning that permits them to live without difficulties[14] with their effective average earning.

The judgement of a labourer on the amount of monetary entitlements that he/she would reckon sufficient to live without difficulties is, when available, a precious piece of information because it can be interpreted as a revealed conversion rate, which is indeed different between different people and families. In this way we can detect a sufficiency, abundance or scarcity of monetary entitlement.

The second indicator proposed, *monetary enrichment,* is intended to look at average wages and make a comparison between them.

The average wage of a specific group of labourers is taken as a point of reference (a sort of threshold) and the distance between this one and the other average wages in the economy is analysed. If this distance is narrowing it may mean that the other wages are lowering through the threshold, or that the threshold is rising. If the growth rate of this distance is falling it can mean that there is a general levelling towards the threshold.

The second *relations* indicator is *educational enrichment* (EE).

The concept that every job should be meaningful is part of the frame of constitutional democracies,[15] and it is noticeable, especially in a *knowledge society*, that a worker gets a personal reward in being continuously educated while working; at the same time it is a gain in productivity for the working organization and a personal resource inseparable from the worker, who becomes in this way more valuable.

The indicator is the share of the employed population which has attended in the last 12 months a course in relation to his/her occupation. 'Education ... improves the quality of life directly ... [it] also increases a person's ability to earn an income and be free of income-poverty as well' (Sen 1999, p. 90).

The indicator here is proposed identically to the 'employees with recent job training' which Anker *et al.* (2002) insert in the aspect called 'adequate earnings and productive work'. Here, the highest percentage possible is desired, but a low one is not considered as an *unfreedom.*

The last indicator of this profile is *freedom to voice* (FV).

Strikes (number, participation, hours) are chosen as an indicator for the freedom of pointing out workers' voices on work matters. The same information is chosen by Anker *et al.* (2002) among indicators for 'social dialogue and workplace relations'.

A useful proxy could be union density (as suggested by Ghai 2002), but for some countries, including Italy, this information is harder to find at a territorial level.

Unfortunately, information about strikes is tricky because it can happen that a circumstance characterized by many strikes is more linked to difficult circumstances in the labour market rather than to moments of larger freedom.

Moreover 'it is possible to attach importance to having opportunities that are not taken up' (Sen 1999, p. 76), such as the opportunity to call a strike without having reasons to actually do it. It is important to keep in mind these issues while using this information.

2.2.2   Fairness profile

The third aspect – *fairness profile* – collects indicators that show how people with every kind of personal characteristics other than the professional ones can equally access every job, and that show how working conditions don't fall into obvious lacks of significance.

This profile is composed of two indicators, both deeply influenced by the peculiarities of the analysed labour market and society; no subject is completely identifiable, but the target is the absence of any findable discrimination and absurd working practice.

As in the *basic profile*, this profile adopts the methodology of looking for the *decent work deficit* (again, there are similarities with Bescond *et al.* 2003). If possible, in respect to data availability, it would be meaningful to get percentages on workers experiencing the defect.

The first indicator within this aspect is called *irrelevance of private characteristics defect* (IPCD). Its aim is to detect suspicious parallelisms between the distribution of jobs and other characteristics of the person different from the professional ones, such as sex, religious creed, ethnic group or minority status, or others.

For example, as will be done for the Italian case, sexual discrimination can be detected when looking at the share of women in top employee positions (such as managers, executives, etc.).

The same indicator is proposed in *decent work* approaches under different labels: 'distribution of skilled jobs per sex' or 'occupational segregation by sex' (Ghai 2002), 'female share of employment in managerial and administrative occupations' (Anker *et al.* 2002).

The second indicator is called *hanging work* (HW) and the meaning of it is to record the incidence of extended non-productive working conditions.

In the Italian case, for example, it is the existence of the institution called '*cassa integrazione*', which doesn't affect the status as an employee, but for various economical reasons an enterprise is allowed to temporarily (but to an extreme extent of four years) push aside workers who would only partially or not at all be able to work in the firm, until the current problem is solved.

This institution is socially precious. It is dedicated to big enterprises; the state partially stands in for the employer to fulfil the obligation to pay wages, and this contains the risk of violent social problems, but apart from that the working significance of it is nil.

It is intended that a worker who has decided to enrol for a job has the will to actually perform that work, to be involved and up-to-date with the production system and that it is perceived as vexing or shaming to be prevented from working when one would like to work.

Similarly, in other economies there can be found conditions inside the universe of what is legally recognized as work, which have some disputable characteristics.

The indicator has been called '*hanging work*' to give the idea of suspension. 'A person who is denied the opportunity of employment' – in this case of working – 'but given an handout from the State… may look a lot less deprived in the space of incomes than in terms of the valuable opportunity to having' – in this case of performing – 'a fulfilling occupation' (Sen 1999, p. 94).

In the other *decent work* approaches this indication is recorded in a completely different way. While in the present approach the *hanging work* has a negative sense of interruption of the meaning of work, in other approaches (Ghai 2002; Anker *et al.* 2002) the sense is positive, because this indication is an additive component among the public expenditure on social protection, which is one of the first identified objectives of *decent work* (which in the present proposal, as said before, is not taken into account).

Ghai (2002) raised the question of whether it could be possible to prioritize decent work components, and agreed with Ritter (2005) that trade-offs and synergies between them can only be explained having access to complete micro data, otherwise hypothesized.

The proposed approach ranks by hypothesis two levels in which profiles are co-located: the fundamental level is composed by the *basic profile*, which is intended as indispensable. *Relations* and *fairness profiles* come together in a subordinated level. It would later be significant to identify an amount of acceptable defects for the *basic profile* so to get the possibility to continue analysing work through the other two profiles.

The idea underneath this hypothesis is that no social remuneration can compensate awful personal *basic decent work defects*, and that in judging work practices the presence of wrong conditions (*unfreedoms*) is worse than the absence of right conditions (*unreached functionings*).

As a matter of fact the existence of *unfreedoms* reduces the capability set, while it is easier to change chosen functionings or reach a new functioning once the possibility to enhance it exists.

Furthermore, this distribution in two levels confirms the decision on the identity of the subject to whom *decent work* refers: the worker.

Indicators chosen are analysed separately, the problem of tracing causal relations between them using statistical indicators remains unsolved; still it is possible to make plausible conjectures.

3 The *decent work basic–relations–fairness approach* in a context of crisis in Italy

Italy, as the other European countries, has been affected by the enduring economic crisis of these last years, and its labour market has been compromised. Starting from 2008 the employment rate decreased and the unemployment rate increased[16] (Figure 12.1), returning to the values recorded during the 1990s. Long-term unemployment, that from 2004 has had values similar or lower than the short-term one, after 2010 has overtaken the short-term unemployment rate. This passage could be a symptom of a permanent worsening of labour market and social conditions.

Elements of the labour market, but also general macroeconomic and social indicators, show a situation of diffused slow-down. To evaluate how this context

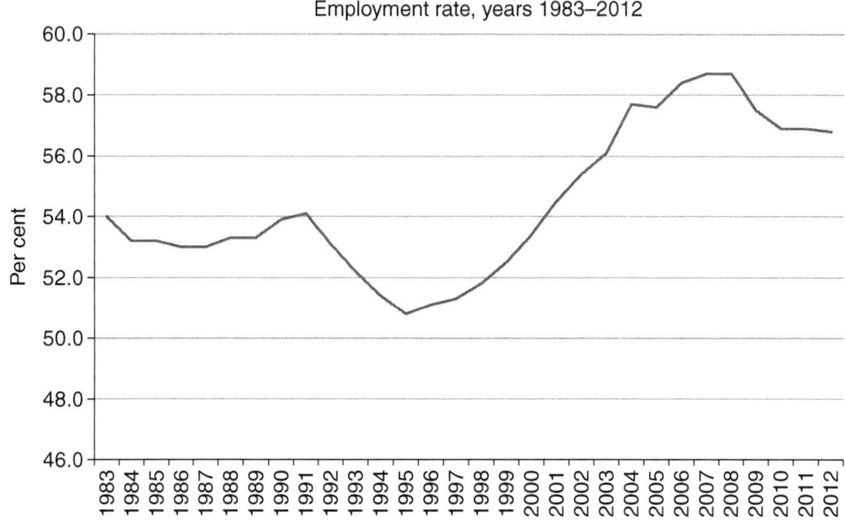

(a)

(b)

Figure 12.1 (a) Unemployment rate 1983–2012; (b) unemployment rate by duration 1992–2012 (source: own elaboration on Eurostat data).

has affected the Italian *decent work* the fundamental level of the previously proposed approach will be analysed.

As it has been presented previously, the basic profile contains four elements: *working hours defect* (WHD), *physical safety defect* (PSD), *legality of jobs defect* (LJD) and *unemployment rate pressure* (URP), which will be calculated as follows.

The right weekly amount of working hours for Italy is reckoned to be between 20 and 40 per week. These limits have been chosen because they correspond to a part- and a full-time employment contract. Due to data availability[17] the WHD is calculated at a national level for 2004–11, summing up people who work more than 40 hours with people who work 1–10 hours and then dividing them all for the totality of the employed people, while for 2000–03 people working more than 40 hours are summed up with those who work 1–15 hours.

It is noteworthy that the survey also reports data about people working 0 hours per week. This information has not been taken into this count because this group includes workers enjoying some form of social security provision (such as sick pay, maternity allowance, Cassa Integrazione Guadagni), and so they escape the group of interest, which is only composed by workers at work.

The second basic indicator is about safety at work. PSD is calculated using data from INAIL, summing up accidents and diseases that happened in the year and then, assuming that every worker could possibly be involved in only one accident or disease, this sum is divided by the total number of employed people (data from ISTAT).

For the third indicator, ISTAT produces an impact of irregular working hours in the frame of national counts. The institution also produces an impact of irregular workers, but here it is chosen to use the information about irregular working hours in the belief that it can be more realistic to imagine that the phenomenon of irregular working hours can concern both people having a regular job and people only working in the irregular sector. The percentage of irregular working hours of the total amount of regular and irregular working hours is given as LJD.

For the last indicator it has been chosen to calculate an unemployment rate which takes into account workers unemployed from more than 12 months,[18] alongside that part of the population called 'discouraged',[19] which is normally counted in the non-active population. The two groups are added and this sum is divided for the ensemble of the labour force[20] and the discouraged.

As Figure 12.2 shows, two elements of the *decent work* basic profile are improving with time (WHD and PSD), while the other two are worsening (LJD and URP).

Looking at the first chart in Figure 12.2, it shows that there is a data break between 2003 and 2004, corresponding to a change in the survey methodology.[21] A descending trend in the *working hours defect* is remarked in both groups of data. In 2004 one-quarter of workers were spending an incorrect amount of time per week at work (25.3 per cent). In recent years, 2009 and 2010, the WHD concerns a little more than one-fifth of workers. The *physical safety defect* trend is falling constantly. In 2000 less than 5 per cent of workers

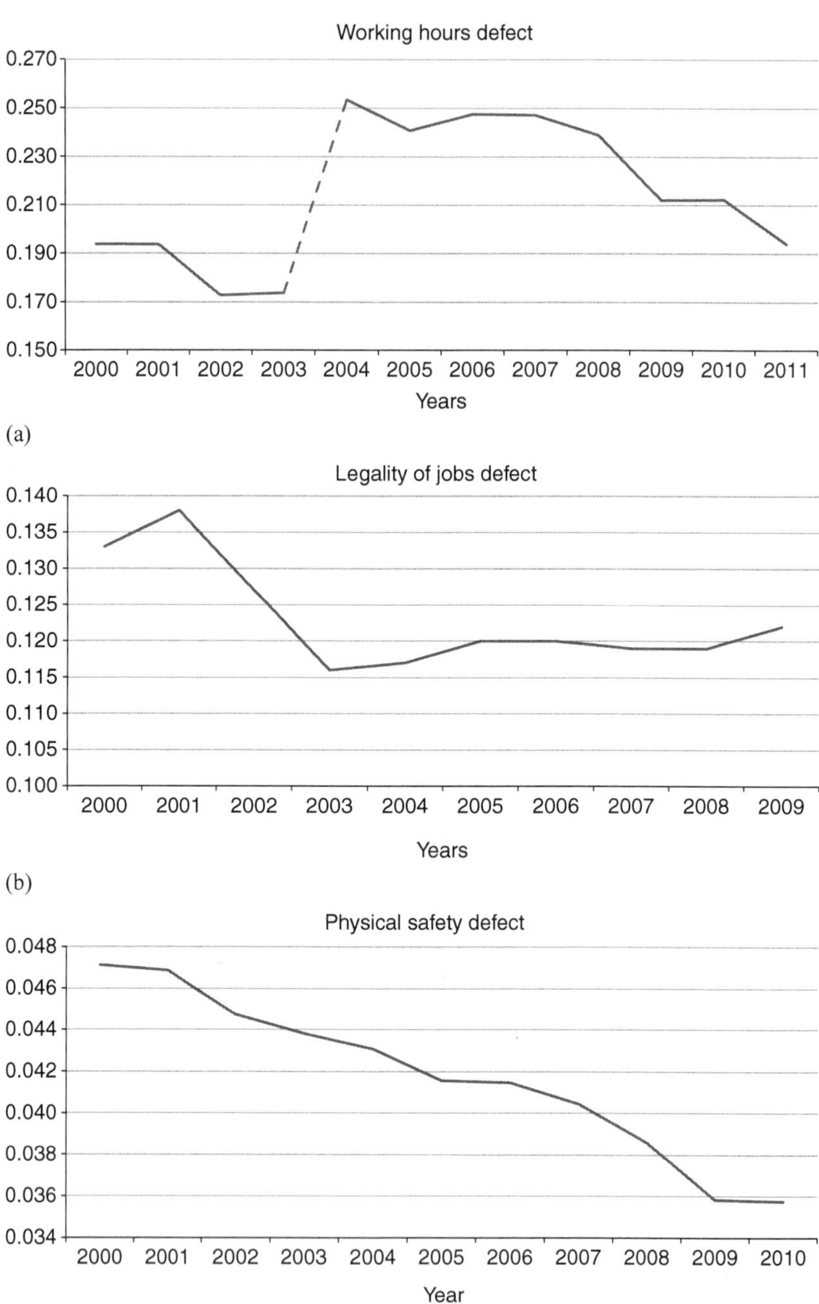

Figure 12.2 Working hours defect, physical safety defect, legality of jobs defect and *unemployment rate pressure* over time (source: own elaboration on ISTAT, INAIL and Eurostat data).

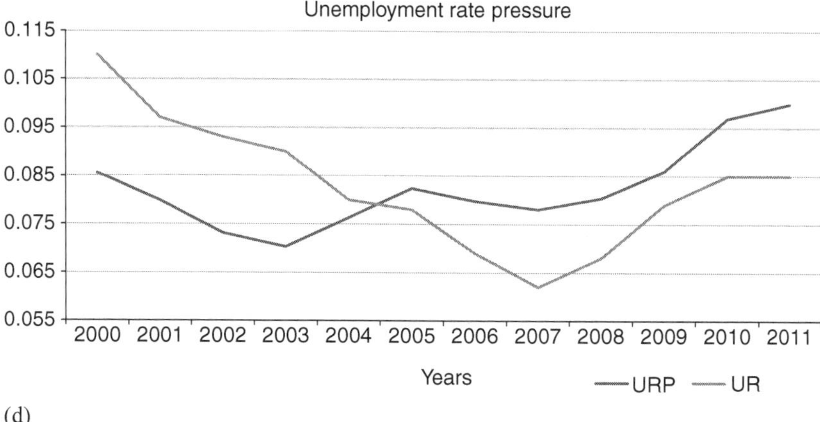

(d)

Figure 12.2 Continued

were involved in accidents or had illness from job activities; in 11 years the trend has always been falling and the recorded percentage declines about one percentage point.[22] It is useful to read this data jointly with the indicator regarding non-regular working. It is appropriate to presume that in areas characterized by high levels of irregular work many working accidents and diseases are not notified. From 2001 to 2003 there is a rapid decrease in the percentage of *legality of jobs defect*, corresponding to the enacting of laws[23] that regulate the employment of familial collaborators. After that a softer but continuous growth continues for years: from 2003 to 2009 the difference is about half a percentage point. Even if it is not possible here to know if there is correspondence between people having these two kinds of working defects, it is possible to make the conjecture that these two indications are linked: one (the *legality of jobs defect*) can prevent the other being realistic.

From 2007 the *unemployment rate pressure* presents an increasing trend. The rate is higher than the commonly used unemployment rate in most of the period considered. In 2004 the URP has lower values than the unemployment rate; this could mean that unemployment of under one year is more incisive than the long-term one onto the general unemployment.

After that year the unemployment rate drops two points up to 2007; the URP falls too, but only half a point. This can be interpreted as if the part of the population considered in URP is less reactive to market opportunity changes.

Afterwards, both rates grow, but when the unemployment rate stops growing from 2010 to 2011, the URP continues. This can be a sign of a shift of people from short-term unemployment to long-term unemployment. In this approach it seemed more interesting to choose this corrected rate because the aim here is to use it as a proxy for the *unfreedom* of the worker to leave his/her job and try to get another.

If the pressure of long-term unemployment and discouragement is high in society, every worker would take this into account when evaluating the choice of whether to continue in the job he/she already has.

From 2008/09 the *decent work* basic profile seems to reflect movements related to the economic crisis. The first indicator, WHD, is constantly improving, but it is possible that a more reasonable amount of working hours is a side-effect of minor employment in terms of working hours rather than a change in the organization of labour.

PSD presents a slow-down of the trend and this should be good news, but in the same period there is an increase of the LJD, with the possibility of connection between the two phenomena that has already been noted. An increase of the LJD could be connected to the desire to escape the complete payment of taxes that can be stronger in a period of perceived fear of the general economic condition, and this could lead to a more unrealistic perception of the dimension of working accidents and deaths.

The URP could be considered the less tricky indicator because, for how it is proposed here, it shows the 'climate' that the worker faces all around his/her work. This indicator has an uninterrupted growth trend since 2007 and inside an environment that is full of people experiencing long-term unemployment a worker feels less and less free to get into any altercations with his/her employer because of the fear of joining the growing group of the unemployed.

In this context of crisis and still considering some multiple meanings that decent work indicators could have,[24] there are various policies that could foster, indirectly and directly, decent work variables. Labour market policies are the most pointed towards these elements and could be part of a wider strategic programme involving growth and development policies (Fadda 2005). In the realm of connecting strategies, industrial policies play a fundamental role in modifying labour market variables. Once the decision about where to co-locate an economy onto the technological frontier is taken, choices on what to produce and how to produce it could activate a virtuous mechanism of revitalization of the entire economy that would eventually effect labour market variables.[25]

Concerning the legality of jobs, an increase in the efficiency of control, such as an augmentation of labour inspectors, could produce a righteous reduction of labour defects.

Tax evasion, which is a tough problem in Italy,[26] could be faced with many different specific subsidies regarding every specific contract, even with tax wedge reductions. Furthermore, it could be argued that the large number of contracts typologies[27] creates confusion about rights and duties that in every case are slightly different, and this is increasing the feeling of non-cohesion that workers experience in Italy nowadays.

Specific labour demand-side policies could affect the working hours defect variable, in particular public support[28] for innovation, concerning not only product innovation but especially organization and process innovation. In this way firms should be able to organize their labour force more efficiently without using overtime work.

Unemployment rate pressure could be positively affected by a strengthening of active labour market policies as public employment services and training activities. Despite the enacting of the reforms concerning the deregulation of the employment agency system,[29] these measures turned out to be inadequate against unemployment. The competition between private (labour agency – LA) and public (public employment service – PES) formal job search channels has produced paltry results: in 2010 only 3.4 per cent of workers had found their job through the PES (most of them relating to compulsory employment) and 2.4 per cent by LA. For about 20 years the mediation power of this system is only 5.8 per cent (Mandrone-Radicchia 2011), which is an insignificant result, especially in comparison with informal recruitment channel (family and friends referrals) that apply to about 30 per cent of workers.

These results are, however, unavoidable for as much as Italy allocates a decreasing share of GDP to labour market policies, in 2011 it was just 0.31 per cent of GDP (Figure 12.3), compared to the EU15 average of 0.56 per cent of GDP. In 2011 Italy dedicated only 0.03 per cent of GDP to labour market services compared to Germany (0.55 per cent) and to the EU15 (0.25 per cent).[30] Only 0.14 per cent of Italian GDP is devoted to training, compared to Germany's 0.26 per cent or to Denmark's 0.50 per cent.

Other Italian labour market reforms try to affect unemployment in its various types. During the last 13 years[31] different reforms significantly changed labour market institutions with the aim to reduce unemployment and increase employment. New kinds of temporary labour contracts have been introduced, reducing what has been considered a rigidity, and increasing flexibility. These policies derive from the European idea, supported by an orthodox economic approach and some empirical evidence,[32] that member states should be inspired by a new social model known as flexicurity. According to this, the deregulation of the labour market should, on the one hand, introduce flexibility, and on the other hand, point to the goal of employability. Italian reforms actually introduced flexibility but measures on security were less incisive (Tridico 2009). The universal scheme for unemployment benefits that has been built in Italy is not systematic enough: the so-called 'Ammortizzatori in deroga'[33] are not sufficient, especially if they are not attached to adequate training programmes that increase human capital and facilitate re-insertion in the labour market, coherently with the perspective of the lifelong learning culture.

Empirical evidence concerning the period in which these reforms have been enforced shows an increase in the number of temporary jobs, whereas there has been a decrease of permanent ones. This shift had produced an increase in precariousness. In this sense, the most important purposes of Italian reforms were partially missed: in these years unemployment increased and temporary workers have been the first to be affected by the crisis.

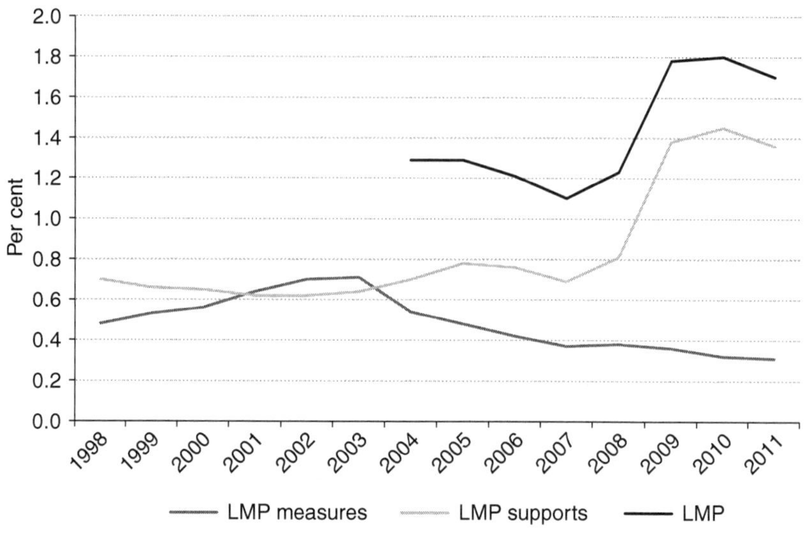

(a)

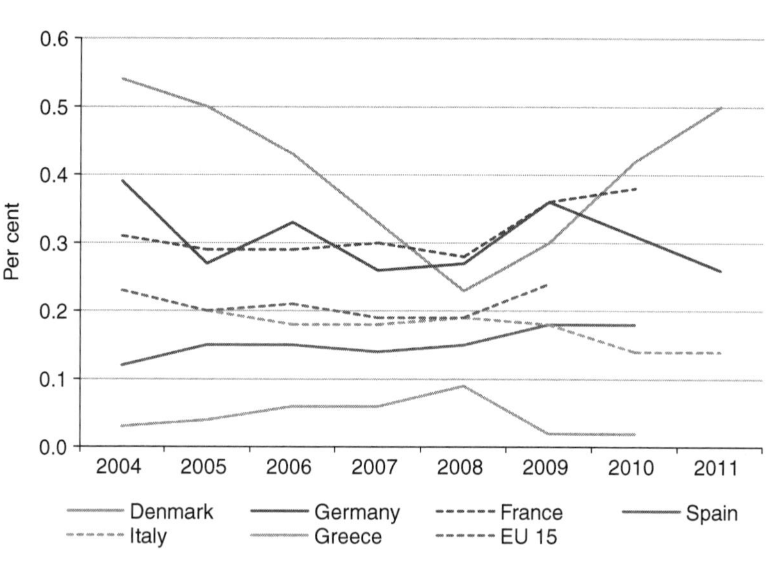

(b)

Figure 12.3 (a) Total labour market policy expenditure in Italy; (b) LMP expenditure (training).

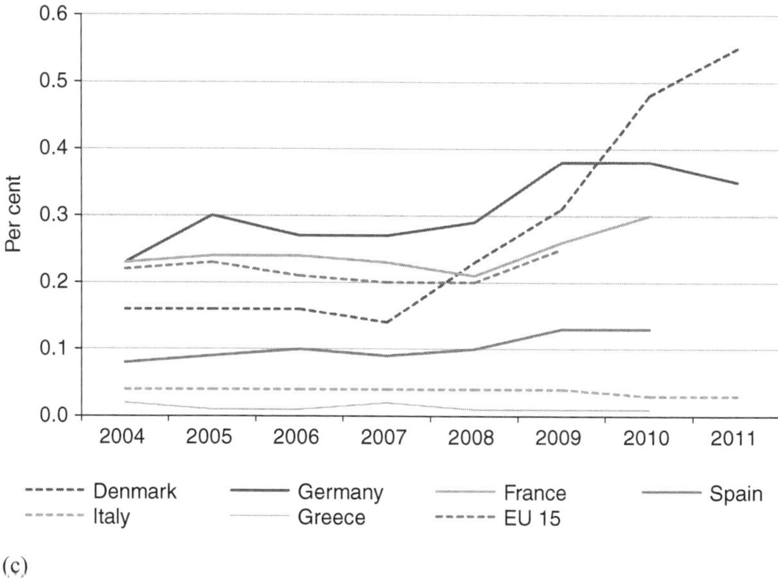

(c)

Figure 12.3 (c) LMP expenditure (LM services) (source: own elaboration on Eurostat data).

4 Conclusions

The aim of this chapter has been to introduce an approach to the ILO *decent work* concept, defining the variables that characterize it in a developed country like Italy. On the basis of this concept, policies concerning *decent work* variables were analysed to evaluate which measures should be implemented to foster it, into a wider scenario of policies to recover from the crises.

This proposal of *decent work* has been articulated into three profiles: basic, relations and fairness. These have been prioritized into two levels: basic is the fundamental one and concerns elements of daily working conditions; relations and fairness are complementary and regroup indicators linked to the social aspect of working.

The approach has been tested by analysing the case of Italy and observing the impact of the crisis on the fundamental level of *decent work*.

The basic profile regroups essential indicators, which are characterized as being the ones more intimately linked to daily working conditions. For these indicators it is possible to point out a chosen desired value, and the gap, whether positive or negative, between the actual and the desired value is recorded as a decent work basic defect. The fundamental level is composed by four variables: *working hours defect* (WHD) indicator shows the percentage of the employed population working an amount of weekly hours different from the ones within the working hours range; *physical safety defect* (PSD) is obtained summing up working accidents and working diseases and dividing all by the number of employed people; *legality of jobs defect* (LJD) shows the share of non-regular working hours on the total amount of regular and non-regular working hours; *unemployment rate pressure* (URP) is meant to be a proxy of the *unfreedom* to change the job that a worker already has. It is built by summing up discouraged people with workers unemployed from more than one year and dividing this sum by the labour force augmented with discouraged people.

The empirical analysis on *decent work* in Italy has been realized using time series data from 2000 to 2011. Different sources have been taken into account, among them the ISTAT labour force survey, statistics on accidents and diseases from INAIL, data from the INPS observatories on workers and EUROSTAT database.

Observing data from the period considered, the four indicators composing the basic level have different trends. WHD and PSD variables show a gradual decrease that could be interpreted as an approach to the *decent work* condition, while the other two indicators (LJD and URP) have an opposite trend of worsening of the defects and estrangement from the desired situation.

Focusing in particular on years affected from the economic crisis, from 2008 the two defects that were decreasing show a moment of stability, while the others get even worse.

In this study, various policies have been taken into account according to their capacity to affect, indirectly and directly, *decent work* variables. Labour market policies are mostly significant and among them some could positively affect those indicators: active policies as strengthen the public employment service and improve training programmes, an increase of labour inspections; or a reform of employment contracts finalized to reduce contract typologies.

Other policies not directly connected to the labour market have been considered for the general effect that they could have in a wider scenario of crisis: fiscal policies addressed to reducing tax burdens, support of ICT innovation, and in particular organization and process innovation, industrial policies and policies against tax evasion.

The proposed approach has tried to detect possible *labour unfreedoms*, in the belief that work is *decent* if it is free from constraints. In a situation of a general downturn of the economy, what is recorded is a non-amelioration of the basic profile indicators.

Recovery from the crisis certainly needs an increase of the employment rate; nevertheless, it would be a partial achievement if it were not associated with an improvement in the quality of labour. In this context the *decent work* analysis could be a useful tool to have a multidimensional view of the matter.

Notes

1 The capability approach, by Amartya Sen, is a way to intend development as the 'process of expanding real freedoms that people enjoy' (Sen 1999, p. 3), so to allow 'people to lead the kind of lives they have reason to value' (Sen 1999, p. 10).

2 In Sen's 1999 theory functionings are actual beings or doings which people have achieved. 'The concept of functionings ... reflects the various things a person may value doing or being' (Sen 1999, p. 75).

3

> We live in a world of unprecedented opulence ... and yet we also live in a world with remarkable deprivation ... individual agency is, ultimately, central to addressing these deprivations ... we have to see individual freedom as a social commitment.
>
> (Sen 1999, pp. xi, xii)

4 The *opportunity cost* is the value of the next best alternative not chosen.

5 *Excessive hours of work* are considered as more than 48 per week, as the ILO Convention N.1/1919 stated, *extreme hours of work* are considered as more than 60 per week.

6 'Percent of employed population working less than hours threshold, but available to work and wanting to work additional hours' (Anker *et al.* 2002, p. 29).

7 In Sen's 1999 theory the 'conversion' is the relation through which every human being can transform income into functionings; it is 'neither constant nor in any sense automatic and irresistible' (Sen 1999, p. 109); it is strongly influenced by environmental contingencies and personal conditions.

8 Or to reach an 'omnilateral development' (see Marx 1875).

9 'A person's capability refers to the alternative combinations of functionings that are feasible for her to achieve ... the substantive freedom to achieve alternative functionings combinations ... the freedom to achieve various lifestyles' (Sen 1999, p. 75). Synthetically, a 'capability set' is the whole of the real opportunities that a person has.

10 One of the most heavy critiques of *decent work* is that it applies better to industrialized countries, so that countries which are more developed in a capitalistic way may seem to have more *decent work* than others where people still have informal non-market economic relationships. Those are not always characterized by awful working conditions, but they may be based on barter, gift or other forms of reciprocity, and people in those systems don't have the difficulties recalled before. As an example it can be seen – even in Western societies – at those experiments of 'local exchange systems', e.g. the time bank, where people produce and exchange services and goods on the basis of time they have used to realize them, so de facto that is a productive situation which can create good conditions of 'work', which cannot be called so because its output is not counted among production in the GDP. This kind of problem arises everywhere there is a non-market relationship that concerns production and exchange of services and goods. In those cases, as that production is not taken into account by the capitalist way of interpreting value, similarly working conditions are not considered. For the aim of this study, which is to adapt a UN concept to an industrialized country, this observation doesn't have an essential quantitative relevance, and it can be assumed that in Italy all economic relationships outside the formal economy are characterized as perpetrating indecent working conditions.

11 Many authors, mostly belonging to the school of new Keynesian economics (NEK), affirm that wages are determined by forces which refer more to social relations rather than to marginal productivity of labour. Wages are viscous and don't follow faithfully or rapidly changes in labour productivity or in the equilibrium between labour demand and labour supply: the presence of unemployment, due to non-equilibrium wages, is not contingent, but it hides mechanisms of complex interactions between economic actors. The insider–outsider theory, developed by Lindbeck and Snower (1986), affirms that wages are influenced by the effective power of labourers already working (often identifiable with the ones belonging to unions), who exploit a privileged position compared to outsiders (workers not yet hired) that allow them to claim and keep

a wage which is higher than the wage demanded by an outsider up to the equivalent of turnover costs (hiring, firing, firm-specific training). This is because replacing an insider worker it costly for the firm and, as long as those costs are high (depending on the level of labour protection and the specificity of the job) insider workers keep their privileged position. The efficiency wage theory, elaborated by Shapiro and Stiglitz (1984), suggests the idea that the productivity of a labourer is incentivized by a high wage (higher than equilibrium wage), and this is convenient to be paid by a firm when control costs are too high, or anyhow higher than the wage incentive. A higher wage, called the efficiency wage, is an instrument for the firm to select, motivate and retain a worker and meanwhile to keep turn-over costs low. The theory of implicit contracts was developed by C. Azariadis (1975), M. Baily (1974) and D. Gordon (1974) (working independently in 1974 and 1975). This theory interprets labour agreements as a insurance formula, so wages are sticky for the interest of both contractors: employers get the certainty that wages won't rise in periods of great earnings, while employees get the certitude of not being fired.

12 An exception is the index of labour morale (Godfrey 2003) which multiplies hourly pay by the share of wage-employed employees to rank countries in the belief that wage-employment is, by hypothesis, the closest to *decent work* conditions.

13 For example, in the Italian Constitution, art. 36, first paragraph, it is stated that the 'worker has the right to a remuneration proportionate to the quantity and quality of his/her work and in any case sufficient to ensure him/herself and his/her family a free and decent existence'.

14 This information, when available, reveals the differences in conversion rates between different people and families.

15 Italian Constitution, art. 35, second paragraph: '[the State] cares after education and professional elevation of workers'.

16 Labour market variables graphs concern workers 15–64 years old.

17 ISTAT 2000–11, *Labour Force Survey*.

18 Due to data availability these data refer to workers aged 15 or older.

19 Due to data availability these data refer to workers aged 15–64.

20 These data refer to workers aged 15 and older.

21 Survey of the cross-section in 2004 became continuous.

22 It is important to specify that these data refer to reported accidents and disease; it is unknown how this picture would change if it were possible to take into account accident and sicknesses not reported, and, because it is possible that this refers to regular and non-regular workers, the problem largely has links with the problem of legality of jobs.

23 Law 30 July 2002, No. 189 *Modifica alla normativa in materia di immigrazione e di asilo*. G.U. 26 August 2002, No. 199; Law 9 October 2002, No. 222 *Conversione in legge, con modificazioni, del decreto-legge 9 settembre 2002, n. 195, recante disposizioni urgenti in materia di legalizzazione del lavoro irregolare di extracomunitari*. G.U. 12 October 2002, No. 240.

24 Those could be explained with the availability of micro data that show connections between different pieces of information.

25 Fields like the green economy and sustainable tourism are new, growing sectors that could offer more and good-quality jobs.

26 See, among others, Tanzi and Shome (1993) and Russo (2010).

27 On the discussion about the number of contracts, see Lapage-Saucier *et al.* (2013).

28 Such as tax credits or non-repayable loans.

29 Law 20 November 1996, No. 608 *Conversione in legge, con modificazioni, del decreto-legge 1 ottobre 1996, n. 510, recante disposizioni urgenti in materia di lavori socialmente utili, di interventi a sostegno del reddito e nel settore previdenziale*. G.U. 30 November 1996, No. 281. D.lgs. 23 December 1997, No. 469 *Conferimento alle regioni e agli enti locali di funzioni e compiti in materia di mercato del lavoro, a*

norma dell'articolo 1 della legge 15 marzo 1997, n. 59. G.U. January 1998, No. 5. Law 15 March 1997, No. 59 *Delega al Governo per il conferimento di funzioni e compiti alle regioni ed enti locali, per la riforma della Pubblica Amministrazione e per la semplificazione amministrativa.* G.U. 17 March 1997, No. 63. Law 24 June 1997, No. 196 *Norme in materia di promozione dell'occupazione.* G.U. 4 July 1997, No. 154. Law 14 February 2003, No. 30 *Delega al Governo in materia di occupazione e mercato del lavoro.* G.U. 26 February 2003, No. 47. A total reorganization of the employment system has been realized with the aim of mediating between labour demand and labour supply. In 2003 it also introduced competition between the private labour agency (LA) and public employment service (PES).

30 Data on EU15 refer to 2009.

31 Law 24 June 1997, No. 196 *Norme in materia di promozione dell'occupazione.* G.U. 4 July 1997, No. 154. Law 14 February 2003, No. 30 about the subject *Delega al Governo in materia di occupazione e mercato del lavoro.* G.U. 26 February 2003, No. 47. Law 28 June 2012, No. 92 *Disposizioni in materia di riforma del mercato del lavoro in una prospettiva di crescita.* G.U. 3 July 2012, No. 153.

32 According to the neoclassical approach, involuntary unemployment derives from the rigidity of the labour market, while, in a flexible market, if unemployment exists it is only voluntary. The empirical evidence concerns the Scandinavian region, where a *flexicurity* model has been implemented with success.

33 These unemployment benefits have been introduced to protect some unemployed who present specific peculiarities; in the recent Fornero reform they are called Mini-Aspi.

References

Anker, R., Chernyshev, I., Egger, P., Mehran, F. and Ritter, J., 2002. Measuring decent work with statistical indicators. *ILO Working Paper*, No. 2.

Azariadis, C., 1975. Implicit contracts and underemployment equilibria. *Journal of Political Economy*, Vol. 83, No. 6, pp. 1183–1202.

Baily, M., 1974. Wages and employment under uncertain demand. *Review of Economic Studies*, Vol. 41, pp. 37–50.

Bescond, D., Chataignier, A. and Mehran, F., 2003. Seven indicators to measure decent work: an international comparison. *International Labour Review*, Vol. 142, No. 2, pp. 179–212.

Eurostat, 2000–2011. Labour market statistics database. Available at http://epp.eurostat.ec.europa.eu/portal/page/portal/statistics/themes (data downloaded between January and July 2012).

Fadda, S., 2005, Per un'integrazione tra politiche del lavoro e politiche di sviluppo. *Argomenti*, n. 14/2005.

Ghai, D., 2002. Decent work: concepts, models and indicators. *ILO Discussion Paper*, No. 139.

Godfrey, M., 2003. Employment dimensions of decent work: trade-offs and complementarities. *International Institute for Labour Studies, Discussion Paper*, No. 148/2003.

Gordon, D.F., 1974. A neoclassical theory of Keynesian unemployment. *Economic Inquiry*, Vol. 12, No. 4, pp. 431–459.

ILO, 1999. *Report of the Director-General: Decent Work*. Geneva, 87th Session of the International Labour Conference.

INAIL, 2000–2010. Statistical data bank archives. Available at bancadati.inail.it/prevenzionale (data downloaded between January and July 2012).

ISTAT, 2000–2011. *Labour force survey*. Available at dati.istat.it (data downloaded between January and July 2012).

ISTAT, 2000–2011. *Monthly survey on employment, working time, earnings and labour cost in large enterprises*. Available at dati.istat.it (data downloaded between January and July 2012).

Krauser, A., 2011. *Work to live or live to work? Unemployment, happiness, and culture. IZA Working Paper*, No. 6101.

Lepage-Saucier, N., Schleich, J. and Wasmer, E. (2013), Moving towards a single labour contract: pros, cons and mixed feelings, *OECD Economics Department Working Papers*, No. 1026.

Lindbeck, A. and Snower, D., 1986. Wage setting, unemployment and insider–outsider relation. *American Economic Review, Papers and Proceedings*, Vol. 76, No. 2, pp. 235–239.

Mandrone, E. and Radicchia, D., 2011. La ricerca di lavoro: i canali di intermediazione e i Centri per l'impiego. *Collana studi Isfol*, 2/2011.

Marx, K., 1875. *Critica al programma di Gotha*. Roma: Samonà e Savelli.

Ritter, J.A., 2005. Patterns of job quality attributes in the European Union. *ILO Working Paper*, No. 51.

Russo, F.S., 2010, Tax evasion and community effects in Italy, *CSEF Working Paper*, no. 254.

Saith, A., 2004. Social protection, decent work and development. *Discussion Paper*, No. 152.

Sen, A., 1999. *Development as freedom*. Oxford: Oxford University Press.

Shapiro, C. and Stiglitz, J., 1984. Equilibrium unemployment as a worker discipline device. *American Economic review*, Vol. 74, No. 3, pp. 433–434.

Tanzi, V. and Shome, P., 1993. A primer on tax evasion, *IMF Staff Paper*, Vol. 40, No. 4, pp. 808–828.

Tridico, P., 2009. Flessibilità, sicurezza e ammortizzatori sociali in Italia. *Departmental Working Papers of Economics, University Roma Tre*, No. 107.

13 The cooperative firm

A non-capitalist model for the Occupy Movement

Andrea Bernardi and Anna Greenwood

1 Time of crisis

It is possible to trace the origin of the current crisis back to the United States, the symbolic centre of world capitalism. A few causes are commonly recognized as the triggers to the 2007–08 US financial crisis, the consequences of which have been spreading around the globe ever since. The causes (Crotty 2009) have, of course, been hotly debated, but among the most commonly recognized causes identified as having paved the way for the collapse have been: subprime lending; the existence of excessively easy credit conditions and the consequent housing bubble; the predatory practices of negligent lending; and the after-effects of fraudulent underwriting. Additional causes (Goodchild 2012) are framed in terms of financial deregulation (as occurred under both Democrat and Republican administrations), the negative effects of over-leveraging (which started as early as in the mid 1990s) and the general regrettable aftermath of a heaving over-complex financial management regulatory system.

Although no single moment can be pinpointed, these preconditions worked together to create a series of interacting effects culminating in the, previously unthinkable, collapse of Lehman Brothers in September 2008. In a rush to take remedial action, the US administration managed to prevent a wider systemic failure through a massive injection of public money, asking the FED to take unprecedented action. A few financial institutions were either nationalized or bailed out. Although these actions did alleviate some of the local damage, they could not prevent the crisis spreading to both European financial markets and the wider global economy. Other pre-existing factors, such as the global imbalances and the crisis of the welfare state, made the situation worse (Tridico 2012).

Similarly, in Europe, between 2008 and 2013, private banks had to be nationalized or bailed out by European governments in Britain, Germany, France, the Netherlands, Belgium, Luxembourg, Sweden, Denmark, Portugal and Greece. As in North America, governments and central banks initiated responses on an unprecedented scale. As the problems spread, however, so too did logistical challenges, particularly those associated with coordination between the two sides of the Atlantic and with delays and mistakes within Europe in terms of creating a united response between the actions of EU institutions, Euro area institutions and national governments.

In Europe, the US-born financial crisis destabilized the common monetary area through the stress it placed on the sovereign debt market. This triggered conflicts between member states and resulted in a very slow and expensive process of stabilization. As we write, in mid-2013, the crisis appears under control, but to get to this point required very unconventional actions by the European Central Bank (ECB) and several high-level meetings between EU member states, Euro area member states and international institutions. The need to lend money to Greece, Spain and later Cyprus, and the need to stabilize the Italian sovereign debt market, pushed forward the so-called 'fiscal compact' and the now well-known austerity policies at both national and European levels.

Given the explicit nature of corporate mistakes and offences, the American debate reached not only the media, but also resulted in a series of high-profile tribunals and parliamentary inquiries. Great expectations were placed on these events, but sadly, despite the initial clamour and spectacularization, disappointment followed in terms of policies, legislation and court sentences.

The scientific (Blankenburg and Palma 2009) and political debates were nevertheless huge in North America and in Europe, receiving extensive media coverage and being widely debated in alternative fora such as social media and also within universities, public meetings and political events. The American debates had originally focused on the excesses of the finance industry and their actors. Protesters typically asked for better regulation and control, protesting specifically against banks and their top executives. Attention was also paid to the conflicts of interest that were highlighted as existing between the financial industry, the government and the legislature. In Europe the character of the debates were slightly different, with the targets of resentment shifting early on to criticize government austerity policies, singling out distinct European and international institutions such as the IMF, ECB and the European Commission, as the responsible culprits.

All the so-called Occupy movements, in the United States and in Europe had a common enemy: the market and the corporations. In a context of growing unemployment and government budget cuts, it was not difficult to motivate and fuel public enthusiasm for the cause in the form of massive street protests, which proliferated alongside an increased influx of newspaper articles, books, films and documentaries against the market and its excesses. The market and corporations were blamed for unemployment, the housing bubble, lost savings and properties. More than two decades of market fundamentalism were, according to many, to blame. In the words of Stiglitz (2009, p. 346): 'From a historical point of view, for a quarter of a century the prevailing religion of the West has been market fundamentalism. I say it is a religion because it was not based on economic science or historical evidence.'

The current crisis of capitalism seems to have also precipitated the emergence of doubts, not only over the modern mess capitalism had got itself into, but also concerning the beneficent effects of returning to the old order. The systems of power as described by Elias in *The Civilizing Process* (1939) or within Boulding's *Organizational Revolution* (1953) were acceptable during periods of economic growth, but seem to have become unbearable during times of crisis. In a rush for action a series of high-profile head-hunting campaigns were undertaken to satisfy a growing public dissatisfaction over the structural inequalities of the old order. We have observed executives of prestigious financial institutions being publically humiliated live by enquiry commissions,[1] we have seen bankers being forced to resign or to 'voluntarily' renounce their outrageous bonuses,[2] we have seen powerful politicians or businessmen resigning from their positions or being ousted by public outrage.[3] The most violent protests took place in Greece; the country most affected by the consequences of the crisis the most.

We will now review in details the origin and the nature of Occupy Wall Street (OWS).

2 The protest movements

It is possible to trace the origins of these protests historically (Castells 2012). Indeed, protest has become one of a number of likely normative reactions to unpopular national and international policies. The last decade of the twentieth century and the first decade of the twenty-first century have been characterized by periodic protests such as those organized at the G8, later G20, meetings. Fear of these reactions have meant that, increasingly, these sorts of official gatherings have needed to meet in secluded and well-protected locations. In a similar vein, the World Economic Forum meetings in Davos, an informal gathering of world financial and political leaders, found itself to be a favourite target for protests against globalization and neoliberal policies. Partly as a response to this increasingly critical and reflective climate, an alternative organization to the World Economic Forum was established and became a successful voice. The World Social Forum held its first meeting in Porto Alegre, Brazil, in 2001.

Criticisms have also increasingly appeared in print. The beginning of the new century has seen a proliferation of publications about non-proprietary standards, anti-globalization, about the ethical dilemmas of consumerism, the aftermath of social conflict and the need for sustainability. Examples of these sorts of publications are numerous, but include *Empire* by Toni Negri and Michael Hardt (2000), *No Logo* by Naomi Klein (2000) and *Petit Traité de la Décroissance Sereine* by Serge Latouche (2007).

After the outbreak of the 2008 financial crisis a plurality of protest movements and organizations came to be collectively called Occupy Movements, with OWS symbolizing the Occupy Movement in its most eponymous and inspiring form. The chronological order of events leading to this type of fashionable protest action is known, although the connections and causal relations between all the lead-up events is still not entirely clear. The key inspiring events are commonly said to have been the establishment of Democracy Village in 2010 outside the British Parliament in London, the protests in Spain that started in May 2011, the earlier events of the so-called Arab Spring and the Occupy Dataran movement in Kuala Lumpur of July 2011. A few national examples can be useful to portray some of the common threads of the overall movement. It should be noted, however, that the debates and situations are still evolving; even in June 2013, the events surrounding the so-called Occupy Gezi Park movement in Turkey were dominating the world press.

2.1 National cases of protest movements

Sweden and Germany can be regarded as pioneers of direct political involvement and action of the protest movements, particularly as a direct result of agitations stimulated by their Pirate Parties. The first Pirate Party was the Swedish 'Piratpartiet', founded in 2006. Other parties were subsequently formed in Austria, Denmark, Finland, Germany, Ireland, the Netherlands, Poland and Spain. More recently, the national organizations have started to establish formal coordination at the European level, given the very similar nature of objectives and methods. In some countries their success has been really tangible; in Sweden, for example, the party in 2009 obtained 7.1 per cent of the votes in the European Parliament elections. Similar success was achieved in Germany in the 2011 elections.

Spain was disturbed in May 2011 by a protest movement that is still alive and active. This was the Indignants' Movement, alternatively known as 'Take the Square'. The street protests which occurred during 2011 against the political class paradoxically helped the conservative party to win the 2011 general election. All the blame for unemployment, state debt and the real-estate bubble was piled at the feet of the socialist government of José Luis Rodríguez Zapatero, who had been in power since 2008.

The United States was also the scene of similar discontent. In September 2011 the first Occupy protest that gained national and international media attention was OWS, in New York. Suggestively, gatherings, talks and camping took place in Zuccotti Park, in the heart of New York's financial district (Chomsky 2012). Showing the power of such movements, in less than a month related gatherings were organized in dozens of other American cities (including even the occupation of the Wisconsin State Capitol building), as well as in about 80 other countries around the world. Another inspiring event occurring on American soil was 'Bank Transfer Day'. This was a consumer activism initiative that called for 'a voluntary switch from commercial banks to not-for-profit credit unions'. In the spirit of the times, everything started on Facebook as an event planned for 5 November 2011. Within a few days the event was joined virtually by tens of thousands of people and was replicated in other places and times in North America. The basic idea behind this collective action was to complain about the fees and service quality of the Bank of America, suggesting that those members of the public in agreement with the protestors should collectively swap their bank accounts to a cooperative bank, or a credit union as it is defined in the United States and Canada. The participants of OWS supported the event, although it did not satisfy every one of their members, as a few radicals complained that cooperative banks should still ultimately be considered a bank, one of the foremost villains of the Occupy Movement.

Italy, so far, has not seen massive street protests such as those that have occurred in Spain or Greece. Even the peaceful gatherings that have occurred can be seen to have been very limited when compared to their counterparts in France or the United States. It seems that the anger of citizens and their participation has been diverted to a political movement, the 'Movimento Cinque Stelle', that in 2013 gained third place in the general elections. The only exception to this Italian tendency towards a muted public response has been the so-called NO TAV movement (it reached its apex of conflict and activities in 2011). NO TAV is an informal organization fighting against high-speed railways. In this case the gatherings often ended with violence against the police and the construction site facilities.

Last but not least, China has been only gently awakened by minor events that followed the inspirational Arab Spring, in what has been described as the failed Jasmine Chinese revolution, started in February 2011. Nevertheless, the Special Administrative Region of Hong Kong has hosted a very interesting protest, the Occupy Central. The protest took place in a square, Central, in front of the headquarters of the international bank HSBC, near the Hong Kong Stock Exchange. Protesters have added to the traditional global economic issues an additional local topic: the request for a reform blueprint towards universal suffrage in Hong Kong. The protest camp stayed in place between 15 October 2011 and 11 September 2012 and was removed after court rules and police intervention. It is interesting to note that the movement has survived the camp and is still active. Currently intellectuals and activists are working on the political manifesto of the so-called Occupy Central 2014 that will take place physically with similar objectives in July 2014, 'to press the government for a democratic reform blueprint to achieve universal suffrage'.

2.2 Common values: heroes and villains

With so many plentiful examples of success, the Occupy Movement is now recognized as a viable means of international protest against economic and democratic power imbalances, against social and economic inequality and for those advocating the need for direct participation in economic and political relations. The movements, locally, have focused on different national issues, but nevertheless they share common methods and common sets of villains and heroes. The common method (Castells 2012) is that of direct participation, which recently has increasingly involved the internet as a means of organizing events, sharing information and making decisions (Soule 2012 ; Castells 2012). The common heroes are the writers and the scholars (such as Negri, Latouche, Chomsky, Stiglitz) whose vision is shared and advocated by the movement. Inevitably there are a few politicians and corporation bosses among the enemies and among the heroes who are inevitably the individuals who spearhead the campaigns and increase media excitement, but it is very hard to map the leadership of the movement, the official demands and the political elaboration, given the extremely informal and participative nature of the organization.

The ideological, scientific and political propositions behind these national movements also share some common points (Gamson and Sifry 2012). There is a common protest against the causes of the crisis (neoliberal policies, excesses of market and finance, big corporations and unethical business, education debt, unfair tax structure, inequality, erosion of democracy), against the consequences of the crisis (unemployment, fiscal consolidation, welfare and labour market reform). There is also a common accusation against either the current or past political class. It is common to see expressed a shared vision in support of sustainable growth (if not de-growth), open software and free access to resources such as water, healthcare and education (Chomsky 2012; Roberts 2012).

We will now consider the nature, origin and contemporary global role of cooperative firms.

3 An old institution

The apex of the crisis was reached in 2012, which was also the UN international year of cooperatives. It is interesting that more connections have not been made between the potential embedded within cooperative models and solutions that are aired for the ending of the economic crisis.

The cooperative firm is a very old institution. The roots of modern cooperation can be historically seen to lie in several forms of collective or communitarian work, such as those that existed within the Roman Empire, ancient Egypt, ancient Asian societies or the Latin American pre-Columbian peoples (Douglas 1987). In 1844, the first modern cooperative organized around a formal business model was established in Rochdale, near Manchester, UK. At the end of the industrial revolution, and as a response to its collateral social problems, the Western world developed the cooperative model, together with the workers' and democratic movements, trade unions, the Communist Manifesto and later the Rerum Novarum encyclical. In the following 150 years the modern cooperative became a worldwide model of economic organization of production in the manufacturing, services and banking sectors.

A cooperative is an enterprise owned not by investors but rather by other, non-capitalist, actors. It can come in many guises. There are producer-owned enterprises (such as employee-owned firms, agricultural cooperatives). There are customer-owned enterprises (such as retail, wholesale or supply firms, cooperative utilities, clubs and other associative organizations, housing cooperatives). There are also non-profit and mutual enterprises (such as mutual savings banks, cooperative banks, loan associations, credit unions, life insurance, insurance companies).

Both socialist thought and Catholic social doctrine have inspired the development of the cooperative movement. In fact, the cooperative model is often mistakenly associated with being closely aligned to communism or state-planned economies. Although the cooperative model does represent an alternative to capitalism, it is not, however, intrinsically mismatched to functioning within a market economy (Jossa 2005). Indeed, quite the contrary, cooperatives have actively flourished in the most liberal Western nations. According to Hansmann (1996, p. 297), while:

> freedom of enterprise is a fundamental characteristic of the most advanced modern economies. Capitalism, on the contrary, is contingent; it is simply the particular form of ownership that most often, but certainly not always, proves efficient with the technologies presently at hand.[4]

In short, cooperatives are primarily representative of an alternative ownership model, and should be seen as successfully operating in market economies and contributing to the plurality of market actors, despite the fact that they are fundamentally non-capitalist in orientation.

3.1 The cooperative sector today

The productive role that cooperative firms play in the market economies of both Western nations and developing countries has nevertheless been frequently overlooked. Likewise, it tends to be forgotten that the International Cooperative Alliance (ICA) is the world's largest NGO. The figures of the current size of the cooperative sector are impressive. According to the ICA, there are one billion members worldwide.[5] With regards to the banking and finance sectors, in 2011 the World Council of Credit Unions counted about 49,000 credit unions among their member institutions, equalling around 177 million individual members in 96 countries. In Europe there are 4,200 local cooperative banks with about 60,000 branches holding an average market share of about 20 per cent of the European banking market. These banks serve 45 million members and 159 million customers. At national levels the figures are even more impressive: the market share of cooperative banks in France is said to be higher than the average; in the Netherlands, Rabobank can count 50 per cent of all Dutch citizens in its membership.

Some national cases are particularly impressive. In Canada, for instance, one out of three citizens are members of a credit union. In the United States 42 million people receive their electricity supply from a cooperative. In Germany the cooperative sector represents 25 per cent of the banking sector. World-leading products are produced by cooperatives, such as most French champagne, all Danish Lurpak butter or 90 per cent of Italian parmigiano. Although not the primary focus of this chapter, it is notable that this situation is also to be found in the developing world. In India, for example, 55 million farmers are members of the Indian Farmers' Cooperative (IFFCO), and in Kenya 45 per cent of national GDP comes from cooperatives.

International organizations such as the UN and the International Labour Organisation (ILO 2002) have always devoted a special interest to cooperatives and their role worldwide. Also, the EU (Commission of the European Communities 2001) and most of its member states have justified and deployed special legislation and policies in recognition and support of the cooperative sector.

As a source of credit, food, social protection, shelter and employment, co-operatives play an important role. The United Nations estimated (in 1994) that the livelihood of three billion people was made more secure by co-operatives. At least 800 million are members of co-operatives and 100 million are employed by them.

(Birchall and Ketilson 2009)

There are several types of cooperatives; a few countries – for instance Chile, Brazil, Italy, the United Kingdom, Spain, France, the United States and Japan – are rich in every kind of them (consumer, worker, user and financial cooperatives). In other nations, the presence of the cooperative model is mostly limited to a few types (the most common model is the consumer cooperative and the supply cooperative). Both consumer and the worker cooperatives operate in a variety of sectors: from retail to electricity, from school to university education, from manufacturing to housing, from performing arts to funeral services and health care.

3.2 *The cooperative diversity*

A true cooperative is owned by either its workers or consumers or users, and this intrinsically makes them more socially responsible and participatory than their capitalist counterparts. Apart from the system of ownership rights, the diversity of cooperative firms can be mapped in a different way in each sector (Bernardi 2007).

The advantages of cooperatives have been empirically observed by a number of scholars. The worker cooperatives have been argued, for example, to represent in both theory and practice an alternative to traditional capital–labour conflict (Jossa 2005; Bernardi *et al.* 2011). Namely, the fact that they are owned by the consumers or the user means they represent a more transparent and fair business model. In the event of market failure they have been shown to be more efficient (Olsen 2002; Jussila *et al.* 2008) and resilient under difficulties (Zanotti 2013). Furthermore, cooperative enterprises represent worldwide distributed alternatives to the investor-owned limited company model (Spear 2000; Chaves and Monzòn 2007). They respond to the expectations of consumers or workers better than firms driven only by the need to remunerate the investment of their owners (Jussila *et al.* 2008). It is also possible to argue that cooperatives offer better health and safety conditions to workers. Research by Guiol and Muñoz (2007) has demonstrated the existence of a strong relationship between safety, well-being and workers' participation.

Cooperatives are rooted in their local communities and therefore often represent a respected and powerful institution at the local level. It is much more likely that a firm owned by the community (for instance, an electric cooperative owned by the whole village) will produce positive externalities (such as social capital and investments in corporate social responsibility) rather than negative ones such as pollution. Those positive externalities can vary quite considerably among different countries because each community, in any specific moment of social development of a nation, or during a specific economic cycle, use cooperatives slightly differently, to solve a specific problem, a peculiar market failure or a local institutional inefficiency. Cooperatives represent not only a good service provider or a responsible employer, but also an opportunity to reinforce rather than consume social capital (Bernardi *et al.* 2011; Fukuyama 1999; Putnam 1993; Sabatini 2013).

3.3 Market plurality

As Stiglitz (2009) has argued, market plurality is a desirable and positive state for national economies. In striving for a balance between market, state and other institutions, there should also be a role for not-for-profits and cooperatives.[6] It was not so long ago that the European continent was a model of a modern mixed social economy and used to represent an alternative to market fundamentalism, although over time this wider focus has gradually become eroded. Even the United States, despite not being commonly associated with cooperatives, can be shown to be home to an abundance of them, once you scratch beneath its capitalist surface. Indeed, although the role of credit unions and saving banks used to be much greater in America, millions of Americans benefit daily from services and goods provided in an efficient, alternative way. As in the case of the United Kingdom, some of the problems in the finance industry occurred just at the end of a process of demutualization during which several cooperative banks and building societies were transformed into traditional banks.[7]

We will now explain how the cooperative model has been particularly successful around the globe during past socio-economic difficulties and has shown resilience during the current crisis.

4 Cooperatives in times of crisis

In the nineteenth and twentieth centuries the purpose of establishing a cooperative was primarily to provide a job or a shop or a service; whereas today the rationale has been subtly refocused to provide good jobs, socially and environmentally responsible products and alternative services which the state or the market were commonly perceived as having failed to provide.

The cooperative sector has not been immune to the current financial crisis. In Spain, for example, the cooperative banks found themselves facing even harder problems than those experienced by the traditional banks during the crisis. Nevertheless, despite this and other inevitable exceptions, it is still possible to argue that the cooperative sector has shown itself to be remarkably resilient during times of crisis. A recent work (Birchall and Ketilson 2009) has measured the durability of cooperatives on the basis of several performance indicators. The findings show in the case of the cooperative banks, for instance, that during the crisis the cooperative sector worldwide actually increased its volume of lending and offered better interest rates compared to its traditional competitors. Despite obvious pressures, these banks cumulatively increased their assets, deposits and membership levels.

4.1 Cooperation and past crises

Cooperatives were well familiar with weathering the storms of financial crises. In part this success is inherently entwined with the investment and management structures of cooperatives themselves, and in part this is to do with the experiential lessons the movement has gained through its not always easy historical past. The modern cooperative was born during the difficult social and economic consequences of the industrial revolution in Northern Europe and this trajectory of turning to the cooperative model during troubled times has been one that has repeated itself throughout history. It is possible to mention several national crises where either individuals or governments have looked to cooperatives as a solution to a problem.

To take an early example, the German rural cooperative bank model, exported all over the world, was invented by Friedrich Raiffeisen, during a deep agricultural depression in 1860s Germany. Similarly, the Great Depression of the 1930s in the United States formed the backdrop to new national policies that established large numbers of agricultural, dairy, electricity, telecommunication and petroleum cooperatives. During this period a cooperative bank was also established to explicitly provide credit to farmers. Furthermore, the Federal Credit Union Act was passed to support the working class that was unable to address the big traditional banks. Somewhat later, in the spirit of rebuilding after the Second World War, agricultural cooperatives in Italy were developed as part of reforms that recognized that the large rural properties needed to be redistributed and allocated more efficiently. Perhaps most dramatically, in the 1960s, the cooperative housing model in Chile emerged after a powerful earthquake disrupted the effectiveness of the traditional market providers. In the same period in New York, for different reasons, the cooperative ownership of the residential buildings (cooperative housing and condominium) became the most commonly favoured ownership system for residential blocks of flats.[8] Again, during the 1960s and 1970s in China the Rural Cooperative Medical Scheme was deployed by Mao to provide basic health care to millions of peasants who did not have any (Bernardi and Greenwood 2014).

4.2 State, market and large corporations

The big corporation has definitely been a common villain for members of the Occupy Movements. In the United States it has become the symbol of the abuses of market power and unethical business, and the site of numerous conflicts of interest. The outrageous bonuses and stock options afforded to CEOs have been seized upon as powerfully demonstrating the greed and systemic corruption endemic in many mega corporations. In terms of looking for solutions, attention has been often focused on American law, criticizing the rights that have too often been collectively attributed to corporations as players within the judiciary.

It is interesting that although there has been much academic debate within the realms of both economics and sociology about the role of state and market (Hayek 1944; Polanyi 1944; Sennet 1998; Clemens 2009), the way the Occupy Movements have vulgarized the alleged dangers of the big corporation remains imprecise or extreme. As Wilkinson *et al.* have argued (2010), many of the problems of big enterprises could be addressed through supporting different forms and practices of worker participation: ranging over a growing scale from information, to communication, consultation, codetermination and control (Wilkinson *et al.* 2010). The cooperative firm would be at the top level of this ranking of participation models. A rejection of corporations *per se*, does not seem to be the answer, especially if the corporation is controlled by a good governance system, is well regulated and is organized with a high degree of worker participation.

It seems that the protest movements too often suggest that the state can be the only sole alternative to the excesses of the market. This is not so. A third alternative would be for protesters and policy makers to consider the option of cooperative ownership. Indeed, it is wrong to:

> take it for granted that, in the absence of government intervention, large-scale enterprise will be organized in the form of investor-owned firm.... Yet investor ownership is not a logically necessary concomitant of free markets and free enterprise. Rather, it is quite contingent, a form of organization that is often but not always dominant given the current technologies.
>
> (Hansmann 1996, p. 1)

4.3 The cooperative sector and this crisis

Support for the cooperative model, anyhow, should not only be justified on the grounds of their ethically superior theoretical or ideological underpinnings.[9] Cooperatives might deserve support by policy makers and by members of the protest movements because they tangibly contribute to the effectiveness of the market by providing them with competition in the form of an alternative model of ownership and governance (ILO 2002). Furthermore, they can be provably shown to be more sustainable and resilient in times of crisis (Massagli and Sorci 2012). For instance, the figures on the performance of the UK cooperative sector compared to those of the overall economy provide some food for thought. Between 2008 and 2011 the number of cooperatives in the United Kingdom grew steadily, rising by 23 per cent between 2008 and 2011. The membership level also increased by 19.7 per cent between 2008 and 2011, currently recording some 13.5 million members. In terms of results, the UK cooperative economy has outperformed the UK economy every year between 2008 and 2011. Cooperative turnover in 2011 was 35.6 billion pounds and has raised an average of +5.9 per cent compared to a negative average of –0.6 per cent for the total UK economy.[10] Similarly positive figures are also available for the Italian economy. In this context, the cooperative sector has raised its productivity between 2008 and 2011, despite the fact that overall national productivity has been decreasing (Bernardi *et al.* 2011; Massagli and Sorci 2012; Zanotti 2013).

Going back to the origins of the crisis (excesses of finance and gigantism of the banking and finance institutions) the case of the Italian cooperative banking sector provides an illustrative example. In this case a plurality of actors are involved, but the most important one is the Banca di Credito Cooperativo (BCC). This is a network[11] of 400 independent banks that share core central operations such as asset management, marketing, information systems and procurement. Although the system is big enough to offer a wide variety of services and an efficient allocation and management of capital, the 400 banks are independent, and the failure of one, or several of them, would not compromise the whole system. This is surely a persuasive advertisement for the benefits of the cooperative model, not least because of the stark contrast it presents to the damage created to the national financial sector in the case of the collapse of big traditional banks. While the European central banks and the ECB itself are debating how to solve the 'too big to fail' paradox, such a federation of banks shows how to be local, but at the same time big, yet big in a way that crucially avoids putting all eggs in the same basket.

As we have exemplified, the cooperative firm may provide some of the answers and solutions sought by OWS. In the next section we will review the values shared by OWS and the Cooperative Movement. The failure of OWS in delivering feasible proposals and real impact will be described.

5 Proposal within protest

From the establishment of the first modern cooperative in Rochdale, the international cooperative movement has prided itself on its seven core inspiring principles. The inspiring principles are 'Voluntary and Open Membership', 'Democratic Member Control', 'Member Economic Participation', 'Autonomy and Independence', 'Education, Training, and Information', 'Cooperation among Cooperatives' and 'Concern for the Community'. Finally, we argue that these principles should make cooperatives a natural choice of ally for members of the protest movements as they have main points of approach in common.

5.1 Shared principles

One point of convergence that has been rarely discussed is that which lies between the values of the Cooperative Movement (ILO 2002) and those espoused by the core supporters of OWS. It is a central contention of this chapter that members of OWS should recognize the importance of shifting from critical (some might say even naive) protests against the market towards a more informed and constructive set of proposals for a better regulated market, responsible consumer choices and the presence of alternative non-capitalist market actors such as cooperatively owned or local authority-owned enterprises.

Taking each of the principles of cooperatives one by one, a number of similarities and points of potential dialogue can be identified (all quotations from the modern definition of the seven cooperative principles as adopted in 1995 by the ICA).

Voluntary and open membership: 'Cooperatives are voluntary organizations, open to all persons able to use their services and willing to accept the responsibilities of membership, without gender, social, racial, political, or religious discrimination.' In a similar way it could be said that one of the central objectives of the protest movements have been their consistent clamour for the free and direct involvement of consumers and workers. Worker and user or consumer cooperatives could be set up in virtually any sector or industry, aside from the very capital-intensive ones. Chomsky (2012) himself, a key actor of OWS, argues for economic democratization, suggesting the cooperative model to allow workers to control the means of production.

Democratic member control:

> Cooperatives are democratic organizations controlled by their members, who actively participate in setting their policies and making decisions. Men and women serving as elected representatives are accountable to the membership. In primary cooperatives members have equal voting rights (one member, one vote).

All the protest movements, but in particular those that have managed to actively run for local or national elections, have argued in favour of economic democracy, at a macro level, and for democratic control of their organizations themselves at a micro level. This is another common point. The Visa and MasterCard network is an example of a technology and platform owned by the member banks, either big or small. This can be applied to many other business sectors, but more generally, a democratic organization such as is presented through the ideal of the cooperative should be treasured by all the movements sharing a concern for the erosion of democracy[12] in contemporary societies.

Economic participation:

> Members contribute equitably to, and democratically control, the capital of their cooperative. At least part of that capital is usually the common property of the cooperative. They usually receive limited compensation, if any, on capital subscribed as a condition of membership. Members allocate surpluses for the following purposes: developing the cooperative, setting up reserves (part of which indivisible), benefiting members in proportion to their transactions with the cooperative business.

The protest movements have not always proposed a formal platform to transform their proposals into actions (Roberts 2012). It could be suggested, however, that principles of collective economic participation and the reinvestment of profits could be more rigorously discussed by members of the protest movements. Rather than outright rejecting the need for profit and capital, cooperatives provide alternative ways to manage them.

Autonomy and independence: 'Cooperatives are autonomous, self-help organizations controlled by their members.' This is an important point of contact between the cooperative movement and the protest movement, because in different ways they both claim the importance of independent businesses. Both concur that the current dominance of big corporations or banks is a threat to economic plurality and indirectly also a threat to democracy and intellectual freedom (Graeber 2011). They both see the importance of having a plural and participatory system. To this end, Wikipedia, which has been widely used in protest campaigns, provides an appropriate example of a knowledge platform that is democratically owned and controlled by its users and contributors.

Education, training and information:

> Cooperatives provide education and training for their members, elected representatives, managers, and employees so they can contribute effectively to the development of their cooperatives. They inform the general public – particularly young people and opinion leaders – about the nature and benefits of cooperation.

Members of the protest movement have often raised issues surrounding the freedom of the press, recognizing the regular conflicts of interest that commonly exist between politics, the press and economic power. As part of these vocal campaigns several independent documentaries and training films have been produced, spreading the message of the evils of the market and in favour of alternative models. The cooperative model, since its beginning, has been investing in cooperative education, marketing and training. Numerous examples exist from documentaries to the funding of schools, universities or new businesses.

Cooperation among cooperatives: 'Cooperatives serve their members most effectively and strengthen the cooperative movement by working together through local, national, regional, and international structures.' As in the protest movement, the basis of the movement is one centred upon horizontal help between members, as opposed to the vertical, hierarchical corporate structures so despised by protestors.

Concern for community: 'While focusing on member needs, cooperatives work for the sustainable development of their communities through policies accepted by their members.' This is perhaps the most important point of connection, as a concern for the community and sustainability is a clear common goal for both movements.

5.2 Reform or revolution?

As Noam Chomsky has argued, the demands of the protest movements have been either very moderate (so much so that even the *Financial Times* columnists have welcomed them) or they have been too vague and implausible (overthrow capitalism, establish direct democracy, etc.), meaning they do not appear to seriously contest the existing capitalist interests and power systems (Chomsky

2012). As Graeber has argued, the Occupy Movements have failed to suggest feasible alternatives to the model they have been opposing (Graeber 2013). The emphasis on the method (transparency, information, direct democracy) is not enough if it is not supported by a strong policy platform. Even Joseph Stiglitz[13] has publically argued that the Occupy Movements have failed to deliver because of their lack of organization and pragmatism.

Furthermore, some of the approaches seem to be worryingly articulated instead. For example, the common depiction of the market as a public enemy could be a dangerous over-simplification of a complicated economic situation with few absolute heroes or villains (Roberts 2012). Similarly, the idea that the state, by definition, would be a better supplier of services than the market, regardless of the sector, the service and the efficiency, could be considered excessively reductionist. Another big taboo for the protestors centres upon the idea of profit, which is generally characterized by members of these movements as evil, dangerous or wrong. Indeed, advocates of cooperatives would argue that profit is actually good, if achieved in a fair and sustainable way. Most cooperatives see profit as a measure of their efficiency and financial sustainability, allowing the organization to keep offering services and goods to their members and providing its workers with employment.

Other issues, such as the public ownership of the national currency and the seigniorage have been debated in an overtly polemical way as well. They are actually complex topics, which arguably suffer rather than advance through the popular public activism of street protests. Nevertheless, at the local level, cooperatives have for a long time been offering successful experiments of collective lending and public currency at the very micro level. Another example of a recurrent oversight of the Occupy Movement is the way their activism seems to be articulated via anger and attacks against banks and financial systems, which are in reality institutions as neutral as the market. Indeed, it seems limiting to reduce banks to public enemies and, as explained by advocates of the Bank Transfer Day movement, there are alternatives to the traditional banking market, and consumers and savers should be aware of the diversity and make wise choices.

Different models of employee ownership[14] are possible over and beyond those promoted by cooperative supporters. The political and scientific debate on alternative forms of ownership is rather developed in Europe and could be harnessed by members of the Occupy Movements to constructively discuss alternative policies. A strong debate about mutual ownership is occurring in the United Kingdom. Very advanced proposals have been produced, in particular with regards to the processes of privatization or transformation occurring within the public sector, such as in the cases of the NHS, the Post Office or the newly nationalized banks (Michie and Llewellyn 2010; Michie *et al.* 2010).

Given the complementarities between the Cooperative Movement and OWS, we will call for dialogue and collaboration between the two movements.

6 Conclusions: ownership not occupation

The Occupy Movement needs a feasible and pragmatic alternative proposal to make protests constructive and consequently more effective. Their emphasis to date on methods rather than on solutions has proved to be largely ineffective. Without a feasible and sound proposal, the Occupy Movement will either decline (Roberts 2012) or, even worse, will end up reinventing itself more radically.

The Cooperative Movement needs to attract a new generation of members with motivations different from those of the previous generations. Indeed, to this end the ICA has already recently developed a new corporate image with the logo, slogan and flag of the next 150 years of cooperation. The old ideological membership of the fathers (either socialist or Christian) and the grandfathers is gone forever, and a new set of reasons to join that resonates with the young and the socially aware needs to be written and promoted.

Cooperatives see that they need both membership and active participation to survive. If the cooperatives and the protest movements worked together there is a great potential for synergy between the two groups. The Occupy Movement has the energy, youth and participation to reinforce the Cooperative Movement. The cooperative sector has the organization and the infrastructure to support the Occupy Movement. Above all, it provides a historically tried and tested practical alternative to current market fundamentalism.

This collaboration between the Cooperative and the Occupy Movements requires effort and dialogue between the two parties and many observers feel that this is not likely to happen (Shepard 2012), especially on account of the international and informal nature of the latter. Nevertheless, several projects at national and local levels may be deployed to start such a dialogue. The finance and banking sector could be a very powerful starting point, if only the protest movement would formally consider cooperative banking as a model of sustainability, fairness and ethics. The consumer cooperative sector might also be promoted to protest movement supporters as a model of ownership, responsible consumer behaviour and fairness. Together, both movements could pool their many common concerns and raise a common voice. Where possible the cooperative ownership should be supported as a model of transferring utilities, services and public goods infrastructures from the state to the community, rather than to a large capitalist corporation.

The protest movement needs the cooperative sector. The cooperative movement needs the energy and youth involved in the Occupy Movements. Citizens of the North and the South of the world need both: a competitive alternative actor for the market and a strong advocate against the excesses of capitalism through ownership, not occupation.

Notes

1 For instance, the US Financial Crisis Inquiry Commission.
2 For instance, the United Kingdom's Royal Bank of Scotland top executives Frederick Goodwin and Stephen Hester.

3 For instance, Italy's bank Monte dei Paschi di Siena president or Greek and Spanish national and local politicians.

4 The comparative efficiency of a system of ownership rights can be calculated by measuring the transaction costs connected with one solution or another: costs of politics, value of voting, cost of contracting, cost of monitoring managers, efficiency of capital allocation, value of entrepreneurism, value of culture and ideology, cost of ownership. The non-capitalist form of ownership is not rare at all if we consider that in the world there are 900 million members of cooperatives and only 320 million direct shareholders.

5 The World Watch Institute, *Vital Signs Report 2012*.

6 Stiglitz also argues that the years of the crisis of the Western world, and in particular of those countries that are more market fundamentalist, have been the years of the rise of China. A country with a large role played by government that has based its growth upon a greater array of institutional arrangements, including the township and village enterprises and cooperatives in the 1990s.

7 For instance, Bradford and Bingley and Northern Rock.

8

> In the United States in 1960, more than 99 percent of all residential apartments in multi-unit buildings were rented from commercial landlords. Since then, a rapidly increasing number of apartment buildings have come to be owned collectively by their occupants through a cooperative or, more commonly, a condominium. By 1991 cooperatives and condominium accounted for 16 percent of all multi-unit housing.
>
> (Hansmann 1996, p. 195)

9 In fact, 'much of the existing literature on ownership, and particularly on worker-owned and consumer-owned enterprise, reflects some degree of ideological commitment' (Hansmann 1996, p. 7).

10 Figures from Cooperatives UK, *The UK Cooperative Economy 2012, Alternatives to Austerity*.

11 The overall network counts 4,400 branches, serving more than 1,100,000 members through almost 35,000 employees.

12 According to Chomsky (2012), democracy is a key topic in defining the Occupy Movement that:

> should be regarded as a response, the first major public response, in fact, to about thirty years of a really quite bitter class war that has led to social, economic and political arrangements in which the system of democracy has been shredded.

13 On 18 October 2012 in an interview on the New York public network Channel 13.

14 Employee ownership (where employees own more than 50 per cent of the shares); co-ownership (employees hold substantial minority stake of more than 25 per cent); employee stock ownership plan (ESOP) (minor employee-owner schemes to provide a company's workforce with an ownership interest in the company); workers' cooperative (employees own the firm indirectly as members, not as shareholders, with rights to be represented at board and/or management level).

References

Bernardi, A., 2007, The co-operative difference: economic, organisational and policy issues. *International Journal of Co-operative Management*, 3, 11–23.

Bernardi A. and Greenwood A., 2014, The Usefulness of a Historical Comparative Perspective: The Rural Co-operative Medical System in China, *Asia Pacific Business Review*. Forthcoming.

Bernardi, A., Treu, T. and Tridico, P., 2011, *Lavoro e Impresa Cooperativa in Italia*, Passigli, Firenze.

Birchall, J. and Ketilson, L.H., 2009, *Resilience of the Cooperative Business Model in Times of Crisis*, Geneva: International Labour Office.

Blankenburg, S. and Palma, J.G., 2009, Introduction: the global financial crisis, *Cambridge Journal of Economics*, 33, 531–538.

Boulding, K., 1953, *The Organizational Revolution: A Study in the Ethics of Economic Organization*, New York: Harper & Brothers.

Castells, M., 2012, *Networks of Outrage and Hope: Social Movements in the Internet Age*, Cambridge: Polity Press.

Chaves, R. and Monzón, J.L., 2007, *The Social Economy in the European Union, European Economic and Social Committee (EESC)*, N° CESE/COMM/05/2005.

Chomsky, N., 2012, *Occupy*, London: Penguin.

Clemens, E.S., 2009, The problem of the corporation: liberalism and the large organization, in Adler, P.S. (ed,), *The Oxford Handbook of Sociology and Organization Studies*, Oxford: Oxford University Press.

Commission of the European Communities, 2001, *Cooperatives in Enterprise Europe*, Brussels, consultation paper.

Crotty, J., 2009, Structural causes of the global financial crisis: a critical assessment of the 'new financial architecture', *Cambridge Journal of Economics*, 33 (4): 563–580.

Douglas, M., 1987, *How Institutions Think*, London: Routledge.

Elias, N., 1939, *The Civilizing Process: Sociogenetic and Psychogenetic Investigations*, Oxford: Blackwell.

Fukuyama, F., 1999, *The Great Disruption: Human Nature and the Reconstitution of Social Order*, New York: Free Press.

Gamson, W.A. and Sifry, M.L., 2012, The #Occupy Movement: an introduction, *The Sociological Quarterly*, 54 (2): 159–163.

Goodchild, P., 2012, What is wrong with the global financial system?, *Journal of Interdisciplinary Economics*, 24 (1): 7–28.

Graeber, D., 2011, *Debt: The First 5000 Years*, Brooklyn: Melville House.

Graeber, D., 2013, *Democracy Project, A History, a Crisis, a Movement*, New York: Spiegel & Grau, Random House.

Guiol, P. and Muñoz, J., 2007, Management, participation et santé des salariés: des médecins et des salariés parlent, *RECMA*, no. 304, 76–96.

Hansmann, H., (1996), *The Ownership of Enterprise*, Cambridge, MA: Harvard University Belknap Press.

Hayek, F.A., 1944, *The Road to Serfdom*, Chicago, IL: Chicago university Press.

ILO (International Labour Organisation), 2002, *Promotion of Cooperatives Recommendation*, No. 193.

Jossa, B., 2005, Marx, Marxism and the cooperative movement, *Cambridge Journal of Economics*, 29 (1): 3–18.

Jussila, I., Tuominen, P. and Saksa, J.M. 2008, Following a different mission: where and how do consumer co-operatives compete?, *Journal of Co-operative Studies*, 41 (3), 28–39.

Klein, N., 2000, *No Logo*, London: Harper Collins Publishers.

Latouche, S., 2007, *Petit Traité de la Décroissance Sereine*, Paris: Mille et Une Nuits.

Massagli, E. and Sorci, V., a cura di, 2012, Il ruolo della Cooperazione ai tempi della Crisi, *Bollettino speciale Adapt*, no. 23, 4 December.

Michie, J. and Llewellyn, D.T., 2010, Converting failed financial institutions into mutual organisations, *Journal of Social Entrepreneurship*, 1 (1): 146–170.

Michie, J., Ham, C. and Mills, C., 2010, *A Mutual Health Service*, Oxford Centre for Mutual and Employee-owned Business, Kellogg College, University of Oxford.

Negri, T. and Hardt, M., 2000, *Empire*, Cambridge, MA: Harvard University Press.

Olsen, O.J., 2002, Consumer ownership in liberalized electricity markets: the case of Denmark, *Annals of Public and Co-operative Economics*, 73, 69–88.

Polanyi, K., 1944, *The Great Transformation: The Political and Economic Origins of Our Time*, Boston, MA: Beacon.

Putnam, R., 1993, *Making Democracy Work: Civic Traditions in Modern Italy*, Princeton, NJ: Princeton University Press.

Roberts, A., 2012, Why the Occupy Movement failed, *Public Administration Review*, 72 (5): 754–762.

Sabatini, F., Modena, F. and Tortia, E., 2013, Do cooperative enterprises create social trust?, *Small Business Economics*. Forthcoming.

Sennet, R., 1998, *The Corrosion of Character: The Personal Consequences of Work in the New Capitalism*, New York: Norton.

Shepard, B., 2012, Labor and Occupy Wall Street: common causes and uneasy alliances, *Working USA, the Journal of Labor and Society*, 15 (1): 121–134.

Soule, S.A., 2012, Social movements and markets, industries, and firms, *Organization Studies*, 33 (12): 1715–1733.

Spear, R., 2000, The co-operative advantage, *Annals of Public and Co-operative Economics*, 71, 4: 507–523.

Stiglitz, D.J., 2009, Moving beyond market fundamentalism to a more balanced economy, *Annals of Public and Cooperative Economics*, 80 (3): 345–360.

Tridico, P., 2012, Financial crisis and global imbalance: its labor market origins and the aftermath, *Cambridge Journal of Economics*, 36: 17–42.

Wilkinson, A., Gollan, P.J., Marchington, M. and Lewin, D., 2010, Conceptualizing Employee participation in organizations, in *The Oxford Handbook of Participation in Organizations*, Oxford: Oxford University Press.

Zanotti, A., 2013, Le performance delle cooperative di servizi durante la crisi: un'analisi nel periodo 2099–2011, *Euricse Working Paper*, no. 51.13.

14 Active employment policy in the EU and in Poland

A Gordian knot or inertia enchanted in words?

Leszek Cybulski and Ewa Pancer-Cybulska

1 Macroeconomic trends and unemployment in the EU

The global economic crisis moved to Europe in the second half of 2008. It caused a sharp deterioration in the labor market, which statistically occurred in the following year. The average annual unemployment rate in 2008 was the lowest in the last quarter of this century. Four years later, in 2012, the unemployment rate in the EU27 exceeded the highest historical level.[1]

The obvious inverse relationship of GDP growth and the unemployment rate do not require special economic reasons. It is illustrated by the divergent slopes of trend lines of GDP and the unemployment rate (Figure 14.1).

Both variables are interdependent, but it should be acknowledged that the unemployment rate is a dependent variable and constitutes a function of the product. If we assume a linear dependence of the form:

$$U_t = ar_t + b \tag{1}$$

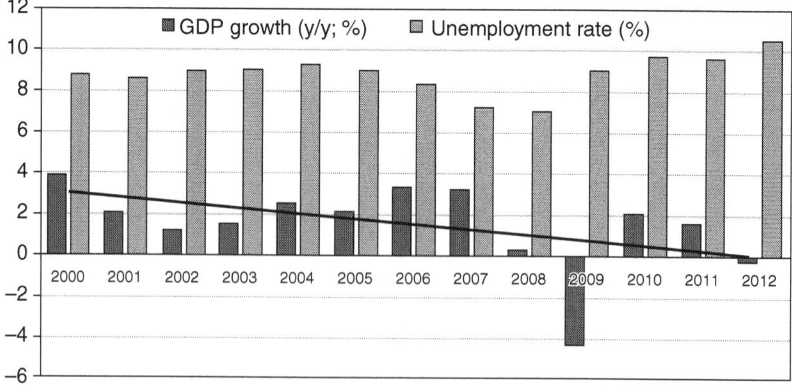

Figure 14.1 Comparison of GDP growth with the unemployment rate in the EU27.

where:

    U is the unemployment rate;
    r is change in GDP
    a, b are parameters
    t represents consecutive years

there emerge two typical practical problems:

1   the effect of the time shift in unemployment in relation to economic growth,
2   the current value of the b parameter, i.e., the volume of the necessary economic dynamics by which employment begins to rise, while unemployment falls.

The EU27 reached a small positive rise of GDP in 2008 (0.3 percent y/y), although the rapid advancement of the economic crisis made societies aware that we are dealing with the most serious financial crisis at least since the 1970s' oil shocks, and perhaps since the Great Depression. At the same time, as we have remarked, in 2008 the unemployment rate was the lowest in the EU in over a quarter of a century. There was a sharp rise in unemployment in 2009 and it continued through 2010, despite the EU having achieved in that year more than 2 percent in growth dynamics. The nature of these time shifts is well known and it concerns delays in collecting, processing and publishing statistics; the manufacturers', service providers' and consumers' belief that the changes are temporary; late reactions of entrepreneurs and public authorities to the falling demand; and long legal procedures of laying employees off (period of notice). An empirical verification of this shift may be done by simple calculation of the a parameter level – based on the full available time series (for the EU27 referring to the years 2000–11) and forecasts for 2012. The lowest level of this parameter (it should be negative, so it is related to its greatest modulus) refers to the best suited function. For functions:

$$U_t = ar_t + b \tag{1}$$

a equals –0.031 (for 13 observations) and –0.098 (for the last 12)

$$U_t = ar_{t-1} + b \tag{1a}$$

a equals –0.229 (12 observations)

$$U_t = ar_{t-0.5} + b \tag{1b}$$

a equals –0.740 (12 observations).

The results of the authors' own calculations show that the function (1b) best captures the causal dependencies.[2] The purely academic problem would be to test additional quarterly pools of data, but the limited statistical base does not allow one to make calculations on a monthly basis. However, even such a simple study enables rejecting simultaneous analyses and those with the annual shift, for the sake of discerning the effects of employment downturn mainly in a six-month term.

A typical situation is the presence of non-employment economic growth in the developed countries. The explanation lies in the formula-expressed relation between the product, employment and its attribute – productivity (the model is univariate because it uses only one Smithian factor of production – work):

$$P_t = Z_t * W_t \tag{2}$$

where

> Z is employment
> W is labor productivity
> P is gross domestic product

which, when converted, becomes:

$$r = r_z + r_w + r_z * r_w \tag{3}$$

where

> r is GPD dynamics
> r_z is employment dynamics
> r_w is labor productivity dynamics

and after some simplification:

$$r \approx r_z + r_w \tag{3a}$$

This means that the condition of employment growth in the economy is $r > r_w$. Labor productivity dynamics may be regarded as an autonomous independent variable, although in reality it is affected by several factors (mainly innovation and technology, organizational and market development, incentive system, working hours and working conditions, training and experience of employees). Work efficiency dynamics is much less subject to fluctuations than production, sales, demand, employment and unemployment. In the richest countries, productivity grows the most slowly. In the new EU member states (N12) reducing the gap it is significantly faster, while it is the fastest in Asian countries which experience the Industrial Revolution. Stability in the work efficiency dynamics is not absolute in nature, and thus the change is slow. Nevertheless, one can assume that r_w, and thus the b parameter in function (1) in the EU27, oscillate around 2 percent in the long term. This was the case in 1974–89 (Commission of the European Communities 1993, p. 12) and nowadays this is confirmed by the recent observations of the time series. GDP growth of 2.1 percent in 2010 corresponded to the stability of unemployment rate of 9.7 percent in 2010–11 among the economically active population, while the next year's growth of 1.6 percent led to an increase in unemployment in 2011 and 2012. The conclusion is explicit – the economic growth of between 0 and 2 percent in the EU is usually accompanied by a decline in employment and rise in unemployment. In order to overcome the serious problem of unemployment in the EU, the region should have a few years of stable growth rate of 3 percent. At a rate of 2 percent one cannot expect the situation to improve.

The presented data are averaged, and the sensitivity of particular national labor markets to changes in the economic situation may be different. It may best be exemplified by Poland, the only country in the EU to avoid the 2009 recession. In 2007–12 Poland had the fastest economic growth and at the same time recorded a decline in the labor market – in contrast to Germany, showing progress of employment (Austria and Malta also made slight progress; Figure 14.2). The decline in the labor market in Bulgaria, Cyprus, Lithuania and Spain is much higher than one might have expected from the general trend of development. In contrast, the labor market in Germany, Austria, Belgium, Finland and Italy is superior in the context of GDP changes.

The same data presented in the form of scattered points enable presentation of the nature of the regression function, which illustrates the level of inverse proportionality of the two phenomena (Figure 14.3).

A more detailed analysis of annual changes in GDP and unemployment, taking into account the effect of half-yearly displacement (i.e. changes in unemployment rates in the years 2009, 2010, 2011, 2012 were associated with the interpolated dynamics of GDP, respectively, in the second half of 2008 and the

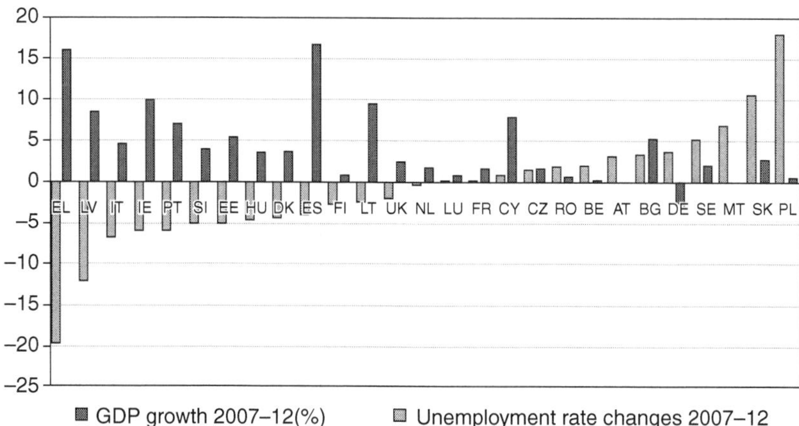

Figure 14.2 The total change in GDP and the unemployment rate in the EU countries during the recession.

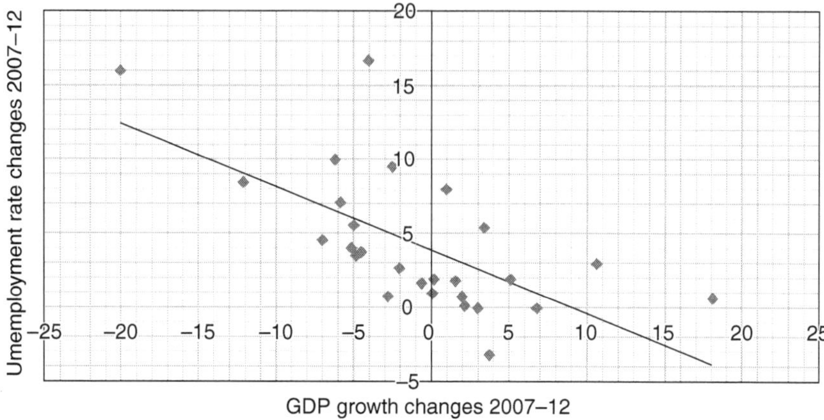

Figure 14.3 Changes in GDP and unemployment in the EU countries during the recession.

first half of 2009, the second part of 2009/first part of 2010, etc.) enabled making 108 observations (27 countries times four periods). One may distinguish the following types of macroeconomic responses:

A   GDP increases (does not decrease), the unemployment rate decreases.
B   GDP increases (does not decrease), the unemployment rate is increasing (not decreasing).
C   GDP declines, the unemployment rate is increasing (not decreasing).
D   GDP declines, the unemployment rate decreases.

As might have been predicted, there was an overwhelming dominance of changes in type A and type C. They found their confirmation in reality, especially in relation to the cases of rapid economic growth (GDP growth above 2 percent: category A+) and large economic regression (from –2 percent: category C–). In light of the comments of non-employment growth at GDP change within the range of 0 to 2 percent, category B is also consistent, but it would be surprising to come across the cases of category D. The calculations made by the authors (see Appendix) indicate that the empirical frequency in the four consecutive periods was as follows:

A   23 cases (including 14 A+) = 21.3 percent of observations
B   32 cases (including 7 B+) = 29.6 percent
C   50 cases (including the 28 C–) = 46.3 percent
D   3 cases = 2.8 percent

All cases involved category D of the second examined year – Germany, Austria, Luxembourg. The occurrence of category B+ may be considered natural only in the case when the observations relate to the new EU member states. However, one of these cases applies to Luxembourg, the other to Sweden. One case concerns Slovakia and four other remaining cases are related to one country – Poland. High growth dynamics in the four consecutive years (from 2.8 percent to 4.2 percent) was accompanied by the increase in unemployment.

The overwhelming dominance of A and C reactions is yet another confirmation of the obvious economic dependence. So is the marginality of reaction D and B+. However, with this repetition one notices a very different behavior of the EU countries, which confirms that the changes in employment are not only the result of the processes of economic growth. Among the factors to be considered when interpreting statistics are as follows:

- Partial incompatibility of employment and unemployment trends, as one should also take into account the differences in demographic structures, employment rates and economic activity and balance of international migrations (to some extent this explains the Polish phenomenon – the return of migrant workers, mostly from Britain and Ireland, which also weakened the growth of unemployment in these countries).
- Different socio-economic models of the EU, as evidenced, among others, by different levels of the social functions of the state (including the EPL indicator) opposing the market decisions dominating in more liberal economies; in practice, it usually means a stronger accommodating response in the countries which foster competitiveness, and a weaker reaction, but extended in time, in socially oriented countries.
- The state of public finance and the role of the public sector in the economy; above-average reactivity to the economic situation in Spain, Ireland, Greece and Cyprus due to sharp budget cuts; these cuts contributed to the reduction of the domestic demand on a larger scale than respectively during the European recession, which occurred in the commercial sector; it is especially important in a situation of an overblown (ante-crisis) public sector.
- The size and efficiency of investments allocated by the individual EU countries to labor market policies (LMPs), and especially to active labor market policies (ALMPs); N12 finances these policies on a much smaller scale, not only in nominal terms, but also in relative ones, with regard to GDP, than the former EU15 countries, particularly Scandinavia and Benelux.
- European employment strategy coordinated with the EU's economic policies and the tasks of the cohesion policy.

The last two factors contribute to the specialized employment policy pursued by the EU and its member states. It determines a large part of the deviations from the main focus for the countries and the regression function (Figure 14.3), because its strength (outlays) and effectiveness vary greatly across the EU. Its effectiveness impacts the development of the macro-economic dependence of growth and unemployment as the employment policy mitigates the effects of the recession and economic slowdown, as well as facilitating the reduction of the value of the *b* parameter and the r_w limit value for the pure market alternative of development. Thus, the range of a typical non-employment economic growth (0 to 2 percent) may be narrowed down on different scales in various member states.

The steps undertaken by national authorities within ALMPs are highly diversified. However, the European Employment Strategy (EES) and the EU activity should at least lead to some compensation of targets, mechanisms and effects in member countries. The authors have devoted their recent studies to the first sphere of activity – national ALMP diversity (Cybulski and Pancer-Cybulska 2013). Therefore, the remaining part of the chapter will be focused on the EES.

2 The origins of and the present European employment strategy: history vitae magistra?

2.1 The beginning of supporting the European labor market

The intensification of the EU activity on the labor market takes place when the employment situation is getting worse. The European Social Fund (ESF), which supports these activities, came into effect by the power of the provisions in the Treaties of Rome, which formed two European communities (1957). However, it was not only the lack of real justification (unemployment), but also a very narrow scope of the authority of the EEC and of financing the courses of action agreed upon by the EEC6 (the importance of the ESF was symbolic) that caused the lack of intervention in the labor market. In the early 1960s budgetary expenditure was 0.03 percent of GDP, while in 1973 it was 0.53 percent of GDP for the EEC9. After the creation of the European Regional Development Fund (ERDF) in 1975 and the conversion into the system of the multiannual financial framework in 1988, at the end of the 1990s the redistribution level increased to 1.2 percent of GDP for the EU15. The most important role was assigned to the ERDF and the European Agricultural Guidance and Guarantee Fund (EAGGF), but after 1988 ESF expenditure started to increase significantly.

The most important actions by the EU to improve the situation on the labor market were as follows:

- 1993: passing of the White Paper (Commission of the European Communities 1993) with the largest ever imminent labor market crisis in the history of the EU15;
- 1997: signing the Treaty of Amsterdam, introducing a new chapter, "employment policy";
- 1998: the launch of the EES;
- 2000–10: The Lisbon Strategy and the 2010–20 strategy *Europe 2020*;
- 2000–06 and 2007–13: the EU financial framework for defining the intensity of the support for the adopted courses of action.

2.2 European Employment Strategy

The EES has been carried out since 1998, with an annual commitment of the most important institutions of the Community/Union. Every year they approve employment guidelines, the member states' reports and recommendations to them and the general report on employment in the Community/Union. The provisions of the primary law in this respect are uncompromising and, as a result, they engage the attention not only of the professional EU staff, but also of the leaders of the countries, regardless of the scale of tensions in the labor market.

The system conceived in such a way was cumbersome to implement. Initially, the number of guidelines exceeded 20 and it was actually modified every year. There were, however, two major problems:

1   It was difficult to introduce new guidelines every year because the "old" ones did not lose their importance: from the beginning an effort was made for the list of the desired actions to be complete.
2   Several months' delay in the implementation of the guidelines by the Ministries of Labour of 15/25/27 countries increased their confusion about which version of the guidelines should be reported and what to implement in a given year.

The emphasis on the constant change led to instability and to what could be called an immunization to the EES. Therefore, guidelines for periods of several years were prepared and their fragmentation became reduced. Nevertheless, their current scope was maintained. The number of passed guidelines for 2003–05 decreased to ten and for the years 2005–08 and for 2008–10 to eight, only to reach four guidelines in 2010 ("super-guidelines," as they cover almost the same tasks as before; Council Decision of 21 October 2010).

While the shortcoming of the White Paper was its incidental character without the adoption of the procedures, the diminished importance and effectiveness of the EES is largely due to its formality and a certain "fatigue" of the decision-making bodies. The Council does adopt guidelines every year, casually stating that the ones which have been issued for the several-year period are still effective. However, they do not have to change for periods of several years, as the rewording of the guidelines for the years 2008–10 compared to 2005–08 guidelines is so minimal that it is difficult to notice when comparing the two documents. Despite the inclusion of the European Parliament in the co-decision process, the EES is currently implemented almost imperceptibly as far as the public are concerned.

2.3 The Lisbon Strategy and Europe 2020

The main objective of the EU's economic strategy adopted at the Lisbon summit in March 2000 was to make the EU the largest and most competitive economy in the world, boasting more and better jobs (Lisbon European Council 2000).

Although the situation on the labor market was much better than in the previous years, the awareness of its invariable importance meant that employment became the "flagship" strategy. The most accentuated indicator in the strategy was to achieve an employment rate of 70 percent in 2010 (67 percent by 2005, 60 percent among women and 50 percent among those nearing retirement). Problems with implementing the strategy contributed to its revitalization ("new start") in 2005 and promoting the slogan "growth and employment" (European Council 2005).

The negative assessment of the Lisbon strategy resulted from basic errors in its construction – an unrealistic level of indicators to be achieved and drawing up a strategy after the approval of the multiannual financial framework (2000–06), which in turn affected the potential for supporting these activities and, consequently, resulted in the designation of targets which indicated only partial implementation of the methods and instruments.

The successor to the Lisbon Strategy, the *Europe 2020* strategy, has emerged in different circumstances, but this has been only partially reflected in its design (European Council 2010; European Commission, 2010). The concentration of attention on the two objectives (growth and jobs) was abandoned for the sake of five more precisely formulated objectives: strengthening innovation (rate of expenditure on R&D to 3 percent of GDP), an eco-energy package (principle of 20/20/20) and the three social economic objectives (social inclusion, education, employment). Employment ceased to be one of the functions of the flagship, which may be surprising, given the higher level of unemployment at the beginning of 2010 than ten years earlier, when the Lisbon Strategy was ratified. The principle of management by objectives was sustained, but the rule of additionality has received more preference, as it enables supporting the objectives from the budget starting in 2014. However, the scope of support in 2010–13, and in fact in 2014, is not large and hence one may expect criticism of the execution of the strategy so far. History repeats itself.

2.4 The multiannual financial framework and European Employment Policy

Stability of the multiannual financial framework was, on the one hand, supposed to enable the realization of investment projects beyond the first year, and, on the other hand, to constitute a remedy to the annual repetition of political conflicts among country leaders during the creation of the Community budget. However, a resulting deficiency consists of low flexibility in meeting the challenges of the changing environment, the state of the economy and the labor market.

When deciding on the financial framework for 2007–13 in December 2005, a compromise was struck which introduced budget cuts in the position *Competitiveness for growth and employment*, which was the denial of the idea of the Lisbon Strategy, aimed at increasing innovation and international competitiveness of the EU in the face of other economic powers. Negative experiences of the past decade in the form of only partial compliance with strategic goals and negotiated directions of funding may be carried over to the present frame-work. Analogous reductions in relation to the financial framework 2014–20 were avoided; however, the conclusions of the EU leaders summit of February 2013 confirm considerable cuts in the outlays on *Smart and inclusive growth* at –8.18 percent in comparison with total commitment cuts of –6.34 percent of the project of the financial framework (European Council 2013; European Commission 2011). One needs to underline that the goals of the EES as a criterion of the distribution of resources are only highlighted exclusively in relation to the most developed regions (Conclusion no. 38). The ESF funds dominate over ERDF funds in those regions; however, in the remaining ones the situation is reversed. The least developed EU areas must concentrate on bridging the gap in terms of infrastructure in the first place and allocate a lot of resources on non-Lisbon goals, so employment goals start to become secondary.

The decision-making mechanism embracing the connection of goals of the EES with the possibilities of funding them is very complicated. In the EU budget there is no separate sheet (division) dedicated to the EES. The basis for the use of ESF funds is the cohesion policy and its guidelines. This is a major reason for the current long-term discussion on the EES guidelines. The following relation-ships are worth noting:

- The EES determined the work and the shape of the Lisbon Strategy.
- The Lisbon Strategy has contributed to the 2007–13 financial framework terminology, but affected the size and structure of expenditure to a lesser extent (as a result of the final reductions in order to achieve a compromise).
- The support for the EES implementation is dependent on the EU and national resolutions pursuing cohesion policy; in terms of execution the EES guidelines are secondary in relation to the cohesion guidelines, although conceptually their order was reversed (Figure 14.4). This fact naturally pet-rifies the EES guidelines, which is a negation of its flexibility and the importance of debating it by most important institutions of the EU, as it was indicated in the Treaty of Amsterdam.
- It may be recognized as the cause of reverse sequencing while creating the *Europe 2020* strategy – first, its goals were announced in March 2010, and then new EES guidelines were set; as a result, three of the four EES guide-lines and five of the *Europe 2020* guidelines are similar in nature.
- The importance of employment targets was diminished since reaching the employment rate of 75 percent in the group of 20–64-year-olds is only one of many reference indicators, as opposed to the Lisbon Strategy, in which the 70 percent employment rate of people aged 15–64 was the most important indicator.
- The presented decision-making mechanism explains the marginalization of the EES in the activities of the EU, but it is completely unjustified in the case of unemployment, which is now higher than in 1997–2000, when the Luxembourg Process was started, the Treaty of Amsterdam adopted, the

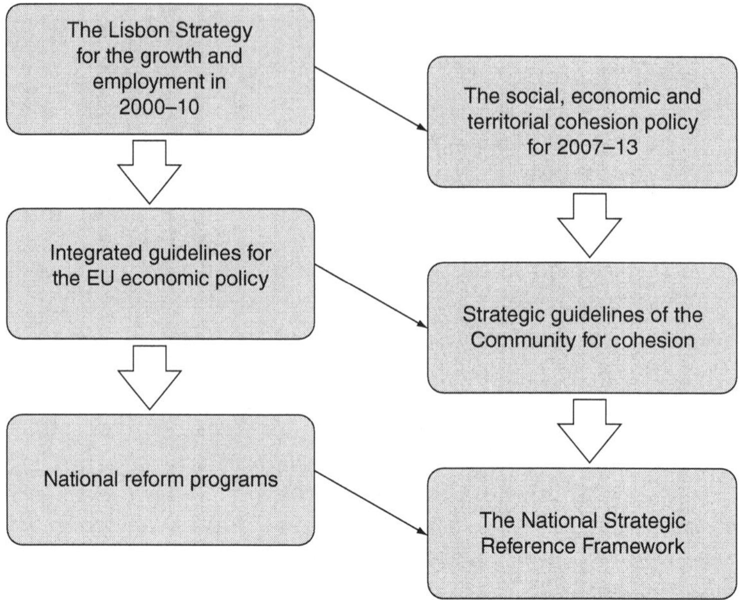

Figure 14.4 Realization interdependencies of the Lisbon Strategy and Cohesion Policy.

EES and the Lisbon Strategy were being executed, giving the labor market problems the highest ranking.

The above-mentioned decision-making mechanism is multi-stage and therefore it is worth presenting the interdependencies of strategic and financial decisions in a graph (Figure 14.4).

3 Experiences of European Employment Policy in Poland

Poland was granted membership of the EU on 1 May 2004. It happened 15 years after the fall of communism and the initiation of market reforms, first resulting in major economic regression and then in progressive liquidation of large companies, especially of industrial ones. Productivity started to increase in the remaining firms as employment was rationalized while production remained the same. It all brought about mass unemployment, which peaked in 1994 (16.9 percent) and only after a temporary improvement in 1998 (9.5 percent), associated with the high annual growth rate of GDP (6–7 percent), the unemployment rate rose in 2002–03 to 20 percent. Under these conditions, Poland was preparing for the membership by executing adjustment processes on three main levels – *legal* (adoption of the Community's *acquis commanautaire*), *programming* (relating to the strategic documents initiated by the EU institutions which set the directions of operating for the member states in the labor market) and *real*, associated with the process of convergence of labor markets in the EU. The last two levels will be the subject of further assessment.

3.1 Polish national employment programs

In compliance with Articles 125–130 of the Treaty of Amsterdam, which form the basis of the EES, in 1999 Poland created its National Employment Strategy, although it was not formally obligatory. In terms of programs, Poland was one of the leaders in the adjustment process among the candidate countries. *The National Strategy for Employment Growth* and *Human Resources Development 2000–2006* (NSEG&HRD) was adopted by the Council of Ministers in January 2000.

The strategic part of NSEG&HRD formulates tasks relating to the four pillars of the EES:

1   improving the quality of human resources
2   development of entrepreneurship
3   encouraging businesses and employees to adapt to changing market conditions
4   strengthening equal opportunities policies.

The main objective until 2006 was for the indicators to achieve an employment rate of 62–64 percent (in fact, only 54.5 percent was achieved; Eurostat 2007). Employment growth was to be accomplished by improving the quality of human resources, freeing up the capital to facilitate the creation of new jobs, especially in the small- and medium-sized enterprises, and making the relationship between labor and capital more flexible. Above all, NSEG&HRD prioritized rules concerning the use of EU support for employment purposes – initially Poland received resources from PHARE (53 percent of the fund) and after the accession from the Structural Funds.

The strategy was incorporated in one of the six sub-programs linked to subsequent *National Development Plan 2004–2006* (NDP). In the 2004–06 programming period on the basis of NSEG&HRD, the Sectoral Operational Programme – Human Resources Development (SOP HRD) was created and it was the only program fully financed from the ESF. Employment-related projects may also have been implemented with the funds from the Integrated Regional Operational Programme (IRDP), which was co-funded (mainly from the ERDF and to a lesser extent from the ESF). Within these two operational programs most of the EES tasks were carried out. The main objective of SOP HRD was to *build an open, knowledge-based society by providing conditions for the development of human resources through education, training and work*. The program laid down the framework for the four areas in line with the EES pillars.

In the 2007–13 programming period the NSEG&HRD successor for 2007–13 was the National Employment Strategy (NES) (adopted in 2005). The pattern of the transposition with regard to the implementation procedures was the same as before – it was executed by means of the National Strategic Reference Framework (NSRF; *Narodowe Strategiczne Ramy Odniesienia* 2007). NES took into account the integrated economic and employment policy guidelines which had been adopted by the Council two months earlier. It directed work on other program documents, even though it was adopted before the decisions on the 2007–13 financial framework were made. NES set three main goals for 2013:

1   reaching an overall employment rate of 58–60 percent and 50–52 percent for women,
2   reduction of unemployment to 10–12 percent,
3   achieving significant progress in the quality of employment.

Seven priorities were established:

1   development of entrepreneurship and innovation;
2   development of continuous learning and improving education;
3   improving the adaptability of workers and enterprises and the flexibility of the labor market;
4   stimulating the activity of people who are at risk of being unemployed and socially excluded;
5   improving the institutional support of the labor market;
6   bridging regional differences;
7   effective migration policy.

The comparison of EES guidelines of 2003 and 2005 with the priorities of the NES indicates that there is no simple adaptation of the EES guidelines. A modified version of the above objectives and priorities was introduced into the NSRF and employment (as a Lisbon target) even found its place in the full title of the document. The main objective of the NSRF is defined as "the creation of conditions for the growth of competitiveness of an economy based on knowledge and entrepreneurship which ensures employment growth and an increase in the level of social, economic and territorial cohesion." Among these six horizontal objectives of cohesion policy in Poland, largely based on the teachings of the Lisbon Strategy, there was an objective of improving the quality of human capital and strengthening social cohesion. It is being implemented by the Human Capital Operational Programme 2007–2013 (HCOP), the successor to the SOP HRD 2004–2006.

The NSRF made a precise distribution of the cohesion policy resources for the period 2007–13. The EU support at €59.7 billion in 2004 prices when converted to 2006 prices amounted to €67.3 billion (19.4 percent of the EU27 cohesion policy). Poland used the funds almost exclusively for the Convergence objective – €66.6 billion, of which the NSRF allocated the amount of €42.5 billion (63.9 percent) to 74 tasks set out in *Annex IV* to the Regulation (Council Regulation (EC) No 1083/2006). ESF funds account for 15 percent of the total support for the Polish cohesion policy and apply only to the HCOP (€9.7 billion).

In the programming period 2014–20, in the light of the decision of the European Council of February 2013 (European Council 2013), Poland is one of the few EU27 countries which has received more funds for cohesion policy than in 2007–13 – €72.9 billion (in 2011prices; 22.4 percent of the EU27 cohesion policy). The details of the usage of this sum will be determined in the future NRSF, but certainly in accordance with the priorities of the *Europe 2020* strategy, the share of the ESF expenditure (the objectives of the EES) will be higher than before. As part of the adjustment process, in September 2012 the government adopted the 2020 National Development Strategy (NDS) and in May 2012 (amended in February 2013) the Ministry of Labour and Social Policy adopted a Human Capital Development Strategy 2020 (HCDS; *Strategia Rozwoju Kapitału Ludzkiego 2020* 2013) which is definitely going to be a starting point for the construction of a new operational program. HCDS takes the current EES guidelines into account but sets more targets and, more importantly, specific indicators to be achieved. The document is a testimony to unrealistic bureaucratic optimism, which assumes the improvement of all indicators.

3.2 The specificity of the Polish labor market and employment policy effects in comparison with the EU

The Polish labor market is unusual in comparison with that of the EU. One should point out its determinants and characteristics:

- Economic shocks (GDP, employment) are asymmetric as opposed to the EU; this particularly applies to the period when Poland was granted an EU membership candidate status and to some extent the years 2008–13.
- In 2001–06 Poland continued to have the highest unemployment rate in the EU (including the candidate countries), but then due to the booming years from 2006 to 2012, the unemployment rate over the period 2008–12 was already slightly lower than the EU average.
- Clearly Poland's economic dynamic, which was the highest in the entire EU in the years 2007–12 (see Appendix), is now somewhat inhibited, and the new forecast for 2013 expects GDP growth at 1.1 percent (vs. –0.1 percent in the EU27) and an increase in the unemployment rate of up to 10.9 percent (11.1 percent in the EU27; European Economic Forecast, 2013).
- After Polish accession to the EU, due to freedom to move and work in another EU country, over two million Poles have benefited (they accounted for over 60 percent of all migrants from the new EU member states prior to the accession of Romania and Bulgaria, and still constitute more than 60 percent of migrant workers to West and North European countries); without opening up the labor markets, unemployment in Poland would still be higher than in Spain and Greece.

- Negative trends in the Polish labor market continue from the point of view of employees: an oversupply of people with higher education causes them to mass emigrate; simultaneously, this category has the highest rate of growth of unemployment; Poland is also a leader in the EU27 in terms of the share of employees with limited duration contracts (26.9 percent vs. 14.1 percent in the EU27; *Eurostat Statistics in Focus*, 2012),
- Spending for social purposes is determined by the level of development, and in the EU15 it constitutes over 30 percent of GDP, and in the N12 countries less than 20 percent of GDP; Polish expenditure on these purposes is 40 percent purchasing power standard (PPS) per capita in the EU27, and the structure of expenditure is dominated by spending on old age and survivors – they amount to 60.9 percent of total spending, which makes up for the highest share in the EU27 (45.0 percent on average; the second place is occupied by Italy). As a result, the other four categories of expenditure are the smallest share in the EU, including resources for the unemployed which represent only 2.2 percent of social expenditure, as compared to 6.0 percent in the EU (*Eurostat News Release*, 2012).
- With insufficient resources, the national budget and EU funds spending particularly neglects the disadvantaged groups (priorities 67 and 71 in *Annex IV*).
- As far as the national legislation in Poland is concerned, for many years only every sixth unemployed person has the right to unemployment benefit; as a result, the share of expenditure on passive labor market instruments (PLMP) in Poland is the smallest in the EU (comparable to Sweden, which has little unemployment and a large share of expenditure on LMP in GDP). As a result, according to the latest available comparative data for 2010, Poland had by far the highest EU27 share of spending on ALMPs (as calculated by the authors, the expenditure on ALMP accounted for 58 percent of total LMP spending compared to 25 percent as the EU average; Cybulski and Pancer-Cybulska 2013).
- In conclusion, the main problem of the Polish labor market on the one hand is continuous employment–unrelated economic growth, and on the other hand, low efficiency of expenditure on ALMPs.

The four EES guidelines, which were adopted in 2010, were based on 2008 statistics. Three of them formulated four key indicators to be achieved (only one guideline did not define any specific measurable objectives). The same indicators are included in three (out of five) *Europe 2020* strategy objectives. The formulation of these goals was dominated by the point of view of Western European countries, which were in a different situation than N12 countries. Therefore, each country could adopt different indicators in its own NDP in accordance with the outlined guidance to be achieved, which corresponds to individual circumstances and capabilities. Poland has adopted two indicators worse than *Europe 2020*, and the other two on a higher level (Table 14.1).

Table 14.1 Strategic employment indicators in EU27 and in Poland

Headline indicator		*European Union 27*			*Poland*		
		Target EES/ Europe 2020	*Statistics*		*Target NDP/* HCDS 2020	*Statistics*	
			2008	*2012*		*2008*	*2012*
Employment	Employment rates (% of the population aged 20–64)	75.0	70.3	68.5	71.0	65.0	64.7
Education	Early leavers from education and training (% of the population aged 18–24)	10.0	14.9	12.8	4.5	5.0	5.7
	Tertiary educational attainment (% of population aged 30–34)	40.0	31.0	35.8	45.0	29.7	39.5
Poverty or social exclusion	People at risk of poverty or social exclusion (million)	−20.0	115.7	116.3	−1.5	11.5	10.4
Other chosen strategic indicators for Poland							
Employment	Share of employees with limited duration contract (% of the population aged 25–49)				23.3		25.1
	Actual age of retirement				64.3		62.3
Unemployment	Unemployment rate among graduates (%)				15.0		20.5
	Average time of being unemployed (in months)				9		11
	Share of permanently unemployed (% of all unemployed)				45.0		50.3
Education	Percentage of people taking part in training or education (% of the population aged 25–64)				min. 10.0		4.4
	Percentage of students in technical or science studies (% of all students)				30.0		26.1

Source: author's study based on: *Strategia Rozwoju Kapitału Ludzkiego 2020*, 2013; *National Reform Programme Europe 2020*, 2011, Eurostat, the Central Statistical Office of Poland.

The pool of data shows that Poland has no quantitative educational problems and outperforms most EU countries. But it does not translate into innovation and job generation. Thus, the strong emphasis which the EES puts on measurable education indicators or recommending use of the flexicurity experience of other countries does not enable Poland to effectively solve problems within the labor market of decreasing employment, low economic activity of society, low demand for qualified personnel, uncertainty of contracts, the bad situation in the labor market for the elderly and long-term unemployment.

4 Conclusions

The research presented in the first part of the chapter confirms the existence of a very strong interrelation between economic growth and the labor market situation of EU member states. This relationship is even tighter when one takes into account a six-month shift of unemployment changes in relation to changes in GDP. However, there are different levels of responsiveness to changes in individual countries which are primarily determined by the level of attained development and the correlated pace of changes in labor productivity. In most countries of the former EU15, economic growth of more than 2 percent per year is sufficient to reduce unemployment, and in some countries (such as Germany) even lower. The new member states (N12), which are catching up with the more developed ones, still need to improve their economic environment so that the situation on the labor market can be amended. This is uniquely exemplified by Poland after 2007, which boasts of the fastest economic growth in the EU27, which is accompanied by a decline in the labor market. In the Polish labor market there is a number of other real differences in comparison with other EU countries, despite the complete legal and program adjustments which occurred before Poland joined the EU.

The EU labor market policy is a necessary complement to the macroeconomic activity which stimulates economic growth. The effectiveness of specialized employment policy has an impact on the described differences in the labor market situation of individual EU members. The EES implemented since 1998 was initially the most important direction of activity of the EU institutions and it influenced the shape of the Lisbon Strategy. In subsequent years, however, there has been a certain routinization and formalization in the treatment of the EES by the EU institutions, which resulted in the disappearance of not only information about the EES from the public domain, but also led to lowering the importance of pro-employment activity in the new *Europe 2020* strategy, although it was adopted in conditions of higher (and rising) unemployment than its predecessor, the Lisbon Strategy.

Depending on the type of labor market policy, the EES guidelines may be implemented without significant amounts of money or the use of funds from national or European funds. The latter are used for cohesion policy and hence the importance of existing and new budget decisions. As for these projects, the EU monitors their compliance with the guidelines of the cohesion policy and

EES guidelines. This is a more effective part of the EES; however, resource-unintensive operations or those dependent on national resources without significant sanctions may diverge from the accepted and agreed strategic objectives. In the authors' view this is the weakness of the EES.

Despite the decisive influence on the economic situation in the labor market emphasized in the first part of the study, one might have expected more of the EES and other EU activities. In its current form, the protection of employment and the efforts for its growth are inadequate, which threatens to deepen the problems and to maintain the unemployment rate at the two-digit level for many years to come.

Appendix

Table 14.A.1

(1)	*GDP growth (%)*					
	y/y					*2007–*
	2008	*2009*	*2010*	*2011*	*2012*	*2012*
(1)	*(2)*	*(3)*	*(4)*	*(5)*	*(6)*	*(7)*
EU27	**0.3**	**−4.3**	**2.1**	**1.6**	*−0.3*	*−0.7*
PL	5.1	1.6	3.9	4.5	*1.9*	*18.1*
SK	5.8	−4.9	4.4	3.2	*2.0*	*10.6*
MT	3.9	−2.6	2.9	1.7	*0.8*	*6.8*
SE	−0.6	−5.0	6.6	3.7	*0.8*	*5.2*
DE	1.1	−5.1	4.2	3.0	*0.7*	*3.7*
BG	6.2	−5.5	0.4	1.8	*0.8*	*3.4*
AT	1.4	−3.8	2.1	2.7	*0.8*	*3.1*
BE	1.0	−2.8	2.4	1.8	*−0.2*	*2.1*
RO	7.3	−6.6	−1.1	2.2	*0.7*	*2.0*
CZ	3.1	−4.5	2.5	1.9	*−1.3*	*1.5*
CY	3.6	−1.9	1.3	0.5	*−2.4*	*1.0*
FR	−0.1	−3.1	1.7	1.7	*0.0*	*0.1*
LU	−0.7	−4.1	2.9	1.7	*0.3*	*0.0*
NL	1.8	−3.7	1.6	1.0	*−1.0*	*−0.4*
UK	−1.0	−4.0	1.8	1.0	*0.3*	*−2.0*
LT	2.9	−14.8	1.5	5.9	*3.6*	*−2.4*
FI	0.3	−8.5	3.3	2.8	*−0.2*	*−2.7*
ES	0.9	−3.7	−0.3	0.4	*−1.4*	*−4.1*
DK	−0.8	−5.7	1.6	1.1	*−0.5*	*−4.4*
HU	0.9	−6.8	1.3	1.6	*−1.7*	*−4.9*
EE	−4.2	−14.1	3.3	8.3	*3.2*	*−5.0*
SI	3.4	−7.8	1.2	0.6	*−2.3*	*−5.2*
PT	0.0	−2.9	1.9	−1.6	*−3.2*	*−5.8*
IE	−2.1	−5.5	−0.8	1.4	*0.9*	*−6.1*
IT	−1.2	−5.5	1.7	0.4	*−2.4*	*−7.0*
LV	−3.3	−17.7	−0.9	5.5	*5.6*	*−12.1*
EL	−0.2	−3.1	−4.9	−7.1	*−6.4*	*−20.0*

Table 14.A.1 *continued*

	GDP growth interpolated (%)			
	II 2008–	II 2009–	II 2010–	II 2011–
	I 2009	I 2010	I 2011	I 2012
	(8)	*(9)*	*(10)*	*(11)*
EU27	**−2.0**	**−1.1**	**1.9**	*0.7*
PL	3.4	2.8	4.2	*3.2*
SK	0.5	−0.3	3.8	*2.6*
MT	0.7	0.2	2.3	*1.3*
SE	−2.8	0.8	5.2	*2.3*
DE	−2.0	−0.5	3.6	*1.9*
BG	0.4	−2.6	1.1	*1.3*
AT	−1.2	−0.9	2.4	*1.8*
BE	−0.9	−0.2	2.1	*0.8*
RO	0.4	−3.9	0.6	*1.5*
CZ	−0.7	−1.0	2.2	*0.3*
CY	0.9	−0.3	0.9	*−1.0*
FR	−1.6	−0.7	1.7	*0.9*
LU	−2.4	−0.6	2.3	*1.0*
NL	−1.0	−1.1	1.3	*0.0*
UK	−2.5	−1.1	1.4	*0.7*
LT	−6.0	−6.7	3.7	*4.8*
FI	−4.1	−2.6	3.1	*1.3*
ES	−1.4	−2.0	0.1	*−0.5*
DK	−3.3	−2.1	1.4	*0.3*
HU	−3.0	−2.8	1.5	*0.0*
EE	−9.2	−5.4	5.8	*5.8*
SI	−2.2	−3.3	0.9	*−0.9*
PT	−1.5	−0.5	0.2	*−2.4*
IE	−3.8	−3.2	0.3	*1.2*
IT	−3.4	−1.9	1.1	*−1.0*
LV	−10.5	−9.3	2.3	*5.6*
EL	−1.7	−4.0	−6.0	*−6.8*

Table 14.A.1 *continued*

	Unemployment rate (%)					
	2007	*2008*	*2009*	*2010*	*2011*	*2012*
	(12)	*(13)*	*(14)*	*(15)*	*(16)*	*(17)*
EU27	**7.2**	**7.1**	**9.0**	**9.7**	**9.7**	**10.5**
PL	9.6	7.0	8.1	9.7	9.7	10.1
SK	11.2	9.6	12.1	14.5	13.6	14.0
MT	6.5	6.0	6.9	6.9	6.5	6.4
SE	6.1	6.2	8.3	8.6	7.8	8.0
DE	8.7	7.5	7.8	7.1	5.9	5.5
BG	6.9	5.6	6.8	10.3	11.3	12.3
AT	4.4	3.8	4.8	4.4	4.2	4.3
BE	7.5	7.0	7.9	8.3	7.2	7.6
RO	6.4	5.8	6.9	7.3	7.4	7.0
CZ	5.3	4.4	6.7	7.3	6.7	7.0
CY	3.9	3.7	5.4	6.3	7.9	11.9
FR	8.4	7.8	9.5	9.7	9.6	10.2
LU	4.2	4.9	5.1	4.6	4.8	5.1
NL	3.6	3.1	3.7	4.5	4.4	5.3
UK	5.3	5.6	7.6	7.8	8.0	7.9
LT	3.8	5.3	13.6	18.0	15.3	13.3
FI	6.9	6.4	8.2	8.4	7.8	7.7
ES	8.3	11.3	18.0	20.1	21.7	25.0
DK	3.8	3.4	6.0	7.5	7.6	7.5
HU	7.4	7.8	10.0	11.2	10.9	10.9
EE	4.6	5.5	13.8	16.9	12.5	10.2
SI	4.9	4.4	5.9	7.3	8.2	8.9
PT	8.9	8.5	10.6	12.0	12.9	15.9
IE	4.7	6.4	12.0	13.9	14.7	14.7
IT	6.1	6.7	7.8	8.4	8.4	10.7
LV	6.5	8.0	18.2	19.8	16.2	14.9
EL	8.3	7.7	9.5	12.6	17.7	24.3

Table 14.A.1 *continued*

	Unemployment rate changes (%)					
	y/y					*2007–*
	2008	*2009*	*2010*	*2011*	*2012*	*2012*
	(18)	*(19)*	*(20)*	*(21)*	*(22)*	*(23)*
EU27	**−0.1**	**1.9**	**0.7**	**0.0**	*0.8*	*3.3*
PL	−2.6	1.1	1.6	0.0	*0.4*	*0.5*
SK	−1.6	2.5	2.4	−0.9	*0.4*	*2.8*
MT	−0.5	0.9	0.0	−0.4	*−0.1*	*−0.1*
SE	0.1	2.1	0.3	−0.8	*0.2*	*1.9*
DE	−1.2	0.3	−0.7	−1.2	*−0.4*	*−3.2*
BG	−1.3	1.2	3.5	1.0	*1.0*	*5.4*
AT	−0.6	1.0	−0.4	−0.2	*0.1*	*−0.1*
BE	−0.5	0.9	0.4	−1.1	*0.4*	*0.1*
RO	−0.6	1.1	0.4	0.1	*−0.4*	*0.6*
CZ	−0.9	2.3	0.6	−0.6	*0.3*	*1.7*
CY	−0.2	1.7	0.9	1.6	*4.0*	*8.0*
FR	−0.6	1.7	0.2	−0.1	*0.6*	*1.8*
LU	0.7	0.2	−0.5	0.2	*0.3*	*0.9*
NL	−0.5	0.6	0.8	−0.1	*0.9*	*1.7*
UK	0.3	2.0	0.2	0.2	*−0.1*	*2.6*
LT	1.5	8.3	4.4	−2.7	*−2.0*	*9.5*
FI	−0.5	1.8	0.2	−0.6	*−0.1*	*0.8*
ES	3.0	6.7	2.1	1.6	*3.3*	*16.7*
DK	−0.4	2.6	1.5	0.1	*−0.1*	*3.7*
HU	0.4	2.2	1.2	−0.3	*0.0*	*3.5*
EE	0.9	8.3	3.1	−4.4	*−2.3*	*5.6*
SI	−0.5	1.5	1.4	0.9	*0.7*	*4.0*
PT	−0.4	2.1	1.4	0.9	*3.0*	*7.0*
IE	1.7	5.6	1.9	0.8	*0.0*	*10.0*
IT	0.6	1.1	0.6	0.0	*2.3*	*4.6*
LV	1.5	10.2	1.6	−3.6	*−1.3*	*8.4*
EL	−0.6	1.8	3.1	5.1	*6.6*	*16.0*

Table 14.A.1 *continued*

	Categories of growth				
	(8)–	*(9)-*	*(10)-*	*(11)-*	*(7)/5-*
	(19)	*(20)*	*(21)*	*(22)*	*(23)*
	(24)	*(25)*	*(26)*	*(27)*	*(28)*
EU27	**C**	**C**	**B**	***B***	**C**
PL	B+	B+	B+	*B+*	***B+***
SK	B	C	A+	*B+*	***B+***
MT	B	B	A+	*A*	***A***
SE	C–	B	A+	*B+*	***B***
DE	C–	D	A+	*A*	***A***
BG	B	C–	B	*B*	***B***
AT	C	D	A+	*B*	***A***
BE	C	C	A+	*B*	***B***
RO	B	C–	B	*A*	***B***
CZ	C	C	A+	*B*	***B***
CY	B	C	B	*C*	***B***
FR	C	C	A	*B*	***B***
LU	C–	D	B+	*B*	***B***
NL	C	C	A	*B*	***C***
UK	C–	C	B	*A*	***C***
LT	C–	C–	A+	*A+*	***C***
FI	C–	C–	A+	*A*	***C***
ES	C	C–	B	*C*	***C***
DK	C–	C–	B	*A*	***C***
HU	C–	C–	A	*C*	***C***
EE	C–	C–	A+	*A+*	***C***
SI	C–	C–	B	*C*	***C***
PT	C	C	B	*C–*	***C***
IE	C–	C–	B	*B*	***C***
IT	C–	C	B	*C*	***C***
LV	C–	C–	A+	*A+*	***C–***
EL	C	C–	C–	*C–*	***C–***

Source for data: Eurostat: (2)–(5), (12)–(16); European Economic Forecast, 2013: (6), (17)

Notes
Bold: summarized data for five years' time or for EU27; italic: forecasts; filled with colour: N12.

Notes

1 The unemployment rate calculated for the EU15 in 1994 reached the level of 10.5 percent. Methodological differences in the EU27 countries do not permit conversion of unemployment statistics for 1994. According to Eurostat data, the EU15 unemployment rate in 2012 was 10.6 percent and 10.5 percent in the EU27. Unemployment rate forecasts for 2013 and 2014 are the same – 0.6 per cent higher than in 2012 (European Commission 2013, p. 35).
2 Eurostat official data as of May 2013 was used herein. A simple interpolation formula was used to calculate the six-month shift.

References

Commission of the European Communities, 1993. *Growth, Competitiveness, Employment: The Challenges and Ways Forward into the 21st Century.* Commission of the European Communities, Luxembourg.

Council Decision of 21 October 2010 on guidelines for the employment policies of the Member States (2010/707/EU). *Official Journal of the EU*, 2010, L 308.

Council Regulation (EC) No 1083/2006 of 11 July 2006 laying down general provisions on the European Regional Development Fund, the European Social Fund and the Cohesion Fund and repealing Regulation (EC) No 1260/1999. *Official Journal of the EU*, 2006, L 210.

Cybulski L. and Pancer-Cybulska, E., 2013. *Aktywna polityka rynku pracy w okresie kryzysu.* Uniwersytet Ekonomiczny, Katowice.

European Commission, 2010. *Europe 2020: A European Strategy for Smart, Sustainable and Inclusive Growth.* Brussels, 3 March, COM (2010) 2020 final.

European Commission, 2011 *Proposal for a Council Regulation laying down the multiannual financial framework for the years 2014–2020.* Brussels, 29 June, COM(2011) 398.

European Commission, 2013 *Statistical Annex of European Economy.* 23 April.

European Council, 2005. *Presidency conclusions.* Council of the European Union, 7619/1/05, Brussels, 23 March.

European Council, 2010. *Conclusions.* European Council, EUCO 13/10, Brussels, 17 June.

European Council, 2013. *Presidency conclusions (Multiannual Financial Framework).* EUCO 37/13, Brussels, 8 February.

European Economic Forecast, 2013. *European Economy*, Vol. 2.

Eurostat News Release, 2007, no. 102, 20 July.

Eurostat News Release, 2012, no. 165, 27 November.

Eurostat Statistics in Focus, 2012, Vol. 40, 5 October.

Lisbon European Council, 2000. *Presidency conclusions.* Council of the European Union, 100/1/00, Brussels, 24 March.

Narodowe Strategiczne Ramy Odniesienia 2007–2013 wspierające wzrost gospodarczy i zatrudnienie. Narodowa Strategia Spójności. MRR, Warszawa, 2007.

National Reform Programme Europe 2020, 2011. Warsaw, April.

Strategia Rozwoju Kapitału Ludzkiego 2020, 2013. MPiPS, Warszawa.

Index

Page numbers in *italics* denote tables, those in **bold** denote figures.

consumers 8, 56, 63, 125, 167, 248, 252, 255, 261; activism initiative 244; cooperatives 3, 248, 253, 256; debt 87, 154; demand 181; goods 71; involvement 253; opinion 204, 210; owned enterprise 257n9; potential 15; preferences 209–10, 213; price expectations 211, 216; responsible 256; unsustainable debt 5, 62; value for 204, 207

cooperative 8, 246, 248, 250–2, 256; banks 244–7, 249; cause 254; consumer 8, 248, 253; financial 248; firms 246–7; market economy 56, 58; members 257n4; model 9, 249–54; movements 8, 254–6; principles 253; sector 247, 249; supporters 255; US 257n8; worker 8, 257n14

Council Decision 267

Council Regulation (EC) 272

credit rating agencies 64, 155

credit unions 3, 8, 244, 246–7, 249; Federal Credit Union Act 250; World Council of Credit Unions 247

Crisis Management Index (CMI) 4, 47, **48**, *49*, **51–4**, 55–6, 58, 58n3

Crockett, A. 141–3

Cybulski, L. 9, 266, 274

Cyprus **42–5**, *46*, **48**, *49*, **57**, 95, 112n9, **185**, 202n5, 242, 263, 265

Czech Republic **42–5**, *46*, **48**, *49*, **57**, 92, 95, 194, 202n5, 211; economy 129n5; nationality *212*

Dawid, H. 165–6

debt 36n12, 41, 70, 135, 144, 167, **171–3**, *173*; constraints 149; consumer 5, 62, 87, 154; crisis 74, 154; default 163; education 246; firms 174; government 22, 150, 158–9, 168, 174; national 157; owned 134; private 151, 159, 175; private sector 164; public 1–2, 6–7, 40, 47, 58, 123, 148–52, 155, 158–60, 174; public sector 152, 155, 165; rising 62; rollover 142; repayment 156, 164, 181; sovereign 8, 40–1, 154, 163, 242; state 244; structure 160n7; system 143

decent work 3, 8, 219–20, 223–4, 235, 237n10, 238n12; basic defect 221, 227, 235; basic profile 229, 232; deficit 221–2, 226; Italian 229, 236

deficit 45, 168, 198; current account 68, 151; decent work 221–2, 226; deficit-GDP ratio 7, 169; deficitsurplus issue

41; federal 204; fiscal 150, 164; government **171**, 174; Greek 41; high 152; large 148; net export 70; profit-stabilizing 159; public sector 165; reduction 150–1, 155, 158; self-imposed 149; spending multiplier 157; *see also* budget deficits

deflationary 47; pressures 50; spiral 164

DeLong, J.B. 164, 184, 190

demand 15, 18, 22–3, 62, 64, 71, 141, 149, 156, 163, 167, 209, 232, 262; aggregate 1–2, 4–5, 21–2, 47, 50, 54, 56, 58, 62, 64, 77, 79, 84–7, 93, 112, 152, 160n4, 164, 167; component 22, 65; for credit 150; depress 63; domestic 72n4, 156, 265; effective 154, 157; employment 109; expected 69; export 72n4; falling 22, 76, 85, 152, 154, 261; for goods 207, 210; insufficient 157; investment 18, 21; labor (labour) 75, 88n3, 93–4, 109, 167, 232, 237n11, 239n29; level of 2, 5, 62–3; low 276; management 68; market 184; money 20, 22, 135; official 245; reduced 181; shocks 90; shortfall 151; transaction 20, 135; uncertainty 109; wage 238n11

Denmark 41, **42–5**, *46*, 47, **48**, 49, **57**, 95, **185**, 208, 233, **234–5**, 241, 244; Danish butter 247; Danish Design Centre 208; *see also* Scandinavia

design 207–10

Design Council 208–9

distribution of income 5, 63, 69, 71; re-distribution 68

division of labor 13, 35n7

DSGE model paradigm 165

Dutt, A.K. 5, 79, 82

economic crisis 2–4, 7, 23, 57, 137, 189, 194, 197, 199, 232, 236, 246, 261; current 4, 56, 58; EU 40, 58n1; EU27 42; global 1, 260; international 8; Italy 227; Mediterranean countries 47

economic efficiency 123, 159

economic growth 7, 50, 109, 181, 184, 204, 243, 276; financialization 58; high levels 72; limited 1; models 24; negative impacts on 3, 6; Polish problem 274; rates 182; restoration of 61, 67; stable 3, 58; sustain 160; technological progress 186; theories 183, 187; unemployment 261266

economic recovery 2–3, 6, 61, 64, 67–8, 72, 151